CAMBRIDGE GREEK AND LATIN CLASSICS

GENERAL EDITORS

E. J. KENNEY
Emeritus Kennedy Professor of Latin, University of Cambridge

AND

P. E. EASTERLING
Professor of Greek, University College London

D0221865

PLATO
PHAEDO

EDITED BY

C. J. ROWE

Henry Overton Wills Professor of Greek,
University of Bristol

CAMBRIDGE
UNIVERSITY PRESS

Published by the Press Syndicate of the University of Cambridge
The Pitt Building, Trumpington Street, Cambridge CB2 1RP
40 West 20th Street, New York, NY 10011-4211, USA
10 Stamford Road, Oakleigh, Melbourne 3166, Australia

First published 1993

Printed in Great Britain at the University Press, Cambridge

A catalogue record for this book is available from the British Library

Library of Congress cataloguing in publication data

Plato.
Phaedo / Plato ; edited by C. J. Rowe.
p.   cm. – (Cambridge Greek and Latin classics)
Includes bibliography and index.
ISBN 0 521 30796 1. – ISBN 0 521 31318 x (pbk.)
1. Immortality (Philosophy) – Early works to 1800.   I. Rowe, C. J.
II. Title.   III. Series.
PA4279.P3P39 1993
184–dc20   92-33958   CIP

ISBN 0 521 30796 1 hardback
ISBN 0 521 31318 x paperback

AO

CONTENTS

PREFACE

The chief aim of this edition and commentary is to provide the basic tools required for an understanding and appreciation of Plato's *Phaedo*. The commentary attempts to anticipate the needs of those who may as yet be relative beginners in Greek language, while also waymarking a path through the maze of ideas and arguments contained in the dialogue. The secondary literature on the *Phaedo* – of which a selection is listed in the Bibliography – is large, and presents a bewildering variety of interpretations of both the whole and its parts, which may itself seem impenetrable without a guide. Considerations of space generally prevent detailed discussion of this literature; instead I have usually contented myself with indicating what seems to me the most promising way forward, referring to the work of others only where I am conscious of having borrowed directly from it, although my own interpretations will often have been formed through consideration of the alternatives offered by others. The fundamental assumption throughout the commentary is that the dialogue is a unified whole, and that the best evidence for the interpretation of any particular part will come from an analysis of its relationship with the parts that precede and follow it. That such an approach allows the work to offer up a complex but consistent sense is, I think, some kind of guarantee of its usefulness. ('Sense' in this context means what I find intelligible, which on the whole seems to coincide with what others find so.) But at no point do I mean to exclude other interpretations, if these can be shown to be better. By their nature, commentaries tend to acquire a certain authority; the present one claims to be no more than a set of reasoned judgements reached by one reader, which he intends as at least a helpful starting-point for others.

My own interest in Plato is primarily in his skills as writer and as philosopher. He is an inconspicuously deliberate and artful author, who repays continual re-reading: each new encounter with his texts tends to reveal new connections, further layers of allusive subtlety. There are sudden changes of pace and tone, between narrative description, quick exchanges of argument, inventive story-telling, solemn, passionate declamation, and ironic humour. The combination of these elements, together with his decision to retire behind his characters, makes Plato's works peculiarly tantalising and elusive. Yet at the same time there is also a remarkable precision in the construction of his arguments, on both the large and the small scale, which belies the informal dramatic and conversational framework in which they are set. Unsuccessful though many of these arguments may be, the quality of the mind behind them is unmistakable (and a large part of the *Phaedo* in fact consists in the criticism by the participants of each other's arguments). There are some aspects of Plato's substantive ideas which we are likely to find unacceptable, even chilling – for example, the fate he proposes in the *Phaedo* for the souls of ordinary mortals who have led ordinary, apparently decent lives. Nevertheless, there is a grandeur and simplicity about the general world-view that underlies some of the longer Platonic dialogues (the *Phaedo* itself, the *Symposium*, the *Republic*, or the *Phaedrus*) which it is hard not to find seductive.

I am grateful to numerous friends and colleagues who have allowed me to try out my ideas on them, or who have commented on parts of the commentary; none of the faults that will remain are theirs. The whole commentary was discussed in draft, over a year or more, at the weekly meetings of the informal Centre for Ancient Philosophy at Bristol, and has benefited greatly from criticism from fellow-members and from students. Important modifications of my views have also stemmed from discussions of papers developing or bringing together ideas in the commentary with audiences at Trinity College, Dublin, Brown and Boston Universities, the Universities of Leiden and Amsterdam, the Università degli Studi di Perugia, and the Université de Paris XII. All of these papers either have been or will be published, and will help to fill out the following Introduction, which has had to contract as the commentary expanded: see Rowe 1992a, which defends my methods of interpretation (cf. also Rowe 1992b); Rowe 1991, 1990–92, 1993.[1] My chief thanks, however, must go to Pauline Hire, of the Cambridge University Press, for her continuing encouragement and flexibility over deadlines, to Susan Moore for her keen copy-editor's eye, and to the general editors, Pat Easterling and Ted Kenney, for their gentle suggestions, admonitions, and attempts to introduce a greater economy of style.

[1] For the style of references to secondary literature, see Select Bibliography, p. 19.

The commentary claims to belong to no particular school of interpretation, although it no doubt especially reflects Anglo-Saxon habits
of mind. It is written in the belief that rational discussion of the issues
is always possible, however different our perspectives and presupposi-
tions may be, and that no one variety of approach is likely to have a
monopoly of understanding. The volume is dedicated to the Interna-
tional Plato Society, one of whose aims is to promote Platonic studies
across national, cultural and other boundaries.

Centre for Ancient Philosophy, Bristol   C.J.R.
June 1992

ABBREVIATIONS

ANCIENT AUTHORS AND WORKS

Aesch.   = Aeschylus; *Ag.* = *Agamemnon*; *Sept.* = *Seven against Thebes*
Ar.   = Aristophanes; *Ach.* = *Acharnians*
Arist.   = Aristotle; *De an.* = *De anima*; *DC* = *De caelo*; *Hist. an.* = *Historia animalium*; *Met.* = *Metaphysics*; *Meteor.* = *Meteorologica*; *Nic. eth.* = *Nicomachean ethics*; *Phys.* = *Physics*; *Po.* = *Poetics*; *Probl.* = [Arist.] *Problemata*; *Top.* = *Topics*
Bacch.   = Bacchylides
Dem.   = Demosthenes; *Cor.* = *De corona*
D. L.   = Diogenes Laertius
Eur.   = Euripides; *Bacch.* = *Bacchae*; *Med.* = *Medea*; *Or.* = *Orestes*
Eust.   = Eustathius; *in Od.* = *in Odysseam*
Hdt.   = Herodotus
Hes.   = Hesiod; *WD* = *Works and days*; *Th.* = *Theogony*
Hom.   = Homer; *Il.* = *Iliad*; *Od.* = *Odyssey*
Lucr.   = Lucretius; *DRN* = *De rerum natura*
Lys.   = Lysias
P.   = Plato; *Ap.* = *Apology*; *Charm.* = *Charmides*; *Cr.* = *Crito*; *Crat.* = *Cratylus*; *Crit.* = *Critias*; *Euth.* = *Euthyphro*; *Euthd.* = *Euthydemus*; *Gorg.* = *Gorgias*; *HMa.* = *Hippias Major*; *La.* = *Laches*; *Parm.* = *Parmenides*; *Phd.* = *Phaedo*; *Phdr.* = *Phaedrus*; *Phil.* = *Philebus*; *Pol.* = *Politicus*; *Prot.* = *Protagoras*; *Rep.* = *Republic*; *Soph.* = *Sophist*; *Symp.* = *Symposium*; *Theaet.* = *Theaetetus*; *Tim.* = *Timaeus*
Pind.   = Pindar; *Ol.* = *Olympians*
Plut.   = Plutarch; *Thes.* = *Theseus*; *Phoc.* = *Phocion*
Soph.   = Sophocles; *El.* = *Electra*; *OC* = *Oedipus at Colonus*; *OT* = *Oedipus Tyrannus*
Theophr. = Theophrastus; *De lap.* = *De lapidibus*
Thuc.   = Thucydides
Xen.   = Xenophon; *Ap.* = *Apology*; *Hell.* = *Hellenica*; *Mem.* = *Memorabilia*; *Symp.* = *Symposium*

('S.', throughout, refers – unless otherwise indicated – to the Socrates of the Platonic dialogues.)

MODERN WORKS

DK   = H. Diels (ed.), revised by W. Kranz, *Die Fragmente der Vorsokratiker*, 6th edition, Berlin 1961

GP   = J. D. Denniston, *The Greek particles*, 2nd edition, Oxford 1954

HGP   = W. K. C. Guthrie, *A history of Greek philosophy* (6 vols.), Cambridge 1967–81

LSJ   = H. G. Liddell, R. Scott, revised by H. S. Jones, *A Greek – English lexicon*, 9th edition, Oxford 1940

MT   = W. W. Goodwin, *Syntax of the moods and tenses of the Greek verb*, London 1889

INTRODUCTION

1. LITERATURE AND PHILOSOPHY

A typical class of British philosophy students, coming to the *Phaedo* for the first time, will probably wonder why they have to wait for so long before getting to any real philosophy; and many recent books and articles on the dialogue, themselves written by philosophers, will encourage them to skip smartly to the four arguments for immortality and the long passage on explanation, looking at the rest – if at all – merely as a place from which to excavate hidden premisses. A typical class of literature students, on the other hand, will be puzzled and irritated when they come to the 'philosophical' parts. This is, of course, a caricature; it is however true that the work makes unfamiliar demands on the modern reader. The closest parallel is with a serious novel, or a play; and there are indeed features which the dialogue shares with tragedy, for example the chorus-like presence of Phaedo and Echecrates, and an Aristotelian-type περιπέτεια or reversal of fortune (see also 115a5,[1] where Socrates compares himself with a tragic hero, albeit ironically).

The analogy should not be pressed too hard. The *Phaedo* is certainly a work of creative fiction (written some twenty years after the events it pretends to relate). But a conversation between philosophers is hardly a promising subject either for the novelist or for the dramatist; and while Plato as writer of dialogues, like the writer of novels or plays, withdraws behind his characters, he probably does so less far and less genuinely in the case of a dialogue like the *Phaedo*, where the directness and singlemindedness of Socrates' delivery of his general message about the importance of the philosophical life makes it hard not to see him in this respect as the authentic voice of Plato himself. If we wish to identify the genre to which the *Phaedo* belongs, it will perhaps best be treated as hovering somewhere between that of serious fiction or

[1] This is the standard form of reference to Platonic works: '115' represents the page number in the relevant volume of H. Stephanus' 1578 edition of Plato, 'a' the relevant section of that page, and '5' the line in that section. (Line-numbers will normally only be given in this volume in references to *Phd.* itself.)

drama on the one hand, and that of the treatises of an Aristotle or a Kant on the other. But there is one respect in which the analogy will certainly hold. It is as perverse to equate reading the *Phaedo* with reading certain portions of it as it would be to stage excerpts of *Oedipus Tyrannus* and call it a performance of Sophocles' play, or to claim to have read *War and Peace* on the strength of having read the first or the middle three hundred pages.

In fact, however, the 'philosophical' sections of the dialogue bulk so large that it is impossible to ignore them. The more pressing task – at least from a modern standpoint, when discussion of the *Phaedo* tends to be dominated by professional philosophers – is to demonstrate the importance of the allegedly 'non-philosophical' parts of the work. What makes it all the more pressing is that the verdict on most or all of the arguments at the core of the conversation reported by Phaedo is generally negative. Thus we have the odd situation that what is generally recognised, even by its philosophical critics, as one of the greatest works of European prose literature, is simultaneously seen as resting on a series of philosophical mistakes. But how can bad philosophy make great literature?

My response is, first, that the critics have been too hasty in condemning Plato's arguments, which are more carefully and ingeniously constructed than they have sometimes supposed; second, and more importantly, that exclusive concentration on these has prevented a proper estimation of the subtlety of Plato's own attitude towards them, which becomes apparent when we begin to look at them in their dramatic context. Analysing the individual arguments may be a useful pedagogical exercise, but is only a part of the process of interpretation. We need also to understand them in their context: how they are received by the characters in the dialogue itself, why each is succeeded by the next, and so on. What emerges is a picture, not of a series of self-standing arguments woodenly inserted into a dramatic framework, but rather of a group of philosophers engaged in debate, listening, criticising, and responding to each other; and this is indeed what philosophy is, according to the *Phaedo*. The *Phaedo* is a written representation of live philosophical conversation, in which failure is, and is acknowledged to be, as much a possibility as success (and perhaps rather more frequent), and where either will have immediate consequences for choice and action: most immediately, we shall be able to judge the reasonableness or otherwise of the contentment with which we see Socrates facing his execution. If none of the arguments proves the immortality of the soul, then on the terms of the discussion, death will be something to be feared; if they are successful, we should not fear death, but rather the manner of our life, which according to Socrates will determine our fate 'in Hades'. Seen in this way, the 'philosophical' and 'non-philosophical' parts of the dialogue together form a perfectly integrated whole.

2. PLATO'S CONCEPTION OF PHILOSOPHY

The distinction between literature and philosophy is certainly not one that would have interested Plato. After all, he had before him examples (Parmenides, Empedocles) of philosophers who wrote in that highest of literary forms, epic verse. (If he sometimes opposes poetry and philosophy, that is because of the lies he claims that most existing poetry tells.) What would have interested him more is the distinction between written representation of philosophical activity and doing philosophy itself (as artistic representation of anything differs from that thing). According to the view he has Socrates develop in the *Phaedrus*, philosophising consists in actual, live conversation between individuals in search of the truth (φιλο-σοφία). Written texts 'contain much that is merely for amusement',[2] and should not be taken too seriously either by their authors or by their readers, because they are incapable of *teaching* anyone anything. The man who knows anything about the most important subjects ('the just, the fine and the good'), if he writes, will do so 'for the sake of amusement . . . , laying up a store of reminders both for himself, when he "reaches a forgetful old age", and for anyone who is following the same track';[3] the best writings 'have really been a way of reminding people who know'.[4] Although Plato's own works are not explicitly included within the scope of these remarks (and cannot be, since from within the dramatic context of the *Phaedrus* they are themselves conversations rather than written texts), it is hard to see any grounds for excluding them. We thus reach the surprising result that neither the writing of a dialogue like the *Phaedo*, nor the reading of it, will count as doing philosophy as such.

[2] *Phdr.* 277e.   [3] *Phdr.* 276d.   [4] *Phdr.* 278a.

We may of course ourselves enter into a kind of conversatic.. with the text, and can indeed hardly avoid doing so: at every point in the dialogue we shall need to ask, like those taking part in it, whether what is being said is acceptable or not. But this will not be a real conversation, since the other party, the text, is dumb, and if you ask it something, it cannot reply, but 'stands there in solemn silence'.[5] According to the *Phaedrus*, the essential feature of philosophical conversation or 'dialectic' (διαλεκτική, the art of διαλέγεσθαι) is that it involves *exchange*: one person (the one who has some knowledge) produces statements, which another person then questions, forcing the first to defend what he has said, and so on. Only so, it is suggested, is any advance, or transfer of knowledge, possible.

It cannot of course be assumed that what Plato (or rather Socrates) says in one dialogue is necessarily applicable to any other. Each dialogue is self-contained; and there are moreover numerous cases in which Plato's views seem to have changed or evolved.[6] However, the conception of philosophy we find in the *Phaedrus* does appear in most respects to be directly transferable to the *Phaedo*. The only significant difference is that whereas the *Phaedrus* seems to presuppose that the conversation will be between unequals (master and pupil), the protagonists in the *Phaedo* appear close to being equals (see §4); but there is no obvious reason why the latter type of situation should be ruled out – if advance is possible between master-philosopher and pupil, it will *a fortiori* also be possible between two or more philosophers working together. Just so Socrates, Simmias and Cebes agree that they have (probably) achieved a definite result, after a long conversation of the type recommended in the *Phaedrus*: statement, followed by questioning, leading to defence of the statement, and so on.

It may have been this view of philosophy – as a two-way process – that determined Plato's initial choice of the dialogue form. The closest approximation to philosophy in writing will be a written portrayal of philosophers in dialogue with each other. Simple declamation, or the rehearsal of arguments without the possibility of criticism or counter-argument, is the province of the rhetorician, not of the philosopher. To the extent that even dialogues cannot be forced to defend themselves, Plato as writer will himself be playing the rhetorician. But in reading them, and entering their fictional context, we become like the audience of a conversation, able like them to learn from it and to share in (or reject) its conclusions.

3. THE AIMS OF PLATO'S PHILOSOPHICAL WRITING

The *Phaedo* has two main conclusions: that the best life is the life of philosophy, and that the soul is immortal. They are inseparably connected, in that the main argument for the choice of the philosophical life is that it will ensure a better fate for us after death, which clearly presupposes that we survive it as conscious beings. That Plato firmly believed in both propositions is hardly in doubt, since he recurs to them repeatedly in other dialogues. But would he have been content if, as philosophers, and using the methods he recommends, we went on to reject the case for immortality? More generally, does he see philosophy as an open-ended process which may lead in unforeseen directions, even to the extent of undermining his own beliefs, or rather as moving ineluctably towards the confirmation of those beliefs? Is he, in other words, a philosopher still groping for the truth, whatever it may be, or one who thinks he already has it, and is trying to confirm it for himself, or even (a third possibility) just looking for ways of allowing us, his readers, to begin to see it?

So far as the *Phaedo* goes, none of the three alternatives is obviously false. Socrates admits that even the last argument for immortality, the one about which he is most optimistic, is based only on hypotheses, on whose precise meaning he has declined to commit himself. Then again, given that he has accepted criticism of previous arguments, he ought also to be prepared to accept criticisms of this one – and Plato's arguments for immortality elsewhere, in the *Republic*, *Phaedrus*, and *Laws*, are in fact of a quite different type. Yet if he could seriously have envisaged dropping the idea of immortality, it is odd that he should have made it so central to the case for the philosophical life, which he would certainly not have given up; and it could be that he in fact had a longer story to tell about his 'hypotheses' which he chose not to allow Socrates to divulge, perhaps because he thought it excessively technical for his intended audience. Similarly, earlier in the dialogue, when he has Socrates complain about his inability to discover the kind of αἰτία or explanation of things that he was looking for, he could mean either that he has abandoned the search, or that he is still hopeful about finding what he wants; or else, again, he has more up his sleeve than he chooses to tell us.

Aristotle certainly attributes to Plato a set of 'unwritten opinions'[7] about the first principles of explanation which might fit the bill – and which he might also have claimed to be capable of converting the hypotheses of the final argument into something more solid. But if he did come to form such opinions (and Aristotle's evidence is hard to write off), we cannot be sure how strongly he held them, or that he had formed them by the time when he wrote the *Phaedo*. There is in my view nothing in the dialogue which compels us to believe that he had. No doubt he could have said more on many subjects, but we have no reason to believe that the projects he suggests (for further investigation of his hypotheses, and for a complete teleological explanation of things) have already been completed. On the other hand, he clearly thinks that they can be successfully completed. In other words, the Plato of the *Phaedo* is a thinker whose mind is neither completely made up nor completely open. Like the Socrates he portrays, he knows what he believes in a general way, but is still busy constructing the arguments he needs to support his opinions, and to convince us of them.

4. THE *PHAEDO* AND PYTHAGOREANISM

The *Phaedo* is set in Phlius in the Peloponnese, where Phaedo, fresh from Athens, relates the story of Socrates' last hours to Echecrates, a native of the city. Echecrates was evidently one of a number of Pythagoreans working in Phlius; he and his friends therefore seem an entirely appropriate choice of audience for a conversation which turns around two ideas which themselves seem to have been quintessentially Pythagorean: that the soul is immortal, and that it may be reincarnated periodically in different bodies. However, the *Phaedo* not only fails to mention Echecrates' Pythagorean credentials, but actually casts doubt upon them, since it represents him as an enthusiastic supporter of the soul-as-harmony theory, which is incompatible with immortality. No doubt he was a Pythagorean, but somewhat unorthodox, and

[7] Arist. *Phys.* 209b14–15.

a rather odd choice if Plato's aim was to introduce us to an ambience of (orthodox) Pythagoreanism. His true role is perhaps just as a philosopher, outside Athens, who is anxious for news of Socrates. Phaedo, we are told, had been taken as a prisoner of war during the Spartan war with Elis, and sold in Athens (apparently as a male prostitute), where his freedom had been bought at Socrates' instigation; he then joined Socrates' circle, and left for his home town of Elis after the execution, calling in at Phlius on the way.[8]

It used to be held[9] that Simmias and Cebes were also Pythagoreans, on the grounds that they are said to have 'associated with' (συγγίγνεσθαι) the famous Pythagorean thinker Philolaus when he was in Thebes.[10] But 'associating with' someone does not necessarily imply adherence to their ideas; and there is no ancient evidence outside the *Phaedo* for the affiliation of either Simmias or Cebes to Pythagoreanism. Again, Simmias' espousal of the harmony theory of soul proves nothing: even if it was held by at least one Pythagorean (Echecrates), and is therefore claimed to be 'Pythagorean', holding a single view in common with a school does not make one a member of it. Rather, Simmias and Cebes are, like Phaedo, members of Socrates' group; they have participated many times before in philosophical discussions ('our questions and answers'),[11] and are less interested in doctrine than in listening to argument, and in finding out what can be established by argument. Paradoxically, it is Socrates himself, the master of those who know nothing, who has acquired 'Pythagorean' beliefs: in the *Apology*, Plato represents him as agnostic about survival after death.[12]

5. THE 'THEORY OF FORMS'

'Forms' (εἴδη) play a fundamental role in much of the conversation in the *Phaedo*. They are the things which 'we' (Socrates and those who have taken part in discussions with him) label as 'what is (equal, or beautiful, or good, or anything else)',[13] and of whose essence 'we' give, or try to give, an account.[14] The standard formula used for referring to forms is αὐτὸ τὸ *F*, i.e., apparently, what is just *F* and nothing else; e.g.

[8] See McQueen and Rowe 1989. [9] See esp. Burnet 1911.
[10] *Phd.* 61d.   [11] *Phd.* 75d, 78d.   [12] *Ap.* 40c.
[13] *Phd.* 75d.   [14] *Phd.* 78d.

8 INTRODUCTION

equality, or *beauty*, not particular examples of equality or beauty. That such things exist is enthusiastically endorsed by Simmias and Cebes; Simmias calls it 'a hypothesis worthy of acceptance'.[15] In fact, the version of the form-hypothesis which appears in the *Phaedo*, and especially its stress on the idea that forms somehow exist separately from particulars, is likely to be Platonic rather than authentically Socratic. But by portraying it as a familiar topic to those present Plato avoids the need to explain in detail what believing in 'forms' might amount to. The implication is perhaps that any philosophically-minded reader will easily come to see that, whatever 'forms' may be, and whatever their relationship with particulars, the assumption that they exist is necessary and uncontroversial. To the extent that it is possible to talk about, and define, something like equality (if not beauty) without special reference to any individual pair of equal things, Plato may seem to have a point; on the other hand, we may well have doubts about whether, as he supposes, what we are talking about in such cases is the sort of thing we could have grasped in some discarnate state, or whether it is capable of 'explaining' (being the αἰτία/αἴτιον of) particulars.[16] The latter proposition is one that 'Socrates' himself treats as a hypothesis: it is one of the two hypotheses that he leaves for further investigation at the end of the final argument,[17] the second being the basic proposition that 'each of the forms is something'.[18] But the difference between us and him is that whereas we would be likely to approach these propositions with scepticism, he clearly thinks that they will turn out to be viable.[19]

6. PLATONIC CONCEPTIONS OF THE SOUL

The word in the *Phaedo* which we translate as 'soul' is ψυχή. What this word refers to is something which inhabits the body while the latter is alive, and is indeed what brings life to it; it is also apparently, in essence, an entity with rational thoughts and desires, which acquires irrational tendencies – desires which are out of line with its rational essence – through its association with the body. Both conceptions have their roots in ordinary Greek language: in non-philosophical contexts, ψυχή ranges in meaning between something close to our 'life',

[15] *Phd.* 98d.   [16] See *Phd.* 100b, etc.   [17] *Phd.* 107b.   [18] *Phd.* 102a.
[19] See above, §3.

and 'mind', as the seat of consciousness, thought and emotion. In yet another role, it is that shadowy, insubstantial version of our former selves which, in Homer and in later poetry, goes to Hades when we die, still with visible shape but impotent and witless. It is from this idea that the main part of the argument of the dialogue begins, since it is what allows Socrates to gain easy acceptance for his definition of death as the separation of the ψυχή from the body. He is then forced to show that the ψυχή which survives this separation is durable and has 'power and intelligence',[20] as he has claimed, so grafting his own view of it (as animator of the body, and as a rational entity) onto the Homeric one, and extending the vague Homeric notion of continued existence into a full-blown immortality. In one partly playful context, Socrates envisages souls which were too attached to the body and its concerns in life as weighed down by corporeal elements, and so visible, like Homeric shades;[21] but in other passages discarnate souls are invisible and incorporeal.

Two problems in the treatment of the 'soul' in the *Phaedo* can be at least partly mitigated. The first problem is that it seems odd to make a rational entity responsible for the life of a biological organism, many of whose aspects are distinctly non-rational. However, Socrates' claim is only that the soul may *become* purely rational, when divested of the body. While incarnated, he hints, it is necessarily involved to some degree in the body's activities. In other dialogues the point is more explicitly recognised, through the division of the soul into rational and irrational parts; the *Phaedo* seems carefully to leave it open whether the soul is composite or unitary,[22] perhaps because it is more interested in its potentiality to achieve a godlike rationality than in what it is forced to be by its conjunction with a body.

The second problem is that whereas Socrates is clearly concerned to establish the immortality of the individual soul (since it is the individual's fear of death that forms the starting-point of the discussion), that is actually incompatible with the belief – to which he appears to be equally committed – in a cycle of reincarnation of souls. He does not propose any continuity of consciousness between one period of incarnation and another: the donkey into which Sardanapallus' soul enters does not remember having been Sardanapallus. The only soul which

---

[20] *Phd.* 70b.   [21] *Phd.* 81c–d (cf. 108a–b).
[22] See esp. *Phd.* 78b–80b, with nn.

will apparently maintain its identity is the truly philosophical one, which will join the company of the gods. That, however, may be enough for Plato's purposes, since philosophy then becomes important just because it is the only way of achieving full immortality – though the cost of achieving it, if it involves giving up everything except the search for knowledge, may seem rather high.

7. MYTHS AND PHILOSOPHY

The conversation Phaedo reports as having taking place in the prison falls into a number of interrelated parts. Socrates begins by defending his cheerfulness at the prospect of death. Challenged on the chief pre-supposition of this defence, the survival of the soul after the demise of the composite thing we call a 'human being', he then mounts a series of three arguments to try to establish it. Simmias and Cebes, however, are unconvinced: they ignore the first argument, claim that the second does not prove enough, and introduce powerful objections to the third – to the dismay of the others present, whose critical powers seem to be markedly inferior to those of the two Thebans. Socrates rallies them, but instead of defending his third argument, mounts an assault on the rival account of the soul proposed by Simmias (the 'harmony' theory), and then, in response to Cebes' objection, introduces a fourth and last argument, prefaced by a long disquisition on types of explanation. Finally, he launches into an elaborate 'myth' or story about the various destinations of the soul after death.

If the 'philosophy' of the *Phaedo* is identified with those parts of it which modern philosophical commentators find interesting,[23] then the myth at the end is certainly not philosophical. But from the point of view of what I claim to be *Plato's* view of philosophy,[24] the issue is rather less clear-cut: the myth, after all, is set within the same conver-sational context as the preceding arguments, and takes its starting-point from them ('if indeed the soul is immortal ...'; 'since the soul is clearly immortal ...').[25] Moreover, elements of Socrates' story link up closely both with his original 'defence' and with the arguments for immortality themselves. The usual explanation of Plato's use of myth is that it is a persuasive device to which he resorts as an adjunct to, or

[23] See above, §1.   [24] Above, §2.   [25] *Phd.* 107c.

support for, rational argument; and yet there are parts of the earlier arguments in the *Phaedo* which themselves rely heavily on persuasive description. Socrates gives his own verdict on the myth: it is something which no one with intelligence would insist on in all its details, and offers at best an approximation to the truth 'about our souls and their abodes'.[26] This perhaps justifies us in saying that he is at least less serious about the myth than he is about what has preceded, the conclusions of which he certainly literally believes. We should beware, however, of supposing that he would have drawn as sharp a distinction between his story-telling and his argumentative ('philosophical') mode as we may be tempted to do ourselves. He appears to be as attached to some of the ideas underlying the myth as he is to the 'hypotheses' on which the final argument for immortality depends. Nor is it likely to be insignificant that the whole series of arguments begins with the question to Cebes, whether 'we should διαμυθολογεῖν' ('talk / tell stories') about the subject of the soul and its fate.[27]

8. THE *PHAEDO* AND THE PLATONIC CORPUS

Among the working hypotheses of most Platonic scholars is that the dialogues can be divided up into three main periods: the early, or more authentically Socratic, period; the middle period, in which Plato developed and expressed some of his most characteristic ideas, in metaphysics, politics, and ethics; and the late period, which includes some of his more problematical and specialised works. This neat picture is based partly on stylistic arguments, partly on arguments relating to content, which assume that apparent differences of doctrine can best be explained in terms of the evolution of Plato's thought. The *Phaedo* is traditionally assigned, on both grounds, to the middle period, in close association with the *Symposium* and the *Republic*, and after *Meno*, which is commonly regarded as a kind of bridge between early and late periods. Such a placing is plausible enough in a number of respects: for example, the theory of recollection is introduced in a way that unmistakably recalls[28] (and perhaps also corrects)[29] the *Meno*; and some central parts of the *Republic* have often been seen as developments or expansions of ideas in the *Phaedo* (the *Symposium*, on the other hand,

----

[26] 104d.   [27] 70b.   [28] *Phd.* 73a–b.   [29] See *Phd.* 77c.

puzzlingly includes much talk about ways of achieving 'immortality',
but nothing about the actual immortality of the soul). However, I shall
suggest in the commentary that a number of the alleged differences
and similarities between the *Phaedo* and other dialogues dissolve on
close inspection. Were the *Phaedo* to declare firmly that the soul is
incomposite, as has sometimes been supposed, then that would raise
interesting questions about its relationship to the *Republic*, where much
of the argument depends on a view of the soul (at least from the perspective of human life) as tripartite; in fact, as I have suggested,[30] it
skirts around the issue. Again, I shall propose that the passage in the
Phaedo in which Socrates describes his 'second sailing' in search of the
αἰτία[31] is best seen in isolation from an apparently similar passage in
the *Republic*, which is talking about a different and only distantly related method; and that the same passage in some respects already
anticipates the first part of the *Parmenides*, which a strong body of
opinion regards as the turning-point between middle and late dialogues. This is not to suggest that there may not still be good grounds
for identifying the *Phaedo* as a 'middle' dialogue. But it does significantly lessen the usefulness of such labelling, in so far as the label
claims to tell us about the general philosophical relationship between
the *Phaedo* and other Platonic works. The genetic hypothesis remains a
hypothesis. Yet a strict unitarianism, which claims that Plato's ideas
never changed, is surely inconceivable. The moral is that we must
begin with close analysis of individual works, as their own form, as
self-standing conversations, encourages us to do in any case. The present volume attempts that task with the *Phaedo*.

9. THE TEXT OF THE *PHAEDO*

The most widely used text of the *Phaedo*, at least in the English-speak-
ing world, is that of Burnet, in the series of Oxford Classical Texts. The
text printed in this edition is based on Burnet, and one of the main
functions of the abbreviated apparatus is to call attention to places
where the text adopted differs from his (numerous changes of punctua-
tion have also been made which are not indicated). The Clarendon
Press some time ago commissioned a new edition of the Oxford text of

---

[30] See above, §6.   [31] *Phd.* 99c–102a.

Plato, and I am fortunate in having been able to call on the assistance of two of those responsible for this new edition, Christopher Strachan, who is the editor primarily responsible for the shape of the apparatus and editorial decisions for the new Oxford *Phaedo*, and David Robinson, in order to ensure that the apparatus should be as accurate as possible. In one or two places, they have persuaded me to return to Burnet's reading (or to adopt a different one); they also convinced me of the need to include rather more information than I had originally intended. Christopher Strachan generously corrected and commented on all the entries in a draft version, and I have accepted virtually all his suggestions (though the choice of these entries, and any residual errors, remain my own). I am extremely grateful for this collaboration, which has allowed me access to the latest scholarly work on the text of the *Phaedo*. It is clear from our discussions that our views on the balance of the arguments for particular readings frequently differ, but that these differences are rarely likely to have any significant impact on the interpretation of the dialogue; the commentary contains a defence of my choices in crucial cases.

For the details of the manuscript tradition of the *Phaedo*, including the relationship between the (ten) primary manuscripts, I refer to the forthcoming new edition of the Oxford text. Two of these primary manuscripts – which fall into three families – contain early corrections, which also count as primary sources. Other evidence for the text comes from quotations of the *Phaedo* in other ancient authors, and from papyri; there are also secondary or derivative manuscripts, which are occasionally the source of useful conjectures. In the apparatus, sigla identify readings as follows:

c = a reading on which there is consensus between the three families of primary manuscripts
m = a reading found in one or more of the primary sources
(m) = a reading found in one of the secondary manuscripts, or inserted by a late or uncertain hand in a primary manuscript
t = a reading found in a quotation of the *Phaedo* by another ancient author
p = a reading found in a papyrus fragment
e = a reading proposed by a modern editor (e.g. Stephanus) which falls into none of the other categories.

It should be emphasised that the apparatus is highly selective, and that there are many other places in the text where alternative readings are available in the tradition, or have been suggested by editors. These will usually be of only passing interest to anyone except the specialist textual critic or philologist, for whom the present edition is not intended. In general, the text of the *Phaedo* seems to be in good shape. It is however salutary to be reminded that, if what we read when we read 'the *Phaedo*' is at least a close approximation to what Plato wrote, as we must hope, it is in many of its details the work of restorers.

10. SELECT BIBLIOGRAPHY

Editions, commentaries, translations, etc.

Archer-Hind, R. D. *The Phaedo of Plato* (2nd edn.), London 1894 / New York 1973 (text and notes).

Bluck, R. S. *Plato's Phaedo*, London 1955 (translation and running commentary).

Burnet, J. *Plato's Phaedo*, Oxford 1911 (a lightly corrected and modified version of his text in the Oxford Classical Texts series, with commentary).

Centrone, B. (ed.) *Platone, Fedone*, Rome / Bari 1991 (Italian translation by M. Valgimigli, with notes).

Dixsaut, M. *Platon, Phédon*, Paris 1991 (translation with extensive notes).

Eggers Lan, C. *El Fedón de Platón*, Buenos Aires 1987[4] (Spanish translation with notes).

Gallop, D. *Plato, Phaedo*, Oxford 1975 (translation and commentary).

Hackforth, R. *Plato's Phaedo*, Cambridge 1955 (translation and commentary).

Loriaux, R. *Le Phédon de Platon* (2 vols.), Namur 1969/75 (commentary and translation).

Robin, L. *Platon, Phédon*, Paris 1926 (text and translation, with introduction and limited notes).

Tredennick, H. *The last days of Socrates* (revised edn), Harmondsworth 1969 (translation of *Phaedo* and three other dialogues).

Verdenius, W. J. 'Notes on Plato's Phaedo', *Mnemosyne* 11 (1958) 133–243 (notes on the text).

Vicaire, P. *Platon, Phédon* Paris 1983 (text and translation, with limited notes: in the same series as Robin, and largely replaces him).
Westerink, L. G. (ed.) *The Greek commentators on Plato's Phaedo,* I: *Olympiodorus*; II: *Damascius*, Amsterdam 1976–77.

The most useful commentaries are those of Burnet, Gallop, and Loriaux: Burnet's is of a traditional philological type, while Gallop caters for a modern philosophical audience; Loriaux gives the most complete account available of different interpretations of individual passages. The best translation is probably Gallop's, though Dixsaut's French version is sometimes more accurate (her notes are also a good supplement to Gallop's commentary).

Studies of the Phaedo

Bolotin, D. 'The life of philosophy and the immortality of the soul: an introduction to Plato's *Phaedo*', *Ancient Philosophy* 7 (1987) 29–56.
Bostock, D. *Plato's Phaedo*, Oxford 1986.
Burger, R. *The Phaedo: a Platonic labyrinth*, New Haven / London 1984.
Dorter, K. *Plato's Phaedo: an interpretation*, Toronto / Buffalo / London 1982.
White, D. A. *Myth and metaphysics in Plato's Phaedo*, London / Toronto 1989.

Other works on or relevant to the Phaedo

Ackrill, J. L. '*Anamnesis* in the *Phaedo*: remarks on 73c–75c', in E. N. Lee et al. (edd.), *Exegesis and argument*, Assen 1973.
Annas, J. 'Aristotle on inefficient causes', *Philosophical Quarterly* 32 (1982) 311–26.
    'Plato's myths of judgement', *Phronesis* 27 (1982) 119–43.
Anscombe, G. E. M. 'The early theory of forms', in *Collected philosophical papers*, I: *from Parmenides to Wittgenstein*, Oxford 1981, 9–20.
Arnott, W. G. 'Swan songs', *Greece and Rome* 24 (1977) 149–53.
Barnes, J. *The Presocratic philosophers* (2 vols.), London / Henley / Boston 1979.
Blank, D. L. 'Socrates' instructions to Cebes: Plato, *Phaedo* 101d–e', *Hermes* 114 (1986) 146–63.

Bluck, R. S. 'ὑποθέσεις in the *Phaedo* and Platonic dialectic', *Phronesis* 2 (1957) 21–31.

   'Forms as standards', *Phronesis* 2 (1957) 115–27.

   'Plato's Form of Equal', *Phronesis* 4 (1959) 4–11.

Brandwood, L. *A word index to Plato*, Manchester 1976.

Bremmer, J. *The ancient Greek concept of the soul*, Princeton 1983.

Brunner, F. 'Le dernier argument du *Phédon* de Platon en faveur de l'immortalité de l'âme', *Revue des sciences philosophiques et théologiques* 70 (1986) 497–520.

Burge, E. L. 'The ideas as *aitiai* in the *Phaedo*', *Phronesis* 16 (1971) 1–13.

Burkert, W. *Lore and science in ancient Pythagoreanism* (English translation), Cambridge, Mass. 1972.

   Greek religion, archaic and classical (English translation), Oxford 1985.

   Ancient mystery cults, Cambridge, Mass. / London 1987.

Calder, W. M., III 'The spherical earth in Plato's *Phaedo*', *Phronesis* 3 (1958) 121–5.

Claus, D. B. *Toward the soul: an inquiry into the meaning of ψυχή before Plato*, New Haven / London 1981.

Clay, D. 'The art of Glaukos', *American Journal of Philology* 106 (1985) 230–6.

   'Plato's first words', *Yale Classical Studies* 29 (1992) 113–29.

Cobb-Stevens, V. 'Mythos and logos in Plato's *Phaedo*', *Analecta Husserliana* 12 (1982) 391–405.

Crombie, I. M. *An examination of Plato's doctrines* (2 vols.), London / New York 1963.

Davidson, D. 'Actions, reasons, and causes', *The Journal of Philosophy* 60 (1963) 685–700.

Dixsaut, M. '*Ousia, eidos* et *idea* dans le *Phédon*', *Revue philosophique* 181 (1991) 479–500.

   'Le sens d'une alternative (*Phédon*, 78b), ou: De l'utilité des commentaires néo-platoniciens', in *Platonisme et néo-platonisme*, Athens 1991, 51–68.

Dodds, E. R. *Plato, Gorgias*, Oxford 1959.

   The Greeks and the irrational, Berkeley / Los Angeles 1963.

Dover, K. J. *Greek popular morality in the time of Plato and Aristotle*, Oxford 1974.

Fine, G. 'Separation', *Oxford Studies in Ancient Philosophy* 2 (1984) 31–87 (see further 3 (1985) 125–73).

   'Immanence', *Oxford Studies in Ancient Philosophy* 4 (1986) 71–97.

Frede, D. 'The final proof of the immortality of the soul in Plato's *Phaedo* 102a–107a', *Phronesis* 23 (1978) 24–41.

Frede, M. 'The original notion of cause', in M. Schofield et al. (edd.), *Doubt and dogmatism*, Oxford, 1980, 217–49.

Furley, D. *Cosmic problems: essays on Greek and Roman philosophy of nature*, Cambridge 1989.

Gallop, D. 'Plato's "Cyclical Argument" recycled', *Phronesis* 27 (1982) 207–22.

Gill, C. 'The death of Socrates', *Classical Quarterly* 23 (1973) 225–8.

Gosling, J. C. B. 'Similarity in *Phaedo* 73 seq.', *Phronesis* 10 (1965) 151–61.

Plato, London 1973.

Gottschalk, H. B. 'Soul as harmonia', *Phronesis* 16 (1971) 179–88.

Greene, W. C. *Scholia Platonica*, Haverford, Penn. 1938.

Griswold, C. L., Jr (ed.) *Platonic writings, Platonic readings*, London 1988.

Guthrie, W. K. C. 'Plato's views on the nature of the soul', reprinted in G. Vlastos (ed.), *Plato: a collection of critical essays*, vol. ii, New York 1971, 230–43.

Haynes, R. P. 'The form equality as a set of equals: *Phaedo* 74b–c', *Phronesis* 9 (1964) 17–26.

Hicken, W. F. '*Phaedo* 93a11–94b3', *Classical Quarterly* 4 (1954) 16–22.

Just, R. 'Freedom, slavery and the female psyche', *History of Political Thought* 6 (1985) 169–88.

Kerferd, G. B. *The sophistic movement*, Cambridge 1981.

Keuls, E. C. *Plato and Greek painting*, Leiden 1978.

Keyt, D. 'The fallacies in *Phaedo* 102a–107b', *Phronesis* 8 (1963) 167–72.

Klagge, J. C. and Smith, Nicholas D. (edd.) *Methods of interpreting Plato and his dialogues*, Oxford Studies in Ancient Philosophy, Supplementary Volume, 1992.

Krämer, H. J. *Plato and the foundations of metaphysics* (English translation), New York 1990.

Lennox, J. G. 'Plato's unnatural teleology', in D. J. O'Meara (ed.), *Platonic investigations*, Washington, D. C. 1985, 195–218.

Lloyd, G. E. R. 'Plato as a natural scientist', *Journal of Hellenic Studies* 88 (1968) 78–92.

Mackenzie, M. M. *Plato on punishment*, Berkeley / Los Angeles / London 1981.

McQueen, E. I. and Rowe, C. J. 'Phaedo, Socrates and the chronology of the Spartan war with Elis', *Méthexis* (*Rivista Argentina de Filosofía Antigua*) 2 (1989) 1–18.

Malcolm, J. *Plato on the self-predication of forms: early and middle dialogues*, Oxford 1991.

Mills, K. W. 'Plato *Phaedo* 74b7–c6', *Phronesis* 2 (1957) 128–47.

Moravcsik, J. 'Learning as recollection', in G. Vlastos (ed.), *Plato: a collection of critical essays*, vol. 1, New York 1971, 53–69.

Morrison, J. S. 'The shape of the earth in Plato's *Phaedo*', *Phronesis* 4 (1959) 110–19.

O'Brien, D. 'The last argument in Plato's *Phaedo*', *Classical Quarterly* 17 (1967) 198–231, 18 (1968) 95–106.

Owen, G. E. L. 'Dialectic and eristic in the treatment of the Forms', in Owen (ed.), *Aristotle on dialectic: the Topics*, Oxford 1968, 103–25.

Patterson, R. *Image and reality in Plato's metaphysics*, Indianapolis 1985.

Plass, P. 'Socrates' method of hypothesis in the *Phaedo*', *Phronesis* 5 (1960) 103–14.

Rist, J. M. 'Equals and intermediates in Plato', *Phronesis* 9 (1964) 27–37.

Robinson, R. *Plato's earlier dialectic*, Oxford 1953.

Robinson, T. M. *Plato's psychology*, Toronto 1970.

Rodis-Lewis, G. 'Limites de la simplicité de l'âme dans le *Phédon*', *Revue philosophique* 155 (1965) 441–54.

Rohde, E. *Psyche* (2 vols.), Freiburg 1894.

Roochnik, D. *The tragedy of reason: towards a Platonic conception of logos*, London 1990.

Ross, W. D. *Plato's Theory of Ideas*, Oxford 1951.

Rowe, C. J. 'The argument and structure of Plato's *Phaedrus*', *Proceedings of the Cambridge Philological Society* n.s. 32 (1986) 106–25.

   'L'argument par "affinité" dans le *Phédon*', *Revue philosophique* 181 (1991) 463–77.

   'Philosophy and literature: the arguments of Plato's *Phaedo*', forthcoming in *Proceedings of the Boston Area Colloquium in Ancient Philosophy* 7 (1991–92).

   'On reading Plato', *Méthexis* 5 (1992) 53–68 (= Rowe 1992a).

   'Parasite or fantasist? The role of the literary commentator', *Cogito* 6 (1992) 9–18 (= Rowe 1992b).

   'Explanation in *Phaedo* 99c6–102a8', forthcoming in *Oxford Studies in Ancient Philosophy* 11 (1993).

Scarrow, D. S. '*Phaedo* 106a–106e', *Philosophical Review* 70 (1961) 245–53.

Schiller, J. '*Phaedo* 104–5: is the soul a form?', *Phronesis* 12 (1967) 50–8.

Scott, D. 'Platonic anamnesis revisited', *Classical Quarterly* 37 (1987) 346–66.

Sedley, D. 'Teleology and myth in the *Phaedo*', forthcoming in *Proceedings of the Boston Area Colloquium in Ancient Philosophy* 5 (1989–90).

Stewart, D. 'Socrates' last bath', *Journal of the History of Philosophy* 10 (1972) 253–9.

Szlezák, T. A. *Platon und die Schriftlichkeit der Philosophie: Interpretationen zu den frühen und mittleren Dialogen*, Berlin / New York 1985.

Tarán, L. 'Plato, *Phaedo* 62a', *American Journal of Philology* 84 (1966) 326–36.

Taylor, C. C. W. 'Forms as causes in the *Phaedo*', *Mind* 78 (1969) 45–59.

Vlastos, G. 'Reasons and causes in the *Phaedo*', *Philosophical Review* 78 (1969) 291–325 (reprinted with corrections and additions in Vlastos, *Platonic Studies*, Princeton 1973, 76–109).

Weiss, R. 'The right exchange: *Phaedo* 69a6–c3', *Ancient Philosophy* 7 (1987) 57–66.

West, M. L. *The Orphic poems*, Oxford 1983.

Westerink, L. G. (ed.) *Anonymous prolegomena to Platonic philosophy*, Amsterdam 1962.

Wiggins, D. 'Teleology and the good in the *Phaedo*', *Oxford Studies in Ancient Philosophy* 4 (1986) 1–18.

Williams, C. J. F. 'On dying', *Philosophy* 44 (1969) 217–30.

Note: references to less frequently cited items among the secondary literature are given in the form 'Williams 1969'; references to commentators on *Phd.* are by author's surname alone.

THE
PHAEDO

ΦΑΙΔΩΝ

ΕΧΕΚΡΑΤΗΣ   ΦΑΙΔΩΝ

ΕΧ. αὐτός, ὦ Φαίδων, παρεγένου Σωκράτει ἐκείνηι τῆι 57
ἡμέραι ἧι τὸ φάρμακον ἔπιεν ἐν τῶι δεσμωτηρίωι, ἢ ἄλλου του
ἤκουσας;

ΦΑΙΔ. αὐτός, ὦ Ἐχέκρατες.

ΕΧ. τί οὖν δή ἐστιν ἅττα εἶπεν ὁ ἀνὴρ πρὸ τοῦ θανά- 5
του; καὶ πῶς ἐτελεύτα; ἡδέως γὰρ ἂν ἐγὼ ἀκούσαιμι. καὶ
γὰρ οὔτε [τῶν πολιτῶν] Φλειασίων οὐδεὶς πάνυ τι ἐπιχωριάζει
τὰ νῦν Ἀθήναζε, οὔτε τις ξένος ἀφῖκται χρόνου συχνοῦ
ἐκεῖθεν ὅστις ἂν ἡμῖν σαφές τι ἀγγεῖλαι οἷός τ᾽ ἦν περὶ b
τούτων, πλήν γε δὴ ὅτι φάρμακον πιὼν ἀποθάνοι· τῶν δὲ
ἄλλων οὐδὲν εἶχεν φράζειν.

ΦΑΙΔ. οὐδὲ τὰ περὶ τῆς δίκης ἄρα ἐπύθεσθε ὃν τρόπον 58
ἐγένετο;

ΕΧ. ναί, ταῦτα μὲν ἡμῖν ἤγγειλέ τις, καὶ ἐθαυμάζομέν
γε ὅτι πάλαι γενομένης αὐτῆς πολλῶι ὕστερον φαίνεται
ἀποθανών. τί οὖν ἦν τοῦτο, ὦ Φαίδων; 5

ΦΑΙΔ. τύχη τις αὐτῶι, ὦ Ἐχέκρατες, συνέβη· ἔτυχεν
γὰρ τῆι προτεραίαι τῆς δίκης ἡ πρύμνα ἐστεμμένη τοῦ πλοίου
ὃ εἰς Δῆλον Ἀθηναῖοι πέμπουσιν.

ΕΧ. τοῦτο δὲ δὴ τί ἐστιν;

ΦΑΙΔ. τοῦτ᾽ ἔστι τὸ πλοῖον, ὥς φασιν Ἀθηναῖοι, ἐν ὧι 10
Θησεύς ποτε εἰς Κρήτην τοὺς "δὶς ἑπτὰ" ἐκείνους ὤιχετο
ἄγων καὶ ἔσωσέ τε καὶ αὐτὸς ἐσώθη. τῶι οὖν Ἀπόλλωνι b
ηὔξαντο ὡς λέγεται τότε, εἰ σωθεῖεν, ἑκάστου ἔτους θεωρίαν
ἀπάξειν εἰς Δῆλον· ἣν δὴ ἀεὶ καὶ νῦν ἔτι ἐξ ἐκείνου κατ᾽
ἐνιαυτὸν τῶι θεῶι πέμπουσιν. ἐπειδὰν οὖν ἄρξωνται τῆς
θεωρίας, νόμος ἐστὶν αὐτοῖς ἐν τῶι χρόνωι τούτωι καθαρεύειν 5
τὴν πόλιν καὶ δημοσίαι μηδένα ἀποκτεινύναι, πρὶν ἂν εἰς
Δῆλόν τε ἀφίκηται τὸ πλοῖον καὶ πάλιν δεῦρο· τοῦτο δ᾽

a7 τῶν πολιτῶν c: secl. e

ἐνίοτε ἐν πολλῶι χρόνωι γίγνεται, ὅταν τύχωσιν ἄνεμοι ἀπο-
c λαβόντες αὐτούς. ἀρχὴ δ' ἐστὶ τῆς θεωρίας ἐπειδὰν ὁ
ἱερεὺς τοῦ Ἀπόλλωνος στέψηι τὴν πρύμναν τοῦ πλοίου·
τοῦτο δ' ἔτυχεν, ὥσπερ λέγω, τῆι προτεραίαι τῆς δίκης γεγο-
νός. διὰ ταῦτα καὶ πολὺς χρόνος ἐγένετο τῶι Σωκράτει ἐν
5 τῶι δεσμωτηρίωι ὁ μεταξὺ τῆς δίκης τε καὶ τοῦ θανάτου.

    ΕΧ. τί δὲ δὴ τὰ περὶ αὐτὸν τὸν θάνατον, ὦ Φαίδων; τί
ἦν τὰ λεχθέντα καὶ πραχθέντα, καὶ τίνες οἱ παραγενόμενοι
τῶν ἐπιτηδείων τῶι ἀνδρί; ἢ οὐκ εἴων οἱ ἄρχοντες παρεῖναι,
ἀλλ' ἔρημος ἐτελεύτα φίλων;
d   ΦΑΙΔ. οὐδαμῶς, ἀλλὰ παρῆσάν τινες, καὶ πολλοί γε.

    ΕΧ. ταῦτα δὴ πάντα προθυμήθητι ὡς σαφέστατα ἡμῖν
ἀπαγγεῖλαι, εἰ μή τίς σοι ἀσχολία τυγχάνει οὖσα.

    ΦΑΙΔ. ἀλλὰ σχολάζω γε καὶ πειράσομαι ὑμῖν διηγή-
5 σασθαι· καὶ γὰρ τὸ μεμνῆσθαι Σωκράτους καὶ αὐτὸν λέγοντα
καὶ ἄλλου ἀκούοντα ἔμοιγε ἀεὶ πάντων ἥδιστον.

    ΕΧ. ἀλλὰ μήν, ὦ Φαίδων, καὶ τοὺς ἀκουσομένους γε
τοιούτους ἑτέρους ἔχεις· ἀλλὰ πειρῶ ὡς ἂν δύνηι ἀκριβέστατα διεξελθεῖν πάντα.
e   ΦΑΙΔ. καὶ μὴν ἔγωγε θαυμάσια ἔπαθον παραγενόμενος.
οὔτε γὰρ ὡς θανάτωι παρόντα με ἀνδρὸς ἐπιτηδείου ἔλεος
εἰσήιει· εὐδαίμων γάρ μοι ἀνὴρ ἐφαίνετο, ὦ Ἐχέκρατες, καὶ
τοῦ τρόπου καὶ τῶν λόγων, ὡς ἀδεῶς καὶ γενναίως ἐτελεύτα,
5 ὥστε μοι ἐκεῖνον παρίστασθαι μηδ' εἰς Ἅιδου ἰόντα ἄνευ
θείας μοίρας ἰέναι, ἀλλὰ καὶ ἐκεῖσε ἀφικόμενον εὖ πράξειν
59 εἴπερ τις πώποτε καὶ ἄλλος. διὰ δὴ ταῦτα οὐδὲν πάνυ μοι
ἐλεινὸν εἰσήιει, ὡς εἰκὸς ἂν δόξειεν εἶναι παρόντι πένθει·
οὔτε αὖ ἡδονὴ ὡς ἐν φιλοσοφίαι ἡμῶν ὄντων ὥσπερ εἰώθεμεν
(καὶ γὰρ οἱ λόγοι τοιοῦτοί τινες ἦσαν), ἀλλ' ἀτεχνῶς
5 ἄτοπόν τί μοι πάθος παρῆν καί τις ἀήθης κρᾶσις ἀπό τε τῆς
ἡδονῆς συγκεκραμένη ὁμοῦ καὶ ἀπὸ τῆς λύπης, ἐνθυμουμένωι
ὅτι αὐτίκα ἐκεῖνος ἔμελλε τελευτᾶν. καὶ πάντες οἱ παρόντες
σχεδόν τι οὕτω διεκείμεθα, τοτὲ μὲν γελῶντες, ἐνίοτε δὲ
δακρύοντες, εἷς δὲ ἡμῶν καὶ διαφερόντως, Ἀπολλόδωρος·
b οἶσθα γάρ που τὸν ἄνδρα καὶ τὸν τρόπον αὐτοῦ.

ΕΧ. πῶς γὰρ οὔ;

ΦΑΙΔ. ἐκεῖνός τε τοίνυν παντάπασιν οὕτως εἶχεν, καὶ
αὐτὸς ἔγωγε ἐτεταράγμην καὶ οἱ ἄλλοι.

ΕΧ. ἔτυχον δέ, ὦ Φαίδων, τίνες παραγενόμενοι;   5

ΦΑΙΔ. οὗτός τε δὴ ὁ Ἀπολλόδωρος τῶν ἐπιχωρίων
παρῆν καὶ Κριτόβουλος καὶ ὁ πατὴρ αὐτοῦ καὶ ἔτι Ἑρμογένης καὶ Ἐπιγένης καὶ Αἰσχίνης καὶ Ἀντισθένης· ἦν δὲ καὶ
Κτήσιππος ὁ Παιανιεὺς καὶ Μενέξενος καὶ ἄλλοι τινὲς τῶν
ἐπιχωρίων. Πλάτων δὲ οἶμαι ἠσθένει.   10

ΕΧ. ξένοι δέ τινες παρῆσαν;

ΦΑΙΔ. ναί, Σιμμίας τέ γε ὁ Θηβαῖος καὶ Κέβης καὶ c
Φαιδώνδης καὶ Μεγαρόθεν Εὐκλείδης τε καὶ Τερψίων.

ΕΧ. τί δέ; Ἀρίστιππος καὶ Κλεόμβροτος παρεγένοντο;

ΦΑΙΔ. οὐ δῆτα· ἐν Αἰγίνηι γὰρ ἐλέγοντο εἶναι.

ΕΧ. ἄλλος δέ τις παρῆν;   5

ΦΑΙΔ. σχεδόν τι οἶμαι τούτους παραγενέσθαι.

ΕΧ. τί οὖν δή; τίνες φὴις ἦσαν οἱ λόγοι;

ΦΑΙΔ. ἐγώ σοι ἐξ ἀρχῆς πάντα πειράσομαι διηγήσασθαι. ἀεὶ γὰρ δὴ καὶ τὰς πρόσθεν ἡμέρας εἰώθεμεν φοιτᾶν d
καὶ ἐγὼ καὶ οἱ ἄλλοι παρὰ τὸν Σωκράτη, συλλεγόμενοι
ἕωθεν εἰς τὸ δικαστήριον ἐν ὧι καὶ ἡ δίκη ἐγένετο· πλησίον
γὰρ ἦν τοῦ δεσμωτηρίου. περιεμένομεν οὖν ἑκάστοτε ἕως
ἀνοιχθείη τὸ δεσμωτήριον, διατρίβοντες μετ᾽ ἀλλήλων, ἀνεῴι- 5
γετο γὰρ οὐ πρώι· ἐπειδὴ δὲ ἀνοιχθείη, εἰσῆιμεν παρὰ τὸν
Σωκράτη καὶ τὰ πολλὰ διημερεύομεν μετ᾽ αὐτοῦ. καὶ δὴ καὶ
τότε πρωιαίτερον συνελέγημεν· τῆι γὰρ προτεραίαι [ἡμέραι]
ἐπειδὴ ἐξήλθομεν ἐκ τοῦ δεσμωτηρίου ἑσπέρας, ἐπυθόμεθα e
ὅτι τὸ πλοῖον ἐκ Δήλου ἀφιγμένον εἴη. παρηγγείλαμεν οὖν
ἀλλήλοις ἥκειν ὡς πρωιαίτατα εἰς τὸ εἰωθός. καὶ ἥκομεν, καὶ
ἡμῖν ἐξελθὼν ὁ θυρωρός, ὅσπερ εἰώθει ὑπακούειν, εἶπεν περιμένειν καὶ μὴ πρότερον παριέναι ἕως ἂν αὐτὸς κελεύσηι· 5
"λύουσι γάρ", ἔφη, "οἱ ἕνδεκα Σωκράτη καὶ παραγγέλλουσιν
ὅπως ἂν τῆιδε τῆι ἡμέραι τελευτᾶι." οὐ πολὺν δ᾽ οὖν χρόνον

e4 περιμένειν *m*: ἐπιμένειν *m*

ἐπισχὼν ἧκεν καὶ ἐκέλευεν ἡμᾶς εἰσιέναι. εἰσιόντες οὖν
60 κατελαμβάνομεν τὸν μὲν Σωκράτη ἄρτι λελυμένον, τὴν δὲ
Ξανθίππην (γιγνώσκεις γάρ) ἔχουσάν τε τὸ παιδίον αὐτοῦ
καὶ παρακαθημένην. ὡς οὖν εἶδεν ἡμᾶς ἡ Ξανθίππη, ἀνηυ-
φήμησέ τε καὶ τοιαῦτ᾽ ἄττα εἶπεν, οἷα δὴ εἰώθασιν αἱ
5 γυναῖκες, ὅτι "ὦ Σώκρατες, ὕστατον δή σε προσεροῦσι νῦν
οἱ ἐπιτήδειοι καὶ σὺ τούτους." καὶ ὁ Σωκράτης βλέψας εἰς
τὸν Κρίτωνα, "ὦ Κρίτων," ἔφη, "ἀπαγέτω τις αὐτὴν
οἴκαδε."

καὶ ἐκείνην μὲν ἀπῆγόν τινες τῶν τοῦ Κρίτωνος βοῶσάν
b τε καὶ κοπτομένην· ὁ δὲ Σωκράτης ἀνακαθιζόμενος εἰς τὴν
κλίνην συνέκαμψέ τε τὸ σκέλος καὶ ἐξέτριψε τῆι χειρί, καὶ
τρίβων ἅμα, "ὡς ἄτοπον," ἔφη, "ὦ ἄνδρες, ἔοικέ τι εἶναι
τοῦτο ὃ καλοῦσιν οἱ ἄνθρωποι ἡδύ· ὡς θαυμασίως πέφυκε
5 πρὸς τὸ δοκοῦν ἐναντίον εἶναι, τὸ λυπηρόν, τὸ ἅμα μὲν
αὐτὼ μὴ θέλειν παραγίγνεσθαι τῶι ἀνθρώπωι, ἐὰν δέ τις
διώκηι τὸ ἕτερον καὶ λαμβάνηι, σχεδόν τι ἀναγκάζεσθαι ἀεὶ
λαμβάνειν καὶ τὸ ἕτερον, ὥσπερ ἐκ μιᾶς κορυφῆς ἡμμένω
c δύ᾽ ὄντε. καί μοι δοκεῖ," ἔφη, "εἰ ἐνενόησεν αὐτὰ Αἴσωπος,
μῦθον ἂν συνθεῖναι ὡς ὁ θεὸς βουλόμενος αὐτὰ διαλλάξαι
πολεμοῦντα, ἐπειδὴ οὐκ ἐδύνατο, συνῆψεν εἰς ταὐτὸν αὐτοῖς
τὰς κορυφάς, καὶ διὰ ταῦτα, ὧι ἂν τὸ ἕτερον παραγένηται
5 ἐπακολουθεῖ ὕστερον καὶ τὸ ἕτερον. ὥσπερ οὖν καὶ αὐτῶι μοι
ἔοικεν· ἐπειδὴ ὑπὸ τοῦ δεσμοῦ ἦν ἐν τῶι σκέλει τὸ ἀλγεινόν,
ἥκειν δὴ φαίνεται ἐπακολουθοῦν τὸ ἡδύ."

ὁ οὖν Κέβης ὑπολαβών, "νὴ τὸν Δία, ὦ Σώκρατες,"
ἔφη, "εὖ γ᾽ ἐποίησας ἀναμνήσας με. περὶ γάρ τοι τῶν
d ποιημάτων ὧν πεποίηκας ἐντείνας τοὺς τοῦ Αἰσώπου λόγους
καὶ τὸ εἰς τὸν Ἀπόλλω προοίμιον καὶ ἄλλοι τινές με ἤδη
ἤροντο, ἀτὰρ καὶ Εὔηνος πρώην, ὅτι ποτὲ διανοηθείς, ἐπειδὴ
δεῦρο ἦλθες, ἐποίησας αὐτά, πρότερον οὐδὲν πώποτε ποιήσας.
5 εἰ οὖν τί σοι μέλει τοῦ ἔχειν ἐμὲ Εὐήνωι ἀποκρίνασθαι ὅταν

e8 εἰσιόντες m: εἰσελθόντες m

με αὖθις ἐρωτᾶι (εὖ οἶδα γὰρ ὅτι ἐρήσεται) εἰπὲ τί χρὴ
λέγειν."

"λέγε τοίνυν", ἔφη, "αὐτῶι, ὦ Κέβης, τἀληθῆ, ὅτι οὐκ
ἐκείνωι βουλόμενος οὐδὲ τοῖς ποιήμασιν αὐτοῦ ἀντίτεχνος
εἶναι ἐποίησα ταῦτα (ἤιδη γὰρ ὡς οὐ ῥάιδιον εἴη), ἀλλ' e
ἐνυπνίων τινῶν ἀποπειρώμενος τί λέγει, καὶ ἀφοσιούμενος
εἰ ἄρα πολλάκις ταύτην τὴν μουσικήν μοι ἐπιτάττοι ποιεῖν.
ἦν γὰρ δὴ ἄττα τοιάδε· πολλάκις μοι φοιτῶν τὸ αὐτὸ ἐνύπνιον ἐν τῶι παρελθόντι βίωι, ἄλλοτ' ἐν ἄλληι ὄψει φαινό- 5
μενον, τὰ αὐτὰ δὲ λέγον, 'ὦ Σώκρατες,' ἔφη, 'μουσικὴν
ποίει καὶ ἐργάζου.' καὶ ἐγὼ ἔν γε τῶι πρόσθεν χρόνωι ὅπερ
ἔπραττον τοῦτο ὑπελάμβανον αὐτό μοι παρακελεύεσθαί τε
καὶ ἐπικελεύειν, ὥσπερ οἱ τοῖς θέουσι διακελευόμενοι, καὶ 61
ἐμοὶ οὕτω τὸ ἐνύπνιον ὅπερ ἔπραττον τοῦτο ἐπικελεύειν,
μουσικὴν ποιεῖν, ὡς φιλοσοφίας μὲν οὔσης μεγίστης μουσι-
κῆς, ἐμοῦ δὲ τοῦτο πράττοντος. νῦν δ' ἐπειδὴ ἥ τε δίκη
ἐγένετο καὶ ἡ τοῦ θεοῦ ἑορτὴ διεκώλυέ με ἀποθνήισκειν, ἔδοξε 5
χρῆναι, εἰ ἄρα πολλάκις μοι προστάττοι τὸ ἐνύπνιον ταύτην
τὴν δημώδη μουσικὴν ποιεῖν, μὴ ἀπειθῆσαι αὐτῶι ἀλλὰ
ποιεῖν· ἀσφαλέστερον γὰρ εἶναι μὴ ἀπιέναι πρὶν ἀφοσιώ-
σασθαι ποιήσαντα ποιήματα καὶ πειθόμενον τῶι ἐνυπνίωι. b
οὕτω δὴ πρῶτον μὲν εἰς τὸν θεὸν ἐποίησα οὗ ἦν ἡ παροῦσα
θυσία· μετὰ δὲ τὸν θεόν, ἐννοήσας ὅτι τὸν ποιητὴν δέοι,
εἴπερ μέλλοι ποιητὴς εἶναι, ποιεῖν μύθους ἀλλ' οὐ λόγους,
καὶ αὐτὸς οὐκ ἦ μυθολογικός, διὰ ταῦτα δὴ οὓς προχείρους 5
εἶχον μύθους καὶ ἠπιστάμην, τοὺς Αἰσώπου, τούτων ἐποίησα
οἷς πρώτοις ἐνέτυχον. ταῦτα οὖν, ὦ Κέβης, Εὐήνωι φράζε,
καὶ ἐρρῶσθαι καί, ἂν σωφρονῆι, ἐμὲ διώκειν ὡς τάχιστα.
ἄπειμι δέ, ὡς ἔοικε, τήμερον· κελεύουσι γὰρ Ἀθηναῖοι." c
καὶ ὁ Σιμμίας, "οἷον παρακελεύηι", ἔφη, "τοῦτο, ὦ Σώκρατες, Εὐήνωι. πολλὰ γὰρ ἤδη ἐντετύχηκα τῶι ἀνδρί·

---

e2 λέγει m: λέγειν m: λέγοι (m)   e3 εἰ ἄρα πολλάκις m: εἰ πολλάκις m
b1 καὶ πειθόμενον m: πειθόμενον m: πιθόμενον e

σχεδὸν οὖν ἐξ ὧν ἐγὼ ἤισθημαι οὐδ᾽ ὁπωστιοῦν σοι ἑκὼν
5 εἶναι πείσεται."

"τί δέ;" ἦ δ᾽ ὅς, "οὐ φιλόσοφος Εὔηνος;"

"ἔμοιγε δοκεῖ," ἔφη ὁ Σιμμίας.

"ἐθελήσει τοίνυν καὶ Εὔηνος καὶ πᾶς ὅτωι ἀξίως τούτου
τοῦ πράγματος μέτεστιν. οὐ μέντοι ἴσως βιάσεται αὐτόν·
10 οὐ γάρ φασι θεμιτὸν εἶναι." καὶ ἅμα λέγων ταῦτα καθῆκε
d τὰ σκέλη ἐπὶ τὴν γῆν, καὶ καθεζόμενος οὕτως ἤδη τὰ λοιπὰ
διελέγετο.

ἤρετο οὖν αὐτὸν ὁ Κέβης· "πῶς τοῦτο λέγεις, ὦ
Σώκρατες, τὸ μὴ θεμιτὸν εἶναι ἑαυτὸν βιάζεσθαι, ἐθέλειν δ᾽
5 ἂν τῶι ἀποθνήισκοντι τὸν φιλόσοφον ἕπεσθαι;"

"τί δέ, ὦ Κέβης; οὐκ ἀκηκόατε σύ τε καὶ Σιμμίας περὶ
τῶν τοιούτων Φιλολάωι συγγεγονότες;"

"οὐδέν γε σαφές, ὦ Σώκρατες."

"ἀλλὰ μὴν καὶ ἐγὼ ἐξ ἀκοῆς περὶ αὐτῶν λέγω· ἃ μὲν
10 οὖν τυγχάνω ἀκηκοὼς φθόνος οὐδεὶς λέγειν. καὶ γὰρ ἴσως
e καὶ μάλιστα πρέπει μέλλοντα ἐκεῖσε ἀποδημεῖν διασκοπεῖν
τε καὶ μυθολογεῖν περὶ τῆς ἀποδημίας τῆς ἐκεῖ, ποίαν τινὰ
αὐτὴν οἰόμεθα εἶναι· τί γὰρ ἄν τις καὶ ποιοῖ ἄλλο ἐν τῶι
μέχρι ἡλίου δυσμῶν χρόνωι;"

5 "κατὰ τί δὴ οὖν ποτε οὔ φασι θεμιτὸν εἶναι αὐτὸν ἑαυτὸν
ἀποκτεινύναι, ὦ Σώκρατες; ἤδη γὰρ ἔγωγε, ὅπερ νυνδὴ σὺ
ἤρου, καὶ Φιλολάου ἤκουσα, ὅτε παρ᾽ ἡμῖν διηιτᾶτο, ἤδη δὲ
καὶ ἄλλων τινῶν, ὡς οὐ δέοι τοῦτο ποιεῖν· σαφὲς δὲ περὶ
αὐτῶν οὐδενὸς πώποτε οὐδὲν ἀκήκοα."

62 "ἀλλὰ προθυμεῖσθαι χρή," ἔφη· "τάχα γὰρ ἂν καὶ ἀκούσαις. ἴσως μέντοι θαυμαστόν σοι φανεῖται εἰ τοῦτο μόνον
τῶν ἄλλων ἁπάντων ἁπλοῦν ἐστιν, καὶ οὐδέποτε τυγχάνει τῶι
ἀνθρώπωι, ὥσπερ καὶ τἆλλα, ἔστιν ὅτε καὶ οἷς βέλτιον
5 τεθνάναι ἢ ζῆν· οἷς δὲ βέλτιον τεθνάναι, θαυμαστὸν ἴσως
σοι φαίνεται εἰ τούτοις τοῖς ἀνθρώποις μὴ ὅσιον αὐτοὺς
ἑαυτοὺς εὖ ποιεῖν, ἀλλὰ ἄλλον δεῖ περιμένειν εὐεργέτην."

a4 βέλτιον ⟨ὂν⟩ e

καὶ ὁ Κέβης ἠρέμα ἐπιγελάσας, "Ἴττω Ζεύς," ἔφη, τῆι
αὑτοῦ φωνῆι εἰπών.

"καὶ γὰρ ἂν δόξειεν", ἔφη ὁ Σωκράτης, "οὕτω γ' εἶναι b
ἄλογον· οὐ μέντοι ἀλλ' ἴσως γ' ἔχει τινὰ λόγον. ὁ μὲν οὖν
ἐν ἀπορρήτοις λεγόμενος περὶ αὐτῶν λόγος, ὡς ἔν τινι
φρουρᾶι ἐσμεν οἱ ἄνθρωποι καὶ οὐ δεῖ δὴ ἑαυτὸν ἐκ ταύτης
λύειν οὐδ' ἀποδιδράσκειν, μέγας τέ τίς μοι φαίνεται καὶ οὐ 5
ῥάιδιος διιδεῖν· οὐ μέντοι ἀλλὰ τόδε γέ μοι δοκεῖ, ὦ Κέβης,
εὖ λέγεσθαι, τὸ θεοὺς εἶναι ἡμῶν τοὺς ἐπιμελουμένους καὶ
ἡμᾶς τοὺς ἀνθρώπους ἓν τῶν κτημάτων τοῖς θεοῖς εἶναι. ἢ
σοὶ οὐ δοκεῖ οὕτως;"

"ἔμοιγε," φησὶν ὁ Κέβης.   10

"οὔκουν", ἦ δ' ὅς, "καὶ σὺ ἂν τῶν σαυτοῦ κτημάτων εἴ c
τι αὐτὸ ἑαυτὸ ἀποκτεινύοι, μὴ σημήναντός σου ὅτι βούλει
αὐτὸ τεθνάναι, χαλεπαίνοις ἂν αὐτῶι καί, εἴ τινα ἔχοις
τιμωρίαν, τιμωροῖο ἄν;"

"πάνυ γ'," ἔφη.   5

"ἴσως τοίνυν ταύτηι οὐκ ἄλογον μὴ πρότερον αὑτὸν
ἀποκτεινύναι δεῖν, πρὶν ἀνάγκην τινὰ θεὸς ἐπιπέμψηι,
ὥσπερ καὶ τὴν νῦν ἡμῖν παροῦσαν."

"ἀλλ' εἰκός", ἔφη ὁ Κέβης, "τοῦτό γε φαίνεται. ὁ μέντοι νυνδὴ ἔλεγες, τὸ τοὺς φιλοσόφους ῥαιδίως ἂν ἐθέλειν 10
ἀποθνήισκειν, ἔοικεν τοῦτο, ὦ Σώκρατες, ἀτόπωι, εἴπερ ὃ d
νυνδὴ ἐλέγομεν εὐλόγως ἔχει, τὸ θεόν τε εἶναι τὸν ἐπιμε-
λούμενον ἡμῶν καὶ ἡμᾶς ἐκείνου κτήματα εἶναι. τὸ γὰρ μὴ
ἀγανακτεῖν τοὺς φρονιμωτάτους ἐκ ταύτης τῆς θεραπείας
ἀπιόντας, ἐν ἧι ἐπιστατοῦσιν αὐτῶν οἵπερ ἄριστοί εἰσιν τῶν 5
ὄντων ἐπιστάται, θεοί, οὐκ ἔχει λόγον· οὐ γάρ που αὐτός γε
αὑτοῦ οἴεται ἄμεινον ἐπιμελήσεσθαι ἐλεύθερος γενόμενος.
ἀλλ' ἀνόητος μὲν ἄνθρωπος τάχ' ἂν οἰηθείη ταῦτα, φευκτέον
εἶναι ἀπὸ τοῦ δεσπότου, καὶ οὐκ ἂν λογίζοιτο ὅτι οὐ δεῖ ἀπό e
γε τοῦ ἀγαθοῦ φεύγειν ἀλλ' ὅτι μάλιστα παραμένειν, διὸ
ἀλογίστως ἂν φεύγοι· ὁ δὲ νοῦν ἔχων ἐπιθυμοῖ που ἂν ἀεὶ

c7 πρὶν ⟨ἂν⟩ e   θεὸς m: ὁ θεὸς m

εἶναι παρὰ τῶι αὐτοῦ βελτίονι. καίτοι οὕτως, ὦ Σώκρατες,
5 τοὐναντίον εἶναι εἰκὸς ἢ ὃ νυνδὴ ἐλέγετο· τοὺς μὲν γὰρ
φρονίμους ἀγανακτεῖν ἀποθνήισκοντας πρέπει, τοὺς δὲ ἄφρονας
χαίρειν."
    ἀκούσας οὖν ὁ Σωκράτης ἡσθῆναί τέ μοι ἔδοξε τῆι τοῦ
63 Κέβητος πραγματείαι, καὶ ἐπιβλέψας εἰς ἡμᾶς, "ἀεί τοι",
ἔφη, "ὁ Κέβης λόγους τινὰς ἀνερευνᾶι, καὶ οὐ πάνυ εὐθέως
ἐθέλει πείθεσθαι ὅτι ἄν τις εἴπηι."
    καὶ ὁ Σιμμίας, "ἀλλὰ μήν," ἔφη, "ὦ Σώκρατες, νῦν γέ μοι
5 δοκεῖ τι καὶ αὐτῶι λέγειν Κέβης· τί γὰρ ἂν βουλόμενοι
ἄνδρες σοφοὶ ὡς ἀληθῶς δεσπότας ἀμείνους αὐτῶν φεύγοιεν
καὶ ῥαιδίως ἀπαλλάττοιντο αὐτῶν; καί μοι δοκεῖ Κέβης εἰς
σὲ τείνειν τὸν λόγον, ὅτι οὕτω ῥαιδίως φέρεις καὶ ἡμᾶς
ἀπολείπων καὶ ἄρχοντας ἀγαθούς, ὡς αὐτὸς ὁμολογεῖς, θεούς."
b   "δίκαια", ἔφη, "λέγετε· οἶμαι γὰρ ὑμᾶς λέγειν ὅτι χρή με
πρὸς ταῦτα ἀπολογήσασθαι ὥσπερ ἐν δικαστηρίωι."
    "πάνυ μὲν οὖν," ἔφη ὁ Σιμμίας.
    "φέρε δή," ἦ δ' ὅς, "πειραθῶ πιθανώτερον πρὸς ὑμᾶς ἀπολο-
5 γήσασθαι ἢ πρὸς τοὺς δικαστάς. ἐγὼ γάρ," ἔφη, "ὦ Σιμμία
τε καὶ Κέβης, εἰ μὲν μὴ ὤιμην ἥξειν πρῶτον μὲν παρὰ
θεοὺς ἄλλους σοφούς τε καὶ ἀγαθούς, ἔπειτα καὶ παρ'
ἀνθρώπους τετελευτηκότας ἀμείνους τῶν ἐνθάδε, ἠδίκουν
ἂν οὐκ ἀγανακτῶν τῶι θανάτωι· νῦν δὲ εὖ ἴστε ὅτι παρ'
c ἄνδρας τε ἐλπίζω ἀφίξεσθαι ἀγαθούς – καὶ τοῦτο μὲν οὐκ ἂν
πάνυ διισχυρισαίμην, ὅτι μέντοι παρὰ θεοὺς δεσπότας πάνυ
ἀγαθοὺς ἥξειν, εὖ ἴστε ὅτι εἴπερ τι ἄλλο τῶν τοιούτων
διισχυρισαίμην ἂν καὶ τοῦτο. ὥστε διὰ ταῦτα οὐχ ὁμοίως
5 ἀγανακτῶ, ἀλλ' εὔελπίς εἰμι εἶναί τι τοῖς τετελευτηκόσι καί,
ὥσπερ γε καὶ πάλαι λέγεται, πολὺ ἄμεινον τοῖς ἀγαθοῖς ἢ
τοῖς κακοῖς."
    "τί οὖν," ἔφη ὁ Σιμμίας, "ὦ Σώκρατες; αὐτὸς ἔχων τὴν
διάνοιαν ταύτην ἐν νῶι ἔχεις ἀπιέναι, ἢ κἂν ἡμῖν μεταδοίης;

c2 ὅτι m: τὸ t(m)

κοινὸν γὰρ δὴ ἔμοιγε δοκεῖ καὶ ἡμῖν εἶναι ἀγαθὸν τοῦτο, καὶ d
ἅμα σοι ἡ ἀπολογία ἔσται, ἐὰν ἅπερ λέγεις ἡμᾶς πείσῃς."

"ἀλλὰ πειράσομαι," ἔφη. "πρῶτον δὲ Κρίτωνα τόνδε
σκεψώμεθα τί ἐστιν ὃ βούλεσθαί μοι δοκεῖ πάλαι εἰπεῖν."

"τί δέ, ὦ Σώκρατες," ἔφη ὁ Κρίτων, "ἄλλο γε ἢ πάλαι 5
μοι λέγει ὁ μέλλων σοι δώσειν τὸ φάρμακον ὅτι χρή σοι
φράζειν ὡς ἐλάχιστα διαλέγεσθαι; φησὶ γὰρ θερμαίνεσθαι
μᾶλλον διαλεγομένους, δεῖν δὲ οὐδὲν τοιοῦτον προσφέρειν
τῶι φαρμάκωι· εἰ δὲ μή, ἐνίοτε ἀναγκάζεσθαι καὶ δὶς καὶ τρὶς e
πίνειν τούς τι τοιοῦτον ποιοῦντας."

καὶ ὁ Σωκράτης, "ἔα", ἔφη, "χαίρειν αὐτόν· ἀλλὰ μόνον
τὸ ἑαυτοῦ παρασκευαζέτω ὡς καὶ δὶς δώσων, ἐὰν δὲ δέῃ,
καὶ τρίς." 5

"ἀλλὰ σχεδὸν μέν τι ἤιδη," ἔφη ὁ Κρίτων· "ἀλλά μοι πάλαι
πράγματα παρέχει."

"ἔα αὐτόν," ἔφη. "ἀλλ' ὑμῖν δὴ τοῖς δικασταῖς βούλομαι
ἤδη τὸν λόγον ἀποδοῦναι, ὥς μοι φαίνεται εἰκότως ἀνὴρ τῶι
ὄντι ἐν φιλοσοφίαι διατρίψας τὸν βίον θαρρεῖν μέλλων 10
ἀποθανεῖσθαι καὶ εὔελπις εἶναι ἐκεῖ μέγιστα οἴσεσθαι ἀγαθὰ 64
ἐπειδὰν τελευτήσῃ. πῶς ἂν οὖν δὴ τοῦθ' οὕτως ἔχοι, ὦ
Σιμμία τε καὶ Κέβης, ἐγὼ πειράσομαι φράσαι.

"κινδυνεύουσι γὰρ ὅσοι τυγχάνουσιν ὀρθῶς ἁπτόμενοι
φιλοσοφίας λεληθέναι τοὺς ἄλλους ὅτι οὐδὲν ἄλλο αὐτοὶ 5
ἐπιτηδεύουσιν ἢ ἀποθνῄσκειν τε καὶ τεθνάναι. εἰ οὖν τοῦτο
ἀληθές, ἄτοπον δήπου ἂν εἴη προθυμεῖσθαι μὲν ἐν παντὶ τῶι
βίωι μηδὲν ἄλλο ἢ τοῦτο, ἥκοντος δὲ δὴ αὐτοῦ ἀγανακτεῖν
ὃ πάλαι προυθυμοῦντό τε καὶ ἐπετήδευον."

καὶ ὁ Σιμμίας γελάσας, "νὴ τὸν Δία," ἔφη, "ὦ Σώκρατες,
οὐ πάνυ γέ με νυνδὴ γελασείοντα ἐποίησας γελάσαι. οἶμαι b
γὰρ ἂν τοὺς πολλοὺς αὐτὸ τοῦτο ἀκούσαντας δοκεῖν εὖ πάνυ
εἰρῆσθαι εἰς τοὺς φιλοσοφοῦντας – καὶ συμφάναι ἂν τοὺς μὲν
παρ' ἡμῖν ἀνθρώπους καὶ πάνυ – ὅτι τῶι ὄντι οἱ φιλοσοφοῦντες θανατῶσι, καὶ σφᾶς γε οὐ λελήθασιν ὅτι ἄξιοί εἰσιν 5
τοῦτο πάσχειν."

"καὶ ἀληθῆ γ᾽ ἂν λέγοιεν, ὦ Σιμμία, πλήν γε τοῦ σφᾶς
μὴ λεληθέναι. λέληθεν γὰρ αὐτοὺς ἧι τε θανατῶσι καὶ ἧι ἄξιοί
εἰσιν θανάτου καὶ οἵου θανάτου οἱ ὡς ἀληθῶς φιλόσοφοι.
c εἴπωμεν γάρ", ἔφη, "πρὸς ἡμᾶς αὐτούς, χαίρειν εἰπόντες ἐκεί-
νοις· ἡγούμεθά τι τὸν θάνατον εἶναι;"
"πάνυ γε," ἔφη ὑπολαβὼν ὁ Σιμμίας.
"ἆρα μὴ ἄλλο τι ἢ τὴν τῆς ψυχῆς ἀπὸ τοῦ σώματος
5 ἀπαλλαγήν; καὶ εἶναι τοῦτο τὸ τεθνάναι, χωρὶς μὲν ἀπὸ τῆς
ψυχῆς ἀπαλλαγὲν αὐτὸ καθ᾽ αὑτὸ τὸ σῶμα γεγονέναι, χωρὶς
δὲ τὴν ψυχὴν ἀπὸ τοῦ σώματος ἀπαλλαγεῖσαν αὐτὴν καθ᾽
αὑτὴν εἶναι; ἆρα μὴ ἄλλο τι ἦι ὁ θάνατος ἢ τοῦτο;"
"οὔκ, ἀλλὰ τοῦτο," ἔφη.
10 "σκέψαι δή, ὠγαθέ, ἐὰν ἄρα καὶ σοὶ συνδοκῆι ἅπερ ἐμοί·
d ἐκ γὰρ τούτων μᾶλλον οἶμαι ἡμᾶς εἴσεσθαι περὶ ὧν σκο-
ποῦμεν. φαίνεταί σοι φιλοσόφου ἀνδρὸς εἶναι ἐσπουδακέναι
περὶ τὰς ἡδονὰς καλουμένας τὰς τοιάσδε, οἷον σιτίων
καὶ ποτῶν;"
5 "ἥκιστα, ὦ Σώκρατες," ἔφη ὁ Σιμμίας.
"τί δὲ τὰς τῶν ἀφροδισίων;"
"οὐδαμῶς."
"τί δὲ τὰς ἄλλας τὰς περὶ τὸ σῶμα θεραπείας; δοκεῖ σοι
ἐντίμους ἡγεῖσθαι ὁ τοιοῦτος; οἷον ἱματίων διαφερόντων
10 κτήσεις καὶ ὑποδημάτων καὶ τοὺς ἄλλους καλλωπισμοὺς
τοὺς περὶ τὸ σῶμα πότερον τιμᾶν δοκεῖ σοι ἢ ἀτιμάζειν,
e καθ᾽ ὅσον μὴ πολλὴ ἀνάγκη μετέχειν αὐτῶν;"
"ἀτιμάζειν ἔμοιγε δοκεῖ," ἔφη, "ὅ γε ὡς ἀληθῶς φιλόσοφος."
"οὐκοῦν ὅλως δοκεῖ σοι", ἔφη, "ἡ τοῦ τοιούτου πραγ-
5 ματεία οὐ περὶ τὸ σῶμα εἶναι, ἀλλὰ καθ᾽ ὅσον δύναται
ἀφεστάναι αὐτοῦ, πρὸς δὲ τὴν ψυχὴν τετράφθαι;"
"ἔμοιγε."
"ἆρ᾽ οὖν πρῶτον μὲν ἐν τοῖς τοιούτοις δῆλός ἐστιν ὁ

φιλόσοφος ἀπολύων ὅτι μάλιστα τὴν ψυχὴν ἀπὸ τῆς τοῦ 65
σώματος κοινωνίας, διαφερόντως τῶν ἄλλων ἀνθρώπων;"

"φαίνεται."

"καὶ δοκεῖ γέ που, ὦ Σιμμία, τοῖς πολλοῖς ἀνθρώποις
ὧι μηδὲν ἡδὺ τῶν τοιούτων μηδὲ μετέχει αὐτῶν οὐκ ἄξιον 5
εἶναι ζῆν, ἀλλ' ἐγγύς τι τείνειν τοῦ τεθνάναι ὁ μηδὲν φρον-
τίζων τῶν ἡδονῶν αἳ διὰ τοῦ σώματός εἰσιν."

"πάνυ μὲν οὖν ἀληθῆ λέγεις."

"τί δὲ δὴ περὶ αὐτὴν τὴν τῆς φρονήσεως κτῆσιν; πότερον ἐμπόδιον τὸ σῶμα ἢ οὔ, ἐάν τις αὐτὸ ἐν τῆι ζητήσει 10
κοινωνὸν συμπαραλαμβάνηι; οἷον τὸ τοιόνδε λέγω· ἆρα ἔχει b
ἀλήθειάν τινα ὄψις τε καὶ ἀκοὴ τοῖς ἀνθρώποις, ἢ τά γε
τοιαῦτα καὶ οἱ ποιηταὶ ἡμῖν ἀεὶ θρυλοῦσιν, ὅτι οὔτ' ἀκούομεν
ἀκριβὲς οὐδὲν οὔτε ὁρῶμεν; καίτοι εἰ αὗται τῶν περὶ τὸ
σῶμα αἰσθήσεων μὴ ἀκριβεῖς εἰσιν μηδὲ σαφεῖς, σχολῆι 5
αἵ γε ἄλλαι· πᾶσαι γάρ που τούτων φαυλότεραί εἰσιν. ἢ
σοὶ οὐ δοκοῦσιν;"

"πάνυ μὲν οὖν," ἔφη.

"πότε οὖν", ἦ δ' ὅς, "ἡ ψυχὴ τῆς ἀληθείας ἅπτεται; ὅταν
μὲν γὰρ μετὰ τοῦ σώματος ἐπιχειρῆι τι σκοπεῖν, δῆλον ὅτι 10
τότε ἐξαπατᾶται ὑπ' αὐτοῦ."

"ἀληθῆ λέγεις." c

"ἆρ' οὖν οὐκ ἐν τῶι λογίζεσθαι εἴπερ που ἄλλοθι κατά-
δηλον αὐτῆι γίγνεταί τι τῶν ὄντων;"

"ναί."

"λογίζεται δέ γέ που τότε κάλλιστα, ὅταν αὐτὴν τούτων 5
μηδὲν παραλυπῆι μήτε ἀκοὴ μήτε ὄψις μήτε ἀλγηδὼν μηδέ
τις ἡδονή, ἀλλ' ὅτι μάλιστα αὐτὴ καθ' αὑτὴν γίγνηται ἐῶσα
χαίρειν τὸ σῶμα, καὶ καθ' ὅσον δύναται μὴ κοινωνοῦσα
αὐτῶι μηδ' ἁπτομένη ὀρέγηται τοῦ ὄντος."

"ἔστι ταῦτα." 10

"οὐκοῦν καὶ ἐνταῦθα ἡ τοῦ φιλοσόφου ψυχὴ μάλιστα
ἀτιμάζει τὸ σῶμα καὶ φεύγει ἀπ' αὐτοῦ, ζητεῖ δὲ αὐτὴ καθ' d
αὑτὴν γίγνεσθαι;"

"φαίνεται."

"τί δὲ δὴ τὰ τοιάδε, ὦ Σιμμία; φαμέν τι εἶναι δίκαιον
5 αὐτὸ ἢ οὐδέν;"

"φαμὲν μέντοι νὴ Δία."

"καὶ αὖ καλόν γέ τι καὶ ἀγαθόν;"

"πῶς δ' οὔ;"

"ἤδη οὖν πώποτέ τι τῶν τοιούτων τοῖς ὀφθαλμοῖς εἶδες;"
10 "οὐδαμῶς," ἦ δ' ὅς.

"ἀλλ' ἄλληι τινὶ αἰσθήσει τῶν διὰ τοῦ σώματος ἐφήψω
αὐτῶν; λέγω δὲ περὶ πάντων, οἷον μεγέθους πέρι, ὑγιείας,
ἰσχύος, καὶ τῶν ἄλλων ἑνὶ λόγωι ἁπάντων τῆς οὐσίας ὃ
e τυγχάνει ἕκαστον ὄν· ἆρα διὰ τοῦ σώματος αὐτῶν τὸ
ἀληθέστατον θεωρεῖται, ἢ ὧδε ἔχει· ὃς ἂν μάλιστα ἡμῶν
καὶ ἀκριβέστατα παρασκευάσηται αὐτὸ ἕκαστον διανοηθῆναι
περὶ οὗ σκοπεῖ, οὗτος ἂν ἐγγύτατα ἴοι τοῦ γνῶναι ἕκαστον;"
5 "πάνυ μὲν οὖν."

"ἆρ' οὖν ἐκεῖνος ἂν τοῦτο ποιήσειεν καθαρώτατα ὅστις
ὅτι μάλιστα αὐτῆι τῆι διανοίαι ἴοι ἐφ' ἕκαστον, μήτε τὴν
ὄψιν παρατιθέμενος ἐν τῶι διανοεῖσθαι μήτε τινὰ ἄλλην
66 αἴσθησιν ἐφέλκων μηδεμίαν μετὰ τοῦ λογισμοῦ, ἀλλ' αὐτῆι
καθ' αὑτὴν εἰλικρινεῖ τῆι διανοίαι χρώμενος αὐτὸ καθ' αὑτὸ εἰλι-
κρινὲς ἕκαστον ἐπιχειροῖ θηρεύειν τῶν ὄντων, ἀπαλλαγεὶς
ὅτι μάλιστα ὀφθαλμῶν τε καὶ ὤτων καὶ ὡς ἔπος εἰπεῖν σύμ-
5 παντος τοῦ σώματος, ὡς ταράττοντος καὶ οὐκ ἐῶντος τὴν
ψυχὴν κτήσασθαι ἀλήθειάν τε καὶ φρόνησιν ὅταν κοινωνῆι;
ἆρ' οὐχ οὗτός ἐστιν, ὦ Σιμμία, εἴπερ τις καὶ ἄλλος, ὁ
τευξόμενος τοῦ ὄντος;"

"ὑπερφυῶς", ἔφη ὁ Σιμμίας, "ὡς ἀληθῆ λέγεις, ὦ
10 Σώκρατες."

b "οὐκοῦν ἀνάγκη", ἔφη, "ἐκ πάντων τούτων παρίστασθαι
δόξαν τοιάνδε τινὰ τοῖς γνησίως φιλοσόφοις, ὥστε καὶ πρὸς
ἀλλήλους τοιαῦτα ἄττα λέγειν, ὅτι 'κινδυνεύει τοι ὥσπερ

e7 τὴν c: τιν' e   e8 μήτε τινὰ m t: μήτε m p t

ἀτραπός τις ἐκφέρειν ἡμᾶς μετὰ τοῦ λόγου ἐν τῆι σκέψει,
ὅτι, ἕως ἂν τὸ σῶμα ἔχωμεν καὶ συμπεφυρμένη ἦι ἡμῶν ἡ 5
ψυχὴ μετὰ τοιούτου κακοῦ, οὐ μή ποτε κτησώμεθα ἱκανῶς
οὗ ἐπιθυμοῦμεν· φαμὲν δὲ τοῦτο εἶναι τὸ ἀληθές. μυρίας
μὲν γὰρ ἡμῖν ἀσχολίας παρέχει τὸ σῶμα διὰ τὴν ἀναγκαίαν
τροφήν· ἔτι δέ, ἄν τινες νόσοι προσπέσωσιν, ἐμποδίζουσιν c
ἡμῶν τὴν τοῦ ὄντος θήραν. ἐρώτων δὲ καὶ ἐπιθυμιῶν καὶ
φόβων καὶ εἰδώλων παντοδαπῶν καὶ φλυαρίας ἐμπίμπλησιν
ἡμᾶς πολλῆς, ὥστε τὸ λεγόμενον ὡς ἀληθῶς τῶι ὄντι ὑπ᾽
αὐτοῦ οὐδὲ φρονῆσαι ἡμῖν ἐγγίγνεται οὐδέποτε οὐδέν. καὶ 5
γὰρ πολέμους καὶ στάσεις καὶ μάχας οὐδὲν ἄλλο παρέχει ἢ
τὸ σῶμα καὶ αἱ τούτου ἐπιθυμίαι. διὰ γὰρ τὴν τῶν χρημάτων κτῆσιν πάντες οἱ πόλεμοι γίγνονται, τὰ δὲ χρήματα
ἀναγκαζόμεθα κτᾶσθαι διὰ τὸ σῶμα, δουλεύοντες τῆι τούτου d
θεραπείαι· καὶ ἐκ τούτου ἀσχολίαν ἄγομεν φιλοσοφίας πέρι
διὰ πάντα ταῦτα. τὸ δ᾽ ἔσχατον πάντων ὅτι, ἐάν τις
ἡμῖν καὶ σχολὴ γένηται ἀπ᾽ αὐτοῦ καὶ τραπώμεθα πρὸς τὸ
σκοπεῖν τι, ἐν ταῖς ζητήσεσιν αὖ πανταχοῦ παραπῖπτον 5
θόρυβον παρέχει καὶ ταραχὴν καὶ ἐκπλήττει, ὥστε μὴ
δύνασθαι ὑπ᾽ αὐτοῦ καθορᾶν τἀληθές. ἀλλὰ τῶι ὄντι ἡμῖν
δέδεικται ὅτι, εἰ μέλλομέν ποτε καθαρῶς τι εἴσεσθαι,
ἀπαλλακτέον αὐτοῦ καὶ αὐτῆι τῆι ψυχῆι θεατέον αὐτὰ τὰ e
πράγματα· καὶ τότε, ὡς ἔοικεν, ἡμῖν ἔσται οὗ ἐπιθυμοῦμέν
τε καί φαμεν ἐρασταὶ εἶναι, φρονήσεως, ἐπειδὰν τελευτή-
σωμεν, ὡς ὁ λόγος σημαίνει, ζῶσιν δὲ οὔ. εἰ γὰρ μὴ οἷόν
τε μετὰ τοῦ σώματος μηδὲν καθαρῶς γνῶναι, δυοῖν θάτερον, 5
ἢ οὐδαμοῦ ἔστιν κτήσασθαι τὸ εἰδέναι ἢ τελευτήσασιν· τότε
γὰρ αὐτὴ καθ᾽ αὑτὴν ἡ ψυχὴ ἔσται χωρὶς τοῦ σώματος, 67
πρότερον δ᾽ οὔ. καὶ ἐν ὧι ἂν ζῶμεν, οὕτως, ὡς ἔοικεν,
ἐγγυτάτω ἐσόμεθα τοῦ εἰδέναι, ἐὰν ὅτι μάλιστα μηδὲν
ὁμιλῶμεν τῶι σώματι μηδὲ κοινωνῶμεν, ὅτι μὴ πᾶσα ἀνάγκη,
μηδὲ ἀναπιμπλώμεθα τῆς τούτου φύσεως, ἀλλὰ καθαρεύωμεν 5

b4 τις om. *m t*   [μετὰ . . . σκέψει] *e*

ἀπ' αὐτοῦ, ἕως ἂν ὁ θεὸς αὐτὸς ἀπολύσηι ἡμᾶς· καὶ οὕτω μὲν
καθαροὶ ἀπαλλαττόμενοι τῆς τοῦ σώματος ἀφροσύνης, ὡς τὸ
εἰκὸς μετὰ τοιούτων τε ἐσόμεθα καὶ γνωσόμεθα δι' ἡμῶν
b αὐτῶν πᾶν τὸ εἰλικρινές, τοῦτο δ' ἐστὶν ἴσως τὸ ἀληθές·
μὴ καθαρῶι γὰρ καθαροῦ ἐφάπτεσθαι μὴ οὐ θεμιτὸν ἦι·
τοιαῦτα οἶμαι, ὦ Σιμμία, ἀναγκαῖον εἶναι πρὸς ἀλλήλους
λέγειν τε καὶ δοξάζειν πάντας τοὺς ὀρθῶς φιλομαθεῖς. ἢ οὐ
5 δοκεῖ σοι οὕτως;"
    "παντός γε μᾶλλον, ὦ Σώκρατες."
    "οὐκοῦν", ἔφη ὁ Σωκράτης, "εἰ ταῦτα ἀληθῆ, ὦ ἑταῖρε,
πολλὴ ἐλπὶς ἀφικομένωι οἷ ἐγὼ πορεύομαι, ἐκεῖ ἱκανῶς,
εἴπερ που ἄλλοθι, κτήσασθαι τοῦτο οὗ ἕνεκα ἡ πολλὴ
10 πραγματεία ἡμῖν ἐν τῶι παρελθόντι βίωι γέγονεν, ὥστε ἥ γε
c ἀποδημία ἡ νῦν ἐμοὶ προστεταγμένη μετὰ ἀγαθῆς ἐλπίδος
γίγνεται, καὶ ἄλλωι ἀνδρὶ ὃς ἡγεῖταί οἱ παρεσκευάσθαι τὴν
διάνοιαν ὥσπερ κεκαθαρμένην."
    "πάνυ μὲν οὖν," ἔφη ὁ Σιμμίας.
5   "κάθαρσις δὲ εἶναι ἄρα οὐ τοῦτο συμβαίνει, ὅπερ πάλαι
ἐν τῶι λόγωι λέγεται, τὸ χωρίζειν ὅτι μάλιστα ἀπὸ τοῦ
σώματος τὴν ψυχὴν καὶ ἐθίσαι αὐτὴν καθ' αὑτὴν παντα-
χόθεν ἐκ τοῦ σώματος συναγείρεσθαί τε καὶ ἀθροίζεσθαι,
καὶ οἰκεῖν κατὰ τὸ δυνατὸν καὶ ἐν τῶι νῦν παρόντι καὶ ἐν τῶι
d ἔπειτα μόνην καθ' αὑτήν, ἐκλυομένην ὥσπερ δεσμῶν ἐκ
τοῦ σώματος;"
    "πάνυ μὲν οὖν," ἔφη.
    "οὐκοῦν τοῦτο γε θάνατος ὀνομάζεται, λύσις καὶ χωρισμὸς
5 ψυχῆς ἀπὸ σώματος;"
    "παντάπασί γε," ἦ δ' ὅς.
    "λύειν δέ γε αὐτήν, ὥς φαμεν, προθυμοῦνται ἀεὶ μάλιστα
καὶ μόνοι οἱ φιλοσοφοῦντες ὀρθῶς, καὶ τὸ μελέτημα αὐτὸ
τοῦτό ἐστιν τῶν φιλοσόφων, λύσις καὶ χωρισμὸς ψυχῆς
10 ἀπὸ σώματος· ἢ οὔ;"
    "φαίνεται."

c1 ἐμοὶ *m t*: μοι *m*   d1 δεσμῶν *m*: ἐκ δεσμῶν *m t*

ΦΑΙΔΩΝ 37

"οὐκοῦν, ὅπερ ἐν ἀρχῆι ἔλεγον, γελοῖον ἂν εἴη ἄνδρα
παρασκευάζονθ' ἑαυτὸν ἐν τῶι βίωι ὅτι ἐγγυτάτω ὄντα τοῦ e
τεθνάναι οὕτω ζῆν, κἄπειθ' ἥκοντος αὐτῶι τούτου ἀγανακτεῖν;"
"γελοῖον· πῶς δ' οὔ;"
"τῶι ὄντι ἄρα," ἔφη, "ὦ Σιμμία, οἱ ὀρθῶς φιλοσοφοῦντες
ἀποθνήισκειν μελετῶσι, καὶ τὸ τεθνάναι ἥκιστα αὐτοῖς 5
ἀνθρώπων φοβερόν. ἐκ τῶνδε δὲ σκόπει. εἰ γὰρ διαβέβληνται μὲν πανταχῆι τῶι σώματι, αὐτὴν δὲ καθ' αὑτὴν
ἐπιθυμοῦσι τὴν ψυχὴν ἔχειν, τούτου δὴ γιγνομένου εἰ
φοβοῖντο καὶ ἀγανακτοῖεν, οὐ πολλὴ ἂν ἀλογία εἴη, εἰ μὴ
ἄσμενοι ἐκεῖσε ἴοιεν, οἷ ἀφικομένοις ἐλπίς ἐστιν οὗ διὰ βίου 68
ἤρων τυχεῖν (ἤρων δὲ φρονήσεως), ὧι τε διεβέβληντο, τούτου
ἀπηλλάχθαι συνόντος αὐτοῖς; ἢ ἀνθρωπίνων μὲν παιδικῶν
καὶ γυναικῶν καὶ ὑέων ἀποθανόντων πολλοὶ δὴ ἑκόντες
ἠθέλησαν εἰς Ἅιδου ἐλθεῖν, ὑπὸ ταύτης ἀγόμενοι τῆς 5
ἐλπίδος, τῆς τοῦ ὄψεσθαί τε ἐκεῖ ὧν ἐπεθύμουν καὶ συνέσε-
σθαι· φρονήσεως δὲ ἄρα τις τῶι ὄντι ἐρῶν, καὶ λαβὼν σφόδρα
τὴν αὐτὴν ταύτην ἐλπίδα, μηδαμοῦ ἄλλοθι ἐντεύξεσθαι αὐτῆι
ἀξίως λόγου ἢ ἐν Ἅιδου, ἀγανακτήσει τε ἀποθνήισκων καὶ b
οὐχ ἄσμενος εἶσιν αὐτόσε; οἴεσθαί γε χρή, ἐὰν τῶι ὄντι γε
ἦι, ὦ ἑταῖρε, φιλόσοφος· σφόδρα γὰρ αὐτῶι ταῦτα δόξει,
μηδαμοῦ ἄλλοθι καθαρῶς ἐντεύξεσθαι φρονήσει ἀλλ' ἢ ἐκεῖ.
εἰ δὲ τοῦτο οὕτως ἔχει, ὅπερ ἄρτι ἔλεγον, οὐ πολλὴ ἂν 5
ἀλογία εἴη εἰ φοβοῖτο τὸν θάνατον ὁ τοιοῦτος;"
"πολλὴ μέντοι νὴ Δία," ἦ δ' ὅς.
"οὐκοῦν ἱκανόν σοι τεκμήριον," ἔφη, "τοῦτο ἀνδρός, ὃν
ἂν ἴδηις ἀγανακτοῦντα μέλλοντα ἀποθανεῖσθαι, ὅτι οὐκ ἄρ'
ἦν φιλόσοφος ἀλλά τις φιλοσώματος; ὁ αὐτὸς δέ που c
οὗτος τυγχάνει ὢν καὶ φιλοχρήματος καὶ φιλότιμος, ἤτοι τὰ
ἕτερα τούτων ἢ ἀμφότερα."
"πάνυ," ἔφη, "ἔχει οὕτως ὡς λέγεις."
"ἆρ' οὖν", ἔφη, "ὦ Σιμμία, οὐ καὶ ἡ ὀνομαζομένη ἀνδρεία 5
τοῖς οὕτω διακειμένοις μάλιστα προσήκει;"

e8 δὴ e: δὲ c   a5 ἐλθεῖν m p: μετελθεῖν m   a6 τε m: τι m "πάντως δήπου," ἔφη.

"οὐκοῦν καὶ ἡ σωφροσύνη, ἣν καὶ οἱ πολλοὶ ὀνομάζουσι σωφροσύνην, τὸ περὶ τὰς ἐπιθυμίας μὴ ἐπτοῆσθαι ἀλλ᾽ 10 ὀλιγώρως ἔχειν καὶ κοσμίως, ἆρ᾽ οὐ τούτοις μόνοις προσήκει, τοῖς μάλιστα τοῦ σώματος ὀλιγωροῦσίν τε καὶ ἐν φιλοσοφίαι ζῶσιν;"

d "ἀνάγκη," ἔφη.

"εἰ γὰρ ἐθέλεις", ἦ δ᾽ ὅς, "ἐννοῆσαι τήν γε τῶν ἄλλων ἀνδρείαν τε καὶ σωφροσύνην, δόξει σοι εἶναι ἄτοπος."

"πῶς δή, ὦ Σώκρατες;"

5 "οἶσθα", ἦ δ᾽ ὅς, "ὅτι τὸν θάνατον ἡγοῦνται πάντες οἱ ἄλλοι τῶν μεγάλων κακῶν;"

"καὶ μάλ᾽," ἔφη.

"οὐκοῦν φόβωι μειζόνων κακῶν ὑπομένουσιν αὐτῶν οἱ ἀνδρεῖοι τὸν θάνατον, ὅταν ὑπομένωσιν;"

10 "ἔστι ταῦτα."

"τῶι δεδιέναι ἄρα καὶ δέει ἀνδρεῖοί εἰσι πάντες πλὴν οἱ φιλόσοφοι· καίτοι ἄλογόν γε δέει τινὰ καὶ δειλίαι ἀνδρεῖον εἶναι."

e "πάνυ μὲν οὖν."

"τί δὲ οἱ κόσμιοι αὐτῶν; οὐ ταὐτὸν τοῦτο πεπόνθασιν· ἀκολασίαι τινὶ σώφρονές εἰσιν; καίτοι φαμέν γε ἀδύνατον εἶναι, ἀλλ᾽ ὅμως αὐτοῖς συμβαίνει τούτωι ὅμοιον τὸ πάθος 5 τὸ περὶ ταύτην τὴν εὐήθη σωφροσύνην· φοβούμενοι γὰρ ἑτέρων ἡδονῶν στερηθῆναι καὶ ἐπιθυμοῦντες ἐκείνων, ἄλλων ἀπέχονται ὑπ᾽ ἄλλων κρατούμενοι. καίτοι καλοῦσί γε ἀκο- 69 λασίαν τὸ ὑπὸ τῶν ἡδονῶν ἄρχεσθαι, ἀλλ᾽ ὅμως συμβαίνει αὐτοῖς κρατουμένοις ὑφ᾽ ἡδονῶν κρατεῖν ἄλλων ἡδονῶν. τοῦτο δ᾽ ὅμοιόν ἐστιν ὧι νυνδὴ ἐλέγετο, τῶι τρόπον τινὰ δι᾽ ἀκολασίαν αὐτοὺς σεσωφρονίσθαι."

5 "ἔοικε γάρ."

"ὦ μακάριε Σιμμία, μὴ γὰρ οὐχ αὕτη ἦι ἡ ὀρθὴ πρὸς ἀρετὴν ἀλλαγή, ἡδονὰς πρὸς ἡδονὰς καὶ λύπας πρὸς λύπας καὶ φόβον πρὸς φόβον καταλλάττεσθαι, καὶ μείζω πρὸς

a8 καὶ² om. t

ἐλάττω, ὥσπερ νομίσματα, ἀλλ᾽ ἦι ἐκεῖνο μόνον τὸ νόμισμα
ὀρθόν, ἀντὶ οὗ δεῖ πάντα ταῦτα καταλλάττεσθαι, φρόνησις, 10
καὶ τούτου μὲν πάντα καὶ μετὰ τούτου ὠνούμενά τε καὶ b
πιπρασκόμενα τῶι ὄντι ἦι καὶ ἀνδρεία καὶ σωφροσύνη καὶ
δικαιοσύνη καὶ συλλήβδην ἀληθὴς ἀρετή, μετὰ φρονήσεως,
καὶ προσγιγνομένων καὶ ἀπογιγνομένων καὶ ἡδονῶν καὶ
φόβων καὶ τῶν ἄλλων πάντων τῶν τοιούτων· χωριζόμενα 5
δὲ φρονήσεως καὶ ἀλλαττόμενα ἀντὶ ἀλλήλων μὴ σκιαγραφία τις ἦι ἡ τοιαύτη ἀρετὴ καὶ τῶι ὄντι ἀνδραποδώδης τε
καὶ οὐδὲν ὑγιὲς οὐδ᾽ ἀληθὲς ἔχηι, τὸ δ᾽ ἀληθὲς τῶι ὄντι ἦι
κάθαρσίς τις τῶν τοιούτων πάντων καὶ ἡ σωφροσύνη καὶ c
ἡ δικαιοσύνη καὶ ἀνδρεία, καὶ αὐτὴ ἡ φρόνησις μὴ καθαρμός τις ἦι. καὶ κινδυνεύουσι καὶ οἱ τὰς τελετὰς ἡμῖν
οὗτοι καταστήσαντες οὐ φαῦλοί τινες εἶναι, ἀλλὰ τῶι ὄντι
πάλαι αἰνίττεσθαι ὅτι ὃς ἂν ἀμύητος καὶ ἀτέλεστος εἰς 5
Ἅιδου ἀφίκηται ἐν βορβόρωι κείσεται, ὁ δὲ κεκαθαρμένος
τε καὶ τετελεσμένος ἐκεῖσε ἀφικόμενος μετὰ θεῶν οἰκήσει.
εἰσὶν γὰρ δή, ὥς φασιν οἱ περὶ τὰς τελετάς, 'ναρθηκοφόροι
μὲν πολλοί, βάκχοι δέ τε παῦροι'. οὗτοι δ᾽ εἰσὶν κατὰ τὴν d
ἐμὴν δόξαν οὐκ ἄλλοι ἢ οἱ πεφιλοσοφηκότες ὀρθῶς. ὧν δὴ
καὶ ἐγὼ κατά γε τὸ δυνατὸν οὐδὲν ἀπέλιπον ἐν τῶι βίωι,
ἀλλὰ παντὶ τρόπωι προυθυμήθην γενέσθαι· εἰ δ᾽ ὀρθῶς
προυθυμήθην καί τι ἠνύσαμεν, ἐκεῖσε ἐλθόντες τὸ σαφὲς 5
εἰσόμεθα, ἂν θεὸς ἐθέληι, ὀλίγον ὕστερον, ὡς ἐμοὶ δοκεῖ.
ταῦτ᾽ οὖν ἐγώ," ἔφη, "ὦ Σιμμία τε καὶ Κέβης, ἀπολογοῦμαι,
ὡς εἰκότως ὑμᾶς τε ἀπολείπων καὶ τοὺς ἐνθάδε δεσπότας οὐ
χαλεπῶς φέρω οὐδ᾽ ἀγανακτῶ, ἡγούμενος κἀκεῖ οὐδὲν ἧττον e
ἢ ἐνθάδε δεσπόταις τε ἀγαθοῖς ἐντεύξεσθαι καὶ ἑταίροις·
τοῖς δὲ πολλοῖς ἀπιστίαν παρέχει. εἴ τι οὖν ὑμῖν πιθανώ-
τερός εἰμι ἐν τῆι ἀπολογίαι ἢ τοῖς Ἀθηναίων δικασταῖς, εὖ
ἂν ἔχοι." 5

εἰπόντος δὴ τοῦ Σωκράτους ταῦτα, ὑπολαβὼν ὁ Κέβης
ἔφη· "ὦ Σώκρατες, τὰ μὲν ἄλλα ἔμοιγε δοκεῖ καλῶς λέγεσθαι,
τὰ δὲ περὶ τῆς ψυχῆς πολλὴν ἀπιστίαν παρέχει τοῖς ἀνθρώποις 70

e3 [τοῖς ... παρέχει] e

μή, ἐπειδὰν ἀπαλλαγῆι τοῦ σώματος, οὐδαμοῦ ἔτι ἦι, ἀλλ᾽ ἐκείνηι
τῆι ἡμέραι διαφθείρηταί τε καὶ ἀπολλύηται ἧι ἂν ὁ ἄνθρωπος ἀπο-
θνήισκηι, εὐθὺς ἀπαλλαττομένη τοῦ σώματος, καὶ ἐκβαίνουσα
5 ὥσπερ πνεῦμα ἢ καπνὸς διασκεδασθεῖσα οἴχηται διαπτομένη
καὶ οὐδὲν ἔτι οὐδαμοῦ ἦι. ἐπεί, εἴπερ εἴη που αὐτὴ καθ᾽
αὑτὴν συνηθροισμένη καὶ ἀπηλλαγμένη τούτων τῶν κακῶν
ὧν σὺ νυνδὴ διῆλθες, πολλὴ ἂν εἴη ἐλπὶς καὶ καλή, ὦ
b Σώκρατες, ὡς ἀληθῆ ἐστιν ἃ σὺ λέγεις· ἀλλὰ τοῦτο δὴ
ἴσως οὐκ ὀλίγης παραμυθίας δεῖται καὶ πίστεως, ὡς ἔστι τε ἡ
ψυχὴ ἀποθανόντος τοῦ ἀνθρώπου καί τινα δύναμιν ἔχει καὶ
φρόνησιν."
5 "ἀληθῆ", ἔφη, "λέγεις," ὁ Σωκράτης, "ὦ Κέβης· ἀλλὰ τί δὴ
ποιῶμεν; ἢ περὶ αὐτῶν τούτων βούλει διαμυθολογῶμεν, εἴτε
εἰκὸς οὕτως ἔχειν εἴτε μή;"
"ἐγὼ γοῦν", ἔφη ὁ Κέβης, "ἡδέως ἂν ἀκούσαιμι ἥντινα
δόξαν ἔχεις περὶ αὐτῶν."
10 "οὔκουν γ᾽ ἂν οἶμαι", ἦ δ᾽ ὃς ὁ Σωκράτης, "εἰπεῖν τινα νῦν
c ἀκούσαντα, οὐδ᾽ εἰ κωμωιδοποιὸς εἴη, ὡς ἀδολεσχῶ καὶ οὐ
περὶ προσηκόντων τοὺς λόγους ποιοῦμαι. εἰ οὖν δοκεῖ, χρὴ
διασκοπεῖσθαι.
"σκεψώμεθα δὲ αὐτὸ τῆιδέ πηι, εἴτ᾽ ἄρα ἐν Ἅιδου εἰσὶν αἱ
5 ψυχαὶ τελευτησάντων τῶν ἀνθρώπων εἴτε καὶ οὔ. παλαιὸς
μὲν οὖν ἔστι τις λόγος οὗ μεμνήμεθα, ὡς εἰσὶν ἐνθένδε
ἀφικόμεναι ἐκεῖ, καὶ πάλιν γε δεῦρο ἀφικνοῦνται καὶ γίγνονται ἐκ τῶν τεθνεώτων· καὶ εἰ τοῦθ᾽ οὕτως ἔχει, πάλιν
γίγνεσθαι ἐκ τῶν ἀποθανόντων τοὺς ζῶντας, ἄλλο τι ἢ εἶεν
d ἂν αἱ ψυχαὶ ἡμῶν ἐκεῖ; οὐ γὰρ ἂν που πάλιν ἐγίγνοντο μὴ
οὖσαι, καὶ τοῦτο ἱκανὸν τεκμήριον τοῦ ταῦτ᾽ εἶναι, εἰ τῶι
ὄντι φανερὸν γίγνοιτο ὅτι οὐδαμόθεν ἄλλοθεν γίγνονται οἱ
ζῶντες ἢ ἐκ τῶν τεθνεώτων· εἰ δὲ μὴ ἔστι τοῦτο, ἄλλου ἂν
5 του δέοι λόγου."
"πάνυ μὲν οὖν," ἔφη ὁ Κέβης.
"μὴ τοίνυν κατ᾽ ἀνθρώπων", ἦ δ᾽ ὅς, "σκόπει μόνον τοῦτο,

b2-3 ἡ ψυχὴ *m* t: ψυχὴ *m*

ΦΑΙΔΩΝ   41

εἰ βούλει ῥᾷον μαθεῖν, ἀλλὰ καὶ κατὰ ζῴων πάντων καὶ
φυτῶν, καὶ συλλήβδην ὅσαπερ ἔχει γένεσιν περὶ πάντων
ἴδωμεν ἆρ' οὑτωσὶ γίγνεται πάντα, οὐκ ἄλλοθεν ἢ ἐκ τῶν e
ἐναντίων τὰ ἐναντία, ὅσοις τυγχάνει ὂν τοιοῦτόν τι, οἷον τὸ
καλὸν τῶι αἰσχρῶι ἐναντίον που καὶ δίκαιον ἀδίκωι, καὶ ἄλλα
δὴ μυρία οὕτως ἔχει. τοῦτο οὖν σκεψώμεθα, ἆρα ἀναγκαῖον
ὅσοις ἔστι τι ἐναντίον, μηδαμόθεν ἄλλοθεν αὐτὸ γίγνεσθαι 5
ἢ ἐκ τοῦ αὐτῶι ἐναντίου. οἷον ὅταν μεῖζόν τι γίγνηται,
ἀνάγκη που ἐξ ἐλάττονος ὄντος πρότερον ἔπειτα μεῖζον
γίγνεσθαι; "
"ναί."
"οὐκοῦν κἂν ἔλαττον γίγνηται, ἐκ μείζονος ὄντος πρότερον 10
ὕστερον ἔλαττον γενήσεται; "   71
"ἔστιν οὕτω," ἔφη.
"καὶ μὴν ἐξ ἰσχυροτέρου γε τὸ ἀσθενέστερον καὶ ἐκ βρα-
δυτέρου τὸ θᾶττον; "
"πάνυ γε."   5
"τί δέ; ἄν τι χεῖρον γίγνηται, οὐκ ἐξ ἀμείνονος, καὶ ἂν
δικαιότερον, ἐξ ἀδικωτέρου; "
"πῶς γὰρ οὔ; "
"ἱκανῶς οὖν", ἔφη, "ἔχομεν τοῦτο, ὅτι πάντα οὕτω γίγνεται,
ἐξ ἐναντίων τὰ ἐναντία πράγματα; "   10
"πάνυ γε."
"τί δ' αὖ; ἔστι τι καὶ τοιόνδε ἐν αὐτοῖς, οἷον μεταξὺ
ἀμφοτέρων πάντων τῶν ἐναντίων δυοῖν ὄντοιν δύο γενέσεις,
ἀπὸ μὲν τοῦ ἑτέρου ἐπὶ τὸ ἕτερον, ἀπὸ δ' αὖ τοῦ ἑτέρου b
πάλιν ἐπὶ τὸ ἕτερον· μείζονος μὲν πράγματος καὶ ἐλάττονος
μεταξὺ αὔξησις καὶ φθίσις, καὶ καλοῦμεν οὕτω τὸ μὲν αὐξά-
νεσθαι, τὸ δὲ φθίνειν; "
"ναί," ἔφη.   5
"οὐκοῦν καὶ διακρίνεσθαι καὶ συγκρίνεσθαι, καὶ ψύχεσθαι
καὶ θερμαίνεσθαι, καὶ πάντα οὕτω, κἂν εἰ μὴ χρώμεθα τοῖς
ὀνόμασιν ἐνιαχοῦ, ἀλλ' ἔργωι γοῦν πανταχοῦ οὕτως ἔχειν
ἀναγκαῖον, γίγνεσθαί τε αὐτὰ ἐξ ἀλλήλων γένεσίν τε εἶναι
ἑκατέρου εἰς ἄλληλα; "   10

42 ΠΛΑΤΩΝΟΣ

"πάνυ γε," ἦ δ' ὅς.

c "τί οὖν;" ἔφη, "τῶι ζῆν ἐστί τι ἐναντίον, ὥσπερ τῶι ἐγρηγορέναι τὸ καθεύδειν;"
"πάνυ μὲν οὖν," ἔφη.
"τί;"

5 "τὸ τεθνάναι," ἔφη.

"οὐκοῦν ἐξ ἀλλήλων τε γίγνεται ταῦτα, εἴπερ ἐναντία ἐστιν, καὶ αἱ γενέσεις εἰσὶν αὐτοῖν μεταξὺ δύο δυοῖν ὄντοιν;"
"πῶς γὰρ οὔ;"
"τὴν μὲν τοίνυν ἑτέραν συζυγίαν ὧν νυνδὴ ἔλεγον ἐγώ
10 σοι", ἔφη, "ἐρῶ," ὁ Σωκράτης, "καὶ αὐτὴν καὶ τὰς γενέσεις· σὺ δέ μοι τὴν ἑτέραν. λέγω δὲ τὸ μὲν καθεύδειν, τὸ δὲ ἐγρη-γορέναι, καὶ ἐκ τοῦ καθεύδειν τὸ ἐγρηγορέναι γίγνεσθαι καὶ
d ἐκ τοῦ ἐγρηγορέναι τὸ καθεύδειν, καὶ τὰς γενέσεις αὐτοῖν τὴν μὲν καταδαρθάνειν εἶναι, τὴν δ' ἀνεγείρεσθαι. ἱκανῶς σοι," ἔφη, "ἢ οὔ;"
"πάνυ μὲν οὖν."

5 "λέγε δή μοι καὶ σύ", ἔφη, "οὕτω περὶ ζωῆς καὶ θανάτου. οὐκ ἐναντίον μὲν φὴς τῶι ζῆν τὸ τεθνάναι εἶναι;"
"ἔγωγε."
"γίγνεσθαι δὲ ἐξ ἀλλήλων;"
"ναί."

10 "ἐξ οὖν τοῦ ζῶντος τί τὸ γιγνόμενον;"
"τὸ τεθνηκός," ἔφη.
"τί δέ", ἦ δ' ὅς, "ἐκ τοῦ τεθνεῶτος;"
"ἀναγκαῖον", ἔφη, "ὁμολογεῖν ὅτι τὸ ζῶν."
"ἐκ τῶν τεθνεώτων ἄρα, ὦ Κέβης, τὰ ζῶντά τε καὶ οἱ
15 ζῶντες γίγνονται;"
e "φαίνεται," ἔφη.
"εἰσὶν ἄρα", ἔφη, "αἱ ψυχαὶ ἡμῶν ἐν Ἅιδου."
"ἔοικεν."
"οὐκοῦν καὶ τοῖν γενεσέοιν τοῖν περὶ ταῦτα ἥ γ' ἑτέρα

b 11 γε m: μὲν οὖν m

σαφὴς οὖσα τυγχάνει· τὸ γὰρ ἀποθνήισκειν σαφὲς δήπου, 5
ἢ οὔ;"

"πάνυ μὲν οὖν," ἔφη.

"πῶς οὖν", ἦ δ' ὅς, "ποιήσομεν; οὐκ ἀνταποδώσομεν τὴν
ἐναντίαν γένεσιν, ἀλλὰ ταύτηι χωλὴ ἔσται ἡ φύσις; ἢ ἀνάγκη
ἀποδοῦναι τῶι ἀποθνήισκειν ἐναντίαν τινὰ γένεσιν;" 10

"πάντως που," ἔφη.

"τίνα ταύτην;"

"τὸ ἀναβιώσκεσθαι."

"οὐκοῦν", ἦ δ' ὅς, "εἴπερ ἔστι τὸ ἀναβιώσκεσθαι, ἐκ τῶν
τεθνεώτων ἂν εἴη γένεσις εἰς τοὺς ζῶντας αὕτη, τὸ ἀνα- 72
βιώσκεσθαι;"

"πάνυ γε."

"ὁμολογεῖται ἄρα ἡμῖν καὶ ταύτηι τοὺς ζῶντας ἐκ τῶν
τεθνεώτων γεγονέναι οὐδὲν ἧττον ἢ τοὺς τεθνεῶτας ἐκ τῶν 5
ζώντων, τούτου δὲ ὄντος ἱκανόν που ἐδόκει τεκμήριον εἶναι
ὅτι ἀναγκαῖον τὰς τῶν τεθνεώτων ψυχὰς εἶναί που, ὅθεν δὴ
πάλιν γίγνεσθαι."

"δοκεῖ μοι," ἔφη, "ὦ Σώκρατες, ἐκ τῶν ὡμολογημένων
ἀναγκαῖον οὕτως ἔχειν." 10

"ἰδὲ τοίνυν οὕτως," ἔφη, "ὦ Κέβης, ὅτι οὐδ' ἀδίκως ὡμο-
λογήκαμεν, ὡς ἐμοὶ δοκεῖ. εἰ γὰρ μὴ ἀεὶ ἀνταποδιδοίη τὰ
ἕτερα τοῖς ἑτέροις γιγνόμενα, ὡσπερεὶ κύκλωι περιιόντα, ἀλλ' b
εὐθεῖά τις εἴη ἡ γένεσις ἐκ τοῦ ἑτέρου μόνον εἰς τὸ καταντικρὺ καὶ μὴ ἀνακάμπτοι πάλιν ἐπὶ τὸ ἕτερον μηδὲ καμπὴν
ποιοῖτο, οἶσθ' ὅτι πάντα τελευτῶντα τὸ αὐτὸ σχῆμα ἂν σχοίη
καὶ τὸ αὐτὸ πάθος ἂν πάθοι καὶ παύσαιτο γιγνόμενα;" 5

"πῶς λέγεις;" ἔφη.

"οὐδὲν χαλεπόν", ἦ δ' ὅς, "ἐννοῆσαι ὃ λέγω· ἀλλ' οἶον εἰ
τὸ καταδαρθάνειν μὲν εἴη, τὸ δ' ἀνεγείρεσθαι μὴ ἀνταποδιδοίη
γιγνόμενον ἐκ τοῦ καθεύδοντος, οἶσθ' ὅτι τελευτῶντα πάντ'
⟨ἂν⟩ λῆρον τὸν Ἐνδυμίωνα ἀποδείξειεν καὶ οὐδαμοῦ ἂν c
φαίνοιτο διὰ τὸ καὶ τἆλλα πάντα ταὐτὸν ἐκείνωι πεπονθέναι,
καθεύδειν. κἂν εἰ συγκρίνοιτο μὲν πάντα, διακρίνοιτο δὲ

μή, ταχὺ ἂν τὸ τοῦ Ἀναξαγόρου γεγονὸς εἴη, 'ὁμοῦ πάντα
5 χρήματα'. ὡσαύτως δέ, ὦ φίλε Κέβης, καὶ εἰ ἀποθνήισκοι
μὲν πάντα ὅσα τοῦ ζῆν μεταλάβοι, ἐπειδὴ δὲ ἀποθάνοι,
μένοι ἐν τούτωι τῶι σχήματι τὰ τεθνεῶτα καὶ μὴ πάλιν
ἀναβιώσκοιτο, ἆρ' οὐ πολλὴ ἀνάγκη τελευτῶντα πάντα
d τεθνάναι καὶ μηδὲν ζῆν; εἰ γὰρ ἐκ μὲν τῶν ἄλλων τὰ
ζῶντα γίγνοιτο, τὰ δὲ ζῶντα θνήισκοι, τίς μηχανὴ μὴ οὐχὶ
πάντα καταναλωθῆναι εἰς τὸ τεθνάναι;"
"οὐδὲ μία μοι δοκεῖ," ἔφη ὁ Κέβης, "ὦ Σώκρατες, ἀλλά μοι
5 δοκεῖς παντάπασιν ἀληθῆ λέγειν."
"ἔστιν γάρ," ἔφη, "ὦ Κέβης, ὡς ἐμοὶ δοκεῖ, παντὸς μᾶλλον
οὕτω, καὶ ἡμεῖς αὐτὰ ταῦτα οὐκ ἐξαπατώμενοι ὁμολογοῦμεν,
ἀλλ' ἔστι τῶι ὄντι καὶ τὸ ἀναβιώσκεσθαι καὶ ἐκ τῶν τεθνεώτων τοὺς ζῶντας γίγνεσθαι καὶ τὰς τῶν τεθνεώτων ψυχὰς
e εἶναι [καὶ ταῖς μέν γε ἀγαθαῖς ἄμεινον εἶναι, ταῖς δὲ κακαῖς
κάκιον]."
"καὶ μήν", ἔφη ὁ Κέβης ὑπολαβών, "καὶ κατ' ἐκεῖνόν γε
τὸν λόγον, ὦ Σώκρατες, εἰ ἀληθής ἐστιν, ὃν σὺ εἴωθας
5 θαμὰ λέγειν, ὅτι ἡμῖν ἡ μάθησις οὐκ ἄλλο τι ἢ ἀνάμνησις
τυγχάνει οὖσα, καὶ κατὰ τοῦτον ἀνάγκη που ἡμᾶς ἐν προτέρωι
τινὶ χρόνωι μεμαθηκέναι ἃ νῦν ἀναμιμνηισκόμεθα. τοῦτο δὲ
73 ἀδύνατον, εἰ μὴ ἦν που ἡμῖν ἡ ψυχὴ πρὶν ἐν τῶιδε τῶι ἀνθρωπίνωι εἴδει γενέσθαι· ὥστε καὶ ταύτηι ἀθάνατόν τι ἡ ψυχή
ἔοικεν εἶναι."
"ἀλλά, ὦ Κέβης," ἔφη ὁ Σιμμίας ὑπολαβών, "ποῖαι τούτων
5 αἱ ἀποδείξεις; ὑπόμνησόν με· οὐ γὰρ σφόδρα ἐν τῶι παρόντι
μέμνημαι."
"ἑνὶ μὲν λόγωι", ἔφη ὁ Κέβης, "καλλίστωι, ὅτι ἐρωτώμενοι
οἱ ἄνθρωποι, ἐάν τις καλῶς ἐρωτᾶι, αὐτοὶ λέγουσιν πάντα ἧι
ἔχει· καίτοι εἰ μὴ ἐτύγχανεν αὐτοῖς ἐπιστήμη ἐνοῦσα καὶ
10 ὀρθὸς λόγος, οὐκ ἂν οἷοί τ' ἦσαν τοῦτο ποιῆσαι. ἔπειτα,
b ἐάν τις ἐπὶ τὰ διαγράμματα ἄγηι ἢ ἄλλο τι τῶν τοιούτων,
ἐνταῦθα σαφέστατα κατηγορεῖ ὅτι τοῦτο οὕτως ἔχει."
"εἰ δὲ μὴ ταύτηι γε", ἔφη, "πείθηι, ὦ Σιμμία," ὁ Σωκράτης,

"σκέψαι ἂν τῆιδέ πήι σοι σκοπουμένωι συνδόξηι. ἀπιστεῖς γὰρ
δὴ πῶς ἡ καλουμένη μάθησις ἀνάμνησίς ἐστιν;" 5
"ἀπιστῶ μὲν ἔγωγε", ἦ δ' ὃς ὁ Σιμμίας, "οὔ, αὐτὸ δὲ
τοῦτο", ἔφη, "δέομαι παθεῖν περὶ οὗ ὁ λόγος, ἀναμνησθῆναι.
καὶ σχεδόν γε ἐξ ὧν Κέβης ἐπεχείρησε λέγειν ἤδη μέμνημαι
καὶ πείθομαι· οὐδὲν μεντἂν ἧττον ἀκούοιμι νῦν πῆι σὺ ἐπ-
εχείρησας λέγειν." 10
"τῆιδ' ἔγωγε," ἦ δ' ὅς. "ὁμολογοῦμεν γὰρ δήπου, εἴ τίς τι c
ἀναμνησθήσεται, δεῖν αὐτὸν τοῦτο πρότερόν ποτε ἐπίστασθαι."
"πάνυ γ'," ἔφη.
"ἆρ' οὖν καὶ τόδε ὁμολογοῦμεν, ὅταν ἐπιστήμη παραγίγνηται τρόπωι τοιούτωι, ἀνάμνησιν εἶναι; λέγω δὲ τινα 5
τρόπον τόνδε. ἐάν τίς τι ἕτερον ἢ ἰδὼν ἢ ἀκούσας ἤ τινα
ἄλλην αἴσθησιν λαβὼν μὴ μόνον ἐκεῖνο γνῶι, ἀλλὰ καὶ
ἕτερον ἐννοήσηι οὗ μὴ ἡ αὐτὴ ἐπιστήμη ἀλλ' ἄλλη, ἆρα
οὐχὶ τοῦτο δικαίως λέγομεν ὅτι ἀνεμνήσθη, οὗ τὴν ἔννοιαν
ἔλαβεν;" d
"πῶς λέγεις;"
"οἷον τὰ τοιάδε· ἄλλη που ἐπιστήμη ἀνθρώπου καὶ λύρας."
"πῶς γὰρ οὔ;"
"οὐκοῦν οἶσθα ὅτι οἱ ἐρασταί, ὅταν ἴδωσιν λύραν ἢ ἱμάτιον 5
ἢ ἄλλο τι οἷς τὰ παιδικὰ αὐτῶν εἴωθε χρῆσθαι, πάσχουσι
τοῦτο· ἔγνωσάν τε τὴν λύραν καὶ ἐν τῆι διανοίαι ἔλαβον τὸ
εἶδος τοῦ παιδὸς οὗ ἦν ἡ λύρα; τοῦτο δέ ἐστιν ἀνάμνησις·
ὥσπερ γε καὶ Σιμμίαν τις ἰδὼν πολλάκις Κέβητος ἀνεμνήσθη,
καὶ ἄλλα που μυρία τοιαῦτ' ἂν εἴη." 10
"μυρία μέντοι νὴ Δία," ἔφη ὁ Σιμμίας.
"οὐκοῦν", ἦ δ' ὅς, "τὸ τοιοῦτον ἀνάμνησίς τίς ἐστι; μάλιστα e
μέντοι ὅταν τις τοῦτο πάθηι περὶ ἐκεῖνα ἃ ὑπὸ χρόνου καὶ τοῦ
μὴ ἐπισκοπεῖν ἤδη ἐπελέληστο;"
"πάνυ μὲν οὖν," ἔφη.
"τί δέ;" ἦ δ' ὅς· "ἔστιν ἵππον γεγραμμένον ἰδόντα καὶ 5

b6 μὲν m: μέν σοι m

λύραν γεγραμμένην ἀνθρώπου ἀναμνησθῆναι, καὶ Σιμμίαν
ἰδόντα γεγραμμένον Κέβητος ἀναμνησθῆναι;"

"πάνυ γε."

"οὐκοῦν καὶ Σιμμίαν ἰδόντα γεγραμμένον αὐτοῦ Σιμμίου
10 ἀναμνησθῆναι;"

74   "ἔστι μέντοι," ἔφη.

"ἆρ' οὖν οὐ κατὰ πάντα ταῦτα συμβαίνει τὴν ἀνάμνησιν
εἶναι μὲν ἀφ' ὁμοίων, εἶναι δὲ καὶ ἀπὸ ἀνομοίων;"

"συμβαίνει."

5   "ἀλλ' ὅταν γε ἀπὸ τῶν ὁμοίων ἀναμιμνήισκηταί τίς τι, ἆρ'
οὐκ ἀναγκαῖον τόδε προσπάσχειν, ἐννοεῖν εἴτε τι ἐλλείπει
τοῦτο κατὰ τὴν ὁμοιότητα εἴτε μὴ ἐκείνου οὗ ἀνεμνήσθη;"

"ἀνάγκη," ἔφη.

"σκόπει δή", ἦ δ' ὅς, "εἰ ταῦτα οὕτως ἔχει. φαμέν πού τι
10 εἶναι ἴσον, οὐ ξύλον λέγω ξύλωι οὐδὲ λίθον λίθωι οὐδ' ἄλλο
τῶν τοιούτων οὐδέν, ἀλλὰ παρὰ ταῦτα πάντα ἕτερόν τι, αὐτὸ
τὸ ἴσον· φῶμέν τι εἶναι ἢ μηδέν;"

b   "φῶμεν μέντοι νὴ Δί'," ἔφη ὁ Σιμμίας, "θαυμαστῶς γε."

"ἦ καὶ ἐπιστάμεθα αὐτὸ ὃ ἔστιν;"

"πάνυ γε," ἦ δ' ὅς.

"πόθεν λαβόντες αὐτοῦ τὴν ἐπιστήμην; ἆρ' οὐκ ἐξ ὧν
5 νυνδὴ ἐλέγομεν, ἢ ξύλα ἢ λίθους ἢ ἄλλα ἄττα ἰδόντες
ἴσα, ἐκ τούτων ἐκεῖνο ἐνενοήσαμεν, ἕτερον ὂν τούτων; ἢ
οὐχ ἕτερόν σοι φαίνεται; σκόπει δὲ καὶ τῆιδε. ἆρ' οὐ λίθοι
μὲν ἴσοι καὶ ξύλα ἐνίοτε ταὐτὰ ὄντα τῶι μὲν ἴσα φαίνεται,
τῶι δ' οὔ;"

10   "πάνυ μὲν οὖν."

c   "τί δέ; αὐτὰ τὰ ἴσα ἔστιν ὅτε ἄνισά σοι ἐφάνη, ἢ ἡ ἰσότης
ἀνισότης;"

"οὐδεπώποτέ γε, ὦ Σώκρατες."

"οὐ ταὐτὸν ἄρα ἐστίν," ἦ δ' ὅς, "ταῦτά τε τὰ ἴσα καὶ αὐτὸ
5 τὸ ἴσον."

"οὐδαμῶς μοι φαίνεται, ὦ Σώκρατες."

b8–9 τῶι ... τῶι m: τότε ... τότε m

"ἀλλὰ μὴν ἐκ τούτων γ'", ἔφη, "τῶν ἴσων, ἑτέρων ὄντων
ἐκείνου τοῦ ἴσου, ὅμως αὐτοῦ τὴν ἐπιστήμην ἐννενόηκάς τε
καὶ εἴληφας;"

"ἀληθέστατα", ἔφη, "λέγεις." 10

"οὐκοῦν ἢ ὁμοίου ὄντος τούτοις ἢ ἀνομοίου;"

"πάνυ γε."

"διαφέρει δέ γε", ἦ δ' ὅς, "οὐδέν· ἕως ἂν ἄλλο ἰδὼν ἀπὸ
ταύτης τῆς ὄψεως ἄλλο ἐννοήσῃς, εἴτε ὅμοιον εἴτε ἀνόμοιον, d
ἀναγκαῖον", ἔφη, "αὐτὸ ἀνάμνησιν γεγονέναι."

"πάνυ μὲν οὖν."

"τί δέ;" ἦ δ' ὅς· "ἦ πάσχομέν τι τοιοῦτον περὶ τὰ ἐν τοῖς
ξύλοις τε καὶ οἷς νυνδὴ ἐλέγομεν τοῖς ἴσοις; ἆρα φαίνεται 5
ἡμῖν οὕτως ἴσα εἶναι ὥσπερ αὐτὸ τὸ ὃ ἔστιν ἴσον, ἢ ἐνδεῖ τι
ἐκείνου τῶι τοιοῦτον εἶναι οἷον τὸ ἴσον, ἢ οὐδέν;"

"καὶ πολύ γε", ἔφη, "ἐνδεῖ."

"οὐκοῦν ὁμολογοῦμεν, ὅταν τίς τι ἰδὼν ἐννοήσῃ ὅτι 'βούλεται μὲν τοῦτο ὃ νῦν ἐγὼ ὁρῶ εἶναι οἷον ἄλλο τι τῶν ὄντων, 10
ἐνδεῖ δὲ καὶ οὐ δύναται τοιοῦτον εἶναι [ἴσον] οἷον ἐκεῖνο, ἀλλ' e
ἔστιν φαυλότερον', ἀναγκαῖόν που τὸν τοῦτο ἐννοοῦντα τυχεῖν
προειδότα ἐκεῖνο ὧι φησιν αὐτὸ προσεοικέναι μέν, ἐνδεεστέρως
δὲ ἔχειν;"

"ἀνάγκη." 5

"τί οὖν; τὸ τοιοῦτον πεπόνθαμεν καὶ ἡμεῖς ἢ οὒ περί τε
τὰ ἴσα καὶ αὐτὸ τὸ ἴσον;"

"παντάπασί γε."

"ἀναγκαῖον ἄρα ἡμᾶς προειδέναι τὸ ἴσον πρὸ ἐκείνου τοῦ
χρόνου ὅτε τὸ πρῶτον ἰδόντες τὰ ἴσα ἐνενοήσαμεν ὅτι 75
ὀρέγεται μὲν πάντα ταῦτα εἶναι οἷον τὸ ἴσον, ἔχει δὲ
ἐνδεεστέρως."

"ἔστι ταῦτα."

"ἀλλὰ μὴν καὶ τόδε ὁμολογοῦμεν, μὴ ἄλλοθεν αὐτὸ ἐν- 5
νενοηκέναι μηδὲ δυνατὸν εἶναι ἐννοῆσαι ἀλλ' ἢ ἐκ τοῦ ἰδεῖν

ἢ ἅψασθαι ἢ ἔκ τινος ἄλλης τῶν αἰσθήσεων· ταὐτὸν δὲ
πάντα ταῦτα λέγω."
"ταὐτὸν γὰρ ἔστιν, ὦ Σώκρατες, πρός γε ὃ βούλεται
10 δηλῶσαι ὁ λόγος."
"ἀλλὰ μὲν δὴ ἔκ γε τῶν αἰσθήσεων δεῖ ἐννοῆσαι ὅτι
b πάντα τὰ ἐν ταῖς αἰσθήσεσιν ἐκείνου τε ὀρέγεται τοῦ ὃ
ἔστιν ἴσον, καὶ αὐτοῦ ἐνδεέστερά ἐστιν· ἢ πῶς λέγομεν;"
"οὕτως."
"πρὸ τοῦ ἄρα ἄρξασθαι ἡμᾶς ὁρᾶν καὶ ἀκούειν καὶ τἆλλα
5 αἰσθάνεσθαι τυχεῖν ἔδει που εἰληφότας ἐπιστήμην αὐτοῦ
τοῦ ἴσου ὅτι ἔστιν, εἰ ἐμέλλομεν τὰ ἐκ τῶν αἰσθήσεων ἴσα
ἐκεῖσε ἀνοίσειν, ὅτι προθυμεῖται μὲν πάντα τοιαῦτ' εἶναι οἷον
ἐκεῖνο, ἔστιν δὲ αὐτοῦ φαυλότερα."
"ἀνάγκη ἐκ τῶν προειρημένων, ὦ Σώκρατες."
10 "οὐκοῦν γενόμενοι εὐθὺς ἑωρῶμέν τε καὶ ἠκούομεν καὶ τὰς
ἄλλας αἰσθήσεις εἴχομεν;"
"πάνυ γε."
c "ἔδει δέ γε, φαμέν, πρὸ τούτων τὴν τοῦ ἴσου ἐπιστήμην
εἰληφέναι;"
"ναί."
"πρὶν γενέσθαι ἄρα, ὡς ἔοικεν, ἀνάγκη ἡμῖν αὐτὴν εἰλη-
5 φέναι."
"ἔοικεν."
"οὐκοῦν εἰ μὲν λαβόντες αὐτὴν πρὸ τοῦ γενέσθαι ἔχοντες
ἐγενόμεθα, ἠπιστάμεθα καὶ πρὶν γενέσθαι καὶ εὐθὺς γενόμενοι οὐ μόνον τὸ ἴσον καὶ τὸ μεῖζον καὶ τὸ ἔλαττον ἀλλὰ
10 καὶ σύμπαντα τὰ τοιαῦτα; οὐ γὰρ περὶ τοῦ ἴσου νῦν ὁ λόγος
ἡμῖν μᾶλλόν τι ἢ καὶ περὶ αὐτοῦ τοῦ καλοῦ καὶ αὐτοῦ τοῦ
d ἀγαθοῦ καὶ δικαίου καὶ ὁσίου καί, ὅπερ λέγω, περὶ ἁπάντων
οἷς ἐπισφραγιζόμεθα τοῦτο, τὸ 'ὃ ἔστι', καὶ ἐν ταῖς ἐρωτή-
σεσιν ἐρωτῶντες καὶ ἐν ταῖς ἀποκρίσεσιν ἀποκρινόμενοι.
ὥστε ἀναγκαῖον ἡμῖν τούτων πάντων τὰς ἐπιστήμας πρὸ τοῦ
5 γενέσθαι εἰληφέναι."

d2 τοῦτο τὸ e: τοῦτο c: τὸ αὐτὸ e, fort. t: τὸ t

"ἔστι ταῦτα."

"καὶ εἰ μέν γε λαβόντες ἑκάστοτε μὴ ἐπιλελήσμεθα, εἰδότας ἀεὶ γίγνεσθαι καὶ ἀεὶ διὰ βίου εἰδέναι· τὸ γὰρ εἰδέναι τοῦτ᾽ ἔστιν, λαβόντα του ἐπιστήμην ἔχειν καὶ μὴ ἀπολωλεκέναι· ἢ οὐ τοῦτο λήθην λέγομεν, ὦ Σιμμία, ἐπι- 10 στήμης ἀποβολήν;"

"πάντως δήπου," ἔφη, "ὦ Σώκρατες." e

"εἰ δέ γε οἶμαι λαβόντες πρὶν γενέσθαι γιγνόμενοι ἀπω-λέσαμεν, ὕστερον δὲ ταῖς αἰσθήσεσι χρώμενοι περὶ αὐτὰ ἐκείνας ἀναλαμβάνομεν τὰς ἐπιστήμας ἅς ποτε καὶ πρὶν εἴχομεν, ἆρ᾽ οὐχ ὃ καλοῦμεν μανθάνειν οἰκείαν ἂν ἐπιστήμην 5 ἀναλαμβάνειν εἴη; τοῦτο δέ που ἀναμιμνήισκεσθαι λέγοντες ὀρθῶς ἂν λέγοιμεν;"

"πάνυ γε."

"δυνατὸν γὰρ δὴ τοῦτό γε ἐφάνη, αἰσθόμενόν τι ἢ ἰδόντα 76 ἢ ἀκούσαντα ἤ τινα ἄλλην αἴσθησιν λαβόντα ἕτερόν τι ἀπὸ τούτου ἐννοῆσαι ὃ ἐπελέληστο, ὧι τοῦτο ἐπλησίαζεν ἀνόμοιον ὂν ἢ ὧι ὅμοιον· ὥστε, ὅπερ λέγω, δυοῖν θάτερον, ἤτοι ἐπι-στάμενοί γε αὐτὰ γεγόναμεν καὶ ἐπιστάμεθα διὰ βίου πάντες, 5 ἢ ὕστερον, οὕς φαμεν μανθάνειν, οὐδὲν ἀλλ᾽ ἢ ἀναμιμνήι-σκονται οὗτοι, καὶ ἡ μάθησις ἀνάμνησις ἂν εἴη."

"καὶ μάλα δὴ οὕτως ἔχει, ὦ Σώκρατες."

"πότερον οὖν αἱρῆι, ὦ Σιμμία; ἐπισταμένους ἡμᾶς γεγο-νέναι, ἢ ἀναμιμνήισκεσθαι ὕστερον ὧν πρότερον ἐπιστήμην b εἰληφότες ἦμεν;"

"οὐκ ἔχω, ὦ Σώκρατες, ἐν τῶι παρόντι ἑλέσθαι."

"τί δέ; τόδε ἔχεις ἑλέσθαι, καὶ πῆι σοι δοκεῖ περὶ αὐτοῦ; ἀνὴρ ἐπιστάμενος περὶ ὧν ἐπίσταται ἔχοι ἂν δοῦναι λόγον 5 ἢ οὔ;"

"πολλὴ ἀνάγκη," ἔφη, "ὦ Σώκρατες."

"ἦ καὶ δοκοῦσί σοι πάντες ἔχειν διδόναι λόγον περὶ τού-των ὧν νυνδὴ ἐλέγομεν;"

"βουλοίμην μεντἄν," ἔφη ὁ Σιμμίας· "ἀλλὰ πολὺ μᾶλλον 10

d7 ἑκάστοτε μὴ *m*: μὴ ἑκάστοτε *m*   a4 θάτερον *m*: τὰ ἕτερα *m*

φοβοῦμαι μὴ αὔριον τηνικάδε οὐκέτι ἦι ἀνθρώπων οὐδεὶς
ἀξίως οἷός τε τοῦτο ποιῆσαι."

c "οὐκ ἄρα δοκοῦσί σοι ἐπίστασθαί γε," ἔφη, "ὦ Σιμμία,
πάντες αὐτά; "

"οὐδαμῶς."

"ἀναμιμνήισκονται ἄρα ἃ ποτε ἔμαθον; "

5 "ἀνάγκη."

"πότε λαβοῦσαι αἱ ψυχαὶ ἡμῶν τὴν ἐπιστήμην αὐτῶν; οὐ
γὰρ δὴ ἀφ' οὗ γε ἄνθρωποι γεγόναμεν."

"οὐ δῆτα."

"πρότερον ἄρα."

10 "ναί."

"ἦσαν ἄρα, ὦ Σιμμία, αἱ ψυχαὶ καὶ πρότερον, πρὶν
εἶναι ἐν ἀνθρώπου εἴδει, χωρὶς σωμάτων, καὶ φρόνησιν
εἶχον."

"εἰ μὴ ἄρα ἅμα γιγνόμενοι λαμβάνομεν, ὦ Σώκρατες,
15 ταύτας τὰς ἐπιστήμας· οὗτος γὰρ λείπεται ἔτι ὁ χρόνος."

d "εἶεν, ὦ ἑταῖρε· ἀπόλλυμεν δὲ αὐτὰς ἐν ποίωι ἄλλωι χρόνωι;
οὐ γὰρ δὴ ἔχοντές γε αὐτὰς γιγνόμεθα, ὡς ἄρτι ὡμολογήσαμεν. ἢ ἐν τούτωι ἀπόλλυμεν ἐν ὧιπερ καὶ λαμβάνομεν; ἢ
ἔχεις ἄλλον τινὰ εἰπεῖν χρόνον; "

5 "οὐδαμῶς, ὦ Σώκρατες, ἀλλὰ ἔλαθον ἐμαυτὸν οὐδὲν εἰπών."

"ἀρ' οὖν οὕτως ἔχει", ἔφη, "ἡμῖν, ὦ Σιμμία; εἰ μὲν ἔστιν
ἃ θρυλοῦμεν ἀεί, καλόν τέ τι καὶ ἀγαθὸν καὶ πᾶσα ἡ τοιαύτη
οὐσία, καὶ ἐπὶ ταύτην τὰ ἐκ τῶν αἰσθήσεων πάντα ἀνα-
e φέρομεν, ὑπάρχουσαν πρότερον ἀνευρίσκοντες ἡμετέραν
οὖσαν, καὶ ταῦτα ἐκείνηι ἀπεικάζομεν, ἀναγκαῖον, οὕτως ὥσπερ
καὶ ταῦτα ἔστιν, οὕτως καὶ τὴν ἡμετέραν ψυχὴν εἶναι καὶ
πρὶν γεγονέναι ἡμᾶς· εἰ δὲ μὴ ἔστι ταῦτα, ἄλλως ἂν ὁ λόγος
5 οὗτος εἰρημένος εἴη; ἀρ' οὕτως ἔχει, καὶ ἴση ἀνάγκη ταῦτά
τε εἶναι καὶ τὰς ἡμετέρας ψυχὰς πρὶν καὶ ἡμᾶς γεγονέναι,
καὶ εἰ μὴ ταῦτα, οὐδὲ τάδε; "

"ὑπερφυῶς, ὦ Σώκρατες," ἔφη ὁ Σιμμίας, "δοκεῖ μοι ἡ
αὐτὴ ἀνάγκη εἶναι, καὶ εἰς καλόν γε καταφεύγει ὁ λόγος εἰς

τὸ ὁμοίως εἶναι τήν τε ψυχὴν ἡμῶν πρὶν γενέσθαι ἡμᾶς καὶ 77
τὴν οὐσίαν ἣν σὺ νῦν λέγεις. οὐ γὰρ ἔχω ἔγωγε οὐδὲν
οὕτω μοι ἐναργὲς ὂν ὡς τοῦτο, τὸ πάντα τὰ τοιαῦτ᾽ εἶναι ὡς
οἷόν τε μάλιστα, καλόν τε καὶ ἀγαθὸν καὶ τἄλλα πάντα ἃ
σὺ νυνδὴ ἔλεγες· καὶ ἔμοιγε ἱκανῶς ἀποδέδεικται." 5
"τί δὲ δὴ Κέβητι;" ἔφη ὁ Σωκράτης· "δεῖ γὰρ καὶ Κέβητα
πείθειν."
"ἱκανῶς," ἔφη ὁ Σιμμίας, "ὡς ἔγωγε οἶμαι· καίτοι καρτερώ-
τατος ἀνθρώπων ἐστὶν πρὸς τὸ ἀπιστεῖν τοῖς λόγοις. ἀλλ᾽
οἶμαι οὐκ ἐνδεῶς τοῦτο πεπεῖσθαι αὐτόν, ὅτι πρὶν γενέσθαι 10
ἡμᾶς ἦν ἡμῶν ἡ ψυχή· εἰ μέντοι καὶ ἐπειδὰν ἀποθάνωμεν b
ἔτι ἔσται, οὐδὲ αὐτῶι μοι δοκεῖ," ἔφη, "ὦ Σώκρατες, ἀποδεδεῖχθαι, ἀλλ᾽ ἔτι ἐνέστηκεν ὃ νυνδὴ Κέβης ἔλεγε, τὸ τῶν
πολλῶν, ὅπως μὴ ἅμα ἀποθνήισκοντος τοῦ ἀνθρώπου διασκεδάννυται ἡ ψυχὴ καὶ αὐτῆι τοῦ εἶναι τοῦτο τέλος ἦι. τί 5
γὰρ κωλύει γίγνεσθαι μὲν αὐτὴν καὶ συνίστασθαι ἄλλοθέν
ποθεν καὶ εἶναι πρὶν καὶ εἰς ἀνθρώπειον σῶμα ἀφικέσθαι,
ἐπειδὰν δὲ ἀφίκηται καὶ ἀπαλλάττηται τούτου, τότε καὶ αὐτὴν
τελευτᾶν καὶ διαφθείρεσθαι;"
"εὖ λέγεις," ἔφη, "ὦ Σιμμία," ὁ Κέβης. "φαίνεται γὰρ c
ὥσπερ ἥμισυ ἀποδεδεῖχθαι οὗ δεῖ, ὅτι πρὶν γενέσθαι ἡμᾶς
ἦν ἡμῶν ἡ ψυχή, δεῖ δὲ προσαποδεῖξαι ὅτι καὶ ἐπειδὰν
ἀποθάνωμεν οὐδὲν ἧττον ἔσται ἢ πρὶν γενέσθαι, εἰ μέλλει
τέλος ἡ ἀπόδειξις ἕξειν." 5
"ἀποδέδεικται μέν," ἔφη, "ὦ Σιμμία τε καὶ Κέβης," ὁ
Σωκράτης, "καὶ νῦν, εἰ θέλετε συνθεῖναι τοῦτόν τε τὸν
λόγον εἰς ταὐτὸν καὶ ὃν πρὸ τούτου ὡμολογήσαμεν, τὸ
γίγνεσθαι πᾶν τὸ ζῶν ἐκ τοῦ τεθνεῶτος. εἰ γὰρ ἔστιν μὲν
ἡ ψυχὴ καὶ πρότερον, ἀνάγκη δὲ αὐτῆι εἰς τὸ ζῆν ἰούσηι τε d
καὶ γιγνομένηι μηδαμόθεν ἄλλοθεν ἢ ἐκ θανάτου καὶ τοῦ
τεθνάναι γίγνεσθαι, πῶς οὐκ ἀνάγκη αὐτὴν καὶ ἐπειδὰν
ἀποθάνηι εἶναι, ἐπειδή γε δεῖ αὖθις αὐτὴν γίγνεσθαι; ἀπο-

a5 ἔμοιγε m: ἐμοὶ ἐδόκει m: ἐμοὶ δοκεῖ m   b6 ἄλλοθέν c: ἀμόθεν e   c5 ἕξειν m:
ἔχειν m

5 δέδεικται μὲν οὖν ὅπερ λέγεται καὶ νῦν· ὅμως δέ μοι δοκεῖς
σύ τε καὶ Σιμμίας ἡδέως ἂν καὶ τοῦτον διαπραγματεύσασθαι
τὸν λόγον ἔτι μᾶλλον, καὶ δεδιέναι τὸ τῶν παίδων, μὴ ὡς
ἀληθῶς ὁ ἄνεμος αὐτὴν ἐκβαίνουσαν ἐκ τοῦ σώματος δια-
e φυσᾷ καὶ διασκεδάννυσιν, ἄλλως τε καὶ ὅταν τύχηι τις μὴ ἐν
νηνεμίαι ἀλλ᾽ ἐν μεγάλωι τινὶ πνεύματι ἀποθνήισκων."
καὶ ὁ Κέβης ἐπιγελάσας, "ὡς δεδιότων," ἔφη, "ὦ Σώκρατες,
πειρῶ ἀναπείθειν· μᾶλλον δὲ μὴ ὡς ἡμῶν δεδιότων, ἀλλ᾽
5 ἴσως ἔνι τις καὶ ἐν ἡμῖν παῖς ὅστις τὰ τοιαῦτα φοβεῖται.
τοῦτον οὖν πειρῶ μεταπείθειν μὴ δεδιέναι τὸν θάνατον ὥσπερ
τὰ μορμολύκεια."
"ἀλλὰ χρή", ἔφη ὁ Σωκράτης, "ἐπάιδειν αὐτῶι ἑκάστης ἡμέρας
ἕως ἂν ἐξεπάισητε."
78 "πόθεν οὖν," ἔφη, "ὦ Σώκρατες, τῶν τοιούτων ἀγαθὸν ἐπωιδὸν
ληψόμεθα, ἐπειδὴ σύ", ἔφη, "ἡμᾶς ἀπολείπεις; "
"πολλὴ μὲν ἡ Ἑλλάς," ἔφη, "ὦ Κέβης, ἐν ἧι ἔνεισί που
ἀγαθοὶ ἄνδρες, πολλὰ δὲ καὶ τὰ τῶν βαρβάρων γένη, οὓς
5 πάντας χρὴ διερευνᾶσθαι ζητοῦντας τοιοῦτον ἐπωιδόν, μήτε
χρημάτων φειδομένους μήτε πόνων, ὡς οὐκ ἔστιν εἰς ὅτι
ἂν εὐκαιρότερον ἀναλίσκοιτε χρήματα. ζητεῖν δὲ χρὴ καὶ
αὐτοὺς μετ᾽ ἀλλήλων· ἴσως γὰρ ἂν οὐδὲ ῥαιδίως εὕροιτε
μᾶλλον ὑμῶν δυναμένους τοῦτο ποιεῖν."
10 "ἀλλὰ ταῦτα μὲν δή", ἔφη, "ὑπάρξει," ὁ Κέβης· "ὅθεν δὲ
b ἀπελίπομεν ἐπανέλθωμεν, εἴ σοι ἡδομένωι ἐστίν."
"ἀλλὰ μὴν ἡδομένωι γε· πῶς γὰρ οὐ μέλλει; "
"καλῶς", ἔφη, "λέγεις."
"οὐκοῦν τοιόνδε τι", ἦ δ᾽ ὃς ὁ Σωκράτης, "δεῖ ἡμᾶς ἀνερέσθαι
5 ἑαυτούς, τῶι ποίωι τινὶ ἄρα προσήκει τοῦτο τὸ πάθος πάσχειν,
τὸ διασκεδάννυσθαι, καὶ ὑπὲρ τοῦ ποίου τινὸς δεδιέναι μὴ
πάθηι αὐτό, καὶ τῶι ποίωι τινὶ ⟨οὔ⟩· καὶ μετὰ τοῦτο αὖ
ἐπισκέψασθαι πότερον ψυχή ἐστιν, καὶ ἐκ τούτων θαρρεῖν
ἢ δεδιέναι ὑπὲρ τῆς ἡμετέρας ψυχῆς; "

d5 λέγεται c: λέγετε (m) e   e6 πειρῶ μεταπείθειν m: πειρώμεθα πείθειν m p
e9 ἐξεπάισητε m: ἐξεπάισηται m: ἐξιάσηται m: ἐξιάσητε m   b8 ψυχή m: ἡ
ψυχή m

"ἀληθῆ", ἔφη, "λέγεις." 10

"ἆρ' οὖν τῶι μὲν συντεθέντι τε καὶ συνθέτωι ὄντι φύσει c
προσήκει τοῦτο πάσχειν, διαιρεθῆναι ταύτηι ἧιπερ συνετέθη·
εἰ δέ τι τυγχάνει ὂν ἀσύνθετον, τούτωι μόνωι προσήκει μὴ
πάσχειν ταῦτα, εἴπερ τωι ἄλλωι; "

"δοκεῖ μοι", ἔφη, "οὕτως ἔχειν," ὁ Κέβης. 5

"οὐκοῦν ἅπερ ἀεὶ κατὰ ταὐτὰ καὶ ὡσαύτως ἔχει, ταῦτα
μάλιστα εἰκὸς εἶναι τὰ ἀσύνθετα, τὰ δὲ ἄλλοτ' ἄλλως καὶ
μηδέποτε κατὰ ταὐτά, ταῦτα δὲ σύνθετα; "

"ἔμοιγε δοκεῖ οὕτως."

"ἴωμεν δή", ἔφη, "ἐπὶ ταὐτὰ ἐφ' ἅπερ ἐν τῶι ἔμπροσθεν 10
λόγωι. αὐτὴ ἡ οὐσία ἧς λόγον δίδομεν τοῦ εἶναι καὶ ἐρω- d
τῶντες καὶ ἀποκρινόμενοι, πότερον ὡσαύτως ἀεὶ ἔχει κατὰ
ταὐτὰ ἢ ἄλλοτ' ἄλλως; αὐτὸ τὸ ἴσον, αὐτὸ τὸ καλόν, αὐτὸ
ἕκαστον ὃ ἔστιν, τὸ ὄν, μή ποτε μεταβολὴν καὶ ἡντινοῦν
ἐνδέχεται; ἢ ἀεὶ αὐτῶν ἕκαστον ὃ ἔστι, μονοειδὲς ὂν αὐτὸ 5
καθ' αὑτό, ὡσαύτως κατὰ ταὐτὰ ἔχει καὶ οὐδέποτε οὐδαμῆι
οὐδαμῶς ἀλλοίωσιν οὐδεμίαν ἐνδέχεται; "

"ὡσαύτως", ἔφη, "ἀνάγκη", ὁ Κέβης, "κατὰ ταὐτὰ ἔχειν, ὦ
Σώκρατες."

"τί δὲ τῶν πολλῶν καλῶν, οἷον ἀνθρώπων ἢ ἵππων ἢ 10
ἱματίων ἢ ἄλλων ὡντινωνοῦν τοιούτων, ἢ ἴσων [ἢ καλῶν] ἢ e
πάντων τῶν ἐκείνοις ὁμωνύμων; ἆρα κατὰ ταὐτὰ ἔχει, ἢ πᾶν
τοὐναντίον ἐκείνοις οὔτε αὐτὰ αὑτοῖς οὔτε ἀλλήλοις οὐδέποτε
ὡς ἔπος εἰπεῖν οὐδαμῶς κατὰ ταὐτά; "

"οὕτως αὖ", ἔφη, "ταῦτα," ὁ Κέβης· "οὐδέποτε ὡσαύτως ἔχει." 5

"οὐκοῦν τούτων μὲν κἂν ἅψαιο κἂν ἴδοις κἂν ταῖς ἄλλαις 79
αἰσθήσεσιν αἴσθοιο, τῶν δὲ κατὰ ταὐτὰ ἐχόντων οὐκ ἔστιν
ὅτωι ποτ' ἂν ἄλλωι ἐπιλάβοιο ἢ τῶι τῆς διανοίας λογισμῶι,
ἀλλ' ἔστιν ἀιδῆ τὰ τοιαῦτα καὶ οὐχ ὁρατά; "

"παντάπασιν", ἔφη, "ἀληθῆ λέγεις." 5

"θῶμεν οὖν βούλει", ἔφη, "δύο εἴδη τῶν ὄντων, τὸ μὲν
ὁρατόν, τὸ δὲ ἀιδές; "

a4 ἀιδῆ m: ἀειδῆ m et sic in seqq.

"θῶμεν," ἔφη.

"καὶ τὸ μὲν ἀιδὲς ἀεὶ κατὰ ταὐτὰ ἔχον, τὸ δὲ ὁρατὸν
10 μηδέποτε κατὰ ταὐτά;"

"καὶ τοῦτο", ἔφη, "θῶμεν."

b "φέρε δή," ἦ δ᾽ ὅς, "ἄλλο τι ἡμῶν αὐτῶν τὸ μὲν σῶμά ἐστι,
τὸ δὲ ψυχή;"

"οὐδὲν ἄλλο," ἔφη.

"ποτέρωι οὖν ὁμοιότερον τῶι εἴδει φαμὲν ἂν εἶναι καὶ
5 συγγενέστερον τὸ σῶμα;"

"παντί", ἔφη, "τοῦτό γε δῆλον, ὅτι τῶι ὁρατῶι."

"τί δὲ ἡ ψυχή; ὁρατὸν ἢ ἀιδές;"

"οὐχ ὑπ᾽ ἀνθρώπων γε, ὦ Σώκρατες," ἔφη.

"ἀλλὰ μὴν ἡμεῖς γε τὰ ὁρατὰ καὶ τὰ μὴ τῆι τῶν ἀνθρώπων
10 φύσει ἐλέγομεν· ἢ ἄλληι τινὶ οἴει;"

"τῆι τῶν ἀνθρώπων."

"τί οὖν περὶ ψυχῆς λέγομεν; ὁρατὸν ἢ ἀόρατον εἶναι;"

"οὐχ ὁρατόν."

"ἀιδὲς ἄρα;"

15 "ναί."

"ὁμοιότερον ἄρα ψυχὴ σώματός ἐστιν τῶι ἀιδεῖ, τὸ δὲ τῶι
ὁρατῶι."

c "πᾶσα ἀνάγκη, ὦ Σώκρατες."

"οὐκοῦν καὶ τόδε πάλαι ἐλέγομεν, ὅτι ἡ ψυχή, ὅταν μὲν
τῶι σώματι προσχρῆται εἰς τὸ σκοπεῖν τι ἢ διὰ τοῦ ὁρᾶν ἢ
διὰ τοῦ ἀκούειν ἢ δι᾽ ἄλλης τινὸς αἰσθήσεως (τοῦτο γάρ
5 ἐστιν τὸ διὰ τοῦ σώματος, τὸ δι᾽ αἰσθήσεως σκοπεῖν τι),
τότε μὲν ἕλκεται ὑπὸ τοῦ σώματος εἰς τὰ οὐδέποτε κατὰ
ταὐτὰ ἔχοντα, καὶ αὐτὴ πλανᾶται καὶ ταράττεται καὶ εἰλιγγιᾶι
ὥσπερ μεθύουσα, ἅτε τοιούτων ἐφαπτομένη;"

"πάνυ γε."

d "ὅταν δέ γε αὐτὴ καθ᾽ αὑτὴν σκοπῆι, ἐκεῖσε οἴχεται εἰς
τὸ καθαρόν τε καὶ ἀεὶ ὂν καὶ ἀθάνατον καὶ ὡσαύτως ἔχον,
καὶ ὡς συγγενὴς οὖσα αὐτοῦ ἀεὶ μετ᾽ ἐκείνου τε γίγνεται,
ὅτανπερ αὐτὴ καθ᾽ αὑτὴν γένηται καὶ ἐξῆι αὐτῆι, καὶ πέπαυταί
5 τε τοῦ πλάνου καὶ περὶ ἐκεῖνα ἀεὶ κατὰ ταὐτὰ ὡσαύτως ἔχει,

ἅτε τοιούτων ἐφαπτομένη· καὶ τοῦτο αὐτῆς τὸ πάθημα φρόνησις κέκληται;"

"παντάπασιν", ἔφη, "καλῶς καὶ ἀληθῆ λέγεις, ὦ Σώκρατες."

"ποτέρωι οὖν αὖ σοι δοκεῖ τῶι εἴδει καὶ ἐκ τῶν πρόσθεν καὶ ἐκ
τῶν νῦν λεγομένων ψυχὴ ὁμοιότερον εἶναι καὶ συγγενέστερον;" e

"πᾶς ἄν μοι δοκεῖ", ἦ δ' ὅς, "συγχωρῆσαι, ὦ Σώκρατες, ἐκ
ταύτης τῆς μεθόδου, καὶ ὁ δυσμαθέστατος, ὅτι ὅλωι καὶ
παντὶ ὁμοιότερόν ἐστι ψυχὴ τῶι ἀεὶ ὡσαύτως ἔχοντι μᾶλλον
ἢ τῶι μή."   5

"τί δὲ τὸ σῶμα;"

"τῶι ἑτέρωι."

"ὅρα δὴ καὶ τῆιδε, ὅτι ἐπειδὰν ἐν τῶι αὐτῶι ὦσι ψυχὴ καὶ
σῶμα, τῶι μὲν δουλεύειν καὶ ἄρχεσθαι ἡ φύσις προστάττει, 8ο
τῆι δὲ ἄρχειν καὶ δεσπόζειν· καὶ κατὰ ταῦτα αὖ πότερόν σοι
δοκεῖ ὅμοιον τῶι θείωι εἶναι καὶ πότερον τῶι θνητῶι; ἢ οὐ
δοκεῖ σοι τὸ μὲν θεῖον οἷον ἄρχειν τε καὶ ἡγεμονεύειν πεφυκέναι, τὸ δὲ θνητὸν ἄρχεσθαί τε καὶ δουλεύειν;"   5

"ἔμοιγε."

"ποτέρωι οὖν ἡ ψυχὴ ἔοικεν;"

"δῆλα δή, ὦ Σώκρατες, ὅτι ἡ μὲν ψυχὴ τῶι θείωι, τὸ δὲ
σῶμα τῶι θνητῶι."

"σκόπει δή," ἔφη, "ὦ Κέβης, εἰ ἐκ πάντων τῶν εἰρημένων 10
τάδε ἡμῖν συμβαίνει, τῶι μὲν θείωι καὶ ἀθανάτωι καὶ νοητῶι b
καὶ μονοειδεῖ καὶ ἀδιαλύτωι καὶ ἀεὶ ὡσαύτως κατὰ ταὐτὰ
ἔχοντι ἑαυτῶι ὁμοιότατον εἶναι ψυχή, τῶι δὲ ἀνθρωπίνωι καὶ
θνητῶι καὶ πολυειδεῖ καὶ ἀνοήτωι καὶ διαλυτῶι καὶ μηδέποτε
κατὰ ταὐτὰ ἔχοντι ἑαυτῶι ὁμοιότατον αὖ εἶναι σῶμα. ἔχομέν 5
τι παρὰ ταῦτα ἄλλο λέγειν, ὦ φίλε Κέβης, ἧι οὐχ οὕτως ἔχει;"

"οὐκ ἔχομεν."

"τί οὖν; τούτων οὕτως ἐχόντων ἆρ' οὐχὶ σώματι μὲν
ταχὺ διαλύεσθαι προσήκει, ψυχῆι δὲ αὖ τὸ παράπαν ἀδιαλύτωι εἶναι ἢ ἐγγύς τι τούτου;"   10

"πῶς γὰρ οὔ;"   c

b4 πολυειδεῖ καὶ ἀνοήτωι m: ἀν. καὶ πολ. m t

"ἐννοεῖς οὖν," ἔφη, "ἐπειδὰν ἀποθάνηι ὁ ἄνθρωπος, τὸ μὲν
ὁρατὸν αὐτοῦ, τὸ σῶμα, καὶ ἐν ὁρατῶι κείμενον, ὃ δὴ νεκρὸν
καλοῦμεν, ὧι προσήκει διαλύεσθαι καὶ διαπίπτειν καὶ δια-
5 πνεῖσθαι, οὐκ εὐθὺς τούτων οὐδὲν πέπονθεν, ἀλλ᾽ ἐπιεικῶς
συχνὸν ἐπιμένει χρόνον· ἐὰν μέν τις καὶ χαριέντως ἔχων τὸ
σῶμα τελευτήσηι καὶ ἐν τοιαύτηι ὥραι, καὶ πάνυ μάλα.
συμ-
πεσὸν γὰρ τὸ σῶμα καὶ ταριχευθέν, ὥσπερ οἱ ἐν Αἰγύπτωι
ταριχευθέντες, ὀλίγου ὅλον μένει ἀμήχανον ὅσον χρόνον·
d ἔνια δὲ μέρη τοῦ σώματος, καὶ ἂν σαπῆι, ὀστᾶ τε καὶ νεῦρα
καὶ τὰ τοιαῦτα πάντα, ὅμως ὡς ἔπος εἰπεῖν ἀθάνατά ἐστιν·
ἢ οὔ;"
"ναί."
5 "ἡ δὲ ψυχὴ ἄρα, τὸ ἀιδές, τὸ εἰς τοιοῦτον τόπον ἕτερον
οἰχόμενον γενναῖον καὶ καθαρὸν καὶ ἀιδῆ, εἰς Ἅιδου ὡς
ἀληθῶς, παρὰ τὸν ἀγαθὸν καὶ φρόνιμον θεόν, οἷ, ἂν θεὸς
θέληι, αὐτίκα καὶ τῆι ἐμῆι ψυχῆι ἰτέον, αὕτη δὲ δὴ ἡμῖν ἡ
τοιαύτη καὶ οὕτω πεφυκυῖα ἀπαλλαττομένη τοῦ σώματος
10 εὐθὺς διαπεφύσηται καὶ ἀπόλωλεν, ὥς φασιν οἱ πολλοὶ
e ἄνθρωποι; πολλοῦ γε δεῖ, ὦ φίλε Κέβης τε καὶ Σιμμία,
ἀλλὰ πολλῶι μᾶλλον ὧδ᾽ ἔχει· ἐὰν μὲν καθαρὰ ἀπαλλάττηται,
μηδὲν τοῦ σώματος συνεφέλκουσα, ἅτε οὐδὲν κοινωνοῦσα
αὐτῶι ἐν τῶι βίωι ἑκοῦσα εἶναι, ἀλλὰ φεύγουσα αὐτὸ καὶ
5 συνηθροισμένη αὐτὴ εἰς ἑαυτήν, ἅτε μελετῶσα ἀεὶ τοῦτο,
τὸ δὲ οὐδὲν ἄλλο ἐστὶν ἢ ὀρθῶς φιλοσοφοῦσα καὶ τῶι ὄντι
81 τεθνάναι μελετῶσα ῥαιδίως· ἢ οὐ τοῦτ᾽ ἂν εἴη μελέτη
θανάτου;"
"παντάπασί γε."
"οὐκοῦν οὕτω μὲν ἔχουσα εἰς τὸ ὅμοιον αὐτῆι τὸ ἀιδὲς
5 ἀπέρχεται, τὸ θεῖόν τε καὶ ἀθάνατον καὶ φρόνιμον, οἷ
ἀφικομένηι ὑπάρχει αὐτῆι εὐδαίμονι εἶναι, πλάνης καὶ ἀνοίας
καὶ φόβων καὶ ἀγρίων ἐρώτων καὶ τῶν ἄλλων κακῶν τῶν
ἀνθρωπείων ἀπηλλαγμένηι, ὥσπερ δὲ λέγεται κατὰ τῶν με-
μυημένων, ὡς ἀληθῶς τὸν λοιπὸν χρόνον μετὰ θεῶν διάγουσα;
10 οὕτω φῶμεν, ὦ Κέβης, ἢ ἄλλως;"
"οὕτω νὴ Δία," ἔφη ὁ Κέβης.

"ἐὰν δέ γε οἶμαι μεμιασμένη καὶ ἀκάθαρτος τοῦ σώματος b
ἀπαλλάττηται, ἅτε τῶι σώματι ἀεὶ συνοῦσα καὶ τοῦτο θερα-
πεύουσα καὶ ἐρῶσα, καὶ γεγοητευμένη ὑπ᾽ αὐτοῦ ὑπό τε τῶν
ἐπιθυμιῶν καὶ ἡδονῶν, ὥστε μηδὲν ἄλλο δοκεῖν εἶναι ἀληθὲς
ἀλλ᾽ ἢ τὸ σωματοειδές, οὗ τις ἂν ἅψαιτο καὶ ἴδοι καὶ πίοι 5
καὶ φάγοι καὶ πρὸς τὰ ἀφροδίσια χρήσαιτο, τὸ δὲ τοῖς
ὄμμασι σκοτῶδες καὶ ἀιδές, νοητὸν δὲ καὶ φιλοσοφίαι αἱρετόν,
τοῦτο δὲ εἰθισμένη μισεῖν τε καὶ τρέμειν καὶ φεύγειν, οὕτω
δὴ ἔχουσαν οἴει ψυχὴν αὐτὴν καθ᾽ αὑτὴν εἰλικρινῆ ἀπαλ- c
λάξεσθαι; "
"οὐδ᾽ ὁπωστιοῦν," ἔφη.
"ἀλλὰ διειλημμένην γε οἶμαι ὑπὸ τοῦ σωματοειδοῦς,
ὃ αὐτῆι ἡ ὁμιλία τε καὶ συνουσία τοῦ σώματος διὰ τὸ ἀεὶ 5
συνεῖναι καὶ διὰ τὴν πολλὴν μελέτην ἐνεποίησε σύμφυτον; "
"πάνυ γε."
"ἐμβριθὲς δέ γε, ὦ φίλε, τοῦτο οἴεσθαι χρὴ εἶναι καὶ
βαρὺ καὶ γεῶδες καὶ ὁρατόν· ὃ δὴ καὶ ἔχουσα ἡ τοιαύτη
ψυχὴ βαρύνεταί τε καὶ ἕλκεται πάλιν εἰς τὸν ὁρατὸν τόπον 10
φόβωι τοῦ ἀιδοῦς τε καὶ Ἅιδου, ὥσπερ λέγεται, περὶ τὰ
μνήματά τε καὶ τοὺς τάφους κυλινδουμένη, περὶ ἃ δὴ καὶ d
ὤφθη ἄττα ψυχῶν σκιοειδῆ φαντάσματα, οἷα παρέχονται αἱ
τοιαῦται ψυχαὶ εἴδωλα, αἱ μὴ καθαρῶς ἀπολυθεῖσαι ἀλλὰ
τοῦ ὁρατοῦ μετέχουσαι, διὸ καὶ ὁρῶνται."
"εἰκός γε, ὦ Σώκρατες." 5
"εἰκὸς μέντοι, ὦ Κέβης· καὶ οὔ τί γε τὰς τῶν ἀγαθῶν
αὐτὰς εἶναι, ἀλλὰ τὰς τῶν φαύλων, αἳ περὶ τὰ τοιαῦτα
ἀναγκάζονται πλανᾶσθαι δίκην τίνουσαι τῆς προτέρας τροφῆς κακῆς οὔσης. καὶ μέχρι γε τούτου πλανῶνται, ἕως ἂν τῆι
τοῦ συνεπακολουθοῦντος, τοῦ σωματοειδοῦς, ἐπιθυμίαι πάλιν e
ἐνδεθῶσιν εἰς σῶμα· ἐνδοῦνται δέ, ὥσπερ εἰκός, εἰς τοιαῦτα
ἤθη ὁποῖ᾽ ἄττ᾽ ἂν καὶ μεμελετηκυῖαι τύχωσιν ἐν τῶι βίωι."
"τὰ ποῖα δὴ ταῦτα λέγεις, ὦ Σώκρατες; "
"οἷον τοὺς μὲν γαστριμαργίας τε καὶ ὕβρεις καὶ φιλοποσίας 5

b3 γεγοητευμένη m t: γοητευομένη m p t   c4 ἀλλὰ m p t: ἀλλὰ καὶ m

μεμελετηκότας καὶ μὴ διευλαβουμένους εἰς τὰ τῶν ὄνων γένη
82 καὶ τῶν τοιούτων θηρίων εἰκὸς ἐνδύεσθαι. ἢ οὐκ οἴει; "
"πάνυ μὲν οὖν εἰκὸς λέγεις."
"τοὺς δέ γε ἀδικίας τε καὶ τυραννίδας καὶ ἁρπαγὰς προ-
τετιμηκότας εἰς τὰ τῶν λύκων τε καὶ ἱεράκων καὶ ἰκτίνων
5 γένη· ἢ ποῖ ἂν ἄλλοσέ φαμεν τὰς τοιαύτας ἰέναι; "
"ἀμέλει," ἔφη ὁ Κέβης, "εἰς τὰ τοιαῦτα."
"οὐκοῦν", ἦ δ' ὅς, "δῆλα δὴ καὶ τἆλλα ἧι ἂν ἕκαστα ἴοι
κατὰ τὰς αὐτῶν ὁμοιότητας τῆς μελέτης; "
"δῆλον δή," ἔφη· "πῶς δ' οὔ; "
10 "οὐκοῦν εὐδαιμονέστατοι", ἔφη, "καὶ τούτων εἰσὶ καὶ εἰς
βέλτιστον τόπον ἰόντες οἱ τὴν δημοτικὴν καὶ πολιτικὴν
b ἀρετὴν ἐπιτετηδευκότες, ἣν δὴ καλοῦσι σωφροσύνην τε καὶ
δικαιοσύνην, ἐξ ἔθους τε καὶ μελέτης γεγονυῖαν ἄνευ φιλοσοφίας τε καὶ νοῦ; "
"πῆι δὴ οὗτοι εὐδαιμονέστατοι; "
5 "ὅτι τούτους εἰκός ἐστιν εἰς τοιοῦτον πάλιν ἀφικνεῖσθαι
πολιτικὸν καὶ ἥμερον γένος, ἤ που μελιττῶν ἢ σφηκῶν ἢ
μυρμήκων, ἢ καὶ εἰς ταὐτόν γε πάλιν τὸ ἀνθρώπινον γένος,
καὶ γίγνεσθαι ἐξ αὐτῶν ἄνδρας μετρίους."
"εἰκός."
10 "εἰς δέ γε θεῶν γένος μὴ φιλοσοφήσαντι καὶ παντελῶς
c καθαρῷ ἀπιόντι οὐ θέμις ἀφικνεῖσθαι ἀλλ' ἢ τῷ φιλομαθεῖ.
ἀλλὰ τούτων ἕνεκα, ὦ ἑταῖρε Σιμμία τε καὶ Κέβης, οἱ
ὀρθῶς φιλόσοφοι ἀπέχονται τῶν κατὰ τὸ σῶμα ἐπιθυμιῶν
ἁπασῶν καὶ καρτεροῦσι καὶ οὐ παραδιδόασιν αὐταῖς ἑαυτούς,
5 οὔ τι οἰκοφθορίαν τε καὶ πενίαν φοβούμενοι, ὥσπερ οἱ
πολλοὶ καὶ φιλοχρήματοι· οὐδὲ αὖ ἀτιμίαν τε καὶ ἀδοξίαν
μοχθηρίας δεδιότες, ὥσπερ οἱ φίλαρχοί τε καὶ φιλότιμοι,
ἔπειτα ἀπέχονται αὐτῶν."
"οὐ γὰρ ἂν πρέποι," ἔφη, "ὦ Σώκρατες," ὁ Κέβης.
d "οὐ μέντοι μὰ Δία," ἦ δ' ὅς. "τοιγάρτοι τούτοις μὲν

ἄπασιν, ὦ Κέβης, ἐκεῖνοι οἷς τι μέλει τῆς ἑαυτῶν ψυχῆς
ἀλλὰ μὴ σώματα πλάττοντες ζῶσι, χαίρειν εἰπόντες, οὐ
κατὰ ταὐτὰ πορεύονται αὐτοῖς ὡς οὐκ εἰδόσιν ὅπηι ἔρχονται,
αὐτοὶ δὲ ἡγούμενοι οὐ δεῖν ἐναντία τῆι φιλοσοφίαι πράττειν 5
καὶ τῆι ἐκείνης λύσει τε καὶ καθαρμῶι, ταύτηι δὴ τρέπονται
ἐκείνηι ἑπόμενοι, ἧι ἐκείνη ὑφηγεῖται.''
    "πῶς, ὦ Σώκρατες; "
    "ἐγὼ ἐρῶ," ἔφη. "γιγνώσκουσι γάρ", ἦ δ᾽ ὅς, "οἱ φιλομαθεῖς
ὅτι παραλαβοῦσα αὐτῶν τὴν ψυχὴν ἡ φιλοσοφία ἀτεχνῶς e
διαδεδεμένην ἐν τῶι σώματι καὶ προσκεκολλημένην, ἀναγκα-
ζομένην δὲ ὥσπερ διὰ εἱργμοῦ διὰ τούτου σκοπεῖσθαι τὰ
ὄντα ἀλλὰ μὴ αὐτὴν δι᾽ αὑτῆς, καὶ ἐν πάσηι ἀμαθίαι κυλιν-
δουμένην, καὶ τοῦ εἱργμοῦ τὴν δεινότητα κατιδοῦσα ὅτι δι᾽ 5
ἐπιθυμίας ἐστίν, ὡς ἂν μάλιστα αὐτὸς ὁ δεδεμένος συλλήπτωρ
εἴη τοῦ δεδέσθαι· ὅπερ οὖν λέγω, γιγνώσκουσιν οἱ φιλομα- 83
θεῖς ὅτι οὕτω παραλαβοῦσα ἡ φιλοσοφία ἔχουσαν αὐτῶν
τὴν ψυχὴν ἠρέμα παραμυθεῖται καὶ λύειν ἐπιχειρεῖ, ἐνδεικνυ-
μένη ὅτι ἀπάτης μὲν μεστὴ ἡ διὰ τῶν ὀμμάτων σκέψις,
ἀπάτης δὲ ἡ διὰ τῶν ὤτων καὶ τῶν ἄλλων αἰσθήσεων, 5
πείθουσα δὲ ἐκ τούτων μὲν ἀναχωρεῖν, ὅσον μὴ ἀνάγκη
αὐτοῖς χρῆσθαι, αὐτὴν δὲ εἰς αὑτὴν συλλέγεσθαι καὶ
ἀθροίζεσθαι παρακελευομένη, πιστεύειν δὲ μηδενὶ ἄλλωι ἀλλ᾽
ἢ αὐτὴν αὑτῆι, ὅτι ἂν νοήσηι αὐτὴ καθ᾽ αὑτὴν αὐτὸ καθ᾽ b
αὑτὸ τῶν ὄντων· ὅτι δ᾽ ἂν δι᾽ ἄλλων σκοπῆι ἐν ἄλλοις ὂν
ἄλλο, μηδὲν ἡγεῖσθαι ἀληθές· εἶναι δὲ τὸ μὲν τοιοῦτον
αἰσθητόν τε καὶ ὁρατόν, ὃ δὲ αὐτὴ ὁρᾶι νοητόν τε καὶ ἀιδές.
ταύτηι οὖν τῆι λύσει οὐκ οἰομένη δεῖν ἐναντιοῦσθαι ἡ τοῦ ὡς 5
ἀληθῶς φιλοσόφου ψυχὴ οὕτως ἀπέχεται τῶν ἡδονῶν τε
καὶ ἐπιθυμιῶν καὶ λυπῶν καὶ φόβων καθ᾽ ὅσον δύναται,
λογιζομένη ὅτι, ἐπειδάν τις σφόδρα ἡσθῆι ἢ λυπηθῆι ἢ
φοβηθῆι ἢ ἐπιθυμήσηι, οὐδὲν τοσοῦτον κακὸν ἔπαθεν ἀπ᾽

---

d3 σώματα *m*: σώματι *m*   d6 δὴ *p*: om. *c t*   a1 τοῦ *e*: τῶι *c p t*   b7 καὶ
φόβων om. *m p t*   b8–9 ἢ λυπηθῆι ἢ φοβηθῆι *m p t*: καὶ λυπ. ἢ φοβ. *m*: ἢ φοβ.
ἢ λυπ. *m*: ἢ φοβ. *m*

6

60   ΠΛΑΤΩΝΟΣ

c αὐτῶν ὧν ἄν τις οἰηθείη, οἷον ἢ νοσήσας ἤ τι ἀναλώσας
διὰ τὰς ἐπιθυμίας, ἀλλ' ὃ πάντων μέγιστόν τε κακῶν καὶ
ἔσχατόν ἐστι, τοῦτο πάσχει καὶ οὐ λογίζεται αὐτό."
"τί τοῦτο, ὦ Σώκρατες;" ἔφη ὁ Κέβης.

5   "ὅτι ψυχὴ παντὸς ἀνθρώπου ἀναγκάζεται ἅμα τε ἡσθῆναι
σφόδρα ἢ λυπηθῆναι ἐπί τωι καὶ ἡγεῖσθαι περὶ ὃ ἂν μάλιστα
τοῦτο πάσχηι, τοῦτο ἐναργέστατόν τε εἶναι καὶ ἀληθέστατον,
οὐχ οὕτως ἔχον· ταῦτα δὲ μάλιστα ὁρατά· ἢ οὔ;"
"πάνυ γε."

d   "οὐκοῦν ἐν τούτωι τῶι πάθει μάλιστα καταδεῖται ψυχὴ ὑπὸ
σώματος;"
"πῶς δή;"
"ὅτι ἑκάστη ἡδονὴ καὶ λύπη ὥσπερ ἧλον ἔχουσα προσηλοῖ
5   αὐτὴν πρὸς τὸ σῶμα καὶ προσπερονᾶι καὶ ποιεῖ σωματοειδῆ,
δοξάζουσαν ταῦτα ἀληθῆ εἶναι ἅπερ ἂν καὶ τὸ σῶμα φῆι.
ἐκ γὰρ τοῦ ὁμοδοξεῖν τῶι σώματι καὶ τοῖς αὐτοῖς χαίρειν
ἀναγκάζεται οἶμαι ὁμότροπός τε καὶ ὁμότροφος γίγνεσθαι
καὶ οἷα μηδέποτε εἰς Ἅιδου καθαρῶς ἀφικέσθαι, ἀλλὰ ἀεὶ
10 τοῦ σώματος ἀναπλέα ἐξιέναι, ὥστε ταχὺ πάλιν πίπτειν εἰς
e   ἄλλο σῶμα καὶ ὥσπερ σπειρομένη ἐμφύεσθαι, καὶ ἐκ τούτων
ἄμοιρος εἶναι τῆς τοῦ θείου τε καὶ καθαροῦ καὶ μονοειδοῦς
συνουσίας."
"ἀληθέστατα", ἔφη, "λέγεις," ὁ Κέβης, "ὦ Σώκρατες."

5   "τούτων τοίνυν ἕνεκα, ὦ Κέβης, οἱ δικαίως φιλομαθεῖς
κόσμιοί εἰσι καὶ ἀνδρεῖοι, οὐχ ὧν οἱ πολλοὶ ἕνεκά φασιν·
ἢ σὺ οἴει;"
84 "οὐ δῆτα ἔγωγε."

"οὐ γάρ· ἀλλ' οὕτω λογίσαιτ' ἂν ψυχὴ ἀνδρὸς φιλοσόφου,
καὶ οὐκ ἂν οἰηθείη τὴν μὲν φιλοσοφίαν χρῆναι ἑαυτὴν λύειν,
λυούσης δὲ ἐκείνης, αὐτὴν παραδιδόναι ταῖς ἡδοναῖς καὶ
5   λύπαις ἑαυτὴν πάλιν αὖ ἐγκαταδεῖν, καὶ ἀνήνυτον ἔργον πράττειν Πηνελόπης τινὰ ἐναντίως ἱστὸν μεταχειριζομένης, ἀλλὰ
γαλήνην τούτων παρασκευάζουσα, ἑπομένη τῶι λογισμῶι καὶ
ἀεὶ ἐν τούτωι οὖσα, τὸ ἀληθὲς καὶ τὸ θεῖον καὶ τὸ ἀδόξαστον

c2 κακῶν m t: κακὸν m

θεωμένη καὶ ὑπ᾽ ἐκείνου τρεφομένη, ζῆν τε οἴεται οὕτω b
δεῖν ἕως ἂν ζῆι, καὶ ἐπειδὰν τελευτήσηι, εἰς τὸ συγγενὲς
καὶ εἰς τὸ τοιοῦτον ἀφικομένη ἀπηλλάχθαι τῶν ἀνθρωπίνων
κακῶν. ἐκ δὴ τῆς τοιαύτης τροφῆς οὐδὲν δεινὸν μὴ φοβηθῆι,
[ταῦτα δ᾽ ἐπιτηδεύσασα,] ὦ Σιμμία τε καὶ Κέβης, ὅπως μὴ 5
διασπασθεῖσα ἐν τῆι ἀπαλλαγῆι τοῦ σώματος ὑπὸ τῶν ἀνέ-
μων διαφυσηθεῖσα καὶ διαπτομένη οἴχηται καὶ οὐδὲν ἔτι
οὐδαμοῦ ἦι."

σιγὴ οὖν ἐγένετο ταῦτα εἰπόντος τοῦ Σωκράτους ἐπὶ c
πολὺν χρόνον, καὶ αὐτός τε πρὸς τῶι εἰρημένωι λόγωι ἦν ὁ
Σωκράτης, ὡς ἰδεῖν ἐφαίνετο, καὶ ἡμῶν οἱ πλεῖστοι· Κέβης
δὲ καὶ Σιμμίας σμικρὸν πρὸς ἀλλήλω διελεγέσθην. καὶ ὁ
Σωκράτης ἰδὼν αὐτὼ ἤρετο, "τί;" ἔφη, "ὑμῖν τὰ λεχθέντα μῶν 5
μὴ δοκεῖ ἐνδεῶς λέγεσθαι; πολλὰς γὰρ δὴ ἔτι ἔχει ὑποψίας
καὶ ἀντιλαβάς, εἴ γε δή τις αὐτὰ μέλλει ἱκανῶς διεξιέναι. εἰ
μὲν οὖν τι ἄλλο σκοπεῖσθον, οὐδὲν λέγω· εἰ δέ τι περὶ
τούτων ἀπορεῖτον, μηδὲν ἀποκνήσητε καὶ αὐτοὶ εἰπεῖν καὶ
διελθεῖν, εἴ πηι ὑμῖν φαίνεται βέλτιον ⟨ἂν⟩ λεχθῆναι, καὶ d
αὖ καὶ ἐμὲ συμπαραλαβεῖν, εἴ τι μᾶλλον οἴεσθε μετ᾽ ἐμοῦ
εὐπορήσειν."

καὶ ὁ Σιμμίας ἔφη· "καὶ μήν, ὦ Σώκρατες, τἀληθῆ σοι
ἐρῶ. πάλαι γὰρ ἡμῶν ἑκάτερος ἀπορῶν τὸν ἕτερον προωθεῖ 5
καὶ κελεύει ἐρέσθαι διὰ τὸ ἐπιθυμεῖν μὲν ἀκοῦσαι, ὀκνεῖν δὲ
ὄχλον παρέχειν, μή σοι ἀηδὲς ἦι διὰ τὴν παροῦσαν συμφοράν."

καὶ ὃς ἀκούσας ἐγέλασέν τε ἠρέμα καί φησιν· "βαβαί,
ὦ Σιμμία· ἦ που χαλεπῶς ἂν τοὺς ἄλλους ἀνθρώπους πείσαιμι ὡς οὐ συμφορὰν ἡγοῦμαι τὴν παροῦσαν τύχην, ὅτε e
γε μηδ᾽ ὑμᾶς δύναμαι πείθειν, ἀλλὰ φοβεῖσθε μὴ δυσκολώ-
τερόν τι νῦν διάκειμαι ἢ ἐν τῶι πρόσθεν βίωι· καί, ὡς ἔοικε,
τῶν κύκνων δοκῶ φαυλότερος ὑμῖν εἶναι τὴν μαντικήν, οἳ
ἐπειδὰν αἴσθωνται ὅτι δεῖ αὐτοὺς ἀποθανεῖν, ἄιδοντες καὶ ἐν 5
τῶι πρόσθεν χρόνωι, τότε δὴ πλεῖστα καὶ μάλιστα ἄιδουσι, 85
γεγηθότες ὅτι μέλλουσι παρὰ τὸν θεὸν ἀπιέναι οὗπέρ εἰσι
θεράποντες. οἱ δ᾽ ἄνθρωποι διὰ τὸ αὐτῶν δέος τοῦ θανάτου

b5 ταῦτα δ᾽ ἐπιτηδεύσασα secl. e: ταῦτα γ᾽ ἐπ. e   a1 μάλιστα m t: κάλλιστα e

καὶ τῶν κύκνων καταψεύδονται, καί φασιν αὐτοὺς θρηνοῦντας
5 τὸν θάνατον ὑπὸ λύπης ἐξᾴδειν, καὶ οὐ λογίζονται ὅτι οὐδὲν
ὄρνεον ᾄδει ὅταν πεινῇ ἢ ῥιγῶι ἤ τινα ἄλλην λύπην λυπῆται,
οὐδὲ αὐτὴ ἥ τε ἀηδὼν καὶ χελιδὼν καὶ ὁ ἔποψ, ἃ δή φασι
διὰ λύπην θρηνοῦντα ᾄδειν. ἀλλ᾽ οὔτε ταῦτά μοι φαίνεται
b λυπούμενα ᾄδειν οὔτε οἱ κύκνοι, ἀλλ᾽ ἅτε οἶμαι τοῦ Ἀπόλλωνος ὄντες, μαντικοί τέ εἰσι καὶ προειδότες τὰ ἐν Ἅιδου
ἀγαθὰ ᾄδουσι καὶ τέρπονται ἐκείνην τὴν ἡμέραν διαφερόντως
ἢ ἐν τῶι ἔμπροσθεν χρόνωι. ἐγὼ δὲ καὶ αὐτὸς ἡγοῦμαι
5 ὁμόδουλός τε εἶναι τῶν κύκνων καὶ ἱερὸς τοῦ αὐτοῦ θεοῦ,
καὶ οὐ χεῖρον ἐκείνων τὴν μαντικὴν ἔχειν παρὰ τοῦ δεσπότου,
οὐδὲ δυσθυμότερον αὐτῶν τοῦ βίου ἀπαλλάττεσθαι. ἀλλὰ
τούτου γ᾽ ἕνεκα λέγειν τε χρὴ καὶ ἐρωτᾶν ὅτι ἂν βούλησθε,
ἕως ἂν Ἀθηναίων ἐῶσιν ἄνδρες ἕνδεκα."
10 "καλῶς", ἔφη, "λέγεις," ὁ Σιμμίας· "καὶ ἐγώ τέ σοι ἐρῶ ὃ
c ἀπορῶ, καὶ αὖ ὅδε, ἧι οὐκ ἀποδέχεται τὰ εἰρημένα. ἐμοὶ
γὰρ δοκεῖ, ὦ Σώκρατες, περὶ τῶν τοιούτων ἴσως ὥσπερ καὶ
σοὶ τὸ μὲν σαφὲς εἰδέναι ἐν τῶι νῦν βίωι ἢ ἀδύνατον εἶναι
ἢ παγχάλεπόν τι, τὸ μέντοι αὖ τὰ λεγόμενα περὶ αὐτῶν μὴ
5 οὐχὶ παντὶ τρόπωι ἐλέγχειν καὶ μὴ προαφίστασθαι πρὶν ἂν
πανταχῇ σκοπῶν ἀπείπῃ τις, πάνυ μαλθακοῦ εἶναι ἀνδρός·
δεῖν γὰρ περὶ αὐτὰ ἕν γέ τι τούτων διαπράξασθαι, ἢ μαθεῖν
ὅπῃ ἔχει ἢ εὑρεῖν ἤ, εἰ ταῦτα ἀδύνατον, τὸν γοῦν βέλτιστον τῶν ἀνθρωπίνων λόγων λαβόντα καὶ δυσεξελεγκτό-
d τατον, ἐπὶ τούτου ὀχούμενον ὥσπερ ἐπὶ σχεδίας κινδυνεύοντα
διαπλεῦσαι τὸν βίον, εἰ μή τις δύναιτο ἀσφαλέστερον καὶ
ἀκινδυνότερον ἐπὶ βεβαιοτέρου ὀχήματος, [ἢ] λόγου θείου
τινός, διαπορευθῆναι. καὶ δὴ καὶ νῦν ἔγωγε οὐκ ἐπαισχυν-
5 θήσομαι ἐρέσθαι, ἐπειδὴ καὶ σὺ ταῦτα λέγεις, οὐδ᾽ ἐμαυτὸν αἰτιάσομαι ἐν ὑστέρωι χρόνωι ὅτι νῦν οὐκ εἶπον ἅ μοι
δοκεῖ. ἐμοὶ γάρ, ὦ Σώκρατες, ἐπειδὴ καὶ πρὸς ἐμαυτὸν
καὶ πρὸς τόνδε σκοπῶ τὰ εἰρημένα, οὐ πάνυ φαίνεται ἱκανῶς
10 εἰρῆσθαι."
e καὶ ὁ Σωκράτης, "ἴσως γάρ," ἔφη, "ὦ ἑταῖρε, ἀληθῆ σοι
φαίνεται· ἀλλὰ λέγε ὅπῃ δὴ οὐχ ἱκανῶς."

"ταύτηι ἔμοιγε," ἦ δ᾽ ὅς, "ἧι δὴ καὶ περὶ ἁρμονίας ἄν τις καὶ
λύρας τε καὶ χορδῶν τὸν αὐτὸν τοῦτον λόγον εἴποι, ὡς ἡ
μὲν ἁρμονία ἀόρατον καὶ ἀσώματον καὶ πάγκαλόν τι καὶ 5
θεῖόν ἐστιν ἐν τῆι ἡρμοσμένηι λύραι, αὐτὴ δ᾽ ἡ λύρα καὶ 86
αἱ χορδαὶ σώματά τε καὶ σωματοειδῆ καὶ σύνθετα καὶ
γεώδη ἐστὶ καὶ τοῦ θνητοῦ συγγενῆ. ἐπειδὰν οὖν ἢ κατάξηι
τις τὴν λύραν ἢ διατέμηι καὶ διαρρήξηι τὰς χορδάς, εἴ τις
διισχυρίζοιτο τῶι αὐτῶι λόγωι ὥσπερ σύ, ὡς ἀνάγκη ἔτι εἶναι 5
τὴν ἁρμονίαν ἐκείνην καὶ μὴ ἀπολωλέναι (οὐδεμία γὰρ
μηχανὴ ἂν εἴη τὴν μὲν λύραν ἔτι εἶναι διερρωγυιῶν τῶν
χορδῶν καὶ τὰς χορδὰς θνητοειδεῖς οὔσας, τὴν δὲ ἁρμονίαν
ἀπολωλέναι τὴν τοῦ θείου τε καὶ ἀθανάτου ὁμοφυῆ τε καὶ b
συγγενῆ, προτέραν τοῦ θνητοῦ ἀπολομένην), ἀλλά, φαίη,
ἀνάγκη ἔτι που εἶναι αὐτὴν τὴν ἁρμονίαν, καὶ πρότερον τὰ
ξύλα καὶ τὰς χορδὰς κατασαπήσεσθαι πρίν τι ἐκείνην
παθεῖν – καὶ γὰρ οὖν, ὦ Σώκρατες, οἶμαι ἔγωγε καὶ αὐτόν 5
σε τοῦτο ἐντεθυμῆσθαι, ὅτι τοιοῦτόν τι μάλιστα ὑπολαμ-
βάνομεν τὴν ψυχὴν εἶναι, ὥσπερ ἐντεταμένου τοῦ σώματος
ἡμῶν καὶ συνεχομένου ὑπὸ θερμοῦ καὶ ψυχροῦ καὶ ξηροῦ
καὶ ὑγροῦ καὶ τοιούτων τινῶν, κρᾶσιν εἶναι καὶ ἁρμονίαν
αὐτῶν τούτων τὴν ψυχὴν ἡμῶν, ἐπειδὰν ταῦτα καλῶς καὶ c
μετρίως κραθῆι πρὸς ἄλληλα· εἰ οὖν τυγχάνει ἡ ψυχὴ οὖσα
ἁρμονία τις, δῆλον ὅτι, ὅταν χαλασθῆι τὸ σῶμα ἡμῶν
ἀμέτρως ἢ ἐπιταθῆι ὑπὸ νόσων καὶ ἄλλων κακῶν, τὴν μὲν
ψυχὴν ἀνάγκη εὐθὺς ὑπάρχει ἀπολωλέναι, καίπερ οὖσαν 5
θειοτάτην, ὥσπερ καὶ αἱ ἄλλαι ἁρμονίαι αἵ τ᾽ ἐν τοῖς
φθόγγοις καὶ ἐν τοῖς τῶν δημιουργῶν ἔργοις πᾶσι, τὰ δὲ
λείψανα τοῦ σώματος ἑκάστου πολὺν χρόνον παραμένειν,
ἕως ἂν ἢ κατακαυθῆι ἢ κατασαπῆι. ὅρα οὖν πρὸς τοῦτον τὸν d
λόγον τί φήσομεν, ἐάν τις ἀξιοῖ κρᾶσιν οὖσαν τὴν ψυχὴν
τῶν ἐν τῶι σώματι ἐν τῶι καλουμένωι θανάτωι πρώτην ἀπόλλυσθαι."
    διαβλέψας οὖν ὁ Σωκράτης, ὥσπερ τὰ πολλὰ εἰώθει, 5

e3 ἧι δὴ m: ἤδη m   a2 σώματα m: σῶμα m

64 ΠΛΑΤΩΝΟΣ

καὶ μειδιάσας, "δίκαια μέντοι", ἔφη, "λέγει ὁ Σιμμίας. εἰ
οὖν τις ὑμῶν εὐπορώτερος ἐμοῦ, τί οὐκ ἀπεκρίνατο; καὶ γὰρ
οὐ φαύλως ἔοικεν ἁπτομένωι τοῦ λόγου. δοκεῖ μέντοι μοι
χρῆναι πρὸ τῆς ἀποκρίσεως ἔτι πρότερον Κέβητος ἀκοῦσαι
e τί αὖ ὅδε ἐγκαλεῖ τῶι λόγωι, ἵνα χρόνου ἐγγενομένου βου-
λευσώμεθα τί ἐροῦμεν, ἔπειτα δὲ ἀκούσαντας ἢ συγχωρεῖν
αὐτοῖς ἐάν τι δοκῶσι προσάιδειν, ἐὰν δὲ μή, οὕτως ἤδη
ὑπερδικεῖν τοῦ λόγου. ἀλλ' ἄγε," ἦ δ' ὅς, "ὦ Κέβης, λέγε,
5 τί ἦν τὸ σὲ αὖ θρᾶττον [ἀπιστίαν παρέχει]."
"λέγω δή," ἦ δ' ὃς ὁ Κέβης. "ἐμοὶ γὰρ φαίνεται ἔτι ἐν
τῶι αὐτῶι ὁ λόγος εἶναι, καί ὅπερ ἐν τοῖς πρόσθεν ἐλέγομεν,
87 ταὐτὸν ἔγκλημα ἔχειν. ὅτι μὲν γὰρ ἦν ἡμῶν ἡ ψυχὴ καὶ
πρὶν εἰς τόδε τὸ εἶδος ἐλθεῖν, οὐκ ἀνατίθεμαι μὴ οὐχὶ πάνυ
χαριέντως καί, εἰ μὴ ἐπαχθές ἐστιν εἰπεῖν, πάνυ ἱκανῶς
ἀποδεδεῖχθαι· ὡς δὲ καὶ ἀποθανόντων ἡμῶν ἔτι που ἔσται,
5 οὔ μοι δοκεῖ τῇδε. ὡς μὲν οὐκ ἰσχυρότερον καὶ πολυχρονιώτερον ψυχὴ σώματος, οὐ συγχωρῶ τῇ Σιμμίου ἀντι-
λήψει· δοκεῖ γάρ μοι πᾶσι τούτοις πάνυ πολὺ διαφέρειν. τί
οὖν, ἂν φαίη ὁ λόγος, ἔτι ἀπιστεῖς, ἐπειδὴ ὁρᾶις ἀποθανόντος
τοῦ ἀνθρώπου τό γε ἀσθενέστερον ἔτι ὄν; τὸ δὲ πολυ-
b χρονιώτερον οὐ δοκεῖ σοι ἀναγκαῖον εἶναι ἔτι σώιζεσθαι ἐν
τούτωι τῶι χρόνωι; πρὸς δὴ τοῦτο τόδε ἐπίσκεψαι, εἴ τι λέγω·
εἰκόνος γάρ τινος, ὡς ἔοικεν, κἀγὼ ὥσπερ Σιμμίας δέομαι.
ἐμοὶ γὰρ δοκεῖ ὁμοίως λέγεσθαι ταῦτα ὥσπερ ἄν τις περὶ
5 ἀνθρώπου ὑφάντου πρεσβύτου ἀποθανόντος λέγοι τοῦτον
τὸν λόγον, ὅτι οὐκ ἀπόλωλεν ὁ ἄνθρωπος ἀλλ' ἔστι που
σῶς, τεκμήριον δὲ παρέχοιτο θοἰμάτιον ὃ ἠμπείχετο αὐτὸς
ὑφηνάμενος ὅτι ἐστὶ σῶν καὶ οὐκ ἀπόλωλεν, καὶ εἴ τις
c ἀπιστοίη αὐτῶι, ἀνερωτῶιη πότερον πολυχρονιώτερόν ἐστι
τὸ γένος ἀνθρώπου ἢ ἱματίου ἐν χρείαι τε ὄντος καὶ φορου-
μένου, ἀποκριναμένου δή τινος ὅτι πολὺ τὸ τοῦ ἀνθρώπου,
οἴοιτο ἀποδεδεῖχθαι ὅτι παντὸς ἄρα μᾶλλον ὅ γε ἄνθρωπος

e2 δὲ om. m   a4 ἔσται m: ἐστιν m   b7 σῶς (m): ἴσως c: p incert.
c1 ἀπιστοίη e: ἀπιστῶν c p   c3 δή τινος m p: δέ τινος m: δὴ [τινος] e

σῶς ἐστιν, ἐπειδὴ τό γε ὀλιγοχρονιώτερον οὐκ ἀπόλωλεν. 5
τὸ δ' οἶμαι, ὦ Σιμμία, οὐχ οὕτως ἔχει· σκόπει γὰρ καὶ σὺ
ἃ λέγω. πᾶς γὰρ ἂν ὑπολάβοι ὅτι εὔηθες λέγει ὁ τοῦτο
λέγων· ὁ γὰρ ὑφάντης οὗτος πολλὰ κατατρίψας τοιαῦτα
ἱμάτια καὶ ὑφηνάμενος ἐκείνων μὲν ὕστερος ἀπόλωλεν πολλῶν ὄντων, τοῦ δὲ τελευταίου οἶμαι πρότερος, καὶ οὐδέν τι d
μᾶλλον τούτου ἕνεκα ἄνθρωπός ἐστιν ἱματίου φαυλότερον
οὐδ' ἀσθενέστερον. τὴν αὐτὴν δὲ ταύτην οἶμαι εἰκόνα
δέξαιτ' ἂν ψυχὴ πρὸς σῶμα, καί τις λέγων αὐτὰ ταῦτα περὶ
αὐτῶν μέτρι' ἄν μοι φαίνοιτο λέγειν, ὡς ἡ μὲν ψυχὴ 5
πολυχρόνιόν ἐστι, τὸ δὲ σῶμα ἀσθενέστερον καὶ ὀλιγο-
χρονιώτερον· ἀλλὰ γὰρ ἂν φαίη ἑκάστην τῶν ψυχῶν πολλὰ
σώματα κατατρίβειν, ἄλλως τε κἂν πολλὰ ἔτη βιῶι· εἰ γὰρ
ῥέοι τὸ σῶμα καὶ ἀπολλύοιτο ἔτι ζῶντος τοῦ ἀνθρώπου,
ἀλλ' ἡ ψυχὴ ἀεὶ τὸ κατατριβόμενον ἀνυφαίνοι· ἀναγκαῖον e
μεντἂν εἴη, ὁπότε ἀπολλύοιτο ἡ ψυχή, τὸ τελευταῖον ὕφασμα
τυχεῖν αὐτὴν ἔχουσαν καὶ τούτου μόνου προτέραν ἀπόλλυσθαι, ἀπολομένης δὲ τῆς ψυχῆς τότ' ἤδη τὴν φύσιν τῆς
ἀσθενείας ἐπιδεικνύοι τὸ σῶμα καὶ ταχὺ σαπὲν διοίχοιτο. 5
ὥστε τούτωι τῶι λόγωι οὔπω ἄξιον πιστεύσαντα θαρρεῖν ὡς
ἐπειδὰν ἀποθάνωμεν ἔτι που ἡμῶν ἡ ψυχὴ ἔστιν. εἰ γάρ 88
τις καὶ πλέον ἔτι τῶι λέγοντι [ἢ] ἃ σὺ λέγεις συγχωρήσειεν,
δοὺς αὐτῶι μὴ μόνον ἐν τῶι πρὶν καὶ γενέσθαι ἡμᾶς χρόνωι
εἶναι ἡμῶν τὰς ψυχάς, ἀλλὰ μηδὲν κωλύειν καὶ ἐπειδὰν
ἀποθάνωμεν ἐνίων ἔτι εἶναι καὶ ἔσεσθαι καὶ πολλάκις γενή- 5
σεσθαι καὶ ἀποθανεῖσθαι αὖθις (οὕτω γὰρ αὐτὸ φύσει
ἰσχυρὸν εἶναι, ὥστε πολλάκις γιγνομένην ψυχὴν ἀντέχειν)·
δοὺς δὲ ταῦτα ἐκεῖνο μηκέτι συγχωροῖ, μὴ οὐ πονεῖν
αὐτὴν ἐν ταῖς πολλαῖς γενέσεσιν, καὶ τελευτῶσάν γε ἔν
τινι τῶν θανάτων παντάπασιν ἀπόλυσθαι, τοῦτον δὲ τὸν 10
θάνατον καὶ ταύτην τὴν διάλυσιν τοῦ σώματος ἢ τῆι ψυχῆι b
φέρει ὄλεθρον μηδένα φαίη εἰδέναι, ἀδύνατον γὰρ εἶναι
ὁτωιοῦν αἰσθέσθαι ἡμῶν· εἰ δὲ τοῦτο οὕτως ἔχει, οὐδενὶ
προσήκει θάνατον θαρροῦντι μὴ οὐκ ἀνοήτως θαρρεῖν, ὃς ἂν
μὴ ἔχηι ἀποδεῖξαι ὅτι ἔστι ψυχὴ παντάπασιν ἀθάνατόν τε 5

καὶ ἀνώλεθρον· εἰ δὲ μή, ἀνάγκην εἶναι ἀεὶ τὸν μέλλοντα
ἀποθανεῖσθαι δεδιέναι ὑπὲρ τῆς αὐτοῦ ψυχῆς μὴ ἐν τῆι νῦν
τοῦ σώματος διαζεύξει παντάπασιν ἀπόληται."

c   πάντες οὖν ἀκούσαντες εἰπόντων αὐτῶν ἀηδῶς διετέθημεν, ὡς ὕστερον ἐλέγομεν πρὸς ἀλλήλους, ὅτι ὑπὸ τοῦ
ἔμπροσθεν λόγου σφόδρα πεπεισμένους ἡμᾶς πάλιν ἐδόκουν
ἀναταράξαι καὶ εἰς ἀπιστίαν καταβαλεῖν οὐ μόνον τοῖς
5   προειρημένοις λόγοις, ἀλλὰ καὶ εἰς τὰ ὕστερον μέλλοντα
ῥηθήσεσθαι, μὴ οὐδενὸς ἄξιοι εἶμεν κριταὶ ἢ καὶ τὰ πράγματα αὐτὰ ἄπιστα ἦι.

ΕΧ.   νὴ τοὺς θεούς, ὦ Φαίδων, συγγνώμην γε ἔχω ὑμῖν.
καὶ γὰρ αὐτόν με νῦν ἀκούσαντά σου τοιοῦτόν τι λέγειν
d   πρὸς ἐμαυτὸν ἐπέρχεται· "τίνι οὖν ἔτι πιστεύσομεν λόγωι;
ὡς γὰρ σφόδρα πιθανὸς ὤν, ὃν ὁ Σωκράτης ἔλεγε λόγον,
νῦν εἰς ἀπιστίαν καταπέπτωκεν." θαυμαστῶς γάρ μου ὁ
λόγος οὗτος ἀντιλαμβάνεται καὶ νῦν καὶ ἀεί, τὸ ἁρμονίαν
5   τινὰ ἡμῶν εἶναι τὴν ψυχήν, καὶ ὥσπερ ὑπέμνησέν με ῥηθεὶς
ὅτι καὶ αὐτῶι μοι ταῦτα προυδέδοκτο. καὶ πάνυ δέομαι
πάλιν ὥσπερ ἐξ ἀρχῆς ἄλλου τινὸς λόγου ὅς με πείσει ὡς
τοῦ ἀποθανόντος οὐ συναποθνήισκει ἡ ψυχή. λέγε οὖν πρὸς
Διός, πῆι ὁ Σωκράτης μετῆλθε τὸν λόγον; καὶ πότερον
e   κἀκεῖνος, ὥσπερ ὑμᾶς φῄς, ἔνδηλός τι ἐγένετο ἀχθόμενος, ἢ
οὔ, ἀλλὰ πρᾴως ἐβοήθει τῶι λόγωι; ἢ καὶ ἱκανῶς ἐβοήθησεν
ἢ ἐνδεῶς; πάντα ἡμῖν δίελθε ὡς δύνασαι ἀκριβέστατα.

ΦΑΙΔ.   καὶ μήν, ὦ Ἐχέκρατες, πολλάκις θαυμάσας
5   Σωκράτη οὐ πώποτε μᾶλλον ἠγάσθην ἢ τότε παραγενόμενος.
89   τὸ μὲν οὖν ἔχειν ὅτι λέγοι ἐκεῖνος ἴσως οὐδὲν ἄτοπον· ἀλλὰ
ἔγωγε μάλιστα ἐθαύμασα αὐτοῦ πρῶτον μὲν τοῦτο, ὡς ἡδέως
καὶ εὐμενῶς καὶ ἀγαμένως τῶν νεανίσκων τὸν λόγον ἀπ-
εδέξατο, ἔπειτα ἡμῶν ὡς ὀξέως ἡισθετο ὃ ἐπεπόνθεμεν ὑπὸ
5   τῶν λόγων, ἔπειτα ὡς εὖ ἡμᾶς ἰάσατο καὶ ὥσπερ πεφευγότας
καὶ ἡττημένους ἀνεκαλέσατο καὶ προύτρεψεν πρὸς τὸ παρ-
έπεσθαί τε καὶ συσκοπεῖν τὸν λόγον.

e2 ἦ m: ἢ m: om. m

ΕΧ. πῶς δή;

ΦΑΙΔ. ἐγὼ ἐρῶ. ἔτυχον γὰρ ἐν δεξιᾶι αὐτοῦ καθή-
μενος παρὰ τὴν κλίνην ἐπὶ χαμαιζήλου τινός, ὁ δὲ ἐπὶ πολὺ b
ὑψηλοτέρου ἢ ἐγώ. καταψήσας οὖν μου τὴν κεφαλὴν καὶ
συμπιέσας τὰς ἐπὶ τῶι αὐχένι τρίχας (εἰώθει γάρ, ὁπότε
τύχοι, παίζειν μου εἰς τὰς τρίχας), "αὔριον δή", ἔφη, "ἴσως, ὦ
Φαίδων, τὰς καλὰς ταύτας κόμας ἀποκερῆι."   5

"ἔοικεν," ἦν δ' ἐγώ, "ὦ Σώκρατες."

"οὔκ, ἄν γε ἐμοὶ πείθηι."

"ἀλλὰ τί;" ἦν δ' ἐγώ.

"τήμερον", ἔφη, "κἀγὼ τὰς ἐμὰς καὶ σὺ ταύτας, ἐάνπερ γε
ἡμῖν ὁ λόγος τελευτήσηι καὶ μὴ δυνώμεθα αὐτὸν ἀναβιώ- 10
σασθαι. καὶ ἔγωγ' ἄν, εἰ σὺ εἴην καί με διαφεύγοι ὁ c
λόγος, ἔνορκον ἂν ποιησαίμην ὥσπερ Ἀργεῖοι, μὴ πρότερον
κομήσειν, πρὶν ἂν νικήσω ἀναμαχόμενος τὸν Σιμμίου τε καὶ
Κέβητος λόγον."

"ἀλλ'", ἦν δ' ἐγώ, "πρὸς δύο λέγεται οὐδ' ὁ Ἡρακλῆς οἷός 5
τε εἶναι."

"ἀλλὰ καὶ ἐμέ", ἔφη, "τὸν Ἰόλεων παρακάλει, ἕως ἔτι
φῶς ἐστιν."

"παρακαλῶ τοίνυν," ἔφην, "οὐχ ὡς Ἡρακλῆς, ἀλλ' ὡς
Ἰόλεως τὸν Ἡρακλῆ."   10

"οὐδὲν διοίσει," ἔφη. "ἀλλὰ πρῶτον εὐλαβηθῶμέν τι πάθος
μὴ πάθωμεν."

"τὸ ποῖον;" ἦν δ' ἐγώ.

"μὴ γενώμεθα", ἦ δ' ὅς, "μισόλογοι, ὥσπερ οἱ μισάνθρωποι d
γιγνόμενοι· ὡς οὐκ ἔστιν", ἔφη, "ὅτι ἄν τις μεῖζον τούτου
κακὸν πάθοι ἢ λόγους μισήσας. γίγνεται δὲ ἐκ τοῦ αὐτοῦ
τρόπου μισολογία τε καὶ μισανθρωπία. ἥ τε γὰρ μισανθρωπία ἐνδύεται ἐκ τοῦ σφόδρα τινὶ πιστεῦσαι ἄνευ τέχνης, 5
καὶ ἡγήσασθαι παντάπασί γε ἀληθῆ εἶναι καὶ ὑγιῆ καὶ
πιστὸν τὸν ἄνθρωπον, ἔπειτα ὀλίγον ὕστερον εὑρεῖν τοῦτον
πονηρόν τε καὶ ἄπιστον, καὶ αὖθις ἕτερον· καὶ ὅταν τοῦτο
πολλάκις πάθηι τις καὶ ὑπὸ τούτων μάλιστα οὓς ἂν ἡγήσαιτο
οἰκειοτάτους τε καὶ ἑταιροτάτους, τελευτῶν δὴ θαμὰ προσ- e

κρούων μισεῖ τε πάντας καὶ ἡγεῖται οὐδενὸς οὐδὲν ὑγιὲς
εἶναι τὸ παράπαν. ἢ οὐκ ᾔσθησαι σύ πω τοῦτο γιγνόμενον; "
"πάνυ γε," ἦν δ᾽ ἐγώ.

5   "οὐκοῦν", ἦ δ᾽ ὅς, "αἰσχρόν, καὶ δῆλον ὅτι ἄνευ τέχνης τῆς
περὶ τἀνθρώπεια ὁ τοιοῦτος χρῆσθαι ἐπιχειρεῖ τοῖς ἀνθρώποις; εἰ γάρ που μετὰ τέχνης ἐχρῆτο, ὥσπερ ἔχει οὕτως
90 ἂν ἡγήσατο, τοὺς μὲν χρηστοὺς καὶ πονηροὺς σφόδρα
ὀλίγους εἶναι ἑκατέρους, τοὺς δὲ μεταξὺ πλείστους."
"πῶς λέγεις; " ἔφην ἐγώ.

"ὥσπερ", ἦ δ᾽ ὅς, "περὶ τῶν σφόδρα σμικρῶν καὶ μεγάλων·
5   οἴει τι σπανιώτερον εἶναι ἢ σφόδρα μέγαν ἢ σφόδρα σμικρὸν
ἐξευρεῖν ἄνθρωπον ἢ κύνα ἢ ἄλλο ὁτιοῦν; ἢ αὖ ταχὺν ἢ
βραδὺν ἢ αἰσχρὸν ἢ καλὸν ἢ λευκὸν ἢ μέλανα; ἢ οὐχὶ
ᾔσθησαι ὅτι πάντων τῶν τοιούτων τὰ μὲν ἄκρα τῶν ἐσχάτων
σπάνια καὶ ὀλίγα, τὰ δὲ μεταξὺ ἄφθονα καὶ πολλά; "
10   "πάνυ γε," ἦν δ᾽ ἐγώ.
b   "οὐκοῦν οἴει," ἔφη, "εἰ πονηρίας ἀγὼν προτεθείη, πάνυ ἂν
ὀλίγους καὶ ἐνταῦθα τοὺς πρώτους φανῆναι; "
"εἰκός γε," ἦν δ᾽ ἐγώ.

"εἰκὸς γάρ," ἔφη. "ἀλλὰ ταύτηι μὲν οὐχ ὅμοιοι οἱ λόγοι
5   τοῖς ἀνθρώποις, ἀλλὰ σοῦ νυνδὴ προάγοντος ἐγὼ ἐφεσπόμην,
ἀλλ᾽ ἐκείνηι ἧι, ἐπειδάν τις πιστεύσηι λόγωι τινὶ ἀληθεῖ
εἶναι ἄνευ τῆς περὶ τοὺς λόγους τέχνης, κἄπειτα ὀλίγον
ὕστερον αὐτῶι δόξηι ψευδὴς εἶναι, ἐνίοτε μὲν ὤν, ἐνίοτε δ᾽
οὐκ ὤν, καὶ αὖθις ἕτερος καὶ ἕτερος – καὶ μάλιστα δὴ οἱ
c   περὶ τοὺς ἀντιλογικοὺς λόγους διατρίψαντες οἶσθ᾽ ὅτι τελευ-
τῶντες οἴονται σοφώτατοι γεγονέναι καὶ κατανενοηκέναι
μόνοι ὅτι οὔτε τῶν πραγμάτων οὐδενὸς οὐδὲν ὑγιὲς οὐδὲ
βέβαιον οὔτε τῶν λόγων, ἀλλὰ πάντα τὰ ὄντα ἀτεχνῶς ὥσπερ
5   ἐν Εὐρίπωι ἄνω κάτω στρέφεται καὶ χρόνον οὐδένα ἐν
οὐδενὶ μένει."

"πάνυ μὲν οὖν", ἔφην ἐγώ, "ἀληθῆ λέγεις."

"οὐκοῦν, ὦ Φαίδων," ἔφη, "οἰκτρὸν ἂν εἴη τὸ πάθος, εἰ

e3 σύ πω m: σὺ m t: οὔπω m   e6 ἐπιχειρεῖ c: ἐπεχείρει t

ὄντος δή τινος ἀληθοῦς καὶ βεβαίου λόγου καὶ δυνατοῦ
κατανοῆσαι, ἔπειτα διὰ τὸ παραγίγνεσθαι τοιούτοις τισὶ d
λόγοις, τοῖς αὐτοῖς τοτὲ μὲν δοκοῦσιν ἀληθέσιν εἶναι, τοτὲ
δὲ μή, μὴ ἑαυτόν τις αἰτιῶιτο μηδὲ τὴν ἑαυτοῦ ἀτεχνίαν,
ἀλλὰ τελευτῶν διὰ τὸ ἀλγεῖν ἄσμενος ἐπὶ τοὺς λόγους ἀφ᾽
ἑαυτοῦ τὴν αἰτίαν ἀπώσαιτο καὶ ἤδη τὸν λοιπὸν βίον μισῶν 5
τε καὶ λοιδορῶν τοὺς λόγους διατελοῖ, τῶν δὲ ὄντων τῆς
ἀληθείας τε καὶ ἐπιστήμης στερηθείη.''

''νὴ τὸν Δία,'' ἦν δ᾽ ἐγώ, ''οἰκτρὸν δῆτα.''

''πρῶτον μὲν τοίνυν'', ἔφη, ''τοῦτο εὐλαβηθῶμεν, καὶ μὴ
παρίωμεν εἰς τὴν ψυχὴν ὡς τῶν λόγων κινδυνεύει οὐδὲν e
ὑγιὲς εἶναι, ἀλλὰ πολὺ μᾶλλον ὅτι ἡμεῖς οὔπω ὑγιῶς ἔχομεν,
ἀλλὰ ἀνδριστέον καὶ προθυμητέον ὑγιῶς ἔχειν, σοὶ μὲν οὖν
καὶ τοῖς ἄλλοις καὶ τοῦ ἔπειτα βίου παντὸς ἕνεκα, ἐμοὶ δὲ
αὐτοῦ ἕνεκα τοῦ θανάτου, ὡς κινδυνεύω ἔγωγε ἐν τῶι παρόντι 91
περὶ αὐτοῦ τούτου οὐ φιλοσόφως ἔχειν ἀλλ᾽ ὥσπερ οἱ πάνυ
ἀπαίδευτοι φιλονίκως. καὶ γὰρ ἐκεῖνοι ὅταν περί του ἀμ-
φισβητῶσιν, ὅπηι μὲν ἔχει περὶ ὧν ἂν ὁ λόγος ἦι οὐ φροντί-
ζουσιν, ὅπως δὲ ἃ αὐτοὶ ἔθεντο ταῦτα δόξει τοῖς παροῦσιν, 5
τοῦτο προθυμοῦνται. καὶ ἐγώ μοι δοκῶ ἐν τῶι παρόντι
τοσοῦτον μόνον ἐκείνων διοίσειν· οὐ γὰρ ὅπως τοῖς παροῦσιν
ἃ ἐγὼ λέγω δόξει ἀληθῆ εἶναι προθυμήσομαι, εἰ μὴ εἴη
πάρεργον, ἀλλ᾽ ὅπως αὐτῶι ἐμοὶ ὅτι μάλιστα δόξει οὕτως
ἔχειν. λογίζομαι γάρ, ὦ φίλε ἑταῖρε (θέασαι ὡς πλεο- b
νεκτικῶς), εἰ μὲν τυγχάνει ἀληθῆ ὄντα ἃ λέγω, καλῶς δὴ
ἔχει τὸ πεισθῆναι· εἰ δὲ μηδέν ἐστι τελευτήσαντι, ἀλλ᾽ οὖν
τοῦτόν γε τὸν χρόνον αὐτὸν τὸν πρὸ τοῦ θανάτου ἧττον τοῖς
παροῦσιν ἀηδὴς ἔσομαι ὀδυρόμενος, ἡ δὲ ἄνοιά μοι αὕτη οὐ 5
συνδιατελεῖ (κακὸν γὰρ ἂν ἦν), ἀλλ᾽ ὀλίγον ὕστερον ἀπολεῖται. παρεσκευασμένος δή,'' ἔφη, ''ὦ Σιμμία τε καὶ Κέβης,
οὑτωσὶ ἔρχομαι ἐπὶ τὸν λόγον· ὑμεῖς μέντοι, ἂν ἐμοὶ πεί-
θησθε, σμικρὸν φροντίσαντες Σωκράτους, τῆς δὲ ἀληθείας c
πολὺ μᾶλλον, ἐὰν μέν τι ὑμῖν δοκῶ ἀληθὲς λέγειν, συνομο-

b5 ἄνοια m: διάνοια m

λογήσατε, εἰ δὲ μή, παντὶ λόγωι ἀντιτείνετε, εὐλαβούμενοι
ὅπως μὴ ἐγὼ ὑπὸ προθυμίας ἅμα ἐμαυτόν τε καὶ ὑμᾶς ἐξα-
5 πατήσας, ὥσπερ μέλιττα τὸ κέντρον ἐγκαταλιπὼν οἰχήσομαι.

"ἀλλ᾽ ἰτέον," ἔφη. "πρῶτόν με ὑπομνήσατε ἃ ἐλέγετε, ἐὰν
μὴ φαίνωμαι μεμνημένος. Σιμμίας μὲν γάρ, ὡς ἐγῶιμαι,
ἀπιστεῖ τε καὶ φοβεῖται μὴ ἡ ψυχὴ ὅμως καὶ θειότερον καὶ
d κάλλιον ὂν τοῦ σώματος προαπολλύηται ἐν ἁρμονίας εἴδει
οὖσα· Κέβης δέ μοι ἔδοξε τοῦτο μὲν ἐμοὶ συγχωρεῖν,
πολυχρονιώτερόν γε εἶναι ψυχὴν σώματος, ἀλλὰ τόδε
ἄδηλον παντί, μὴ πολλὰ δὴ σώματα καὶ πολλάκις κατα-
5 τρίψασα ἡ ψυχὴ τὸ τελευταῖον σῶμα καταλιποῦσα νῦν
αὐτὴ ἀπολλύηται, καὶ ἦι αὐτὸ τοῦτο θάνατος, ψυχῆς ὄλεθρος, ἐπεὶ σῶμά γε ἀεὶ ἀπολλύμενον οὐδὲν παύεται. ἆρα
ἄλλ᾽ ἢ ταῦτ᾽ ἐστίν, ὦ Σιμμία τε καὶ Κέβης, ἃ δεῖ ἡμᾶς
ἐπισκοπεῖσθαι;"
e   συνωμολογείτην δὴ ταῦτ᾽ εἶναι ἄμφω.

"πότερον οὖν", ἔφη, "πάντας τοὺς ἔμπροσθε λόγους οὐκ
ἀποδέχεσθε, ἢ τοὺς μέν, τοὺς δ᾽ οὔ;"

"τοὺς μέν," ἐφάτην, "τοὺς δ᾽ οὔ."

5   "τί οὖν", ἦ δ᾽ ὅς, "περὶ ἐκείνου τοῦ λόγου λέγετε ἐν ὧι
ἔφαμεν τὴν μάθησιν ἀνάμνησιν εἶναι, καὶ τούτου οὕτως
ἔχοντος ἀναγκαίως ἔχειν ἄλλοθι πρότερον ἡμῶν εἶναι τὴν
92 ψυχήν, πρὶν ἐν τῶι σώματι ἐνδεθῆναι;"

"ἐγὼ μέν", ἔφη ὁ Κέβης, "καὶ τότε θαυμαστῶς ὡς ἐπείσθην
ὑπ᾽ αὐτοῦ καὶ νῦν ἐμμένω ὡς οὐδενὶ λόγωι."

"καὶ μήν", ἔφη ὁ Σιμμίας, "καὶ αὐτὸς οὕτως ἔχω, καὶ πάνυ
5 ἂν θαυμάζοιμι εἴ μοι περί γε τούτου ἄλλο ποτέ τι δόξειεν."

καὶ ὁ Σωκράτης, "ἀλλὰ ἀνάγκη σοι," ἔφη, "ὦ ξένε Θηβαῖε,
ἄλλα δοξάσαι, ἐάνπερ μείνηι ἥδε ἡ οἴησις, τὸ ἁρμονίαν μὲν εἶναι
σύνθετον πρᾶγμα, ψυχὴν δὲ ἁρμονίαν τινὰ ἐκ τῶν κατὰ τὸ
σῶμα ἐντεταμένων συγκεῖσθαι· οὐ γάρ που ἀποδέξηι γε
b σαυτοῦ λέγοντος ὡς πρότερον ἦν ἁρμονία συγκειμένη, πρὶν
ἐκεῖνα εἶναι ἐξ ὧν ἔδει αὐτὴν συντεθῆναι. ἢ ἀποδέξηι;"

c3 εὐλαβούμενοι om. m   a7 δοξάσαι m: δόξαι m(?) p t

"οὐδαμῶς," ἔφη, "ὦ Σώκρατες."

"αἰσθάνηι οὖν", ἦ δ᾽ ὅς, "ὅτι ταῦτά σοι συμβαίνει λέγειν, ὅταν φῆις μὲν εἶναι τὴν ψυχὴν πρὶν καὶ εἰς ἀνθρώπου εἶδός 5 τε καὶ σῶμα ἀφικέσθαι, εἶναι δὲ αὐτὴν συγκειμένην ἐκ τῶν οὐδέπω ὄντων; οὐ γὰρ δὴ ἁρμονία γέ σοι τοιοῦτόν ἐστιν ὧι ἀπεικάζεις, ἀλλὰ πρότερον καὶ ἡ λύρα καὶ αἱ χορδαὶ καὶ οἱ φθόγγοι ἔτι ἀνάρμοστοι ὄντες γίγνονται, τελευταῖον δὲ c πάντων συνίσταται ἡ ἁρμονία καὶ πρῶτον ἀπόλλυται. οὗτος οὖν σοι ὁ λόγος ἐκείνωι πῶς συνάισεται;"

"οὐδαμῶς," ἔφη ὁ Σιμμίας.

"καὶ μήν", ἦ δ᾽ ὅς, "πρέπει γε εἴπερ τωι ἄλλωι λόγωι συνωιδῶι 5 εἶναι καὶ τῶι περὶ ἁρμονίας."

"πρέπει γάρ," ἔφη ὁ Σιμμίας.

"οὗτος τοίνυν", ἔφη, "σοὶ οὐ συνωιδός· ἀλλ᾽ ὅρα πότερον αἱρῆι τῶν λόγων, τὴν μάθησιν ἀνάμνησιν εἶναι ἢ ψυχὴν ἁρμονίαν;" 10

"πολὺ μᾶλλον", ἔφη, "ἐκεῖνον, ὦ Σώκρατες. ὅδε μὲν γάρ d μοι γέγονεν ἄνευ ἀποδείξεως μετὰ εἰκότος τινὸς καὶ εὐπρε- πείας, ὅθεν καὶ τοῖς πολλοῖς δοκεῖ ἀνθρώποις· ἐγὼ δὲ τοῖς διὰ τῶν εἰκότων τὰς ἀποδείξεις ποιουμένοις λόγοις σύνοιδα οὖσιν ἀλαζόσιν, καὶ ἄν τις αὐτοὺς μὴ φυλάττηται εὖ μάλα, ἐξαπατῶσι, καὶ ἐν γεωμετρίαι καὶ ἐν τοῖς ἄλλοις ἅπασιν. 5 ὁ δὲ περὶ τῆς ἀναμνήσεως καὶ μαθήσεως λόγος δι᾽ ὑποθέσεως ἀξίας ἀποδέξασθαι εἴρηται. ἐρρήθη γάρ που οὕτως ἡμῶν εἶναι ἡ ψυχὴ καὶ πρὶν εἰς σῶμα ἀφικέσθαι, ὥσπερ αὐτή ἐστιν ἡ οὐσία ἔχουσα τὴν ἐπωνυμίαν τὴν τοῦ ὅ ἐστιν. ἐγὼ δὲ ταύτην, ὡς ἐμαυτὸν πείθω, ἱκανῶς τε καὶ ὀρθῶς ἀπο- e δέδεγμαι. ἀνάγκη οὖν μοι, ὡς ἔοικε, διὰ ταῦτα μήτε ἐμαυτοῦ μήτε ἄλλου ἀποδέχεσθαι λέγοντος ὡς ψυχή ἐστιν ἁρμονία."

"τί δέ," ἦ δ᾽ ὅς, "ὦ Σιμμία, τῆιδε; δοκεῖ σοι ἁρμονίαι ἢ ἄλληι τινὶ συνθέσει προσήκειν ἄλλως πως ἔχειν ἢ ὡς ἂν ἐκεῖνα 93 ἔχηι ἐξ ὧν ἂν συγκέηται;"

"οὐδαμῶς."

b8 ὧι m t: ὅ m   d8 αὐτὴ (m) e: αὐτῆς c t

"οὐδὲ μὴν ποιεῖν τι, ὡς ἐγῶιμαι, οὐδέ τι πάσχειν ἄλλο
5 παρ' ἃ ἂν ἐκεῖνα ἢ ποιῆι ἢ πάσχηι;" συνέφη.
"οὐκ ἄρα ἡγεῖσθαί γε προσήκει ἁρμονίαν τούτων ἐξ ὧν ἂν
συντεθῆι, ἀλλ' ἕπεσθαι." συνεδόκει.
"πολλοῦ ἄρα δεῖ ἐναντία γε ἁρμονία κινηθῆναι ἢ
φθέγξασθαι ἤ τι ἄλλο ἐναντιωθῆναι τοῖς αὑτῆς μέρεσιν."
10 "πολλοῦ μέντοι," ἔφη.
"τί δέ; οὐχ οὕτως ἁρμονία πέφυκεν εἶναι ἑκάστη ἁρμονία
ὡς ἂν ἁρμοσθῆι;"
"οὐ μανθάνω," ἔφη.
"ἢ οὐχί," ἦ δ' ὅς, "ἂν μὲν μᾶλλον ἁρμοσθῆι καὶ ἐπὶ πλέον,
b εἴπερ ἐνδέχεται τοῦτο γίγνεσθαι, μᾶλλόν τε ἂν ἁρμονία εἴη καὶ
πλείων, εἰ δ' ἧττόν τε καὶ ἐπ' ἔλαττον, ἥττων τε καὶ ἐλάττων;"
"πάνυ γε."
"ἢ οὖν ἔστι τοῦτο περὶ ψυχήν, ὥστε καὶ κατὰ τὸ σμικρό-
5 τατον μᾶλλον ἑτέραν ἑτέρας ψυχῆς ἐπὶ πλέον καὶ μᾶλλον
ἢ ἐπ' ἔλαττον καὶ ἧττον αὐτὸ τοῦτο εἶναι, ψυχήν;"
"οὐδ' ὁπωστιοῦν," ἔφη.
"φέρε δή," ἔφη, "πρὸς Διός· λέγεται ψυχὴ ἡ μὲν νοῦν τε
ἔχειν καὶ ἀρετὴν καὶ εἶναι ἀγαθή, ἡ δὲ ἄνοιάν τε καὶ μοχθηρίαν
c καὶ εἶναι κακή; καὶ ταῦτα ἀληθῶς λέγεται;"
"ἀληθῶς μέντοι."
"τῶν οὖν θεμένων ψυχὴν ἁρμονίαν εἶναι τί τις φήσει
ταῦτα ὄντα εἶναι ἐν ταῖς ψυχαῖς, τήν τε ἀρετὴν καὶ τὴν
5 κακίαν; πότερον ἁρμονίαν αὖ τινα ἄλλην καὶ ἀναρμοστίαν;
καὶ τὴν μὲν ἡρμόσθαι, τὴν ἀγαθήν, καὶ ἔχειν ἐν αὑτῆι
ἁρμονίαι οὔσηι ἄλλην ἁρμονίαν, τὴν δὲ ἀνάρμοστον αὐτήν τε
εἶναι καὶ οὐκ ἔχειν ἐν αὑτῆι ἄλλην;"
"οὐκ ἔχω ἔγωγ'," ἔφη ὁ Σιμμίας, "εἰπεῖν· δῆλον δ' ὅτι
10 τοιαῦτ' ἄττ' ἂν λέγοι ὁ ἐκεῖνο ὑποθέμενος."
d "ἀλλὰ προωμολόγηται", ἔφη, "μηδὲν μᾶλλον μηδ' ἧττον
ἑτέραν ἑτέρας ψυχὴν ψυχῆς εἶναι· τοῦτο δ' ἔστι τὸ ὁμο-

α8 κινηθῆναι ἂν *t*

λόγημα, μηδὲν μᾶλλον μηδ' ἐπὶ πλέον μηδ' ἧττον μηδ' ἐπ'
ἔλαττον ἑτέραν ἑτέρας ἁρμονίαν ἁρμονίας εἶναι. ἦ γάρ; "

"πάνυ γε." 5

"τὴν δέ γε μηδὲν μᾶλλον μηδὲ ἧττον ἁρμονίαν οὖσαν μηδὲ
μᾶλλον μηδὲ ἧττον ἡρμόσθαι· ἔστιν οὕτως; "

"ἔστιν."

"ἡ δὲ μήτε μᾶλλον μήτε ἧττον ἡρμοσμένη ἔστιν ὅτι πλέον
ἢ ἔλαττον ἁρμονίας μετέχει, ἢ τὸ ἴσον; " 10

"τὸ ἴσον."

"οὐκοῦν ψυχὴ ἐπειδὴ οὐδὲν μᾶλλον οὐδ' ἧττον ἄλλη
ἄλλης αὐτὸ τοῦτο, ψυχή, ἐστίν, οὐδὲ δὴ μᾶλλον οὐδὲ ἧττον e
ἥρμοσται; "

"οὕτω."

"τοῦτο δέ γε πεπονθυῖα οὐδὲν πλέον ἀναρμοστίας οὐδὲ
ἁρμονίας μετέχοι ἄν; " 5

"οὐ γὰρ οὖν."

"τοῦτο δ' αὖ πεπονθυῖα ἆρ' ἄν τι πλέον κακίας ἢ ἀρετῆς
μετέχοι ἑτέρα ἑτέρας, εἴπερ ἡ μὲν κακία ἀναρμοστία, ἡ δὲ
ἀρετὴ ἁρμονία εἴη; "

"οὐδὲν πλέον." 10

"μᾶλλον δέ γέ που, ὦ Σιμμία, κατὰ τὸν ὀρθὸν λόγον 94
κακίας οὐδεμία ψυχὴ μεθέξει, εἴπερ ἁρμονία ἐστίν· ἁρμονία
γὰρ δήπου παντελῶς αὐτὸ τοῦτο οὖσα, ἁρμονία, ἀναρμοστίας
οὔποτ' ἂν μετάσχοι."

"οὐ μέντοι." 5

"οὐδέ γε δήπου ψυχή, οὖσα παντελῶς ψυχή, κακίας."

"πῶς γὰρ ἔκ γε τῶν προειρημένων; "

"ἐκ τούτου ἄρα τοῦ λόγου ἡμῖν πᾶσαι ψυχαὶ πάντων
ζῴων ὁμοίως ἀγαθαὶ ἔσονται, εἴπερ ὁμοίως ψυχαὶ πεφύκασιν
αὐτὸ τοῦτο, ψυχαί, εἶναι." 10

"ἔμοιγε δοκεῖ," ἔφη, "ὦ Σώκρατες."

"ἦ καὶ καλῶς δοκεῖ", ἦ δ' ὅς, "οὕτω λέγεσθαι, καὶ πάσχειν

d6–7 μήτε . . . μήτε e

b ἂν ταῦτα ὁ λόγος εἰ ὀρθὴ ἡ ὑπόθεσις ἦν, τὸ ψυχὴν ἁρμονίαν
εἶναι; "
"οὐδ' ὁπωστιοῦν," ἔφη.
"τί δέ; " ἦ δ' ὅς· "τῶν ἐν ἀνθρώπωι πάντων ἔσθ' ὅτι ἄλλο
5 λέγεις ἄρχειν ἢ ψυχὴν ἄλλως τε καὶ φρόνιμον; "
"οὐκ ἔγωγε."
"πότερον συγχωροῦσαν τοῖς κατὰ τὸ σῶμα πάθεσιν ἢ καὶ
ἐναντιουμένην; λέγω δὲ τὸ τοιόνδε, οἷον καύματος ἐνόντος
καὶ δίψους ἐπὶ τοὐναντίον ἕλκειν, τὸ μὴ πίνειν, καὶ πείνης
10 ἐνούσης ἐπὶ τὸ μὴ ἐσθίειν, καὶ ἄλλα μυρία που ὁρῶμεν
c ἐναντιουμένην τὴν ψυχὴν τοῖς κατὰ τὸ σῶμα· ἢ οὔ; "
"πάνυ μὲν οὖν."
"οὐκοῦν αὖ ὡμολογήσαμεν ἐν τοῖς πρόσθεν μήποτ' ἂν
αὐτήν, ἁρμονίαν γε οὖσαν, ἐναντία ἄιδειν οἷς ἐπιτείνοιτο
5 καὶ χαλῶιτο καὶ ψάλλοιτο καὶ ἄλλο ὁτιοῦν πάθος πάσχοι
ἐκεῖνα ἐξ ὧν τυγχάνοι οὖσα, ἀλλ' ἕπεσθαι ἐκείνοις καὶ οὔποτ'
ἂν ἡγεμονεύειν; "
"ὡμολογήσαμεν," ἔφη· "πῶς γὰρ οὔ; "
"τί οὖν; νῦν οὐ πᾶν τοὐναντίον ἡμῖν φαίνεται ἐργαζομένη,
10 ἡγεμονεύουσά τε ἐκείνων πάντων ἐξ ὧν φησί τις αὐτὴν
d εἶναι, καὶ ἐναντιουμένη ὀλίγου πάντα διὰ παντὸς τοῦ βίου
καὶ δεσπόζουσα πάντας τρόπους, τὰ μὲν χαλεπώτερον κολά-
ζουσα καὶ μετ' ἀλγηδόνων, τά τε κατὰ τὴν γυμναστικὴν καὶ
τὴν ἰατρικήν, τὰ δὲ πραιότερον, καὶ τὰ μὲν ἀπειλοῦσα, τὰ δὲ
5 νουθετοῦσα, ταῖς ἐπιθυμίαις καὶ ὀργαῖς καὶ φόβοις ὡς ἄλλη
οὖσα ἄλλωι πράγματι διαλεγομένη; οἷόν που καὶ Ὅμηρος ἐν
Ὀδυσσείαι πεποίηκεν, οὗ λέγει τὸν Ὀδυσσέα·

στῆθος δὲ πλήξας κραδίην ἠνίπαπε μύθωι·
e 'τέτλαθι δή, κραδίη· καὶ κύντερον ἄλλο ποτ' ἔτλης.'

ἆρ' οἴει αὐτὸν ταῦτα ποιῆσαι διανοούμενον ὡς ἁρμονίας
αὐτῆς οὔσης καὶ οἵας ἄγεσθαι ὑπὸ τῶν τοῦ σώματος παθημάτων, ἀλλ' οὐχ οἵας ἄγειν τε ταῦτα καὶ δεσπόζειν, καὶ
5 οὔσης αὐτῆς πολὺ θειοτέρου τινὸς πράγματος ἢ καθ'
ἁρμονίαν; "

"νὴ Δία, ὦ Σώκρατες, ἔμοιγε δοκεῖ."

"οὐκ ἄρα, ὦ ἄριστε, ἡμῖν οὐδαμῇ καλῶς ἔχει ψυχὴν ἁρμονίαν τινὰ φάναι εἶναι· οὔτε γὰρ ἄν, ὡς ἔοικεν, Ὁμήρωι 95 θείωι ποιητῇ ὁμολογοῖμεν οὔτε αὐτοὶ ἡμῖν αὐτοῖς."

"ἔχει οὕτως," ἔφη.

"εἶεν δή," ἦ δ' ὃς ὁ Σωκράτης, "τὰ μὲν Ἁρμονίας ἡμῖν τῆς Θηβαϊκῆς ἵλεά πως, ὡς ἔοικε, μετρίως γέγονεν· τί δὲ δὴ τὰ 5 Κάδμου," ἔφη, "ὦ Κέβης, πῶς ἱλασόμεθα καὶ τίνι λόγωι;"

"σύ μοι δοκεῖς", ἔφη ὁ Κέβης, "ἐξευρήσειν· τουτονὶ γοῦν τὸν λόγον τὸν πρὸς τὴν ἁρμονίαν θαυμαστῶς μοι εἶπες ὡς παρὰ δόξαν. Σιμμίου γὰρ λέγοντος ὅτι ἠπόρει, πάνυ ἐθαύμαζον εἴ τι ἕξει τις χρήσασθαι τῶι λόγωι αὐτοῦ· πάνυ οὖν b μοι ἀτόπως ἔδοξεν εὐθὺς τὴν πρώτην ἔφοδον οὐ δέξασθαι τοῦ σοῦ λόγου. ταὐτὰ δὴ οὐκ ἂν θαυμάσαιμι καὶ τὸν τοῦ Κάδμου λόγον εἰ πάθοι."

"ὠγαθέ," ἔφη ὁ Σωκράτης, "μὴ μέγα λέγε, μή τις ἡμῶν 5 βασκανία περιτρέψῃ τὸν λόγον τὸν μέλλοντα ἔσεσθαι. ἀλλὰ δὴ ταῦτα μὲν τῶι θεῶι μελήσει, ἡμεῖς δὲ Ὁμηρικῶς ἐγγὺς ἰόντες πειρώμεθα εἰ ἄρα τι λέγεις. ἔστι δὲ δὴ τὸ κεφάλαιον ὧν ζητεῖς· ἀξιοῖς ἐπιδειχθῆναι ἡμῶν τὴν ψυχὴν ἀνώλεθρόν τε καὶ ἀθάνατον οὖσαν, εἰ φιλόσοφος ἀνὴρ μέλ- c λων ἀποθανεῖσθαι, θαρρῶν τε καὶ ἡγούμενος ἀποθανὼν ἐκεῖ εὖ πράξειν διαφερόντως ἢ εἰ ἐν ἄλλωι βίωι βιοὺς ἐτελεύτα, μὴ ἀνόητόν τε καὶ ἠλίθιον θάρρος θαρρήσει. τὸ δὲ ἀποφαίνειν ὅτι ἰσχυρόν τί ἐστιν ἡ ψυχὴ καὶ θεοειδὲς καὶ ἦν ἔτι 5 πρότερον, πρὶν ἡμᾶς ἀνθρώπους γενέσθαι, οὐδὲν κωλύειν φῂς πάντα ταῦτα μηνύειν ἀθανασίαν μὲν μή, ὅτι δὲ πολυχρόνιόν τέ ἐστιν ψυχὴ καὶ ἦν που πρότερον ἀμήχανον ὅσον χρόνον καὶ ᾔδει τε καὶ ἔπραττεν πολλὰ ἄττα· ἀλλὰ γὰρ οὐδέν τι μᾶλλον ἦν ἀθάνατον, ἀλλὰ καὶ αὐτὸ τὸ εἰς ἀν- d θρώπου σῶμα ἐλθεῖν ἀρχὴ ἦν αὐτῇ ὀλέθρου, ὥσπερ νόσος· καὶ ταλαιπωρουμένη τε δὴ τοῦτον τὸν βίον ζώιη καὶ τελευτῶσά γε ἐν τῶι καλουμένωι θανάτωι ἀπολλύοιτο. διαφέρειν δὲ δὴ

a9 ὅτι *m*: ὅτε *m*

5 φῆις οὐδὲν εἴτε ἅπαξ εἰς σῶμα ἔρχεται εἴτε πολλάκις, πρός
γε τὸ ἕκαστον ἡμῶν φοβεῖσθαι· προσήκει γὰρ φοβεῖσθαι,
εἰ μὴ ἀνόητος εἴη, τῶι μὴ εἰδότι μηδὲ ἔχοντι λόγον διδόναι
e ὡς ἀθάνατόν ἐστι. τοιαῦτ' ἄττα ἐστίν, οἶμαι, ὦ Κέβης, ἃ
λέγεις· καὶ ἐξεπίτηδες πολλάκις ἀναλαμβάνω, ἵνα μή τι
διαφύγηι ἡμᾶς, εἴ τέ τι βούλει, προσθῆις ἢ ἀφέληις.''
κὰι ὁ Κέβης, ''ἀλλ' οὐδὲν ἔγωγε ἐν τῶι παρόντι'', ἔφη,
5 ''οὔτε ἀφελεῖν οὔτε προσθεῖναι δέομαι· ἔστι δὲ ταῦτα ἃ
λέγω.''
ὁ οὖν Σωκράτης συχνὸν χρόνον ἐπισχὼν καὶ πρὸς ἑαυτόν
τι σκεψάμενος, ''οὐ φαῦλον πρᾶγμα,'' ἔφη, ''ὦ Κέβης, ζητεῖς·
ὅλως γὰρ δεῖ περὶ γενέσεως καὶ φθορᾶς τὴν αἰτίαν δια-
96 πραγματεύσασθαι. ἐγὼ οὖν σοι δίειμι περὶ αὐτῶν, ἐὰν
βούληι, τά γε ἐμὰ πάθη· ἔπειτα ἄν τί σοι χρήσιμον
φαίνηται ὧν ἂν λέγω, πρὸς τὴν πειθὼ περὶ ὧν δὴ λέγεις
χρήσηι.''
5 ''ἀλλὰ μήν'', ἔφη ὁ Κέβης, ''βούλομαί γε.''
''ἄκουε τοίνυν ὡς ἐροῦντος. ἐγὼ γάρ,'' ἔφη, ''ὦ Κέβης,
νέος ὢν θαυμαστῶς ὡς ἐπεθύμησα ταύτης τῆς σοφίας ἣν
δὴ καλοῦσι περὶ φύσεως ἱστορίαν· ὑπερήφανος γάρ μοι
ἐδόκει εἶναι, εἰδέναι τὰς αἰτίας ἑκάστου, διὰ τί γίγνεται
10 ἕκαστον καὶ διὰ τί ἀπόλλυται καὶ διὰ τί ἔστι. καὶ πολλάκις
b ἐμαυτὸν ἄνω κάτω μετέβαλλον σκοπῶν πρῶτον τὰ τοιάδε·
ἆρ' ἐπειδὰν τὸ θερμὸν καὶ τὸ ψυχρὸν σηπεδόνα τινὰ
λάβηι, ὡς τινες ἔλεγον, τότε δὴ τὰ ζῶια συντρέφεται; καὶ
πότερον τὸ αἷμά ἐστιν ὧι φρονοῦμεν, ἢ ὁ ἀὴρ ἢ τὸ πῦρ; ἢ
5 τούτων μὲν οὐδέν, ὁ δ' ἐγκέφαλός ἐστιν ὁ τὰς αἰσθήσεις
παρέχων τοῦ ἀκούειν καὶ ὁρᾶν καὶ ὀσφραίνεσθαι, ἐκ τούτων
δὲ γίγνοιτο μνήμη καὶ δόξα, ἐκ δὲ μνήμης καὶ δόξης λα-
βούσης τὸ ἠρεμεῖν, κατὰ ταῦτα γίγνεσθαι ἐπιστήμην; καὶ
αὖ τούτων τὰς φθορὰς σκοπῶν, καὶ τὰ περὶ τὸν οὐρανόν
c τε καὶ τὴν γῆν πάθη, τελευτῶν οὕτως ἐμαυτῶι ἔδοξα πρὸς
ταύτην τὴν σκέψιν ἀφυὴς εἶναι ὡς οὐδὲν χρῆμα. τεκμή-

a3 δὴ λέγεις e: ἂν λέγηις m: λέγεις m t   b2 καὶ τὸ m t: καὶ m: τὸ m

ριον δέ σοι ἐρῶ ἱκανόν· ἐγὼ γὰρ ἃ καὶ πρότερον σαφῶς
ἠπιστάμην, ὥς γε ἐμαυτῶι καὶ τοῖς ἄλλοις ἐδόκουν, τότε
ὑπὸ ταύτης τῆς σκέψεως οὕτω σφόδρα ἐτυφλώθην, ὥστε 5
ἀπέμαθον καὶ ταῦτα ἃ πρὸ τοῦ ὤιμην εἰδέναι, περὶ ἄλλων τε
πολλῶν καὶ διὰ τί ἄνθρωπος αὐξάνεται. τοῦτο γὰρ ὤιμην
πρὸ τοῦ παντὶ δῆλον εἶναι, ὅτι διὰ τὸ ἐσθίειν καὶ πίνειν·
ἐπειδὰν γὰρ ἐκ τῶν σιτίων ταῖς μὲν σαρξὶ σάρκες προσ- d
γένωνται, τοῖς δὲ ὀστοῖς ὀστᾶ, καὶ οὕτω κατὰ τὸν αὐτὸν
λόγον καὶ τοῖς ἄλλοις τὰ αὐτῶν οἰκεῖα ἑκάστοις προσγένηται,
τότε δὴ τὸν ὀλίγον ὄγκον ὄντα ὕστερον πολὺν γεγονέναι,
καὶ οὕτω γίγνεσθαι τὸν σμικρὸν ἄνθρωπον μέγαν. οὕτως 5
τότε ὤιμην· οὐ δοκῶ σοι μετρίως;"
"ἔμοιγε," ἔφη ὁ Κέβης.
"σκέψαι δὴ καὶ τάδε ἔτι. ὤιμην γὰρ ἱκανῶς μοι δοκεῖν,
ὁπότε τις φαίνοιτο ἄνθρωπος παραστὰς μέγας σμικρῶι μείζων
εἶναι αὐτῆι τῆι κεφαλῆι, καὶ ἵππος ἵππου· καὶ ἔτι γε τούτων e
ἐναργέστερα, τὰ δέκα μοι ἐδόκει τῶν ὀκτὼ πλέονα εἶναι διὰ
τὸ δύο αὐτοῖς προσεῖναι, καὶ τὸ δίπηχυ τοῦ πηχυαίου μεῖζον
εἶναι διὰ τὸ ἡμίσει αὐτοῦ ὑπερέχειν."
"νῦν δὲ δή", ἔφη ὁ Κέβης, "τί σοι δοκεῖ περὶ αὐτῶν;" 5
"πόρρω που", ἔφη, "νὴ Δία ἐμὲ εἶναι τοῦ οἴεσθαι περὶ
τούτων του τὴν αἰτίαν εἰδέναι, ὅς γε οὐκ ἀποδέχομαι ἐμαυτοῦ
οὐδὲ ὡς ἐπειδὰν ἑνί τις προσθῆι ἕν, ἢ τὸ ἓν ὧι προσετέθη
δύο γέγονεν, ἢ τὸ προστεθὲν καὶ ὧι προσετέθη
διὰ τὴν πρόσθεσιν τοῦ ἑτέρου τῶι ἑτέρωι δύο ἐγένετο· 97
θαυμάζω γὰρ εἰ ὅτε μὲν ἑκάτερον αὐτῶν χωρὶς ἀλλήλων
ἦν, ἓν ἄρα ἑκάτερον ἦν καὶ οὐκ ἤστην τότε δύο, ἐπεὶ δ'
ἐπλησίασαν ἀλλήλοις, αὕτη ἄρα αἰτία αὐτοῖς ἐγένετο τοῦ δύο
γενέσθαι, ἡ σύνοδος τοῦ πλησίον ἀλλήλων τεθῆναι. οὐδέ 5
γε ὡς ἐάν τις ἓν διασχίσηι, δύναμαι ἔτι πείθεσθαι ὡς αὕτη
αὖ αἰτία γέγονεν, ἡ σχίσις, τοῦ δύο γεγονέναι· ἐναντία γὰρ
γίγνεται ἢ τότε αἰτία τοῦ δύο γίγνεσθαι· τότε μὲν γὰρ ὅτι b

e7 του (m): τοῦ m: om. m   e9 ἤ c p: ⟨ἢ τὸ προστεθὲν⟩ ἢ e et fort. t   b1 ἢ
e: ἡ c t

συνήγετο πλησίον ἀλλήλων καὶ προσετίθετο ἕτερον ἑτέρωι,
νῦν δ᾽ ὅτι ἀπάγεται καὶ χωρίζεται ἕτερον ἀφ᾽ ἑτέρου. οὐδέ
γε δι᾽ ὅτι ἓν γίγνεται ὡς ἐπίσταμαι, ἔτι πείθω ἐμαυτόν,
5 οὐδ᾽ ἄλλο οὐδὲν ἑνὶ λόγωι δι᾽ ὅτι γίγνεται ἢ ἀπόλλυται ἢ
ἔστι, κατὰ τοῦτον τὸν τρόπον τῆς μεθόδου, ἀλλά τιν᾽ ἄλλον
τρόπον αὐτὸς εἰκῆι φύρω, τοῦτον δὲ οὐδαμῆι προσίεμαι.

"ἀλλ᾽ ἀκούσας μέν ποτε ἐκ βιβλίου τινός, ὡς ἔφη, Ἀναξ-
c αγόρου ἀναγιγνώσκοντος, καὶ λέγοντος ὡς ἄρα νοῦς ἐστιν ὁ
διακοσμῶν τε καὶ πάντων αἴτιος, ταύτηι δὴ τῆι αἰτίαι ἥσθην τε
καὶ ἔδοξέ μοι τρόπον τινὰ εὖ ἔχειν τὸ τὸν νοῦν εἶναι πάντων
αἴτιον, καὶ ἡγησάμην, εἰ τοῦθ᾽ οὕτως ἔχει, τόν γε νοῦν
5 κοσμοῦντα πάντα κοσμεῖν καὶ ἕκαστον τιθέναι ταύτηι ὅπηι
ἂν βέλτιστα ἔχηι· εἰ οὖν τις βούλοιτο τὴν αἰτίαν εὑρεῖν
περὶ ἑκάστου ὅπηι γίγνεται ἢ ἀπόλλυται ἢ ἔστι, τοῦτο δεῖν
περὶ αὐτοῦ εὑρεῖν, ὅπηι βέλτιστον αὐτῶι ἐστιν ἢ εἶναι ἢ
d ἄλλο ὁτιοῦν πάσχειν ἢ ποιεῖν· ἐκ δὲ δὴ τοῦ λόγου τούτου
οὐδὲν ἄλλο σκοπεῖν προσήκειν ἀνθρώπωι καὶ περὶ αὐτοῦ ἐκείνου καὶ περὶ τῶν ἄλλων ἀλλ᾽ ἢ τὸ ἄριστον καὶ τὸ βέλτιστον.
ἀναγκαῖον δὲ εἶναι τὸν αὐτὸν τοῦτον καὶ τὸ χεῖρον εἰδέναι·
5 τὴν αὐτὴν γὰρ εἶναι ἐπιστήμην περὶ αὐτῶν. ταῦτα δὴ
λογιζόμενος ἅσμενος ηὑρηκέναι ὤιμην διδάσκαλον τῆς αἰτίας
περὶ τῶν ὄντων κατὰ νοῦν ἐμαυτῶι, τὸν Ἀναξαγόραν, καί
μοι φράσειν πρῶτον μὲν πότερον ἡ γῆ πλατεῖά ἐστιν ἢ
e στρογγύλη, ἐπειδὴ δὲ φράσειεν, ἐπεκδιηγήσεσθαι τὴν αἰτίαν
καὶ τὴν ἀνάγκην, λέγοντα τὸ ἄμεινον καὶ ὅτι αὐτὴν ἄμεινον
ἦν τοιαύτην εἶναι· καὶ εἰ ἐν μέσωι φαίη εἶναι αὐτήν, ἐπεκδιηγήσεσθαι ὡς ἄμεινον ἦν αὐτὴν ἐν μέσωι εἶναι· καὶ εἴ μοι
98 ταῦτα ἀποφαίνοι, παρεσκευάσμην ὡς οὐκέτι ποθεσόμενος
αἰτίας ἄλλο εἶδος. καὶ δὴ καὶ περὶ ἡλίου οὕτω παρεσκευάσμην ὡσαύτως πευσόμενος, καὶ σελήνης καὶ τῶν ἄλλων
ἄστρων, τάχους τε πέρι πρὸς ἄλληλα καὶ τροπῶν καὶ τῶν
5 ἄλλων παθημάτων, πῆι ποτε ταῦτ᾽ ἄμεινόν ἐστιν ἕκαστον
καὶ ποιεῖν καὶ πάσχειν ἃ πάσχει. οὐ γὰρ ἄν ποτε αὐτὸν

d2 ἐκείνου om. m t

ὤιμην, φάσκοντά γε ὑπὸ νοῦ αὐτὰ κεκοσμῆσθαι, ἄλλην τινὰ
αὐτοῖς αἰτίαν ἐπενεγκεῖν ἢ ὅτι βέλτιστον αὐτὰ οὕτως ἔχειν
ἐστὶν ὥσπερ ἔχει· ἑκάστωι οὖν αὐτῶν ἀποδιδόντα τὴν αἰτίαν b
καὶ κοινῆι πᾶσι, τὸ ἑκάστωι βέλτιστον ὤιμην καὶ τὸ κοινὸν
πᾶσιν ἐπεκδιηγήσεσθαι ἀγαθόν· καὶ οὐκ ἂν ἀπεδόμην πολλοῦ
τὰς ἐλπίδας, ἀλλὰ πάνυ σπουδῆι λαβὼν τὰς βίβλους ὡς
τάχιστα οἷός τ' ἦ ἀνεγίγνωσκον, ἵν' ὡς τάχιστα εἰδείην τὸ 5
βέλτιστον καὶ τὸ χεῖρον.
"ἀπὸ δὴ θαυμαστῆς, ὦ ἑταῖρε, ἐλπίδος ὠιχόμην φερόμενος,
ἐπειδὴ προϊὼν καὶ ἀναγιγνώσκων ὁρῶ ἄνδρα τῶι μὲν νῶι
οὐδὲν χρώμενον οὐδέ τινας αἰτίας ἐπαιτιώμενον εἰς τὸ
διακοσμεῖν τὰ πράγματα, ἀέρας δὲ καὶ αἰθέρας καὶ ὕδατα c
αἰτιώμενον καὶ ἄλλα πολλὰ καὶ ἄτοπα. καί μοι ἔδοξεν
ὁμοιότατον πεπονθέναι ὥσπερ ἂν εἴ τις λέγων ὅτι Σωκράτης
πάντα ὅσα πράττει νῶι πράττει, κἄπειτα ἐπιχειρήσας λέγειν
τὰς αἰτίας ἑκάστων ὧν πράττω, λέγοι πρῶτον μὲν ὅτι διὰ 5
ταῦτα νῦν ἐνθάδε κάθημαι, ὅτι σύγκειταί μου τὸ σῶμα ἐξ
ὀστῶν καὶ νεύρων, καὶ τὰ μὲν ὀστᾶ ἐστιν στερεὰ καὶ
διαφυὰς ἔχει χωρὶς ἀπ' ἀλλήλων, τὰ δὲ νεῦρα οἷα ἐπι-
τείνεσθαι καὶ ἀνίεσθαι, περιαμπέχοντα τὰ ὀστᾶ μετὰ τῶν d
σαρκῶν καὶ δέρματος ὃ συνέχει αὐτά· αἰωρουμένων οὖν τῶν
ὀστῶν ἐν ταῖς αὐτῶν συμβολαῖς χαλῶντα καὶ συντείνοντα
τὰ νεῦρα κάμπτεσθαί που ποιεῖ οἷόν τ' εἶναι ἐμὲ νῦν τὰ
μέλη, καὶ διὰ ταύτην τὴν αἰτίαν συγκαμφθεὶς ἐνθάδε κά- 5
θημαι· καὶ αὖ περὶ τοῦ διαλέγεσθαι ὑμῖν ἑτέρας τοιαύτας
αἰτίας λέγοι, φωνάς τε καὶ ἀέρας καὶ ἀκοὰς καὶ ἄλλα μυρία
τοιαῦτα αἰτιώμενος, ἀμελήσας τὰς ὡς ἀληθῶς αἰτίας λέγειν, e
ὅτι, ἐπειδὴ Ἀθηναίοις ἔδοξε βέλτιον εἶναι ἐμοῦ καταψη-
φίσασθαι, διὰ ταῦτα δὴ καὶ ἐμοὶ βέλτιον αὖ δέδοκται ἐνθάδε
καθῆσθαι, καὶ δικαιότερον παραμένοντα ὑπέχειν τὴν δίκην
ἣν ἂν κελεύσωσιν· ἐπεὶ νὴ τὸν κύνα, ὡς ἐγῶμαι, πάλαι ἂν 5
ταῦτα τὰ νεῦρα καὶ τὰ ὀστᾶ ἢ περὶ Μέγαρα ἢ Βοιωτοὺς ἦν, 99
ὑπὸ δόξης φερόμενα τοῦ βελτίστου, εἰ μὴ δικαιότερον ὤιμην

b7 ὦ ἑταῖρε ἐλπίδος *m t*: ἐλπ. ὦ ἑτ. *m*

καὶ κάλλιον εἶναι πρὸ τοῦ φεύγειν τε καὶ ἀποδιδράσκειν
ὑπέχειν τῆι πόλει δίκην ἥντιν᾽ ἂν τάττηι. ἀλλ᾽ αἴτια μὲν
5 τὰ τοιαῦτα καλεῖν λίαν ἄτοπον· εἰ δέ τις λέγοι ὅτι ἄνευ
τοῦ τὰ τοιαῦτα ἔχειν καὶ ὀστᾶ καὶ νεῦρα καὶ ὅσα ἄλλα ἔχω,
οὐκ ἂν οἷός τ᾽ ἦ ποιεῖν τὰ δόξαντά μοι, ἀληθῆ ἂν λέγοι· ὡς
μέντοι διὰ ταῦτα ποιῶ ἃ ποιῶ, καὶ ταῦτα νῶι πράττω, ἀλλ᾽ οὐ
b τῆι τοῦ βελτίστου αἱρέσει, πολλὴ ἂν καὶ μακρὰ ῥαιθυμία εἴη
τοῦ λόγου. τὸ γὰρ μὴ διελέσθαι οἷόν τ᾽ εἶναι ὅτι ἄλλο μέν
τί ἐστι τὸ αἴτιον τῶι ὄντι, ἄλλο δὲ ἐκεῖνο ἄνευ οὗ τὸ αἴτιον
οὐκ ἄν ποτ᾽ εἴη αἴτιον· ὃ δή μοι φαίνονται ψηλαφῶντες οἱ
5 πολλοὶ ὥσπερ ἐν σκότει, ἀλλοτρίωι ὀνόματι προσχρώμενοι,
ὡς αἴτιον αὐτὸ προσαγορεύειν. διὸ δὴ καὶ ὁ μέν τις δίνην
περιτιθεὶς τῆι γῆι ὑπὸ τοῦ οὐρανοῦ μένειν δὴ ποιεῖ τὴν γῆν,
ὁ δὲ ὥσπερ καρδόπωι πλατείαι βάθρον τὸν ἀέρα ὑπερείδει·
c τὴν δὲ τοῦ ὡς οἷόν τε βέλτιστα αὐτὰ τεθῆναι δύναμιν οὕτω
νῦν κεῖσθαι, ταύτην οὔτε ζητοῦσιν οὔτε τινὰ οἴονται δαι-
μονίαν ἰσχὺν ἔχειν, ἀλλὰ ἡγοῦνται τούτου Ἄτλαντα ἄν
ποτε ἰσχυρότερον καὶ ἀθανατώτερον καὶ μᾶλλον ἅπαντα
5 συνέχοντα ἐξευρεῖν, καὶ ὡς ἀληθῶς τὸ ἀγαθὸν καὶ δέον
συνδεῖν καὶ συνέχειν οὐδὲν οἴονται. ἐγὼ μὲν οὖν τῆς
τοιαύτης αἰτίας ὅπηι ποτὲ ἔχει μαθητὴς ὁτουοῦν ἥδιστ᾽ ἂν
γενοίμην· ἐπειδὴ δὲ ταύτης ἐστερήθην καὶ οὔτ᾽ αὐτὸς εὑρεῖν
οὔτε παρ᾽ ἄλλου μαθεῖν οἷός τε ἐγενόμην, τὸν δεύτερον
d πλοῦν ἐπὶ τὴν τῆς αἰτίας ζήτησιν ἧι πεπραγμάτευμαι βούλει
σοι", ἔφη, "ἐπίδειξιν ποιήσωμαι, ὦ Κέβης;"

"ὑπερφυῶς μὲν οὖν", ἔφη, "ὡς βούλομαι."

"ἔδοξε τοίνυν μοι", ἦ δ᾽ ὅς, "μετὰ ταῦτα, ἐπειδὴ ἀπειρήκη
5 τὰ ὄντα σκοπῶν, δεῖν εὐλαβηθῆναι μὴ πάθοιμι ὅπερ οἱ
τὸν ἥλιον ἐκλείποντα θεωροῦντες καὶ σκοπούμενοι·
διαφθείρονται γάρ που ἔνιοι τὰ ὄμματα, ἐὰν μὴ ἐν ὕδατι ἢ
e τινι τοιούτωι σκοπῶνται τὴν εἰκόνα αὐτοῦ. τοιοῦτόν τι καὶ
ἐγὼ διενοήθην, καὶ ἔδεισα μὴ παντάπασι τὴν ψυχὴν τυφλω-

θείην βλέπων πρὸς τὰ πράγματα τοῖς ὄμμασι καὶ ἑκάστηι
τῶν αἰσθήσεων ἐπιχειρῶν ἅπτεσθαι αὐτῶν. ἔδοξε δή μοι
χρῆναι εἰς τοὺς λόγους καταφυγόντα ἐν ἐκείνοις σκοπεῖν 5
τῶν ὄντων τὴν ἀλήθειαν. ἴσως μὲν οὖν ὧι εἰκάζω τρόπον
τινὰ οὐκ ἔοικεν· οὐ γὰρ πάνυ συγχωρῶ τὸν ἐν λόγοις 100
σκοπούμενον τὰ ὄντα ἐν εἰκόσι μᾶλλον σκοπεῖν ἢ τὸν ἐν
ἔργοις. ἀλλ᾽ οὖν δὴ ταύτηι γε ὥρμησα, καὶ ὑποθέμενος
ἑκάστοτε λόγον ὃν ἂν κρίνω ἐρρωμενέστατον εἶναι, ἃ μὲν
ἄν μοι δοκῆι τούτωι συμφωνεῖν τίθημι ὡς ἀληθῆ ὄντα, καὶ 5
περὶ αἰτίας καὶ περὶ τῶν ἄλλων ἁπάντων, ἃ δ᾽ ἂν
μή, ὡς οὐκ ἀληθῆ. βούλομαι δέ σοι σαφέστερον εἰπεῖν
ἃ λέγω· οἶμαι γάρ σε νῦν οὐ μανθάνειν.᾽᾽
    ᾽᾽οὐ μὰ τὸν Δία,᾽᾽ ἔφη ὁ Κέβης, ᾽᾽οὐ σφόδρα.᾽᾽
    ᾽᾽ἀλλ᾽᾽᾽, ἦ δ᾽ ὅς, ᾽᾽ὧδε λέγω, οὐδὲν καινόν, ἀλλ᾽ ἅπερ ἀεί b
τε ἄλλοτε καὶ ἐν τῶι παρεληλυθότι λόγωι οὐδὲν πέπαυμαι
λέγων. ἔρχομαι γὰρ δὴ ἐπιχειρῶν σοι ἐπιδείξασθαι τῆς
αἰτίας τὸ εἶδος ὃ πεπραγμάτευμαι, καὶ εἶμι πάλιν ἐπ᾽ ἐκεῖνα
τὰ πολυθρύλητα καὶ ἄρχομαι ἀπ᾽ ἐκείνων, ὑποθέμενος εἶναί 5
τι καλὸν αὐτὸ καθ᾽ αὑτὸ καὶ ἀγαθὸν καὶ μέγα καὶ τἆλλα
πάντα· ἃ εἴ μοι δίδως τε καὶ συγχωρεῖς εἶναι ταῦτα, ἐλπίζω
σοι ἐκ τούτων τὴν αἰτίαν ἐπιδείξειν καὶ ἀνευρήσειν ὡς
ἀθάνατον ἡ ψυχή.᾽᾽
    ᾽᾽ἀλλὰ μήν᾽᾽, ἔφη ὁ Κέβης, ᾽᾽ὡς διδόντος σοι οὐκ ἂν c
φθάνοις περαίνων.᾽᾽
    ᾽᾽σκόπει δή᾽᾽, ἔφη, ᾽᾽τὰ ἑξῆς ἐκείνοις ἐάν σοι συνδοκῆι ὥσπερ
ἐμοί. φαίνεται γάρ μοι, εἴ τί ἐστιν ἄλλο καλὸν πλὴν αὐτὸ
τὸ καλόν, οὐδὲ δι᾽ ἓν ἄλλο καλὸν εἶναι ἢ διότι μετέχει 5
ἐκείνου τοῦ καλοῦ· καὶ πάντα δὴ οὕτως λέγω. τῆι τοιᾶιδε
αἰτίαι συγχωρεῖς;᾽᾽
    ᾽᾽συγχωρῶ,᾽᾽ ἔφη.
    ᾽᾽οὐ τοίνυν᾽᾽, ἦ δ᾽ ὅς, ᾽᾽ἔτι μανθάνω οὐδὲ δύναμαι τὰς ἄλλας
αἰτίας τὰς σοφὰς ταύτας γιγνώσκειν· ἀλλ᾽ ἐάν τίς μοι λέγηι 10

---

e6 ὧι m: ὡς m   a1 λόγοις m: τοῖς λόγοις m   a3 ἔργοις m: τοῖς ἔργοις
m t   a6 ἁπάντων m ἁπάντων ὄντων m   b9 ἡ ψυχὴ m: ψυχὴ m p

d δι' ὅτι καλόν ἐστιν ὁτιοῦν, ἢ χρῶμα εὐανθὲς ἔχον ἢ σχῆμα
ἢ ἄλλο ὁτιοῦν τῶν τοιούτων, τὰ μὲν ἄλλα χαίρειν ἐῶ
(ταράττομαι γὰρ ἐν τοῖς ἄλλοις πᾶσι), τοῦτο δὲ ἁπλῶς καὶ
ἀτέχνως, καὶ ἴσως εὐήθως ἔχω παρ' ἐμαυτῶι, ὅτι οὐκ ἄλλο τι
5 ποιεῖ αὐτὸ καλὸν ἢ ἡ ἐκείνου τοῦ καλοῦ εἴτε παρουσία εἴτε
κοινωνία εἴτε ὅπηι δὴ καὶ ὅπως προσγενομένου· οὐ γὰρ ἔτι
τοῦτο διισχυρίζομαι, ἀλλ' ὅτι τῶι καλῶι πάντα τὰ καλὰ
γίγνεται καλά. τοῦτο γάρ μοι δοκεῖ ἀσφαλέστατον εἶναι
καὶ ἐμαυτῶι ἀποκρίνασθαι καὶ ἄλλωι, καὶ τούτου ἐχόμενος
e ἡγοῦμαι οὐκ ἄν ποτε πεσεῖν, ἀλλ' ἀσφαλὲς εἶναι καὶ ἐμοὶ
καὶ ὁτωιοῦν ἄλλωι ἀποκρίνασθαι ὅτι τῶι καλῶι τὰ καλὰ
καλά· ἢ οὐ καὶ σοὶ δοκεῖ; "
"δοκεῖ."
5 "καὶ μεγέθει ἄρα τὰ μεγάλα μεγάλα καὶ τὰ μείζω μείζω,
καὶ σμικρότητι τὰ ἐλάττω ἐλάττω; "
"ναί."
"οὐδὲ σὺ ἄρ' ἂν ἀποδέχοιο εἴ τίς τινα φαίη ἕτερον ἑτέρου
τῆι κεφαλῆι μείζω εἶναι, καὶ τὸν ἐλάττω τῶι αὐτῶι τούτωι
101 ἐλάττω, ἀλλὰ διαμαρτύροιο ἂν ὅτι σὺ μὲν οὐδὲν ἄλλο λέγεις
ἢ ὅτι τὸ μεῖζον πᾶν ἕτερον ἑτέρου οὐδενὶ ἄλλωι μεῖζόν ἐστιν
ἢ μεγέθει, καὶ διὰ τοῦτο μεῖζον, διὰ τὸ μέγεθος, τὸ δὲ
ἔλαττον οὐδενὶ ἄλλωι ἔλαττον ἢ σμικρότητι, καὶ διὰ τοῦτο
5 ἔλαττον, διὰ τὴν σμικρότητα, φοβούμενος οἶμαι μή τίς σοι
ἐναντίος λόγος ἀπαντήσηι, ἐὰν τῆι κεφαλῆι μείζονά τινα φῆις
εἶναι καὶ ἐλάττω, πρῶτον μὲν τῶι αὐτῶι τὸ μεῖζον μεῖζον εἶναι
καὶ τὸ ἔλαττον ἔλαττον, ἔπειτα τῆι κεφαλῆι σμικρᾶι οὔσηι τὸν
b μείζω μείζω εἶναι, καὶ τοῦτο δὴ τέρας εἶναι, τὸ σμικρῶι τινι
μέγαν τινὰ εἶναι· ἢ οὐκ ἂν φοβοῖο ταῦτα; "
καὶ ὁ Κέβης γελάσας, "ἔγωγε," ἔφη.
"οὐκοῦν", ἦ δ' ὅς, "τὰ δέκα τῶν ὀκτὼ δυοῖν πλείω εἶναι, καὶ
5 διὰ ταύτην τὴν αἰτίαν ὑπερβάλλειν, φοβοῖο ἂν λέγειν, ἀλλὰ

d6 προσγενομένου e: προσγινομένου m: προσγενομένη m: προσαγορευομένη
e   d8 γίγνεται καλά m: καλά m, p ut vid.: om. m   e3 καλά m: καλά
γίγνεται m: γίγνεται καλά m: om. m

μὴ πλήθει καὶ διὰ τὸ πλῆθος; καὶ τὸ δίπηχυ τοῦ πηχυαίου ἡμίσει μεῖζον εἶναι ἀλλ' οὐ μεγέθει; ὁ αὐτὸς γάρ που φόβος."

"πάνυ γ'," ἔφη.

"τί δέ; ἑνὶ ἑνὸς προστεθέντος τὴν πρόσθεσιν αἰτίαν εἶναι τοῦ δύο γενέσθαι ἢ διασχισθέντος τὴν σχίσιν οὐκ εὐλαβοῖο c ἂν λέγειν; καὶ μέγα ἂν βοῴης ὅτι οὐκ οἶσθα ἄλλως πως ἕκαστον γιγνόμενον ἢ μετασχὸν τῆς ἰδίας οὐσίας ἑκάστου οὗ ἂν μετάσχῃ, καὶ ἐν τούτοις οὐκ ἔχεις ἄλλην τινὰ αἰτίαν τοῦ δύο γενέσθαι ἀλλ' ἢ τὴν τῆς δυάδος μετάσχεσιν, καὶ 5 δεῖν τούτου μετασχεῖν τὰ μέλλοντα δύο ἔσεσθαι, καὶ μονάδος ὃ ἂν μέλλῃ ἓν ἔσεσθαι, τὰς δὲ σχίσεις ταύτας καὶ προσθέσεις καὶ τὰς ἄλλας τὰς τοιαύτας κομψείας ἐῴης ἂν χαίρειν, παρεὶς ἀποκρίνασθαι τοῖς σεαυτοῦ σοφωτέροις· σὺ δὲ δεδιὼς ἄν, τὸ λεγόμενον, τὴν σαυτοῦ σκιὰν καὶ τὴν ἀπειρίαν, ἐχόμενος d ἐκείνου τοῦ ἀσφαλοῦς τῆς ὑποθέσεως, οὕτως ἀποκρίναιο ἄν. εἰ δέ τις αὐτῆς τῆς ὑποθέσεως ἔχοιτο, χαίρειν ἐῴης ἂν καὶ οὐκ ἀποκρίναιο ἕως ἂν τὰ ἀπ' ἐκείνης ὁρμηθέντα σκέψαιο εἴ σοι ἀλλήλοις συμφωνεῖ ἢ διαφωνεῖ· ἐπειδὴ δὲ ἐκείνης 5 αὐτῆς δέοι σε διδόναι λόγον, ὡσαύτως ἂν διδοίης, ἄλλην αὖ ὑπόθεσιν ὑποθέμενος ἥτις τῶν ἄνωθεν βελτίστη φαίνοιτο, ἕως ἐπί τι ἱκανὸν ἔλθοις, ἅμα δὲ οὐκ ἂν φύροιο ὥσπερ οἱ e ἀντιλογικοὶ περί τε τῆς ἀρχῆς διαλεγόμενος καὶ τῶν ἐξ ἐκείνης ὡρμημένων, εἴπερ βούλοιό τι τῶν ὄντων εὑρεῖν; ἐκείνοις μὲν γὰρ ἴσως οὐδὲ εἷς περὶ τούτου λόγος οὐδὲ φροντίς· ἱκανοὶ γὰρ ὑπὸ σοφίας ὁμοῦ πάντα κυκῶντες ὅμως 5 δύνασθαι αὐτοὶ αὑτοῖς ἀρέσκειν· σὺ δ', εἴπερ εἶ τῶν φιλοσόφων, οἶμαι ἂν ὡς ἐγὼ λέγω ποιοῖς." 102

"ἀληθέστατα", ἔφη, "λέγεις," ὅ τε Σιμμίας ἅμα καὶ ὁ Κέβης.

ΕΧ. νὴ Δία, ὦ Φαίδων, εἰκότως γε· θαυμαστῶς γάρ μοι δοκεῖ ὡς ἐναργῶς τῶι καὶ σμικρὸν νοῦν ἔχοντι εἰπεῖν ἐκεῖνος ταῦτα. 5

ΦΑΙΔ. πάνυ μὲν οὖν, ὦ Ἐχέκρατες, καὶ πᾶσι τοῖς παροῦσιν ἔδοξεν.

d3 ἔχοιτο c : ἔφοιτο e

ΕΧ. καὶ γὰρ ἡμῖν τοῖς ἀποῦσι, νῦν δὲ ἀκούουσιν. ἀλλὰ τίνα δὴ ἦν τὰ μετὰ ταῦτα λεχθέντα;

10 ΦΑΙΔ. ὡς μὲν ἐγὼ οἶμαι, ἐπεὶ αὐτῶι ταῦτα συνεχωρήθη,
b καὶ ὡμολογεῖτο εἶναί τι ἕκαστον τῶν εἰδῶν καὶ τούτων τἄλλα μεταλαμβάνοντα αὐτῶν τούτων τὴν ἐπωνυμίαν ἴσχειν, τὸ δὴ μετὰ ταῦτα ἠρώτα· "εἰ δή", ἦ δ' ὅς, "ταῦτα οὕτως λέγεις, ἆρ' οὐχ, ὅταν Σιμμίαν Σωκράτους φῆις μείζω εἶναι, Φαίδωνος
5 δὲ ἐλάττω, λέγεις τότ' εἶναι ἐν τῶι Σιμμίαι ἀμφότερα, καὶ μέγεθος καὶ σμικρότητα;"

"ἔγωγε."

"ἀλλὰ γάρ", ἦ δ' ὅς, "ὁμολογεῖς τὸ τὸν Σιμμίαν ὑπερέχειν Σωκράτους οὐχ ὡς τοῖς ῥήμασι λέγεται οὕτω καὶ τὸ ἀληθὲς
c ἔχειν; οὐ γάρ που πεφυκέναι Σιμμίαν ὑπερέχειν τούτωι, τῶι Σιμμίαν εἶναι, ἀλλὰ τῶι μεγέθει ὃ τυγχάνει ἔχων· οὐδ' αὖ Σωκράτους ὑπερέχειν ὅτι Σωκράτης ὁ Σωκράτης ἐστίν, ἀλλ' ὅτι σμικρότητα ἔχει ὁ Σωκράτης πρὸς τὸ ἐκείνου μέγεθος;"

5 "ἀληθῆ."

"οὐδέ γε αὖ ὑπὸ Φαίδωνος ὑπερέχεσθαι τῶι ὅτι Φαίδων ὁ Φαίδων ἐστίν, ἀλλ' ὅτι μέγεθος ἔχει ὁ Φαίδων πρὸς τὴν Σιμμίου σμικρότητα;"

"ἔστι ταῦτα."

10 "οὕτως ἄρα ὁ Σιμμίας ἐπωνυμίαν ἔχει σμικρός τε καὶ μέγας εἶναι, ἐν μέσωι ὢν ἀμφοτέρων, τοῦ μὲν τῶι μεγέθει
d ὑπερέχειν τὴν σμικρότητα ὑπέχων, τῶι δὲ τὸ μέγεθος τῆς σμικρότητος παρέχων ὑπερέχον." καὶ ἅμα μειδιάσας, "ἔοικα", ἔφη, "καὶ συγγραφικῶς ἐρεῖν, ἀλλ' οὖν ἔχει γέ που ὡς λέγω." συνέφη.

5 "λέγω δὴ τοῦδ' ἕνεκα, βουλόμενος δόξαι σοὶ ὅπερ ἐμοί. ἐμοὶ γὰρ φαίνεται οὐ μόνον αὐτὸ τὸ μέγεθος οὐδέποτ' ἐθέλειν ἅμα μέγα καὶ σμικρὸν εἶναι, ἀλλὰ καὶ τὸ ἐν ἡμῖν μέγεθος οὐδέποτε προσδέχεσθαι τὸ σμικρὸν οὐδ' ἐθέλειν ὑπερέχεσθαι, ἀλλὰ δυοῖν τὸ ἕτερον, ἢ φεύγειν καὶ ὑπεκχωρεῖν ὅταν αὐτῶι
e προσίηι τὸ ἐναντίον, τὸ σμικρόν, ἢ προσελθόντος ἐκείνου ἀπολωλέναι· ὑπομένον δὲ καὶ δεξάμενον τὴν σμικρότητα οὐκ ἐθέλειν εἶναι ἕτερον ἢ ὅπερ ἦν. ὥσπερ ἐγὼ δεξάμενος

καὶ ὑπομείνας τὴν σμικρότητα, καὶ ἔτι ὢν ὅσπερ εἰμί, οὗτος
ὁ αὐτὸς σμικρός εἰμι· ἐκεῖνο δὲ οὐ τετόλμηκεν μέγα ὂν 5
σμικρὸν εἶναι· ὡς δ' αὕτως καὶ τὸ σμικρὸν τὸ ἐν ἡμῖν οὐκ
ἐθέλει ποτὲ μέγα γίγνεσθαι οὐδὲ εἶναι, οὐδ' ἄλλο οὐδὲν τῶν
ἐναντίων, ἔτι ὂν ὅπερ ἦν, ἅμα τοὐναντίον γίγνεσθαί τε
καὶ εἶναι, ἀλλ' ἤτοι ἀπέρχεται ἢ ἀπόλλυται ἐν τούτωι τῶι 103
παθήματι."

"παντάπασιν", ἔφη ὁ Κέβης, "οὕτω φαίνεταί μοι."

καί τις εἶπε τῶν παρόντων ἀκούσας (ὅστις δ' ἦν, οὐ
σαφῶς μέμνημαι), "πρὸς θεῶν, οὐκ ἐν τοῖς πρόσθεν ἡμῖν 5
λόγοις αὐτὸ τὸ ἐναντίον τῶν νυνὶ λεγομένων ὡμολογεῖτο, ἐκ
τοῦ ἐλάττονος τὸ μεῖζον γίγνεσθαι καὶ ἐκ τοῦ μείζονος τὸ
ἔλαττον, καὶ ἀτεχνῶς αὕτη εἶναι ἡ γένεσις τοῖς ἐναντίοις,
ἐκ τῶν ἐναντίων; νῦν δέ μοι δοκεῖ λέγεσθαι ὅτι τοῦτο οὐκ
ἂν ποτε γένοιτο."   10

καὶ ὁ Σωκράτης παραβαλὼν τὴν κεφαλὴν καὶ ἀκούσας,
"ἀνδρικῶς", ἔφη, "ἀπεμνημόνευκας, οὐ μέντοι ἐννοεῖς τὸ b
διαφέρον τοῦ τε νῦν λεγομένου καὶ τοῦ τότε. τότε μὲν
γὰρ ἐλέγετο ἐκ τοῦ ἐναντίου πράγματος τὸ ἐναντίον πρᾶγμα
γίγνεσθαι, νῦν δέ, ὅτι αὐτὸ τὸ ἐναντίον ἑαυτῶι ἐναντίον οὐκ
ἂν ποτε γένοιτο, οὔτε τὸ ἐν ἡμῖν οὔτε τὸ ἐν τῆι φύσει. 5
τότε μὲν γάρ, ὦ φίλε, περὶ τῶν ἐχόντων τὰ ἐναντία ἐλέγομεν, ἐπονομάζοντες αὐτὰ τῆι ἐκείνων ἐπωνυμίαι, νῦν δὲ περὶ
ἐκείνων αὐτῶν ὧν ἐνόντων ἔχει τὴν ἐπωνυμίαν τὰ ὀνομαζό-
μενα· αὐτὰ δ' ἐκεῖνα οὐκ ἂν ποτέ φαμεν ἐθελῆσαι γένεσιν c
ἀλλήλων δέξασθαι." καὶ ἅμα βλέψας πρὸς τὸν Κέβητα
εἶπεν, "ἆρα μή που, ὦ Κέβης," ἔφη, "καὶ σέ τι τούτων
ἐτάραξεν ὧν ὅδε εἶπεν;"

"οὐδ' αὖ", ἔφη ὁ Κέβης, "οὕτως ἔχω· καίτοι οὔτι λέγω 5
ὡς οὐ πολλά με ταράττει."

"συνωμολογήκαμεν ἄρα", ἦ δ' ὅς, "ἁπλῶς τοῦτο, μηδέποτε
ἐναντίον ἑαυτῶι τὸ ἐναντίον ἔσεσθαι."

"παντάπασιν," ἔφη.

a5 ἡμῖν m: ὑμῖν m   c5 καίτοι οὔτι m p: καὶ τοιοῦτό τι m

10   "ἔτι δή μοι καὶ τόδε σκέψαι," ἔφη, "εἰ ἄρα συνομολογήσεις.
θερμόν τι καλεῖς καὶ ψυχρόν; "
"ἔγωγε."
"ἆρ' ὅπερ χιόνα καὶ πῦρ; "
d   "μὰ Δί' οὐκ ἔγωγε."
"ἀλλ' ἕτερόν τι πυρὸς τὸ θερμὸν καὶ ἕτερόν τι χιόνος τὸ
ψυχρόν; "
"ναί."
5   "ἀλλὰ τόδε γ' οἶμαι δοκεῖ σοι, οὐδέποτε χιόνα οὖσαν,
δεξαμένην τὸ θερμόν, ὥσπερ ἐν τοῖς πρόσθεν ἐλέγομεν,
ἔτι ἔσεσθαι ὅπερ ἦν, χιόνα καὶ θερμόν, ἀλλὰ προσιόντος
τοῦ θερμοῦ ἢ ὑπεκχωρήσειν αὐτῶι ἢ ἀπολεῖσθαι."
"πάνυ γε."
10   "καὶ τὸ πῦρ γε αὖ προσιόντος τοῦ ψυχροῦ αὐτῶι ἢ
ὑπεξιέναι ἢ ἀπολεῖσθαι, οὐ μέντοι ποτὲ τολμήσειν δεξάμενον τὴν ψυχρότητα ἔτι εἶναι ὅπερ ἦν, πῦρ καὶ ψυχρόν."
e   "ἀληθῆ", ἔφη, "λέγεις."
"ἔστιν ἄρα", ἦ δ' ὅς, "περὶ ἔνια τῶν τοιούτων, ὥστε μὴ
μόνον αὐτὸ τὸ εἶδος ἀξιοῦσθαι τοῦ αὐτοῦ ὀνόματος εἰς τὸν
ἀεὶ χρόνον, ἀλλὰ καὶ ἄλλο τι ὃ ἔστι μὲν οὐκ ἐκεῖνο, ἔχει
5   δὲ τὴν ἐκείνου μορφὴν ἀεί, ὅτανπερ ἦι. ἔτι δὲ ἐν τῶιδε
ἴσως ἔσται σαφέστερον ὃ λέγω· τὸ γὰρ περιττὸν ἀεί που
δεῖ τούτου τοῦ ὀνόματος τυγχάνειν ὅπερ νῦν λέγομεν· ἢ οὔ; "
"πάνυ γε."
"ἆρα μόνον τῶν ὄντων (τοῦτο γὰρ ἐρωτῶ) ἢ καὶ ἄλλο
104   τι ὃ ἔστι μὲν οὐχ ὅπερ τὸ περιττόν, ὅμως δὲ δεῖ αὐτὸ
μετὰ τοῦ ἑαυτοῦ ὀνόματος καὶ τοῦτο καλεῖν ἀεὶ διὰ τὸ οὕτω
πεφυκέναι ὥστε τοῦ περιττοῦ μηδέποτε ἀπολείπεσθαι; λέγω
δὲ αὐτὸ εἶναι οἷον καὶ ἡ τριὰς πέπονθε καὶ ἄλλα πολλά.
5   σκόπει δὲ περὶ τῆς τριάδος. ἆρα οὐ δοκεῖ σοι τῶι τε αὐτῆς
ὀνόματι ἀεὶ προσαγορευτέα εἶναι καὶ τῶι τοῦ περιττοῦ, ὄντος
οὐχ ὅπερ τῆς τριάδος; ἀλλ' ὅμως οὕτω πως πέφυκε καὶ ἡ
τριὰς καὶ ἡ πεμπτὰς καὶ ὁ ἥμισυς τοῦ ἀριθμοῦ ἅπας, ὥστε
b   οὐκ ὢν ὅπερ τὸ περιττὸν ἀεὶ ἕκαστος αὐτῶν ἐστι περιττός·

ΦΑΙΔΩΝ

ΦΑΙΔΩΝ 87

καὶ αὖ τὰ δύο καὶ τὰ τέτταρα καὶ ἅπας ὁ ἕτερος αὖ στίχος
τοῦ ἀριθμοῦ οὐκ ὢν ὅπερ τὸ ἄρτιον ὅμως ἕκαστος αὐτῶν
ἄρτιός ἐστιν ἀεί· συγχωρεῖς ἢ οὔ;"
"πῶς γὰρ οὔκ;" ἔφη.   5
"ὃ τοίνυν", ἔφη, "βούλομαι δηλῶσαι, ἄθρει. ἔστιν δὲ
τόδε, ὅτι φαίνεται οὐ μόνον ἐκεῖνα τὰ ἐναντία ἄλληλα οὐ
δεχόμενα, ἀλλὰ καὶ ὅσα οὐκ ὄντ' ἀλλήλοις ἐναντία ἔχει ἀεὶ
τἀναντία, οὐδὲ ταῦτα ἔοικε δεχομένοις ἐκείνην τὴν ἰδέαν ἢ
ἂν τῇ ἐν αὑτοῖς οὔσῃ ἐναντία ᾖ, ἀλλ' ἐπιούσης αὐτῆς ἤτοι 10
ἀπολλύμενα ἢ ὑπεκχωροῦντα. ἢ οὐ φήσομεν τὰ τρία καὶ c
ἀπολεῖσθαι πρότερον καὶ ἄλλο ὁτιοῦν πείσεσθαι, πρὶν ὑπο-
μεῖναι ἔτι τρία ὄντα ἄρτια γενέσθαι;"
"πάνυ μὲν οὖν," ἔφη ὁ Κέβης.
"οὐδὲ μήν", ἦ δ' ὅς, "ἐναντίον γέ ἐστι δυὰς τριάδι."   5
"οὐ γὰρ οὖν."
"οὐκ ἄρα μόνον τὰ εἴδη τὰ ἐναντία οὐχ ὑπομένει ἐπιόντα
ἄλληλα, ἀλλὰ καὶ ἄλλ' ἄττα τὰ ἐναντία οὐχ ὑπομένει
ἐπιόντα."
"ἀληθέστατα", ἔφη, "λέγεις."   10
"βούλει οὖν," ἦ δ' ὅς, "ἐὰν οἷοί τ' ὦμεν, ὁρισώμεθα ὁποῖα
ταῦτά ἐστιν;"
"πάνυ γε."
"ἆρ' οὖν," ἔφη, "ὦ Κέβης, τάδε εἴη ἄν, ἃ ὅτι ἂν κατάσχῃ, d
μὴ μόνον ἀναγκάζει τὴν αὑτοῦ ἰδέαν αὐτὸ ἴσχειν, ἀλλὰ καὶ
ἐναντίου τωι ἀεί τινος;"
"πῶς λέγεις;"
"ὥσπερ ἄρτι ἐλέγομεν. οἶσθα γὰρ δήπου ὅτι ἃ ἂν ἡ τῶν 5
τριῶν ἰδέα κατάσχῃ, ἀνάγκη αὐτοῖς οὐ μόνον τρισὶν εἶναι
ἀλλὰ καὶ περιττοῖς."
"πάνυ γε."
"ἐπὶ τὸ τοιοῦτον δή, φαμέν, ἡ ἐναντία ἰδέα ἐκείνῃ τῇ
μορφῇ ἣ ἂν τοῦτο ἀπεργάζηται οὐδέποτ' ἂν ἔλθοι."   10

b2 τὰ² om. m   d3 τωι e: αὐτῶι c   d10 ἢ m: ᾗι m: ἢ m

"οὐ γάρ."

"εἰργάζετο δέ γε ἡ περιττή; "

"ναί."

"ἐναντία δὲ ταύτηι ἡ τοῦ ἀρτίου; "

15 "ναί."

e "ἐπὶ τὰ τρία ἄρα ἡ τοῦ ἀρτίου ἰδέα οὐδέποτε ἥξει."

"οὐ δῆτα."

"ἄμοιρα δὴ τοῦ ἀρτίου τὰ τρία."

"ἄμοιρα."

5 "ἀνάρτιος ἄρα ἡ τριάς."

"ναί."

"ὃ τοίνυν ἔλεγον ὁρίσασθαι, ποῖα οὐκ ἐναντία τινὶ ὄντα
ὅμως οὐ δέχεται αὐτό, τὸ ἐναντίον—οἷον νῦν ἡ τριὰς τῶι
ἀρτίωι οὐκ οὖσα ἐναντία οὐδέν τι μᾶλλον αὐτὸ δέχεται, τὸ
10 γὰρ ἐναντίον ἀεὶ αὐτῶι ἐπιφέρει, καὶ ἡ δυὰς τῶι περιττῶι καὶ
105 τὸ πῦρ τῶι ψυχρῶι καὶ ἄλλα πάμπολλα· ἀλλ᾽ ὅρα δὴ εἰ
οὕτως ὁρίζηι, μὴ μόνον τὸ ἐναντίον τὸ ἐναντίον μὴ δέχεσθαι,
ἀλλὰ καὶ ἐκεῖνο ὃ ἂν ἐπιφέρηι τι ἐναντίον ἐκείνωι, ἐφ᾽ ὅτι
ἂν αὐτὸ ἴηι, αὐτὸ τὸ ἐπιφέρον, τὴν τοῦ ἐπιφερομένου ἐναν-
5 τιότητα μηδέποτε δέξασθαι. πάλιν δὲ ἀναμιμνήισκου· οὐ
γὰρ χεῖρον πολλάκις ἀκούειν. τὰ πέντε τὴν τοῦ ἀρτίου
οὐ δέξεται, οὐδὲ τὰ δέκα τὴν τοῦ περιττοῦ, τὸ διπλάσιον
(τοῦτο μὲν οὖν καὶ αὐτὸ ἄλλωι ἐναντίον, ὅμως δὲ τὴν
b τοῦ περιττοῦ οὐ δέξεται)· οὐδὲ δὴ τὸ ἡμιόλιον οὐδὲ τἆλλα
τὰ τοιαῦτα, τὸ ἥμισυ, τὴν τοῦ ὅλου, καὶ τριτημόριον αὖ
καὶ πάντα τὰ τοιαῦτα, εἴπερ ἔπηι τε καὶ συνδοκεῖ σοι οὕτως."

"πάνυ σφόδρα καὶ συνδοκεῖ," ἔφη, "καὶ ἕπομαι."

5 "πάλιν δή μοι", ἔφη, "ἐξ ἀρχῆς λέγε. καὶ μή μοι ὃ ἂν
ἐρωτῶ ἀποκρίνου, ἀλλὰ μιμούμενος ἐμέ. λέγω δὲ παρ᾽ ἣν
τὸ πρῶτον ἔλεγον ἀπόκρισιν, τὴν ἀσφαλῆ ἐκείνην, ἐκ τῶν
νῦν λεγομένων ἄλλην ὁρῶν ἀσφάλειαν. εἰ γὰρ ἔροιό με
ὧι ἂν τί ἐν τῶι σώματι ἐγγένηται θερμὸν ἔσται, οὐ τὴν
c ἀσφαλῆ σοι ἐρῶ ἀπόκρισιν ἐκείνην τὴν ἀμαθῆ, ὅτι ὧι ἂν

a8 ἐναντίον c: οὐκ ἐναντίον e   b6 δὲ m: δὴ m   b9, c1, c2, c3 ὧι m: ὃ m

θερμότης, ἀλλὰ κομψοτέραν ἐκ τῶν νῦν, ὅτι ὧι ἂν πῦρ· οὐδὲ
ἂν ἔρηι ὧι ἂν σώματι τί ἐγγένηται νοσήσει, οὐκ ἐρῶ ὅτι
ὧι ἂν νόσος, ἀλλ᾽ ὧι ἂν πυρετός· οὐδ᾽ ὧι ἂν ἀριθμῶι τί
ἐγγένηται περιττὸς ἔσται, οὐκ ἐρῶ ὧι ἂν περιττότης, ἀλλ᾽ 5
ὧι ἂν μονάς, καὶ τἆλλα οὕτως. ἀλλ᾽ ὅρα εἰ ἤδη ἱκανῶς
οἶσθ᾽ ὅτι βούλομαι.''

''ἀλλὰ πάνυ ἱκανῶς,'' ἔφη.

''ἀποκρίνου δή,'' ἦ δ᾽ ὅς, ''ὧι ἂν τί ἐγγένηται σώματι ζῶν
ἔσται;'' 10

''ὧι ἂν ψυχή,'' ἔφη.

''οὐκοῦν ἀεὶ τοῦτο οὕτως ἔχει;'' d

''πῶς γὰρ οὐχί;'' ἦ δ᾽ ὅς.

''ψυχὴ ἄρα ὅτι ἂν αὐτὴ κατάσχηι, ἀεὶ ἥκει ἐπ᾽ ἐκεῖνο
φέρουσα ζωήν;''

''ἥκει μέντοι,'' ἔφη. 5

''πότερον δ᾽ ἔστι τι ζωῆι ἐναντίον ἢ οὐδέν;''

''ἔστιν,'' ἔφη.

''τί;''

''θάνατος.''

''οὐκοῦν ψυχὴ τὸ ἐναντίον ὧι αὐτὴ ἐπιφέρει ἀεὶ οὐ μή 10
ποτε δέξηται, ὡς ἐκ τῶν πρόσθεν ὡμολόγηται;''

''καὶ μάλα σφόδρα,'' ἔφη ὁ Κέβης.

''τί οὖν; τὸ μὴ δεχόμενον τὴν τοῦ ἀρτίου ἰδέαν τί νυνδὴ
ὠνομάζομεν;''

''ἀνάρτιον,'' ἔφη. 15

''τὸ δὲ δίκαιον μὴ δεχόμενον καὶ ὃ ἂν μουσικὸν μὴ δέχηται;''

''ἄμουσον,'' ἔφη, ''τὸ δὲ ἄδικον.'' e

''εἶεν· ὃ δ᾽ ἂν θάνατον μὴ δέχηται τί καλοῦμεν;''

''ἀθάνατον,'' ἔφη.

''οὐκοῦν ψυχὴ οὐ δέχεται θάνατον;''

''οὔ.'' 5

''ἀθάνατον ἄρα ψυχή.''

''ἀθάνατον.''

d3, d10, e4, e6 ψυχὴ *m*: ἡ ψυχὴ *m*

"εἶεν," ἔφη· "τοῦτο μὲν δὴ ἀποδεδεῖχθαι φῶμεν; ἢ πῶς δοκεῖ; "
"καὶ μάλα γε ἱκανῶς, ὦ Σώκρατες."

10 "τί οὖν," ἦ δ᾽ ὅς, "ὦ Κέβης; εἰ τῶι ἀναρτίωι ἀναγκαῖον ἦν
106 ἀνωλέθρωι εἶναι, ἄλλο τι τὰ τρία ἢ ἀνώλεθρα ἂν ἦν; "
"πῶς γὰρ οὔ; "
"οὐκοῦν εἰ καὶ τὸ ἄθερμον ἀναγκαῖον ἦν ἀνώλεθρον εἶναι,
ὁπότε τις ἐπὶ χιόνα θερμὸν ἐπάγοι, ὑπεξήιει ἂν ἡ χιὼν οὖσα
5 σῶς καὶ ἄτηκτος; οὐ γὰρ ἂν ἀπώλετό γε, οὐδ᾽ αὖ ὑπο-
μένουσα ἐδέξατο ἂν τὴν θερμότητα."
"ἀληθῆ", ἔφη, "λέγεις."
"ὡς δ᾽ αὕτως οἶμαι κἂν εἰ τὸ ἄψυκτον ἀνώλεθρον ἦν,
ὁπότε ἐπὶ τὸ πῦρ ψυχρόν τι ἐπήιει, οὔποτ᾽ ἂν ἀπεσβέννυτο
10 οὐδ᾽ ἀπώλλυτο, ἀλλὰ σῶν ἂν ἀπελθὸν ὤιχετο."
"ἀνάγκη," ἔφη.

b "οὐκοῦν καὶ ὧδε", ἔφη, "ἀνάγκη περὶ τοῦ ἀθανάτου εἰπεῖν;
εἰ μὲν τὸ ἀθάνατον καὶ ἀνώλεθρόν ἐστιν, ἀδύνατον ψυχῆι,
ὅταν θάνατος ἐπ᾽ αὐτὴν ἴηι, ἀπόλλυσθαι· θάνατον μὲν γὰρ
δὴ ἐκ τῶν προειρημένων οὐ δέξεται οὐδ᾽ ἔσται τεθνηκυῖα,
5 ὥσπερ τὰ τρία οὐκ ἔσται, ἔφαμεν, ἄρτιον, οὐδέ γ᾽ αὖ τὸ
περιττόν, οὐδὲ δὴ πῦρ ψυχρόν, οὐδέ γε ἡ ἐν τῶι πυρὶ θερμότης. ἀλλὰ τί κωλύει, φαίη ἄν τις, ἄρτιον μὲν τὸ
περιττὸν μὴ γίγνεσθαι ἐπιόντος τοῦ ἀρτίου, ὥσπερ ὡμολόγη-
c ται, ἀπολομένου δὲ αὐτοῦ ἀντ᾽ ἐκείνου ἄρτιον γεγονέναι;
τῶι ταῦτα λέγοντι οὐκ ἂν ἔχοιμεν διαμάχεσθαι ὅτι οὐκ
ἀπόλλυται· τὸ γὰρ ἀνάρτιον οὐκ ἀνώλεθρόν ἐστιν· ἐπεὶ εἰ
τοῦτο ὡμολόγητο ἡμῖν, ῥαιδίως ἂν διεμαχόμεθα ὅτι ἐπελ-
5 θόντος τοῦ ἀρτίου τὸ περιττὸν καὶ τὰ τρία οἴχεται ἀπιόντα·
καὶ περὶ πυρὸς καὶ θερμοῦ καὶ τῶν ἄλλων οὕτως ἂν διεμαχόμεθα. ἢ οὔ; "
"πάνυ μὲν οὖν."
"οὐκοῦν καὶ νῦν περὶ τοῦ ἀθανάτου, εἰ μὲν ἡμῖν ὁμολογεῖται
10 καὶ ἀνώλεθρον εἶναι, ψυχὴ ἂν εἴη πρὸς τῶι ἀθάνατος εἶναι
d καὶ ἀνώλεθρος· εἰ δὲ μή, ἄλλου ἂν δέοι λόγου."

a3 ἄθερμον (m): θερμὸν m: ψυχρὸν m

"ἀλλ᾽ οὐδὲν δεῖ," ἔφη, "τούτου γε ἕνεκα· σχολῇι γὰρ ἂν τι ἄλλο φθορὰν μὴ δέχοιτο, εἰ τό γε ἀθάνατον ἀίδιον ὂν φθορὰν δέξεται."

"ὁ δέ γε θεὸς οἶμαι", ἔφη ὁ Σωκράτης, "καὶ αὐτὸ τὸ τῆς 5 ζωῆς εἶδος καὶ εἴ τι ἄλλο ἀθάνατόν ἐστιν, παρὰ πάντων ἂν ὁμολογηθείη μηδέποτε ἀπόλλυσθαι."

"παρὰ πάντων μέντοι νὴ Δί᾽", ἔφη, "ἀνθρώπων τέ γε καὶ ἔτι μᾶλλον, ὡς ἐγῶιμαι, παρὰ θεῶν."

"ὁπότε δὴ τὸ ἀθάνατον καὶ ἀδιάφθορόν ἐστιν, ἄλλο e τι ψυχὴ ἤ, εἰ ἀθάνατος τυγχάνει οὖσα, καὶ ἀνώλεθρος ἂν εἴη;"

"πολλὴ ἀνάγκη."

"ἐπιόντος ἄρα θανάτου ἐπὶ τὸν ἄνθρωπον τὸ μὲν θνητόν, 5 ὡς ἔοικεν, αὐτοῦ ἀποθνῄσκει, τὸ δ᾽ ἀθάνατον σῶν καὶ ἀδιάφθορον οἴχεται ἀπιόν, ὑπεκχωρῆσαν τῶι θανάτωι."

"φαίνεται."

"παντὸς μᾶλλον ἄρα," ἔφη, "ὦ Κέβης, ψυχὴ ἀθάνατον καὶ ἀνώλεθρον, καὶ τῶι ὄντι ἔσονται ἡμῶν αἱ ψυχαὶ ἐν Ἅιδου." 107

"οὔκουν ἔγωγε, ὦ Σώκρατες," ἔφη, "ἔχω παρὰ ταῦτα ἄλλο τι λέγειν οὐδέ πηι ἀπιστεῖν τοῖς λόγοις. ἀλλ᾽ εἰ δή τι Σιμμίας ὅδε ἤ τις ἄλλος ἔχει λέγειν, εὖ ἔχει μὴ κατασιγῆ-σαι· ὡς οὐκ οἶδα εἰς ὅντινά τις ἄλλον καιρὸν ἀναβάλλοιτο 5 ἢ τὸν νῦν παρόντα, περὶ τῶν τοιούτων βουλόμενος ἤ τι εἰπεῖν ἢ ἀκοῦσαι."

"ἀλλὰ μήν", ἦ δ᾽ ὃς ὁ Σιμμίας, "οὐδ᾽ αὐτὸς ἔχω ἔτι ὅπηι ἀπιστῶ ἔκ γε τῶν λεγομένων· ὑπὸ μέντοι τοῦ μεγέθους περὶ ὦν οἱ λόγοι εἰσίν, καὶ τὴν ἀνθρωπίνην ἀσθένειαν ἀτιμάζων, b ἀναγκάζομαι ἀπιστίαν ἔτι ἔχειν παρ᾽ ἐμαυτῶι περὶ τῶν εἰρημένων."

"οὐ μόνον γ᾽," ἔφη, "ὦ Σιμμία," ὁ Σωκράτης, "ἀλλὰ ταῦτά τε εὖ λέγεις καὶ τάς γε ὑποθέσεις τὰς πρώτας, καὶ εἰ 5 πισταὶ ὑμῖν εἰσιν, ὅμως ἐπισκεπτέαι σαφέστερον· καὶ ἐὰν αὐτὰς ἱκανῶς διέλητε, ὡς ἐγῶιμαι, ἀκολουθήσετε τῶι λόγωι,

d3 τό γε m: τό τε t: γε τὸ m

92 ΠΛΑΤΩΝΟΣ

καθ' ὅσον δυνατὸν μάλιστ' ἀνθρώπωι ἐπακολουθῆσαι· κἂν
τοῦτο αὐτὸ σαφὲς γένηται, οὐδὲν ζητήσετε περαιτέρω."

10 "ἀληθῆ", ἔφη, "λέγεις."

c "ἀλλὰ τόδε γ'," ἔφη, "ὦ ἄνδρες, δίκαιον διανοηθῆναι, ὅτι,
εἴπερ ἡ ψυχὴ ἀθάνατος, ἐπιμελείας δὴ δεῖται οὐχ ὑπὲρ τοῦ
χρόνου τούτου μόνον ἐν ὧι καλοῦμεν τὸ ζῆν, ἀλλ' ὑπὲρ τοῦ
παντός, καὶ ὁ κίνδυνος νῦν δὴ καὶ δόξειεν ἂν δεινὸς εἶναι,
5 εἴ τις αὐτῆς ἀμελήσει. εἰ μὲν γὰρ ἦν ὁ θάνατος τοῦ παντὸς
ἀπαλλαγή, ἕρμαιον ἂν ἦν τοῖς κακοῖς ἀποθανοῦσι τοῦ τε
σώματος ἅμ' ἀπηλλάχθαι καὶ τῆς αὐτῶν κακίας μετὰ τῆς
ψυχῆς· νῦν δ' ἐπειδὴ ἀθάνατος φαίνεται οὖσα, οὐδεμία ἂν
d εἴη αὐτῆι ἄλλη ἀποφυγὴ κακῶν οὐδὲ σωτηρία πλὴν τοῦ ὡς
βελτίστην τε καὶ φρονιμωτάτην γενέσθαι. οὐδὲν γὰρ ἄλλο
ἔχουσα εἰς Ἅιδου ἡ ψυχὴ ἔρχεται πλὴν τῆς παιδείας τε καὶ
τροφῆς, ἃ δὴ καὶ μέγιστα λέγεται ὠφελεῖν ἢ βλάπτειν τὸν
5 τελευτήσαντα εὐθὺς ἐν ἀρχῆι τῆς ἐκεῖσε πορείας. λέγεται
δὲ οὕτως, ὡς ἄρα τελευτήσαντα ἕκαστον ὁ ἑκάστου δαίμων,
ὅσπερ ζῶντα εἰλήχει, οὗτος ἄγειν ἐπιχειρεῖ εἰς δή τινα
τόπον, οἷ δεῖ τοὺς συλλεγέντας διαδικασαμένους εἰς Ἅιδου
e πορεύεσθαι μετὰ ἡγεμόνος ἐκείνου ὧι δὴ προστέτακται τοὺς
ἐνθένδε ἐκεῖσε πορεῦσαι· τυχόντας δὲ ἐκεῖ ὧν δεῖ τυχεῖν
καὶ μείναντας ὃν χρὴ χρόνον ἄλλος δεῦρο πάλιν ἡγεμὼν
κομίζει ἐν πολλαῖς χρόνου καὶ μακραῖς περιόδοις. ἔστι δὲ
5 ἄρα ἡ πορεία οὐχ ὡς ὁ Αἰσχύλου Τήλεφος λέγει· ἐκεῖνος
108 μὲν γὰρ ἁπλῆν οἷμόν φησιν εἰς Ἅιδου φέρειν, ἡ δ' οὔτε
ἁπλῆ οὔτε μία φαίνεταί μοι εἶναι. οὐδὲ γὰρ ἂν ἡγεμόνων
ἔδει· οὐ γάρ πού τις ἂν διαμάρτοι οὐδαμόσε μιᾶς ὁδοῦ
οὔσης. νῦν δὲ ἔοικε σχίσεις τε καὶ τριόδους πολλὰς ἔχειν·
5 ἀπὸ τῶν ὁσίων τε καὶ νομίμων τῶν ἐνθάδε τεκμαιρόμενος
λέγω. ἡ μὲν οὖν κοσμία τε καὶ φρόνιμος ψυχὴ ἕπεταί τε
καὶ οὐκ ἀγνοεῖ τὰ παρόντα· ἡ δ' ἐπιθυμητικῶς τοῦ σώματος
ἔχουσα, ὅπερ ἐν τῶι ἔμπροσθεν εἶπον, περὶ ἐκεῖνο πολὺν

e2 δεῖ c: δὴ t   a4 τριόδους t: περιόδους c t   a5 ὁσίων m: θυσιῶν m t:
οὐσιῶν t

χρόνον ἑπτοημένη καὶ περὶ τὸν ὁρατὸν τόπον, πολλὰ b
ἀντιτείνασα καὶ πολλὰ παθοῦσα, βίαι καὶ μόγις ὑπὸ τοῦ
προστεταγμένου δαίμονος οἴχεται ἀγομένη. ἀφικομένην δὲ
ὅθιπερ αἱ ἄλλαι, τὴν μὲν ἀκάθαρτον καί τι πεποιηκυῖαν
τοιοῦτον, ἢ φόνων ἀδίκων ἡμμένην ἢ ἄλλ᾽ ἄττα τοιαῦτα 5
εἰργασμένην, ἃ τούτων ἀδελφά τε καὶ ἀδελφῶν ψυχῶν ἔργα
τυγχάνει ὄντα, ταύτην μὲν ἅπας φεύγει τε καὶ ὑπεκτρέπεται
καὶ οὔτε συνέμπορος οὔτε ἡγεμὼν ἐθέλει γίγνεσθαι, αὐτὴ
δὲ πλανᾶται ἐν πάσηι ἐχομένη ἀπορίαι ἕως ἂν δή τινες c
χρόνοι γένωνται, ὧν ἐλθόντων ὑπ᾽ ἀνάγκης φέρεται εἰς τὴν
αὐτῆι πρέπουσαν οἴκησιν· ἡ δὲ καθαρῶς τε καὶ μετρίως τὸν
βίον διεξελθοῦσα, καὶ συνεμπόρων καὶ ἡγεμόνων θεῶν
τυχοῦσα, ὤικησεν τὸν αὐτῆι ἑκάστηι τόπον προσήκοντα. εἰσὶν 5
δὲ πολλοὶ καὶ θαυμαστοὶ τῆς γῆς τόποι, καὶ αὐτὴ οὔτε οἵα
οὔτε ὅση δοξάζεται ὑπὸ τῶν περὶ γῆς εἰωθότων λέγειν, ὡς
ἐγὼ ὑπό τινος πέπεισμαι."

καὶ ὁ Σιμμίας, "πῶς ταῦτα", ἔφη, "λέγεις, ὦ Σώκρατες; d
περὶ γάρ τοι γῆς καὶ αὐτὸς πολλὰ δὴ ἀκήκοα, οὐ μέντοι
ταῦτα ἃ σὲ πείθει· ἡδέως οὖν ἂν ἀκούσαιμι."

"ἀλλὰ μέντοι, ὦ Σιμμία, οὐχ ἡ Γλαύκου τέχνη γέ μοι
δοκεῖ εἶναι διηγήσασθαι ἅ γ᾽ ἐστίν· ὡς μέντοι ἀληθῆ, 5
χαλεπώτερόν μοι φαίνεται ἢ κατὰ τὴν Γλαύκου τέχνην, καὶ
ἅμα μὲν ἐγὼ ἴσως οὐδ᾽ ἂν οἷός τε εἴην, ἅμα δέ, εἰ καὶ
ἠπιστάμην, ὁ βίος μοι δοκεῖ ὁ ἐμός, ὦ Σιμμία, τῶι μήκει
τοῦ λόγου οὐκ ἐξαρκεῖν. τὴν μέντοι ἰδέαν τῆς γῆς οἵαν
πέπεισμαι εἶναι, καὶ τοὺς τόπους αὐτῆς οὐδέν με κωλύει e
λέγειν."

"ἀλλ᾽ ", ἔφη ὁ Σιμμίας, "καὶ ταῦτα ἀρκεῖ."

"πέπεισμαι τοίνυν", ἦ δ᾽ ὅς, "ἐγὼ ὡς πρῶτον μέν, εἰ ἔστιν
ἐν μέσωι τῶι οὐρανῶι περιφερὴς οὖσα, μηδὲν αὐτῆι δεῖν μήτε 5
ἀέρος πρὸς τὸ μὴ πεσεῖν μήτε ἄλλης ἀνάγκης μηδεμιᾶς 109
τοιαύτης, ἀλλὰ ἱκανὴν εἶναι αὐτὴν ἴσχειν τὴν ὁμοιότητα
τοῦ οὐρανοῦ αὐτοῦ ἑαυτῶι πάντηι καὶ τῆς γῆς αὐτῆς τὴν

c5 ἑκάστηι m: ἑκάστη m t

ἰσορροπίαν· ἰσόρροπον γὰρ πρᾶγμα ὁμοίου τινὸς ἐν μέσωι
5 τεθὲν οὐχ ἕξει μᾶλλον οὐδ᾽ ἧττον οὐδαμόσε κλιθῆναι,
ὁμοίως δ᾽ ἔχον ἀκλινὲς μενεῖ. πρῶτον μὲν τοίνυν", ἦ δ᾽ ὅς,
"τοῦτο πέπεισμαι."

"καὶ ὀρθῶς γε," ἔφη ὁ Σιμμίας.

"ἔτι τοίνυν", ἔφη, "πάμμεγά τι εἶναι αὐτό, καὶ ἡμᾶς οἰκεῖν
b τοὺς μέχρι Ἡρακλείων στηλῶν ἀπὸ Φάσιδος ἐν σμικρῶι
τινι μορίωι, ὥσπερ περὶ τέλμα μύρμηκας ἢ βατράχους περὶ
τὴν θάλατταν οἰκοῦντας, καὶ ἄλλους ἄλλοθι πολλοὺς ἐν
πολλοῖσι τοιούτοις τόποις οἰκεῖν. εἶναι γὰρ πανταχῆι περὶ
5 τὴν γῆν πολλὰ κοῖλα καὶ παντοδαπὰ καὶ τὰς ἰδέας καὶ τὰ
μεγέθη, εἰς ἃ συνερρυηκέναι τό τε ὕδωρ καὶ τὴν ὁμίχλην
καὶ τὸν ἀέρα· αὐτὴν δὲ τὴν γῆν καθαρὰν ἐν καθαρῶι κεῖσθαι
τῶι οὐρανῶι ἐν ὧιπέρ ἐστι τὰ ἄστρα, ὃν δὴ αἰθέρα ὀνομάζειν
c τοὺς πολλοὺς τῶν περὶ τὰ τοιαῦτα [εἰωθότων λέγειν]· οὗ δὴ
ὑποστάθμην ταῦτα εἶναι καὶ συρρεῖν ἀεὶ εἰς τὰ κοῖλα τῆς
γῆς. ἡμᾶς οὖν οἰκοῦντας ἐν τοῖς κοίλοις αὐτῆς λεληθέναι
καὶ οἴεσθαι ἄνω ἐπὶ τῆς γῆς οἰκεῖν, ὥσπερ ἂν εἴ τις ἐν
5 μέσωι τῶι πυθμένι τοῦ πελάγους οἰκῶν οἴοιτό τε ἐπὶ τῆς
θαλάττης οἰκεῖν καὶ διὰ τοῦ ὕδατος ὁρῶν τὸν ἥλιον καὶ τὰ
ἄλλα ἄστρα τὴν θάλατταν ἡγοῖτο οὐρανὸν εἶναι, διὰ δὲ
d βραδυτῆτά τε καὶ ἀσθένειαν μηδεπώποτε ἐπὶ τὰ ἄκρα τῆς
θαλάττης ἀφιγμένος μηδὲ ἑωρακὼς εἴη, ἐκδὺς καὶ ἀνακύψας
ἐκ τῆς θαλάττης εἰς τὸν ἐνθάδε τόπον, ὅσωι καθαρώτερος
καὶ καλλίων τυγχάνει ὢν τοῦ παρὰ σφίσι, μηδὲ ἄλλου
5 ἀκηκοὼς εἴη τοῦ ἑωρακότος. ταὐτὸν δὴ τοῦτο καὶ ἡμᾶς
πεπονθέναι· οἰκοῦντας γὰρ ἔν τινι κοίλωι τῆς γῆς οἴεσθαι
ἐπάνω αὐτῆς οἰκεῖν, καὶ τὸν ἀέρα οὐρανὸν καλεῖν, ὡς διὰ
τούτου οὐρανοῦ ὄντος τὰ ἄστρα χωροῦντα· τὸ δὲ εἶναι ταὐ-
e τόν, ὑπ᾽ ἀσθενείας καὶ βραδυτῆτος οὐχ οἵους τε εἶναι ἡμᾶς
διεξελθεῖν ἐπ᾽ ἔσχατον τὸν ἀέρα· ἐπεί, εἴ τις αὐτοῦ ἐπ᾽ ἄκρα
ἔλθοι ἢ πτηνὸς γενόμενος ἀνάπτοιτο, κατιδεῖν ⟨ἂν⟩ ἀνακύψαντα, ὥσπερ ἐνθάδε οἱ ἐκ τῆς θαλάττης ἰχθύες ἀνακύ-

b4 πολλοῖσι m: πολλοῖς m t   e3 ἂν e: δὴ t

πτοντες ὁρῶσι τὰ ἐνθάδε, οὕτως ἄν τινα καὶ τὰ ἐκεῖ κατιδεῖν, 5
καὶ εἰ ἡ φύσις ἱκανὴ εἴη ἀνασχέσθαι θεωροῦσα, γνῶναι ἂν
ὅτι ἐκεῖνός ἐστιν ὁ ἀληθῶς οὐρανὸς καὶ τὸ ἀληθινὸν φῶς
καὶ ἡ ὡς ἀληθῶς γῆ. ἥδε μὲν γὰρ ἡ γῆ καὶ οἱ λίθοι καὶ 110
ἅπας ὁ τόπος ὁ ἐνθάδε διεφθαρμένα ἐστὶν καὶ καταβεβρω-
μένα, ὥσπερ τὰ ἐν τῆι θαλάττηι ὑπὸ τῆς ἅλμης, καὶ οὔτε
φύεται ἄξιον λόγου οὐδὲν ἐν τῆι θαλάττηι, οὔτε τέλειον ὡς
ἔπος εἰπεῖν οὐδέν ἐστι, σήραγγες δὲ καὶ ἄμμος καὶ πηλὸς 5
ἀμήχανος καὶ βόρβοροί εἰσιν, ὅπου ἂν καὶ ἡ γῆ ἦι, καὶ
πρὸς τὰ παρ' ἡμῖν κάλλη κρίνεσθαι οὐδ' ὁπωστιοῦν ἄξια.
ἐκεῖνα δὲ αὖ τῶν παρ' ἡμῖν πολὺ ἂν ἔτι πλέον φανείη δια-
φέρειν· εἰ γὰρ δὴ καὶ μῦθον λέγειν καλόν, ἄξιον ἀκοῦσαι, ὦ b
Σιμμία, οἷα τυγχάνει τὰ ἐπὶ τῆς γῆς ὑπὸ τῶι οὐρανῶι ὄντα."

"ἀλλὰ μήν," ἔφη ὁ Σιμμίας, "ὦ Σώκρατες, ἡμεῖς γε τούτου
τοῦ μύθου ἡδέως ἂν ἀκούσαιμεν."

"λέγεται τοίνυν," ἔφη, "ὦ ἑταῖρε, πρῶτον μὲν εἶναι τοιαύτη 5
ἡ γῆ αὕτη ἰδεῖν, εἴ τις ἄνωθεν θεῶιτο, ὥσπερ αἱ δωδεκάσκυτοι σφαῖραι, ποικίλη, χρώμασιν διειλημμένη, ὦν καὶ τὰ
ἐνθάδε εἶναι χρώματα ὥσπερ δείγματα, οἷς δὴ οἱ γραφῆς
καταχρῶνται. ἐκεῖ δὲ πᾶσαν τὴν γῆν ἐκ τοιούτων εἶναι, καὶ c
πολὺ ἔτι ἐκ λαμπροτέρων καὶ καθαρωτέρων ἢ τούτων· τὴν
μὲν γὰρ ἁλουργῆ εἶναι καὶ θαυμαστὴν τὸ κάλλος, τὴν δὲ
χρυσοειδῆ, τὴν δὲ ὅση λευκὴ γύψου ἢ χιόνος λευκοτέραν,
καὶ ἐκ τῶν ἄλλων χρωμάτων συγκειμένην ὡσαύτως, καὶ ἔτι 5
πλειόνων καὶ καλλιόνων ἢ ὅσα ἡμεῖς ἑωράκαμεν. καὶ γὰρ
αὐτὰ ταῦτα τὰ κοῖλα αὐτῆς, ὕδατός τε καὶ ἀέρος ἔκπλεα
ὄντα, χρώματός τι εἶδος παρέχεσθαι στίλβοντα ἐν τῆι τῶν d
ἄλλων χρωμάτων ποικιλίαι, ὥστε ἕν τι αὐτῆς εἶδος συνεχὲς
ποικίλον φαντάζεσθαι. ἐν δὲ ταύτηι οὔσηι τοιαύτηι ἀνὰ
λόγον τὰ φυόμενα φύεσθαι, δένδρα τε καὶ ἄνθη καὶ τοὺς
καρπούς· καὶ αὖ τὰ ὄρη ὡσαύτως, καὶ τοὺς λίθους ἔχειν ἀνὰ 5
τὸν αὐτὸν λόγον τήν τε λειότητα καὶ τὴν διαφάνειαν καὶ τὰ

a6 ἡ γῆ m t: γῆ m   b1 δὴ ... λέγειν καλόν m t: δεῖ ... λέγειν καλόν m: δεῖ ...
λέγειν m   b6 αὕτη c t: αὐτὴ t

χρώματα καλλίω· ὧν καὶ τὰ ἐνθάδε λιθίδια εἶναι ταῦτα τὰ
ἀγαπώμενα μόρια, σάρδιά τε καὶ ἰάσπιδας καὶ σμαράγδους
e καὶ πάντα τὰ τοιαῦτα· ἐκεῖ δὲ οὐδὲν ὅτι οὐ τοιοῦτον εἶναι καὶ
ἔτι τούτων καλλίω. τὸ δ᾽ αἴτιον τούτου εἶναι ὅτι ἐκεῖνοι οἱ
λίθοι εἰσὶ καθαροὶ καὶ οὐ κατεδηδεσμένοι οὐδὲ διεφθαρμένοι
ὥσπερ οἱ ἐνθάδε ὑπὸ σηπεδόνος καὶ ἅλμης ὑπὸ τῶν δεῦρο
5 συνερρυηκότων, ἃ καὶ λίθοις καὶ γῆι καὶ τοῖς ἄλλοις ζώιοις τε
καὶ φυτοῖς αἴσχη τε καὶ νόσους παρέχει. τὴν δὲ γῆν αὐτὴν
κεκοσμῆσθαι τούτοις τε ἅπασι καὶ ἔτι χρυσῶι τε καὶ ἀργύρωι καὶ
111 τοῖς ἄλλοις αὖ τοῖς τοιούτοις. ἐκφανῆ γὰρ αὐτὰ πεφυκέναι,
ὄντα πολλὰ πλήθει καὶ μεγάλα καὶ πανταχοῦ τῆς γῆς, ὥστε
αὐτὴν ἰδεῖν εἶναι θέαμα εὐδαιμόνων θεατῶν. ζῶια δ᾽ ἐπ᾽
αὐτῆι εἶναι ἄλλα τε πολλὰ καὶ ἀνθρώπους, τοὺς μὲν ἐν
5 μεσογαίαι οἰκοῦντας, τοὺς δὲ περὶ τὸν ἀέρα ὥσπερ ἡμεῖς
περὶ τὴν θάλατταν, τοὺς δ᾽ ἐν νήσοις ἃς περιρρεῖν τὸν ἀέρα
πρὸς τῆι ἠπείρωι οὔσας· καὶ ἑνὶ λόγωι, ὅπερ ἡμῖν τὸ ὕδωρ τε
καὶ ἡ θάλαττά ἐστι πρὸς τὴν ἡμετέραν χρείαν, τοῦτο ἐκεῖ
b τὸν ἀέρα, ὃ δὲ ἡμῖν ἀήρ, ἐκείνοις τὸν αἰθέρα. τὰς δὲ ὥρας
αὐτοῖς κρᾶσιν ἔχειν τοιαύτην ὥστε ἐκείνους ἀνόσους εἶναι καὶ
χρόνον τε ζῆν πολὺ πλείω τῶν ἐνθάδε, καὶ ὄψει καὶ ἀκοῆι καὶ
φρονήσει καὶ πᾶσι τοῖς τοιούτοις ἡμῶν ἀφεστάναι τῆι αὐτῆι
5 ἀποστάσει ἧιπερ ἀήρ τε ὕδατος ἀφέστηκεν καὶ αἰθὴρ ἀέρος
πρὸς καθαρότητα. καὶ δὴ καὶ θεῶν ἄλση τε καὶ ἱερὰ αὐτοῖς
εἶναι, ἐν οἷς τῶι ὄντι οἰκητὰς θεοὺς εἶναι, καὶ φήμας τε καὶ
μαντείας καὶ αἰσθήσεις τῶν θεῶν, καὶ τοιαύτας συνουσίας
c γίγνεσθαι αὐτοῖς πρὸς αὐτούς· καὶ τόν γε ἥλιον καὶ σελήνην
καὶ ἄστρα ὁρᾶσθαι ὑπ᾽ αὐτῶν οἷα τυγχάνει ὄντα, καὶ τὴν
ἄλλην εὐδαιμονίαν τούτων ἀκόλουθον εἶναι.

"καὶ ὅλην μὲν δὴ τὴν γῆν οὕτω πεφυκέναι καὶ τὰ περὶ
5 τὴν γῆν· τόπους δ᾽ ἐν αὐτῆι εἶναι κατὰ τὰ ἔγκοιλα αὐτῆς
κύκλωι περὶ ὅλην πολλούς, τοὺς μὲν βαθυτέρους καὶ ἀνα-
πεπταμένους μᾶλλον ἢ ἐν ὧι ἡμεῖς οἰκοῦμεν, τοὺς δὲ βαθυτέρους ὄντας τὸ χάσμα αὐτοὺς ἔλαττον ἔχειν τοῦ παρ᾽ ἡμῖν
d τόπου, ἔστι δ᾽ οὓς καὶ βραχυτέρους τῶι βάθει τοῦ ἐνθάδε
εἶναι καὶ πλατυτέρους. τούτους δὲ πάντας ὑπὸ γῆν εἰς

ἀλλήλους συντετρῆσθαί τε πολλαχῆι καὶ κατὰ στενότερα καὶ
εὐρύτερα καὶ διεξόδους ἔχειν, ἧι πολὺ μὲν ὕδωρ ῥεῖν ἐξ
ἀλλήλων εἰς ἀλλήλους ὥσπερ εἰς κρατῆρας, καὶ ἀενάων 5
ποταμῶν ἀμήχανα μεγέθη ὑπὸ τὴν γῆν καὶ θερμῶν ὑδάτων
καὶ ψυχρῶν, πολὺ δὲ πῦρ καὶ πυρὸς μεγάλους ποταμούς,
πολλοὺς δὲ ὑγροῦ πηλοῦ καὶ καθαρωτέρου καὶ βορβορωδεστέρου, ὥσπερ ἐν Σικελίαι οἱ πρὸ τοῦ ῥύακος πηλοῦ ῥέοντες e
ποταμοὶ καὶ αὐτὸς ὁ ῥύαξ· ὧν δὴ καὶ ἑκάστους τοὺς τόπους
πληροῦσθαι, ὡς ἂν ἑκάστοις τύχηι ἑκάστοτε ἡ περιρροὴ γιγνομένη. ταῦτα δὲ πάντα κινεῖν ἄνω καὶ κάτω ὥσπερ αἰώραν
τινὰ ἐνοῦσαν ἐν τῆι γῆι· ἔστι δὲ ἄρα αὕτη ἡ αἰώρα διὰ φύσιν 5
τοιάνδε τινά. ἕν τι τῶν χασμάτων τῆς γῆς ἄλλως τε
μέγιστον τυγχάνει ὂν καὶ διαμπερὲς τετρημένον δι᾽ ὅλης τῆς 112
γῆς, τοῦτο ὅπερ Ὅμηρος εἶπε, λέγων αὐτό

τῆλε μάλ᾽, ἧιχι βάθιστον ὑπὸ χθονός ἐστι βέρεθρον·

ὃ καὶ ἄλλοθι καὶ ἐκεῖνος καὶ ἄλλοι πολλοὶ τῶν ποιητῶν Τάρταρον κεκλήκασιν. εἰς γὰρ τοῦτο τὸ χάσμα συρρέουσί τε 5
πάντες οἱ ποταμοὶ καὶ ἐκ τούτου πάλιν ἐκρέουσιν· γίγνονται
δὲ ἕκαστοι τοιοῦτοι δι᾽ οἵας ἂν καὶ τῆς γῆς ῥέωσιν. ἡ δὲ
αἰτία ἐστὶν τοῦ ἐκρεῖν τε ἐντεῦθεν καὶ εἰσρεῖν πάντα τὰ b
ῥεύματα, ὅτι πυθμένα οὐκ ἔχει οὐδὲ βάσιν τὸ ὑγρὸν τοῦτο.
αἰωρεῖται δὴ καὶ κυμαίνει ἄνω καὶ κάτω, καὶ ὁ ἀὴρ καὶ τὸ
πνεῦμα τὸ περὶ αὐτὸ ταὐτὸν ποιεῖ· συνέπεται γὰρ αὐτῶι καὶ
ὅταν εἰς τὸ ἐπ᾽ ἐκεῖνα τῆς γῆς ὁρμήσηι καὶ ὅταν εἰς τὸ ἐπὶ 5
τάδε, καὶ ὥσπερ τῶν ἀναπνεόντων ἀεὶ ἐκπνεῖ τε καὶ ἀναπνεῖ
ῥέον τὸ πνεῦμα, οὕτω καὶ ἐκεῖ συναιωρούμενον τῶι ὑγρῶι τὸ
πνεῦμα δεινούς τινας ἀνέμους καὶ ἀμηχάνους παρέχεται καὶ
εἰσιὸν καὶ ἐξιόν. ὅταν τε οὖν ὑποχωρήσηι τὸ ὕδωρ εἰς τὸν c
τόπον τὸν δὴ κάτω καλούμενον, τοῖς κατ᾽ ἐκεῖνα τὰ ῥεύματα
διὰ τῆς γῆς εἰσρεῖ τε καὶ πληροῖ αὐτὰ ὥσπερ οἱ ἐπαν-
τλοῦντες· ὅταν τε αὖ ἐκεῖθεν μὲν ἀπολίπηι, δεῦρο δὲ ὁρμήσηι,
τὰ ἐνθάδε πληροῖ αὖθις, τὰ δὲ πληρωθέντα ῥεῖ διὰ τῶν 5

e3 ὡς t: ὧν c

ὀχετῶν καὶ διὰ τῆς γῆς, καὶ εἰς τοὺς τόπους ἔκαστα ἀφικνού-
μενα, εἰς οὓς ἑκάστους ὁδοποιεῖται, θαλάττας τε καὶ λίμνας
καὶ ποταμοὺς καὶ κρήνας ποιεῖ· ἐντεῦθεν δὲ πάλιν δυόμενα
d κατὰ τῆς γῆς, τὰ μὲν μακροτέρους τόπους περιελθόντα καὶ
πλείους, τὰ δὲ ἐλάττους καὶ βραχυτέρους, πάλιν εἰς τὸν
Τάρταρον ἐμβάλλει, τὰ μὲν πολὺ κατωτέρω ἢ ἐπηντλεῖτο, τὰ δὲ ὀλίγον· πάντα δὲ ὑποκάτω εἰσρεῖ τῆς ἐκροῆς,
5 καὶ ἔνια μὲν καταντικρὺ ἧι εἰσρεῖ ἐξέπεσεν, ἔνια δὲ
κατὰ τὸ αὐτὸ μέρος· ἔστι δὲ ἃ παντάπασιν κύκλωι περιελθόντα, ἢ ἅπαξ ἢ καὶ πλεονάκις περιελιχθέντα περὶ τὴν γῆν
ὥσπερ οἱ ὄφεις, εἰς τὸ δυνατὸν κάτω καθέντα πάλιν ἐμβάλλει.
e δυνατὸν δέ ἐστιν ἑκατέρωσε μέχρι τοῦ μέσου καθιέναι, πέρα
δ' οὔ· ἄναντες γὰρ ἀμφοτέροις τοῖς ῥεύμασι τὸ ἑκατέρωθεν
γίγνεται μέρος.

"τὰ μὲν οὖν δὴ ἄλλα πολλά τε καὶ μεγάλα καὶ παντοδαπὰ
5 ῥεύματά ἐστι· τυγχάνει δ' ἄρα ὄντα ἐν τούτοις τοῖς πολλοῖς
τέτταρ' ἄττα ῥεύματα, ὧν τὸ μὲν μέγιστον καὶ ἐξωτάτω ῥέον
περὶ κύκλωι ὁ καλούμενος Ὠκεανός ἐστιν, τούτου δὲ καταντικρὺ καὶ ἐναντίως ῥέων Ἀχέρων, ὃς δι' ἐρήμων τε τόπων
113 ῥεῖ ἄλλων καὶ δὴ καὶ ὑπὸ γῆν ῥέων εἰς τὴν λίμνην ἀφικνεῖται
τὴν Ἀχερουσιάδα, οὗ αἱ τῶν τετελευτηκότων ψυχαὶ τῶν
πολλῶν ἀφικνοῦνται καί τινας εἱμαρμένους χρόνους μείνασαι,
αἱ μὲν μακροτέρους, αἱ δὲ βραχυτέρους, πάλιν ἐκπέμπονται
5 εἰς τὰς τῶν ζώιων γενέσεις. τρίτος δὲ ποταμὸς τούτων κατὰ
μέσον ἐκβάλλει, καὶ ἐγγὺς τῆς ἐκβολῆς ἐκπίπτει εἰς τόπον
μέγαν πυρὶ πολλῶι καόμενον, καὶ λίμνην ποιεῖ μείζω τῆς
παρ' ἡμῖν θαλάττης, ζέουσαν ὕδατος καὶ πηλοῦ· ἐντεῦθεν δὲ
b χωρεῖ κύκλωι θολερὸς καὶ πηλώδης, περιελιττόμενος δὲ τῆι
γῆι ἄλλοσέ τε ἀφικνεῖται καὶ παρ' ἔσχατα τῆς Ἀχερουσιάδος
λίμνης, οὐ συμμειγνύμενος τῶι ὕδατι· περιελιχθεὶς δὲ πολλάκις
ὑπὸ γῆς ἐμβάλλει κατωτέρω τοῦ Ταρτάρου· οὗτος δ' ἐστὶν
5 ὃν ἐπονομάζουσιν Πυριφλεγέθοντα, οὗ καὶ οἱ ῥύακες ἀπο-
σπάσματα ἀναφυσῶσιν ὅπηι ἂν τύχωσι τῆς γῆς. τούτου δὲ

αὖ καταντικρὺ ὁ τέταρτος ἐκπίπτει εἰς τόπον πρῶτον δεινόν
τε καὶ ἄγριον, ὡς λέγεται, χρῶμα δ' ἔχοντα ὅλον οἷον ὁ
κυανός, ὃν δὴ ἐπονομάζουσι Στύγιον, καὶ τὴν λίμνην c
ποιεῖ ὁ ποταμὸς ἐμβάλλων Στύγα· ὁ δ' ἐμπεσὼν ἐνταῦθα
καὶ δεινὰς δυνάμεις λαβὼν ἐν τῶι ὕδατι, δὺς κατὰ τῆς γῆς,
περιελιττόμενος χωρεῖ ἐναντίος τῶι Πυριφλεγέθοντι καὶ
ἀπαντᾶι ἐν τῆι Ἀχερουσιάδι λίμνηι ἐξ ἐναντίας· καὶ οὐδὲ τὸ 5
τούτου ὕδωρ οὐδενὶ μείγνυται, ἀλλὰ καὶ οὗτος κύκλωι περιελ-
θὼν ἐμβάλλει εἰς τὸν Τάρταρον, ἐναντίος τῶι Πυριφλεγέθοντι·
ὄνομα δὲ τούτωι ἐστίν, ὡς οἱ ποιηταὶ λέγουσιν, Κωκυτός.

"τούτων δὲ οὕτως πεφυκότων, ἐπειδὰν ἀφίκωνται οἱ τετε- d
λευτηκότες εἰς τὸν τόπον οἷ ὁ δαίμων ἕκαστον κομίζει,
πρῶτον μὲν διεδικάσαντο οἵ τε καλῶς καὶ ὁσίως βιώσαντες
καὶ οἱ μή. καὶ οἳ μὲν ἂν δόξωσι μέσως βεβιωκέναι, πορευθέντες ἐπὶ τὸν Ἀχέροντα, ἀναβάντες ἃ δὴ αὐτοῖς ὀχήματά 5
ἐστιν, ἐπὶ τούτων ἀφικνοῦνται εἰς τὴν λίμνην, καὶ ἐκεῖ
οἰκοῦσί τε καὶ καθαιρόμενοι τῶν τε ἀδικημάτων διδόντες
δίκας ἀπολύονται, εἴ τίς τι ἠδίκηκεν, τῶν τε εὐεργεσιῶν
τιμὰς φέρονται κατὰ τὴν ἀξίαν ἕκαστος· οἳ δ' ἂν δόξωσιν e
ἀνιάτως ἔχειν διὰ τὰ μεγέθη τῶν ἁμαρτημάτων, ἢ ἱερο-
συλίας πολλὰς καὶ μεγάλας ἢ φόνους ἀδίκους καὶ παρανόμους
πολλοὺς ἐξειργασμένοι ἢ ἄλλα ὅσα τοιαῦτα τυγχάνει ὄντα,
τούτους δὲ ἡ προσήκουσα μοῖρα ῥίπτει εἰς τὸν Τάρταρον, 5
ὅθεν οὔποτε ἐκβαίνουσιν. οἳ δ' ἂν ἰάσιμα μὲν μεγάλα δὲ
δόξωσιν ἡμαρτηκέναι ἁμαρτήματα, οἷον πρὸς πατέρα ἢ μη-
τέρα ὑπ' ὀργῆς βίαιόν τι πράξαντες, καὶ μεταμέλον αὐτοῖς 114
τὸν ἄλλον βίον βιῶσιν, ἢ ἀνδροφόνοι τοιούτωι τινὶ ἄλλωι
τρόπωι γένωνται, τούτους δὲ ἐμπεσεῖν μὲν εἰς τὸν Τάρταρον
ἀνάγκη, ἐμπεσόντας δὲ αὐτοὺς καὶ ἐνιαυτὸν ἐκεῖ γενομένους
ἐκβάλλει τὸ κῦμα, τοὺς μὲν ἀνδροφόνους κατὰ τὸν Κωκυτόν, 5
τοὺς δὲ πατραλοίας καὶ μητραλοίας κατὰ τὸν Πυριφλεγ-
έθοντα· ἐπειδὰν δὲ φερόμενοι γένωνται κατὰ τὴν λίμνην τὴν
Ἀχερουσιάδα, ἐνταῦθα βοῶσί τε καὶ καλοῦσιν, οἱ μὲν οὓς

c1 λίμνην m t: λίμνην ἣν m t

ἀπέκτειναν, οἱ δὲ οὓς ὕβρισαν, καλέσαντες δ' ἱκετεύουσι
b καὶ δέονται ἐᾶσαι σφᾶς ἐκβῆναι εἰς τὴν λίμνην καὶ δέξασθαι,
καὶ ἐὰν μὲν πείσωσιν, ἐκβαίνουσί τε καὶ λήγουσι τῶν
κακῶν, εἰ δὲ μή, φέρονται αὖθις εἰς τὸν Τάρταρον καὶ
ἐκεῖθεν πάλιν εἰς τοὺς ποταμούς, καὶ ταῦτα πάσχοντες οὐ
5 πρότερον παύονται πρὶν ἂν πείσωσιν οὓς ἠδίκησαν· αὕτη γὰρ
ἡ δίκη ὑπὸ τῶν δικαστῶν αὐτοῖς ἐτάχθη.

οἳ δὲ δὴ ἂν δόξωσι
διαφερόντως πρὸς τὸ ὁσίως βιῶναι, οὗτοί εἰσιν οἱ τῶνδε μὲν
τῶν τόπων τῶν ἐν τῇι γῇι ἐλευθερούμενοί τε καὶ ἀπαλλαττό-
c μενοι ὥσπερ δεσμωτηρίων, ἄνω δὲ εἰς τὴν καθαρὰν οἴκησιν
ἀφικνούμενοι καὶ ἐπὶ γῆς οἰκιζόμενοι. τούτων δὲ αὐτῶν οἱ
φιλοσοφίαι ἱκανῶς καθηράμενοι ἄνευ τε σωμάτων ζῶσι τὸ
παράπαν εἰς τὸν ἔπειτα χρόνον, καὶ εἰς οἰκήσεις ἔτι τούτων
5 καλλίους ἀφικνοῦνται, ἃς οὔτε ῥάιδιον δηλῶσαι οὔτε ὁ χρόνος
ἱκανὸς ἐν τῶι παρόντι. ἀλλὰ τούτων δὴ ἕνεκα χρὴ ὧν διεληλύ-
θαμεν, ὦ Σιμμία, πᾶν ποιεῖν ὥστε ἀρετῆς καὶ φρονήσεως ἐν
τῶι βίωι μετασχεῖν· καλὸν γὰρ τὸ ἆθλον καὶ ἡ ἐλπὶς μεγάλη.

d "τὸ μὲν οὖν ταῦτα διισχυρίσασθαι οὕτως ἔχειν ὡς ἐγὼ
διελήλυθα, οὐ πρέπει νοῦν ἔχοντι ἀνδρί· ὅτι μέντοι ἢ ταῦτ'
ἐστὶν ἢ τοιαῦτ' ἄττα περὶ τὰς ψυχὰς ἡμῶν καὶ τὰς οἰκήσεις,
ἐπείπερ ἀθάνατόν γε ἡ ψυχὴ φαίνεται οὖσα, τοῦτο καὶ
5 πρέπειν μοι δοκεῖ καὶ ἄξιον κινδυνεῦσαι οἰομένωι οὕτως
ἔχειν· καλὸς γὰρ ὁ κίνδυνος, καὶ χρὴ τὰ τοιαῦτα ὥσπερ
ἐπάιδειν ἑαυτῶι, διὸ δὴ ἔγωγε καὶ πάλαι μηκύνω τὸν μῦθον.
ἀλλὰ τούτων δὴ ἕνεκα θαρρεῖν χρὴ περὶ τῆι ἑαυτοῦ ψυχῆι
e ἄνδρα ὅστις ἐν τῶι βίωι τὰς μὲν ἄλλας ἡδονὰς τὰς περὶ τὸ
σῶμα καὶ τοὺς κόσμους εἴασε χαίρειν, ὡς ἀλλοτρίους τε
ὄντας, καὶ πλέον θάτερον ἡγησάμενος ἀπεργάζεσθαι, τὰς δὲ
περὶ τὸ μανθάνειν ἐσπούδασέ τε καὶ κοσμήσας τὴν ψυχὴν
5 οὐκ ἀλλοτρίωι ἀλλὰ τῶι αὐτῆς κόσμωι, σωφροσύνηι τε καὶ
115 δικαιοσύνηι καὶ ἀνδρείαι καὶ ἐλευθερίαι καὶ ἀληθείαι, οὕτω
περιμένει τὴν εἰς Ἅιδου πορείαν ὡς πορευσόμενος ὅταν ἡ
εἱμαρμένη καλῆι. ὑμεῖς μὲν οὖν," ἔφη, "ὦ Σιμμία τε καὶ

a2–3 ὡς . . . καλῆι secl. e (cf. a5–6)

Κέβης καὶ οἱ ἄλλοι, εἰς αὖθις ἔν τινι χρόνωι ἕκαστοι πορεύ-
σεσθε· ἐμὲ δὲ νῦν ἤδη καλεῖ, φαίη ἂν ἀνὴρ τραγικός, ἡ 5
εἱμαρμένη, καὶ σχεδόν τί μοι ὥρα τραπέσθαι πρὸς τὸ λουτρόν·
δοκεῖ γὰρ δὴ βέλτιον εἶναι λουσάμενον πιεῖν τὸ φάρμακον
καὶ μὴ πράγματα ταῖς γυναιξὶ παρέχειν νεκρὸν λούειν."

    ταῦτα δὴ εἰπόντος αὐτοῦ ὁ Κρίτων, "εἶεν," ἔφη, "ὦ b
Σώκρατες· τί δὲ τούτοις ἢ ἐμοὶ ἐπιστέλλεις ἢ περὶ τῶν
παίδων ἢ περὶ ἄλλου του, ὅτι ἄν σοι ποιοῦντες ἡμεῖς ἐν
χάριτι μάλιστα ποιοῖμεν;"

    "ἅπερ ἀεὶ λέγω," ἔφη, "ὦ Κρίτων, οὐδὲν καινότερον· ὅτι 5
ὑμῶν αὐτῶν ἐπιμελούμενοι ὑμεῖς καὶ ἐμοὶ καὶ τοῖς ἐμοῖς
καὶ ὑμῖν αὐτοῖς ἐν χάριτι ποιήσετε ἅττ' ἂν ποιῆτε, κἂν μὴ
νῦν ὁμολογήσητε· ἐὰν δὲ ὑμῶν μὲν αὐτῶν ἀμελῆτε καὶ
μὴ θέλητε ὥσπερ κατ' ἴχνη κατὰ τὰ νῦν τε εἰρημένα
καὶ τὰ ἐν τῶι ἔμπροσθεν χρόνωι ζῆν, οὐδὲ ἐὰν πολλὰ ὁμολο- 10
γήσητε ἐν τῶι παρόντι καὶ σφόδρα, οὐδὲν πλέον ποιήσετε." c

    "ταῦτα μὲν τοίνυν προθυμησόμεθα", ἔφη, "οὕτω ποιεῖν·
θάπτωμεν δέ σε τίνα τρόπον;"

    "ὅπως ἄν", ἔφη, "βούλησθε, ἐάνπερ γε λάβητέ με καὶ
μὴ ἐκφύγω ὑμᾶς." γελάσας δὲ ἅμα ἡσυχῆι καὶ πρὸς ἡμᾶς 5
ἀποβλέψας εἶπεν· "οὐ πείθω, ὦ ἄνδρες, Κρίτωνα, ὡς
ἐγώ εἰμι οὗτος Σωκράτης, ὁ νυνὶ διαλεγόμενος καὶ διατάττων ἕκαστον τῶν λεγομένων, ἀλλ' οἴεταί με ἐκεῖνον εἶναι
ὃν ὄψεται ὀλίγον ὕστερον νεκρόν, καὶ ἐρωτᾶι δὴ πῶς με d
θάπτηι. ὅτι δὲ ἐγὼ πάλαι πολὺν λόγον πεποίημαι, ὡς,
ἐπειδὰν πίω τὸ φάρμακον, οὐκέτι ὑμῖν παραμενῶ, ἀλλ'
οἰχήσομαι ἀπιὼν εἰς μακάρων δή τινας εὐδαιμονίας, ταῦτά
μοι δοκῶ αὐτῶι ἄλλως λέγειν, παραμυθούμενος ἅμα μὲν 5
ὑμᾶς, ἅμα δ' ἐμαυτόν. ἐγγυήσασθε οὖν με πρὸς Κρίτωνα",
ἔφη, "τὴν ἐναντίαν ἐγγύην ἢ ἣν οὗτος πρὸς τοὺς δικαστὰς
ἠγγυᾶτο. οὗτος μὲν γὰρ ἦ μὴν παραμενεῖν· ὑμεῖς δὲ ἦ μὴν
μὴ παραμενεῖν ἐγγυήσασθε ἐπειδὰν ἀποθάνω, ἀλλὰ οἰχή-

e σεσθαι ἀπιόντα, ἵνα Κρίτων ῥᾷον φέρῃ, καὶ μὴ ὁρῶν μου τὸ
σῶμα ἢ καόμενον ἢ κατορυττόμενον ἀγανακτῇ ὑπὲρ ἐμοῦ
ὡς δεινὰ πάσχοντος, μηδὲ λέγῃ ἐν τῇ ταφῇ ὡς ἢ προτίθεται
Σωκράτη ἢ ἐκφέρει ἢ κατορύττει. εὖ γὰρ ἴσθι," ἦ δ' ὅς, "ὦ
5 ἄριστε Κρίτων, τὸ μὴ καλῶς λέγειν οὐ μόνον εἰς αὐτὸ τοῦτο
πλημμελές, ἀλλὰ καὶ κακόν τι ἐμποιεῖ ταῖς ψυχαῖς. ἀλλὰ
θαρρεῖν τε χρὴ καὶ φάναι τοὐμὸν σῶμα θάπτειν, καὶ θάπτειν
116 οὕτως ὅπως ἄν σοι φίλον ᾖ καὶ μάλιστα ἡγῇ νόμιμον εἶναι."

ταῦτ' εἰπὼν ἐκεῖνος μὲν ἀνίστατο εἰς οἴκημά τι ὡς λουσό-
μενος, καὶ ὁ Κρίτων εἵπετο αὐτῷ, ἡμᾶς δ' ἐκέλευε περιμένειν.
περιεμένομεν οὖν πρὸς ἡμᾶς αὐτοὺς διαλεγόμενοι περὶ τῶν
5 εἰρημένων καὶ ἀνασκοποῦντες, τοτὲ δ' αὖ περὶ τῆς συμφορᾶς
διεξιόντες ὅση ἡμῖν γεγονυῖα εἴη, ἀτεχνῶς ἡγούμενοι ὥσπερ
πατρὸς στερηθέντες διάξειν ὀρφανοὶ τὸν ἔπειτα βίον. ἐπειδὴ
b δὲ ἐλούσατο καὶ ἠνέχθη παρ' αὐτὸν τὰ παιδία (δύο γὰρ αὐτῷ
ὑιεῖς σμικροὶ ἦσαν, εἷς δὲ μέγας), καὶ αἱ οἰκεῖαι γυναῖκες
ἀφίκοντο ἐκεῖναι, ἐναντίον τοῦ Κρίτωνος διαλεχθείς τε καὶ
ἐπιστείλας ἄττα ἐβούλετο, τὰς μὲν γυναῖκας καὶ τὰ παιδία
5 ἀπιέναι ἐκέλευσεν, αὐτὸς δὲ ἧκε παρ' ἡμᾶς. καὶ ἦν ἤδη
ἐγγὺς ἡλίου δυσμῶν· χρόνον γὰρ πολὺν διέτριψεν ἔνδον.
ἐλθὼν δ' ἐκαθέζετο λελουμένος καὶ οὐ πολλὰ ἄττα μετὰ
ταῦτα διελέχθη, καὶ ἧκεν ὁ τῶν ἕνδεκα ὑπηρέτης καὶ στὰς
c παρ' αὐτόν, "ὦ Σώκρατες," ἔφη, "οὐ καταγνώσομαί γε σοῦ
ὅπερ ἄλλων καταγιγνώσκω, ὅτι μοι χαλεπαίνουσι καὶ κατα-
ρῶνται ἐπειδὰν αὐτοῖς παραγγείλω πίνειν τὸ φάρμακον
ἀναγκαζόντων τῶν ἀρχόντων. σὲ δὲ ἐγὼ καὶ ἄλλως
5 ἔγνωκα ἐν τούτῳ τῷ χρόνῳ γενναιότατον καὶ πραιότατον
καὶ ἄριστον ἄνδρα ὄντα τῶν πώποτε δεῦρο ἀφικομένων, καὶ
δὴ καὶ νῦν εὖ οἶδ' ὅτι οὐκ ἐμοὶ χαλεπαίνεις, γιγνώσκεις γὰρ
τοὺς αἰτίους, ἀλλὰ ἐκείνοις. νῦν οὖν, οἶσθα γὰρ ἃ ἦλθον
d ἀγγέλλων, χαῖρέ τε καὶ πειρῶ ὡς ῥᾷστα φέρειν τὰ ἀναγκαῖα."
καὶ ἅμα δακρύσας μεταστρεφόμενος ἀπῄει.

καὶ ὁ Σωκράτης ἀναβλέψας πρὸς αὐτόν, "καὶ σύ", ἔφη,

b3 ἐκεῖναι m: ἐκείναις m

"χαῖρε, καὶ ἡμεῖς ταῦτα ποιήσομεν." καὶ ἅμα πρὸς ἡμᾶς, "ὡς ἀστεῖος", ἔφη, "ὁ ἄνθρωπος· καὶ παρὰ πάντα μοι τὸν 5 χρόνον προσῄει καὶ διελέγετο ἐνίοτε καὶ ἦν ἀνδρῶν λῷστος, καὶ νῦν ὡς γενναίως με ἀποδακρύει. ἀλλ᾽ ἄγε δή, ὦ Κρίτων, πειθώμεθα αὐτῶι, καὶ ἐνεγκάτω τις τὸ φάρμακον, εἰ τέτριπται· εἰ δὲ μή, τριψάτω ὁ ἄνθρωπος."

καὶ ὁ Κρίτων, "ἀλλ᾽ οἶμαι", ἔφη, "ἔγωγε, ὦ Σώκρατες, ἔτι e ἥλιον εἶναι ἐπὶ τοῖς ὄρεσιν καὶ οὔπω δεδυκέναι. καὶ ἅμα ἐγὼ οἶδα καὶ ἄλλους πάνυ ὀψὲ πίνοντας, ἐπειδὰν παραγγελθῇ αὐτοῖς, δειπνήσαντάς τε καὶ πιόντας εὖ μάλα, καὶ συγγενο- μένους γ᾽ ἐνίους ὧν ἂν τύχωσιν ἐπιθυμοῦντες. ἀλλὰ μηδὲν 5 ἐπείγου· ἔτι γὰρ ἐγχωρεῖ."

καὶ ὁ Σωκράτης, "εἰκότως γε," ἔφη, "ὦ Κρίτων, ἐκεῖνοί τε ταῦτα ποιοῦσιν, οὓς σὺ λέγεις, οἴονται γὰρ κερδανεῖν ταῦτα ποιήσαντες· καὶ ἔγωγε ταῦτα εἰκότως οὐ ποιήσω· οὐδὲν γὰρ οἶμαι κερδαίνειν ὀλίγον ὕστερον πιών, ἄλλο γε ἢ γέλωτα 117 ὀφλήσειν παρ᾽ ἐμαυτῶι, γλιχόμενος τοῦ ζῆν καὶ φειδόμενος οὐ- δενὸς ἔτι ἐνόντος. ἀλλ᾽ ἴθι, ἔφη, πείθου καὶ μὴ ἄλλως ποίει."

καὶ ὁ Κρίτων ἀκούσας ἔνευσε τῶι παιδὶ πλησίον ἑστῶτι. καὶ ὁ παῖς ἐξελθὼν καὶ συχνὸν χρόνον διατρίψας ἧκεν ἄγων 5 τὸν μέλλοντα δώσειν τὸ φάρμακον, ἐν κύλικι φέροντα τετριμ- μένον. ἰδὼν δὲ ὁ Σωκράτης τὸν ἄνθρωπον, "εἶεν," ἔφη, "ὦ βέλτιστε, σὺ γὰρ τούτων ἐπιστήμων, τί χρὴ ποιεῖν; "

"οὐδὲν ἄλλο", ἔφη, "ἢ πιόντα περιιέναι, ἕως ἄν σου βάρος ἐν τοῖς σκέλεσι γένηται, ἔπειτα κατακεῖσθαι· καὶ οὕτως αὐτὸ b ποιήσει." καὶ ἅμα ὤρεξε τὴν κύλικα τῶι Σωκράτει.

καὶ ὃς λαβὼν καὶ μάλα ἵλεως, ὦ Ἐχέκρατες, οὐδὲν τρέσας οὐδὲ διαφθείρας οὔτε τοῦ χρώματος οὔτε τοῦ προσ- ώπου, ἀλλ᾽ ὥσπερ εἰώθει ταυρηδὸν ὑποβλέψας πρὸς τὸν 5 ἄνθρωπον, "τί λέγεις", ἔφη, "περὶ τοῦδε τοῦ πώματος πρὸς τὸ ἀποσπεῖσαί τινι; ἔξεστιν ἢ οὔ; "

"τοσοῦτον," ἔφη, "ὦ Σώκρατες, τρίβομεν ὅσον οἰόμεθα μέτριον εἶναι πιεῖν."

e8 κερδανεῖν m: κερδαίνειν m   a1 κερδαίνειν m: κερδανεῖν m

c   "μανθάνω," ἦ δ' ὅς· "ἀλλ' εὔχεσθαί γέ που τοῖς θεοῖς ἔξεστί
τε καὶ χρή, τὴν μετοίκησιν τὴν ἐνθένδε ἐκεῖσε εὐτυχῆ γενέ-
σθαι· ἃ δὴ καὶ ἐγὼ εὔχομαί τε καὶ γένοιτο ταύτηι." καὶ ἅμ'
εἰπὼν ταῦτα ἐπισχόμενος καὶ μάλα εὐχερῶς καὶ εὐκόλως
5 ἐξέπιεν. καὶ ἡμῶν οἱ πολλοὶ τέως μὲν ἐπιεικῶς οἷοί τε
ἦσαν κατέχειν τὸ μὴ δακρύειν, ὡς δὲ εἴδομεν πίνοντά τε καὶ
πεπωκότα, οὐκέτι, ἀλλ' ἐμοῦ γε βίαι καὶ αὐτοῦ ἀστακτὶ ἐχώρει
τὰ δάκρυα, ὥστε ἐγκαλυψάμενος ἀπέκλαον ἐμαυτόν· οὐ
γὰρ δὴ ἐκεῖνόν γε, ἀλλὰ τὴν ἐμαυτοῦ τύχην, οἵου ἀνδρὸς
d ἑταίρου ἐστερημένος εἴην. ὁ δὲ Κρίτων ἔτι πρότερος ἐμοῦ,
ἐπειδὴ οὐχ οἷός τ' ἦν κατέχειν τὰ δάκρυα, ἐξανέστη.
Ἀπολλόδωρος δὲ καὶ ἐν τῶι ἔμπροσθεν χρόνωι οὐδὲν ἐπαύετο
δακρύων, καὶ δὴ καὶ τότε ἀναβρυχησάμενος κλάων καὶ
5 ἀγανακτῶν οὐδένα ὅντινα οὐ κατέκλασε τῶν παρόντων πλήν
γε αὐτοῦ Σωκράτους.
    ἐκεῖνος δέ, "οἷα", ἔφη, "ποιεῖτε, ὦ θαυμάσιοι. ἐγὼ μέντοι
οὐχ ἥκιστα τούτου ἕνεκα τὰς γυναῖκας ἀπέπεμψα, ἵνα μὴ
e τοιαῦτα πλημμελοῖεν· καὶ γὰρ ἀκήκοα ὅτι ἐν εὐφημίαι χρὴ
τελευτᾶν. ἀλλ' ἡσυχίαν τε ἄγετε καὶ καρτερεῖτε."
    καὶ ἡμεῖς ἀκούσαντες ἠισχύνθημέν τε καὶ ἐπέσχομεν τοῦ
δακρύειν. ὁ δὲ περιελθών, ἐπειδή οἱ βαρύνεσθαι ἔφη τὰ
5 σκέλη, κατεκλίνη ὕπτιος· οὕτω γὰρ ἐκέλευεν ὁ ἄνθρωπος·
καὶ ἅμα ἐφαπτόμενος αὐτοῦ οὗτος ὁ δοὺς τὸ φάρμακον,
διαλιπὼν χρόνον ἐπεσκόπει τοὺς πόδας καὶ τὰ σκέλη,
κἄπειτα σφόδρα πιέσας αὐτοῦ τὸν πόδα ἤρετο εἰ αἰσθάνοιτο,
118 ὁ δ' οὐκ ἔφη. καὶ μετὰ τοῦτο αὖθις τὰς κνήμας· καὶ ἐπανιὼν
οὕτως ἡμῖν ἐπεδείκνυτο ὅτι ψύχοιτό τε καὶ πηγνῦτο. καὶ
αὐτὸς ἥπτετο καὶ εἶπεν ὅτι, ἐπειδὰν πρὸς τῆι καρδίαι γένηται
αὐτῶι, τότε οἰχήσεται.
5 ἤδη οὖν σχεδόν τι αὐτοῦ ἦν τὰ περὶ τὸ ἦτρον ψυχόμενα,
καὶ ἐκκαλυψάμενος, ἐνεκεκάλυπτο γάρ, εἶπεν, ὃ δὴ τελευταῖον ἐφθέγξατο· "ὦ Κρίτων," ἔφη, "τῶι Ἀσκληπιῶι ὀφείλομεν
ἀλεκτρυόνα· ἀλλὰ ἀπόδοτε καὶ μὴ ἀμελήσητε."
    "ἀλλὰ ταῦτα", ἔφη, "ἔσται," ὁ Κρίτων· "ἀλλ' ὅρα εἴ τι ἄλλο
10 λέγεις."

ταῦτα ἐρομένου αὐτοῦ οὐδὲν ἔτι ἀπεκρίνατο, ἀλλ' ὀλίγον χρόνον διαλιπὼν ἐκινήθη τε καὶ ὁ ἄνθρωπος ἐξεκάλυψεν αὐτόν, καὶ ὃς τὰ ὄμματα ἔστησεν· ἰδὼν δὲ ὁ Κρίτων συνέλαβε τὸ στόμα καὶ τοὺς ὀφθαλμούς.

ἥδε ἡ τελευτή, ὦ Ἐχέκρατες, τοῦ ἑταίρου ἡμῖν ἐγένετο, 15 ἀνδρός, ὡς ἡμεῖς φαῖμεν ἄν, τῶν τότε ὧν ἐπειράθημεν ἀρίστου, καὶ ἄλλως φρονιμωτάτου καὶ δικαιοτάτου.

COMMENTARY

57a1–59c7: introductory conversation

Phaedo, who was present at Socrates' death, is asked by Echecrates, his host in Phlius, where the dialogue is set, to report what the great man said before he died, and how he responded to the occasion. In particular, Echecrates wonders why the execution took place so long after the trial. Phaedo explains, and then goes on to describe the feelings of those who were there, and who they were.

57a2 τὸ φάρμακον: the word means 'drug' or 'potion', whether harmful or beneficial; it could be applied either to a poison (as here) or to a medicine. S.'s death from the hemlock turns out to be similarly ambiguous: at 64a–69e, he suggests that death is not an evil but something better than the human condition (cf. 58e–59a, on the mixed feelings of those present; and 118a7–8n.).   **a6 πῶς ἐτελεύτα;** 'How did he meet his end?' The imperfect suggests the series of events leading up to and including his 'end'. The use of τελευτᾶν, though a quite normal way of referring to death, has a certain irony about it here, at the beginning of a dialogue whose chief conclusion will be just that death is not the end.   **a6–7 καὶ γάρ** 'for in fact' (*GP* 108–9); similarly in 58d5.   **a7 [τῶν πολιτῶν]:** bracketed by some editors as a gloss inserted by a later hand to explain the unfamiliar Φλειασίων. Verdenius defends the transmitted text by treating Φλειασίων as an explanation of τῶν πολιτῶν ('none of the citizens (i.e. my fellow-citizens), the Phliasians, …'); cf. *Meno* 70b οἱ τοῦ σοῦ ἑταίρου … πολῖται Λαρισαῖοι. But the reference to Phlius seems to be the important one. (Phlius was a small city-state in the northern Peloponnese, close to the natural route between Athens and Phaedo's native Elis.)   **οὐδεὶς πάνυ τι** 'hardly anyone'. Others prefer 'absolutely no one', which in a colloquial context comes to much the same thing.   **a8 τὰ νῦν:** as against a few years before, when the Phliasians would have been part of the Peloponnesian forces which regularly invaded Attica. ἐπιχωριάζειν in a7 is used here (and apparently nowhere else) instead of the usual ἐπιδημεῖν (of foreigners 'visiting' a city); but then the 'visits' of the Phliasians were not of the usual kind.   **a8 οὔτε τις ξένος … b3 φράζειν** 'nor has any foreigner arrived from there in a long while (χρόνου συχνοῦ, genitive

of 'time within which') who would have been able to report anything
σαφές about these things, except of course that Socrates died after
drinking poison; of the rest, he was not able to relate anything'. The
Greek is compressed (as is natural enough in a plain conversational
context), but the sense is clear.

b1 σαφές is probably 'clear' (or 'definite', Gallop) rather than 'sure',
'trustworthy' (Burnet): someone who obviously doesn't know about a
thing (and doesn't claim to) is more likely to be described as unclear
than as untrustworthy. Phaedo, Echecrates implies, is a man out of the
ordinary: as indeed his attachment to S., and therefore to philosophy,
already suggests. On the idea of the separation of the philosopher from
the common run of mankind, see esp. 64aff.

58a1 τὰ περὶ τῆς δίκης: the trial itself is of course the subject of another
Platonic work, the *Apology*, which gives us (P.'s version of) S.'s speeches
in his defence, including a long and spirited account of his life's work.
Phd., in effect, continues that account – as, in a different way, does the
Crito – by showing us S. actively continuing to live the same kind of life,
of argument and exhortation, right up until the end (or 'end': cf.
57a6n.). **a3–5 ναί, ταῦτα μὲν ...:** P. thus neatly sidesteps the need
to retell any part of the story which he has told elsewhere, and concen-
trates our attention on a particular – and highly ironical – aspect of it.
The execution of S. turns out to have been so long delayed because of
the need to observe an established religious rule (that no public execu-
tions should take place during the embassy to Delos). The charge on
which S. was condemned was one of impiety – specifically, according
to P.'s version, that he does not believe in the gods the city believes in,
and teaches the young to do the same (*Ap.* 24b–c, with 19b–c). Contrast with that, P. implies, the Athenians' punctilious behaviour in
delaying his execution. Later on, it is S. himself who will explicitly
claim to be the real servant of Apollo, as a philosopher (60d–61b,
85b); and philosophy will turn out to be a kind of 'purification' (65e,
66d, 67a, 67b, 80d, 80e, 82c, 82d, 114c; cf. 69b–d). **a6 τύχη:** τύχη is
either 'luck' (good or bad), or simply 'chance'; here, in view of the
following ἔτυχεν, it is primarily the latter. Gallop, following Loriaux,
discovers in this twin reference to τύχη (τύχη ... ἔτυχεν) 'a hint of
supernatural intervention', pointing to 58e5–6 as supporting evidence.
Divine intervention is certainly more than hinted at in the later pas-

sage; but here Phaedo seems to make a straightforward reference to chance or luck – which might itself have been regarded, at the popular level, as a 'supernatural' force, but would not have implied the involvement of other such forces.   **a6 ἔτυχεν γὰρ ... 8 πέμπουσιν:** i.e. during the festival of the Delia (cf. Xen. *Mem.* 4.8.2), in the Attic month of Anthesterion, which corresponds to our February/March. **a7 πρύμνα ἐστεμμένη:** the first stage of the ritual event (see c1–2). **a8 Ἀθηναῖοι** 'the Athenians': the omission of the article in such cases is perfectly regular.   **a9 τοῦτο δὲ δὴ τί ἐστιν;** Echecrates evidently knows nothing at all about the festival: 'what ship is that (δή)?' For Plato's point in going into detail, see a3–5n., 11n.   **a10 ὥς φασιν Ἀθηναῖοι** suggests a certain scepticism – could the ship that carried Theseus to Crete all those years ago really have survived for so long? (Cf. Plut. *Thes.* 23, who reports that this ship was a standard philosophical illustration of the problem of identity: if all the timbers had been replaced, was it the same ship or not?)   **a11 τοὺς "δὶς ἑπτὰ" ἐκείνους:** the demonstrative ἐκείνους ('those, sc. *well-known* ...'), with the unusual phrase δὶς ἑπτά, indicates that 'the twice seven' is a special expression (traditional: see Bacch. 17.2). Seven young men and seven young women, according to the story, used to be sent annually as tribute to Knossos, where they would be fed to the Minotaur. This detail Phaedo does not report, saying merely, in a vague way, that Theseus 'succeeded in saving both [his companions'] lives and his own' (b1). Thus the whole emphasis is thrown on to Theseus' role as saviour – both of others, as Phaedo says, and of himself, which might suggest a comparison with S.

b1 τῶι οὖν Ἀπόλλωνι ηὔξαντο κτλ.: οὖν is perhaps 'resumptive' (*GP* 428–9): Phaedo now goes back and explains the connection between Theseus' voyage to Crete with the 'twice seven' and the mission to Delos. 'They had vowed (ηὔξαντο: as often in Greek, the aorist is used where we might expect the pluperfect) to Apollo, if they [sc. Theseus and his companions] were saved, to send ...' The subject of the main verb appears to be 'the Athenians [of the time]', which is understood easily enough from Ἀθηναῖοι in a10.   **b3 ἀπάξειν:** ἀπάγειν has the connotation of 'making a return', in this case for favours received.   **b3 ἣν δὴ ... 4 πέμπουσιν** 'and that is the very one (δή again emphatic, as in a9 and 57a5) which they have always sent to the god, from that time (ἐξ ἐκείνου, sc. χρόνου), annually, and still do now'. Phaedo lays elaborate emphasis on the *continuity* of the Athenians' adherence to their vow: cf. a3–5n. **b4 οὖν** in this case seems only to mark a new point in the explanation (*GP* 426: 'proceeding to a new point, or a new stage in the march of thought'); contrast b1 above. **b5–6 καθαρεύειν τὴν πόλιν:** sc. φόνου, 'that the city should be clean [from killing]': cf. e.g. Plut. *Phocion* 37. **b6 καὶ δημοσίαι:** καί is frequently used to add an idea which somehow qualifies or explains the one preceding (not discussed in *GP*, but see LSJ s.v. καί A.I.2, and Verdenius 249); so here δημοσίαι μηδένα ἀποκτεινύναι explains the application of the requirement καθαρεύειν τὴν πόλιν to the particular case. **b7 δεῦρο** 'here', in a somewhat loose sense (since Phaedo is speaking in Phlius). **b8–c1 ὅταν τύχωσιν ...:** as evidently happened on the occasion in question; Phaedo is here describing the general situation, which he then applies at c4–5 (διὰ ταῦτα ...) to S.'s particular case. (τύχωσιν recalls τύχη at the beginning of Phaedo's account, in a6: chance was doubly involved in the sequence of events.)

c4 καί here, according to *GP* (307), is to be taken with what precedes it (διὰ ταῦτα): 'it was just because of these things'. (But it could be emphasising πολύς: 'a *rather long* time'.) **c4–5 πολὺς χρόνος ἐγένετο ... ὁ μεταξὺ τῆς δίκης τε καὶ τοῦ θανάτου** 'there turned out to be a long time for S. in the prison, [I mean] the [time] between his trial and his death'. Phaedo's account ends, neatly enough, by mentioning the central event; and that is what Echecrates wants to know about next – c6 'And what then (connective δή: sc. now that you mention it) about the circumstances of the death itself?' **c7–8 τίνες ... τῶι ἀνδρί** 'who were those who were there with him (τῶι ἀνδρί) of his friends?' ὁ ἀνήρ is frequently used, as here, in place of a demonstrative pronoun (similarly, *pace* Verdenius, at e3). **c8 οὐκ εἴων ... παρεῖναι** 'would the prison authorities not allow [sc. his friends] to be there with him?' I.e. did they persist in preventing his friends from seeing him? **c9 ἐτελεύτα:** for the tense cf. 57a6n. and 58e4.

d1 οὐδαμῶς ... γε 'Not at all; there *were* some people there, and what's more (καὶ ... γε: *GP* 157) a whole lot of them (πολλοί).' Some MSS divide the line between the two speakers, so making ἀλλὰ παρῆσάν τινες into a question by Echecrates. καὶ πολλοί γε would then mean 'yes indeed, a lot of them', with adverbial καί and emphatic γε.

But τινὲς καὶ πολλοί is idiomatic: so at *Gorg.* 455c τινὲς καὶ συχνοί, 'not just a few, but a large number'.   **d2 ταῦτα . . . πάντα:** i.e. τὰ λεχθέντα καὶ πραχθέντα (c7).   **d3 εἰ μὴ . . . οὖσα:** this piece of politeness cancels out the sharpness of the plain (aorist) imperative (προθυμήθητι) in d2, which expresses Echecrates' impatience to have Phaedo's report of S.   **d4 ἀλλὰ σχολάζω γε** 'Well, I *have* leisure', i.e. 'Yes, I *do* have the time.' Both ἀλλά and γε here imply assent: see *GP* 16–17 on ἀλλά and 131 on γε.   **d5–6 καὶ γὰρ . . . ἥδιστον** 'for in fact (καὶ γάρ: see 57a6–7n.) to remember S., whether by speaking myself (acc., agreeing with the implied subject of μεμνῆσθαι, i.e. Phaedo) or by listening to someone else . . .': the nature of Phaedo's attachment to S. becomes more explicit. ἔμοιγε 'for me at any rate', i.e. however anyone else may feel about him.   **d7 ἀλλὰ μήν** 'Well, certainly' (*GP* 343: in this kind of use, ἀλλὰ μήν generally indicates 'a favourable reaction to the previous speaker's words').   **καὶ τοὺς ἀκουσομένους γε:** καί and γε are here to be taken separately – καί is 'also', while γε is 'limiting' (in Echecrates and his friends S. will find others, too, of the same mind, except that on this occasion they can only listen, and not contribute anything themselves).   **d8 ὡς ἂν δύνηι ἀκριβέστατα** 'as accurately as you can'. In fact, there is likely to be rather little which is 'accurate' in *Phd.* as a whole (see Introduction).

e1 καὶ μὴν ἔγωγε . . . 'Well then: my experiences when I was there were extraordinary.' With καὶ μήν, Phaedo accepts Echecrates' challenge (*GP* 355). This account of his personal feelings is the most significant part of the introductory section, setting the tone for the whole dialogue. From all that has been said so far, S.'s death was an occasion of unrelieved tragedy, which brought only grief to his supporters and friends (cf. e2–3). Not so, says Phaedo: grief there was, but also a strange admixture of pleasure, so that we laughed as well as crying. What his listeners are to expect, and we are to expect, is no longer simply a tragedy, but a tragi-comedy (see 57a2n., 115a5–6n.).   **e2–3 οὔτε γὰρ . . . εἰσήιει** 'For neither did pity affect me, as being present at a friend's death.' This denial of his having felt pity for S. (though later he appears to modify this: see 59a1–2n.), together with his explanation, occupies almost half of Phaedo's speech (the second half of the sentence is delayed until 59a3).   **e3 εὐδαίμων γὰρ . . . 59a1 ἄλλος:** Phaedo's explanation is complex. S. (*a*) 'appeared fortunate both in his

manner and in what he said, so fearlessly and nobly did he die'. The
ability to behave so well, Phaedo implies, is something enviable in
itself, and therefore an inappropriate object of pity. But (b) at the same
time, and as a result of (ὥστε, e5) his seeing how S. behaved, 'the
thought occurred to me that not even when going to Hades was he
going without a portion from the gods, but that when he came there
too he would fare well, if ever any man yet did'. What 'occurs to'
(παρίστασθαι) him is to compare S. with the heroes, just because of the
nobility of his death (cf. Soph. OC 1585). **e4 τοῦ τρόπου καὶ τῶν
λόγων:** the genitive is used after εὐδαίμων by an easy analogy with
εὐδαιμονίζειν (Burnet compares Crito 43b πολλάκις ... σε ... ηὐδαι-
μόνισα τοῦ τρόπου – again of S., and of his behaviour in the face of
death). **ὡς ἀδεῶς καὶ γενναίως** '[sc. as I saw] how fearlessly and
nobly'. S. later suggests the view that 'virtue' – if that includes philosophical wisdom – is the primary or sole constituent of εὐδαιμονία
(64a–69d); but all that Phaedo implies here is that courage, and nobility in general, are part of what contributes to it (probably the ordinary
Greek view; see Dover 1974, esp. 161–70.) **e5 παρίστασθαι** is used
here impersonally, with acc. + inf. following (ἐκεῖνον ... ἰέναι): '[so
that] it came to [my] mind that'. Where a consequence is reported as
a fact, we should normally expect to find ὥστε followed by the indicative; this seems to be an exception to the rule. **e5–6 μηδ' εἰς Ἅιδου
... ἰέναι:** i.e. that he would 'have a divine portion' in death just as he
did before it. 'Having a divine portion' is evidently equivalent to 'far-
ing well' in the next clause; a man's good 'fortune' may as well be
attributed to the gods (see e.g. Hom. Il. 24.527–38) as to chance (cf.
58a6n.). The expression 'going to Hades' need not be taken literally;
S., for example, can associate death in general with 'being in Hades'
(e.g. 70c4) while also suggesting rather different destinations for at
least some 'dead' souls (see esp. 114b–c).

59a1–2 οὐδὲν πάνυ ... ἐλεινόν 'almost no pity', rather than 'absolutely no pity' (cf. 57a7n.). Phaedo says that he experienced a mixture
of pleasure and pain (a4–6); the pain occurred 'as I reflected that [S.]
was going to die very shortly' (a6–7). The statement at 58e2–3 is
softened by 59a1–2: it is not that he felt no compassion, rather that he
felt surprisingly little; and that was actually mixed with pleasure. For
ἔλεος as painful, see Phil. 47e. **οὐδὲν ἐλεινόν** = 'no feeling of pity': the

positive (and more familiar) form of the expression would be τὸ ἐλεινόν (which is indistinguishable in meaning from ἔλεος). **a2 ὡς εἰκὸς ... πένθει** 'as would appear to be expected (sc. μοι εἰσιέναι), since I was witness to (παρόντι) misfortune' (πένθος in the sense of what causes grief, rather than the feeling itself). **a3 οὔτε αὖ ... εἰώθεμεν:** οὔτε αὖ ... continues and completes the sentence begun in 58e2–3 (hence οὔτε, answering to οὔτε in 58e2, rather than the οὐδέ we would expect after 59a1 οὐδέν). The 'almost' of 59a1–2 is probably meant to carry over into the present line: 'so I felt almost no pity, and [almost] no pleasure [sc. of the kind I might have expected to feel] because we were philosophising as had been our custom before'. ἐν φιλοσοφίαι ... ὄντων = 'occupied with philosophy'. ὥσπερ εἰώθεμεν: not only before Socrates' trial and sojourn in prison, but evidently even during his imprisonment (cf. 59d). **a4 καὶ γὰρ ... ἦσαν** partly justifies Phaedo's earlier reference to S.'s fearlessness (58e4): not everyone would have the stomach (or the head) for close philosophical argument on such an occasion. **a4 ἀλλ' ἀτεχνῶς ... 7 τελευτᾶν:** he sums up his feelings. What he experienced was a peculiar mix of pleasure and pain, which stemmed from the single reflection about the imminence of S.'s death. That caused him pain; on the other hand, he derived a certain plea-sure from the thought that 'this man here, who is behaving so calmly, is actually about to die'. (It is sometimes suggested that what S. says about pleasure and pain at 60b–c would imply the impossibility of the 'mix' Phaedo describes here: cf. esp. 60b5–6 τὸ ἅμα μὲν αὐτὼ μὴ θέλειν παραγίγνεσθαι τῶι ἀνθρώπωι. But see 60b4n., 5n.) **a5** Note the careful word-order, which emphasises first ἄτοπον, then κρᾶσις (through the promotion of the colourless τις before ἀήθης). For καί, cf. 58b6n. **a8 σχεδόν τι οὕτω** 'pretty much like this'. **τότε ... ἐνίοτε:** for (rhetorical) variation in place of the expected τότε ... τότε. There are other traces of rhetorical artifice in this speech of Phaedo's (see e.g. on a5). This contrasts with the generally conversational style of the introductory section as a whole (the other exception is the simple nar-rative in Phaedo's last long speech, 58a10–c5). The loftier style suits what he has to say. **a9 Ἀπολλόδωρος** is the (fictional) narrator of *Symp.*, where he appears as entirely devoted to Socrates, and also as having the nickname μαλακός (*Symp.* 173d: some MSS have the less probable μανικός). From what is said about him here in *Phd.* (and also at 117d), μαλακός ought to mean 'soft' in the sense of 'weak', 'lacking

in control' (cf. especially *Rep.* 556c, Arist. *Nic. eth.* 1150a33), though
the speaker at *Symp.* 173d at least purports (in a spirit of banter?) to
take it rather in the sense of 'gentle'. At Xen. *Ap.* 28 he is 'passionately
attached to Socrates, but otherwise simple-minded'. Apollodorus' behaviour is a perfect foil to S.'s. In 60a, his role is about to be usurped
by Xanthippe, S.'s wife, when S. abruptly orders Crito to remove her.

b1 οἶσθα γάρ που 'For I suppose (που, softening the assertion) you
know the man and his way': anyone who knew S. evidently also
knew Apollodorus (Xen. *Mem.* 3.11.17).   **b3–4 ἐκεῖνός τε τοίνυν κτλ.**
'Well, he certainly lived up to our expectations, and I myself was in a
state of confusion, and the others too.'   **b5 ἔτυχον κτλ.** 'And who
were those who were there?' τυγχάνω is sometimes used without any
strong connotations of 'chance' or 'coincidence' (cf. LSJ s.v. A.II.1:
'frequently τυγχάνω cannot be translated at all'); so perhaps here,
since it was S.'s friends (58c9) who were with him. On the other hand,
it was chance that P. was kept away by illness (if he was; Phaedo says
only '*I think* P. was ill', b10); and no doubt others, like Aristippus and
Cleombrotus (c3) might have been there.   **b6–c6** Phaedo does not
claim that his list is complete, only that 'those, I think, were *pretty much*
(σχεδόν τι) the people who were there' (c6); and he actually mentions
'some other local people' as present, without naming them (b9–10).
There may be various reasons behind the choice and ordering of those
who are actually named (see b7n. for Critobulus); but there is also a
vagueness about the list which suggests a touch of literary realism. P.'s
own absence is mentioned casually (b10), which might reflect its relative unimportance to Phaedo (see c4n.); it also, paradoxically, reminds
us of his presence as author – while also denying it (after all, he wasn't
even *there*).   **b7 Κριτόβουλος καὶ ὁ πατὴρ αὐτοῦ:** for this pairing of
Critobulus with his father Crito (after whom the dialogue *Crito* is
named), compare *Ap.* 33d–e, where S. is challenging the relatives of
the young men whom he is charged with corrupting to come before the
court and accuse him. Crito and Critobulus head that list too; and the
presence of the two of them together in the prison, both equally his
friends, implicitly refutes any suggestion that Socrates had any case to
answer there. If he had corrupted a young man like Critobulus, surely
his father would have had something to say about it? Of Crito, we
know little beyond what we can deduce from P.'s evidence; D. L. tells

us (2.121) that he provided for S.'s material needs (cf. 115c3n.), wrote seventeen dialogues, and had other sons (called, strikingly, Hermogenes, Epigenes, and Ctesippus: either Crito made a habit of naming sons after other acquaintances of S., or, more likely, D. L. – or his source – has misremembered the present passage). **b7–8 καὶ ἔτι Ἑρμογένης καὶ Ἐπιγένης καὶ Αἰσχίνης καὶ Ἀντισθένης:** Hermogenes (son of Hipponicus, and brother of Callias, who according to *Ap.* 20a 'has paid out more money to sophists than everyone else put together') is one of the speakers in *Crat.* Epigenes' only appearance is in the list of νέοι at *Ap.* 33d–e (see b7n.) – where his father's name is given as Ἀντίφων ὁ Κηφισεύς. Aeschines (son of Lysanias, of the deme Sphettus) also appears in that list, but became better known as one of the more widely recognised writers of Socratic dialogues. Antisthenes is yet another dialogue-writer (according to D. L. 2.64, the Stoic Panaetius (2nd cent. B.C.) thought only four writers' dialogues genuinely 'Socratic': those of Antisthenes, Aeschines, P., and Xenophon). For us he is a shadowy figure, but he was well known in antiquity either as a forerunner or as founder of Cynicism, which in its turn was a major influence on the formation of Stoicism. He would perhaps have been in late middle age at the time of S.'s death. **b9 Κτήσιππος . . . καὶ Μενέξενος:** two more of S.'s younger associates, both of whom appear in the *Lysis*; Ctesippus also figures in the *Euthd.*, while Menexenus has one of the minor Platonic works named after him. **b10 Πλάτων . . . :** on the significance of this, see b6–c6n.

c1 Σιμμίας τέ . . . ὁ Θηβαῖος καὶ Κέβης turn out to be Socrates' two main partners in the conversation in the prison. It is frequently said by commentators that they were Pythagoreans. There is not much evidence for this assertion: they come from Thebes, a centre of Pythagoreanism (cf. *HGP* 1.179); they have 'been with' the Pythagorean Philolaus (*Phd.* 61d6–7); and *Phd.* contains many ideas – e.g. the immortality of the soul, and its transmigration from one body to another – which are echoed in Pythagoreanism (so that to have Pythagoreans actually participating in the conversation would be particularly apposite). But συγγίγνεσθαι (61d7) does not necessarily imply the relationship of pupil and master; Simmias turns out to have heard οὐδὲν . . . σαφές from Philolaus, at least about the subjects in hand (61d8, e8–9); and he later (85e–86d) introduces a model for 'soul' which is

inconsistent with the ideas of immortality and transmigration and unlikely to come from a Pythagorean source. It fits better with the evidence, and suits the dramatic situation just as well, to treat him merely
as a young man who is passionate about argument (more so, according
to *Phdr.* 242b, than any of his contemporaries; cf. *Phd.* 62e–63a, on
Cebes). If he has 'been with' Philolaus, he has also been with S. (see
e.g. 59a3); he would thus have as much right to be called a Socratic as
a Pythagorean – and in fact in *Phd.* he enthusiastically shares S.'s belief
in the existence of 'forms' (74b, 76e–77a, etc.), something which (*pace*
Bluck 6) it would be surprising to find a Pythagorean doing. On 'forms',
see Introduction §5. Arist. *Met.* A 6 suggests that this item of Platonic
'doctrine' – of which (as Arist. himself confirms) the historical S. was
innocent – has its roots in Pythagoreanism; but the connection is fairly
remote, and no contemporary Pythagorean (like Philolaus) would
immediately have welcomed P.'s 'forms' as his own. D. L. certainly
makes no link between Simmias and Pythagoreanism; all he reports on
Simmias is that he wrote (twenty-three, named) dialogues – which
again suggests rather the connection with Socrates. The same reasoning applies to Cebes (author of three dialogues, according to D. L.); cf.
especially 72e3–6.   γε 'adds detail to an assent already expressed' (*GP*
136).   **c2 Φαιδώνδης** is otherwise only known from Xen. *Mem.* 1.2.48,
where he is mentioned as a '[true] associate' of S., along with Simmias
and Cebes (see c1n.) and others. But here as often elsewhere Xenophon probably depends on P.   **Εὐκλείδης τε καὶ Τερψίων** appear
in *Theaet.* (the main conversation in the dialogue, chiefly between
Socrates and Theaetetus, has supposedly been recorded by Eucleides,
and is read out to Terpsion). Eucleides is said to have founded the
Megarian 'school' of philosophy; Terpsion is otherwise unknown.   **c3
Ἀρίστιππος:** according to D. L. this is the Aristippus who founded
the Cyrenaic school; but see c4n.   **Κλεόμβροτος** is another unknown
name, though in one of Callimachus' *Epigrams* (23 Pfeiffer) one Cleombrotus of Ambracia throws himself into the sea after reading the *Phd.*
(see following n.).   **c4 οὐ δῆτα· ἐν Αἰγίνηι γὰρ κτλ.:** it was held in
antiquity (see Burnet) that this line contained a slur on Aristippus,
on the assumption that he was the Cyrenaic; allegedly, the distance
from Aegina would not have been sufficient to constitute a genuine
explanation of his absence (the same interpretation probably explains
Callimachus' story about Cleombrotus). But οὐ δῆτα perhaps rather

suggests a tone of simple surprise: 'No, they *weren't* there; they were said to be in Aegina.' Echecrates has shown that he expects them to be mentioned as among those present, and Phaedo's attitude is the same. If there is any real significance in the mention of their absence, it is perhaps that it makes the previous mention of P.'s own absence as inconspicuous as, dramatically, it should be – to Phaedo, after all, Plato is just another of Socrates' associates.

59c8–64a3: two views of death

Phaedo now begins his full account of what happened in the prison. After describing the scene, he reports a first interchange between Socrates and his friends, the chief effect of which is to stress Socrates' positive attitude towards his impending death.

59d1 γὰρ δή: δή emphasises γάρ, which as often marks the beginning of a promised narrative. **d3 καί** is emphatic: 'in which the trial *itself* [had] occurred'. **d5 ἀνοιχθείη:** the optative (after περιεμένομεν) indicates purpose (contrast d6, of repeated action: '*whenever* it was opened'). **d7 τὰ πολλά** 'for the most part', 'usually'. **d7–8 καὶ δὴ καὶ τότε** 'And on this particular occasion …': i.e. whatever they did on previous occasions, they did with even greater urgency now. **d8 τῆι προτεραίαι [ἡμέραι]:** τῆι προτεραίαι usually occurs without the explicit addition of ἡμέραι.

e2 ἀφιγμένον εἴη 'had arrived', 'was already in port'. **e3 εἰς τὸ εἰωθός:** sc. χωρίον. **e4–5 περιμένειν καὶ μὴ πρότερον παριέναι ἕως …:** after the negative μὴ πρότερον we would have expected πρίν (cf. 62c6–7); but the substance of the order is the positive περιμένειν, and ἕως follows appropriately. **ἂν … κελεύσηι:** P. might have written the optative; ἄν + subjunctive retains the form of the warder's original instruction. **e6 λύουσι:** i.e. from his chains, for the sentence to be carried out (but that will 'free' him in another sense: cf. 62b, 67d). **οἱ ἕνδεκα:** a board of public officials charged with enforcing the penalties of the courts. **e7 ὅπως ἂν … τελευτᾶι** is best treated as a final clause (orders are, after all, given for a purpose); ἄν is sometimes found with the subjunctive in such clauses. **δ' οὖν** probably implies a mild contrast (*GP* 461): 'But in fact he came after only a short time' – literally 'having waited (ἐπέχω in an intransitive sense) for no great time' (οὐ πολὺν χρόνον, accusative of duration of time). **e8 οὖν** logically belongs with εἰσιόντες rather than κατελαμβάνομεν: '[he told us to go in,] so we went in, and as we did we found . . . '

60a2 τὸ παιδίον αὐτοῦ: according to *Ap.* 34d, S. had two sons who were still παιδία, i.e. (probably) under seven (see also *Phd.* 116b); presumably this one was the younger (cf. a7–8n.). **a3 οὖν** 'Well, . . .'; cf. 58b4n. **ἀνηυφήμησε** 'shrieked' (see Burnet). **a4–5 τοιαῦτ' ἄττα εἶπεν, οἷα δὴ εἰώθασιν αἱ γυναῖκες** 'she said some things of just (δή) the sort which women usually do, [to the effect] that . . .' (or 'with the effect of . . .': ὅτι is regularly though illogically followed by direct statement). The dismissive or disparaging note which *GP* (220) finds in δή here would clearly be present even without it. In *Rep.*, P.'s S. suggests that some women may possess the capacity to become rulers; but that is consistent with his accepting the usual Greek view of women – as he does here – as typically emotional rather than rational. **a5 δή** is emphatic ('the *very* last time . . .'). **a7–8 ἀπαγέτω τις αὐτὴν οἴκαδε:** S.'s curt dismissal of the distraught Xanthippe, with his infant son, recalls his refusal at his trial to 'make appeals to the dikasts, with floods of tears, bringing on his infant children to achieve the maximum of pity, and many of his other relatives and his friends besides' (*Ap.* 34c). Here, of course, P. has done just that on his behalf; but the last word goes to S., who will not be pitied. **a9 τινες τῶν τοῦ Κρίτωνος** 'some of Crito's people', i.e. of his slaves? **a9–b1 βοῶσάν τε καὶ κοπτομένην** 'crying out and lamenting', 'crying out in lament'; κόπτεσθαι ('beat oneself', sc. in grief) seems to have come to mean no more than 'grieving', as perhaps at *Rep.* 619c.

b1–2 ἀνακαθιζόμενος εἰς τὴν κλίνην 'sitting up onto (εἰς) the bed', so that both his feet are on it (see 61c–d). Since εἰς implies motion towards something, he was evidently not already on the bed; or perhaps he had been sitting with his feet on the floor (to allow his chains to be removed?). **b3 τρίβων ἅμα** 'as he rubbed [it]'. **b4 τοῦτο ὃ καλοῦσιν οἱ ἄνθρωποι ἡδύ** 'this thing (?state: see c6n.) which people call "pleasant"': in *Rep.* (583b–585a) and in other dialogues the question is raised whether the kind of 'pleasure' referred to here (i.e. the experience of relief from pain, a category which turns out to include virtually all varieties of physical enjoyment) really is pleasant, and not rather an intermediate state which only appears pleasant in contrast to the preceding pain. 'Real' pleasure is something which one enjoys in the absence of any pain, whether antecedent or consequent (*Rep.* 584b). This set of ideas is sufficient to explain most of S.'s present speech (b3–c7), if not quite all of it (see c3n.).   **b5 τὸ δοκοῦν ἐναντίον εἶναι, τὸ λυπηρόν** 'what seems to be [its] opposite, the painful', i.e. the state which people call painful. But there is no indication that they are wrong in their description of *this* state (cf. *Rep.* 584e–585a). What is at issue is whether this painful state is really the opposite of the one they call 'pleasant'; if the latter is not really pleasant, then this is not a genuine instance of the (real) opposition between pleasure and pain. Strictly, then, the present passage has no positive bearing on the later passages which make use of the idea of 'opposites' (70d–72e, 102b–107a).   **τὸ ἅμα κτλ.** 'the fact that …' The construction is loose but intelligible: S. has remarked on the strangeness of the relationship between the two things (αὐτώ, b6: i.e. the painful state, on the one hand, and the (supposedly) pleasant state on the other); he now describes that relationship.   **b6 μὴ θέλειν** 'are not willing', 'refuse'.   **b6–7 ἐὰν δέ τις κτλ.:** it is clear enough that people 'pursue' and try to 'catch' physical pleasure; but there will also be cases where someone could be said to be 'pursuing' pains, e.g. where he or she chooses to submit to a painful operation, which will (they hope) be followed by 'pleasure'. S.'s own experience in a way fits the same pattern: he might be said at least to have chosen the pains of imprisonment – now temporarily relieved – in so far as he had the option of avoiding them (cf. *Cr.*). **b8–c1 ὥσπερ ἐκ μιᾶς κτλ.:** i.e. joined at the head like Siamese twins. This does not cancel out the qualification σχεδόν τι (cf. 59a8) in b7: S. is only describing what the relationship between the two things *is like*: it seems that they are like Siamese twins, because they so often go together.

c2 μῦθον ἂν συνθεῖναι: sc. αὐτόν.   **ὁ θεός:** not God, but whichever god was responsible.   **διαλλάξαι** 'reconcile'.   **c3 πολεμοῦντα:** it is difficult to give any literal sense to this idea except in terms of the general opposition between pleasure and pain – in which case both the two things would after all have to be genuine instances of their kind (see b4n., 5n.). Or perhaps it is sufficient that they *appear* to be opposites: people do in fact pay attention to both of them, and weigh them against each other (cf. 69a) – so that there is a natural 'hostility' between them. It is this common view of them which makes the close connection between them so 'strange'. S. says of his own situation only that 'the pleasant *seems* to have come following [the painful]' (c7).   **c5 ὥσπερ οὖν κτλ.** 'Just as in fact (οὖν: *GP* 422) seems [sc. to be happening] in my own case, too (καί)'.   **c6 ὑπὸ τοῦ δεσμοῦ** 'because of the fetter'.   **τὸ ἀλγεινόν** is presumably equivalent to τὸ λυπηρόν in b5; the reference, here as there, is to the state of feeling pain ('when the pain was in my leg').   **c8 ὑπολαβών** 'taking up [what had been said]'.   **c9 εὖ γ' ἐποίησας κτλ.** 'You do well (emphasised by γε) in reminding me': ἐποίησας represents a type of aorist, often found in tragedy, without specific temporal reference; ἀναμνήσας similarly refers merely to the *fact* of the reminding.   **τοι** is 'designed to arrest the attention' (*GP* 547): 'About those poems ...'

d1 ὧν = τούτων ἅ (attraction of relative pronoun into the case of its antecedent).   **ἐντείνας** 'by putting into verse'. Some prefer to take the verb as meaning 'setting to music'; but (*a*) what he 'made' (i.e. composed, ποιεῖν) were ποιήματα, which implies compositions in verse (cf. *Symp.* 205c); (*b*) Aesop's λόγοι, at least (the first object of ἐντείνας), were presumably in prose. (It may be that S. set them to music as well as putting them into verse, but that is neither said nor – despite e3: see n. – necessarily implied.) It is true that ἐντείνας is also applied to 'the proem to Apollo' (d2), which – if the reference is to an existing work – must already have been in verse. But the 'proem' is probably meant to be S.'s own composition (so Hackforth); in any case 'the proem to Apollo' would hardly be sufficient to identify anyone else's work (even Homer's "προοίμιον" Ἀπόλλωνος is attributed to him by name at Thuc. 3.104). It is bracketed with Aesop's λόγοι as an object of ἐντείνας because it formed the introduction to S.'s versification of Aesop, which he dedicated to his master Apollo (cf. 61b2; 85b). Whether such a work existed, or represents an invention of P.'s, is impossible to say (but see 61b5n.); it clearly has a dramatic function, in emphasising S.'s piety and devotion to his calling (see his reply to Crito here, and 58a1n.).   **d2–3 καὶ ... ἀτὰρ καί** 'both ... and [especially] ...'   **d3 Εὔηνος** is reported at *Ap.* 20b as claiming to teach 'what makes a good man and a good citizen' for the princely sum of five minas; at *Phdr.* 267a he is an inventor of recondite rhetorical devices: 'And must we not give public recognition to that most admirable Parian, Evenus, for being the first to discover "covert allusion" and "indirect praise"?

Some say he also utters "indirect censures" in verse as an aid to memory; he's a clever one.' **d3–4 ὅτι ποτὲ διανοηθείς κτλ.** 'what on earth (ποτε) you had in mind in composing them when you came here [sc. of all places] ...' **d5 εἰ οὖν τί σοι μέλει τοῦ ἔχειν ἐμέ κτλ.** 'So if you care at all (τι) about my having [anything] to reply to Evenus ...' ἀποκρίνασθαι is an 'epexegetic' or explanatory infinitive (as e.g. in 'I gave him water *to wash with*'). **d8 λέγε τοίνυν** 'Well, tell him ...' (*GP* 571). **d8–e1 οὐκ ἐκείνωι κτλ.:** that S.'s tone is heavily ironic would be clear even without the *Phdr.* passage cited above (d3n.); so e.g. in e1, which suggests that he had actually considered the possibility of trying to outdo Evenus ('I knew that that was not easy'). His main target, as always when he is attacking sophists and rhetoricians (cf. especially *Gorg.* 462–6), is Evenus' claim to expertise: 'I did not compose out of a desire to be his ἀντίτεχνος (to rival his τέχνη).'

e2 ἐνυπνίων: ἐνύπνια are '[things which come] in one's sleep'; i.e. dreams, or perhaps rather dream–figures, since they can take on different guises, and speak (e5–6). **τί λέγει** 'what they mean'. **e2–3 ἀφοσιούμενος εἰ ἄρα πολλάκις κτλ.** 'fulfilling my obligation in case, perhaps (πολλάκις), after all (ἄρα), it was this [kind of] μουσική which they were ordering me to make (ποιεῖν)'. 'This kind of μουσική' is μουσική 'as popularly understood' (δημώδη, 61a7), which is strictly either poetry in performance (i.e. sung), or music by itself (as at *Symp.* 205c); but presumably written poems in themselves, i.e. viewed apart from their performance, might also come under the same description. **e4 γὰρ δή:** see 59d1n. **ἄττα = τινα.** **τὸ αὐτὸ ἐνύπνιον:** 'the same', because it said the same things (e6), though it appeared in different guises (e5–6). **e7 ποίει καὶ ἐργάζου:** ἐργάζεσθαι seems to make the instruction more specific: 'create [compose] μουσική, and make it your business'. **γε** 'at least' ('before, at least', contrasting with νῦν δέ, 61a4). **ὅπερ** 'the very thing which'. **e8–61a1 παρακελεύεσθαί τε καὶ ἐπικελεύειν:** as with ποιεῖν and ἐργάζεσθαι in e7, the second verb is narrower in its connotations: παρακελεύεσθαι can be used of exhortation to someone to do something *de novo* (as at 61c2), whereas ἐπικελεύειν, as the immediate sequel shows, here means encouraging someone to *go on* doing something.

61a1–2 καὶ ἐμοί κτλ. 'and [I used to suppose] that the dream was exhorting me in this way [to do] ...' ('in this way', i.e. as those who

cheer on runners do).   **a3 ὡς** 'because I thought that' (followed by
two constructions with gen. abs.) – 'whereas now ...' (a4). For the
Platonic or Socratic conceit that philosophy is the highest, or real, 'art
of the Muses' (μουσική, sc. τέχνη), cf. *Rep.* 548b, *Phdr.* 259b–d.   **a4**
πράττοντος 'practising' (cf. ἐργάζεσθαι, 60e7).   **ἐπειδή** is ambiguous
between 'when' (giving 'now' a precise reference) and 'because' (the
fact that his death was being delayed by the festival of Apollo – traditionally associated with the Muses as patron of the arts – caused him
to reconsider his previous interpretation of the dream: cf. b2–3).   **a6**
εἰ ἄρα πολλάκις: see 60e2–3n.

b1 ποιήσαντα ποιήματα καὶ πειθόμενον 'by having composed poems,
and so (καί: cf. 58b6n.) obeying'.   **b2 οὕτω δή κτλ.** 'It was in this way
(οὕτω), then (δή), that I came first to write [a poem] to the god ...'
(i.e. the proem to Apollo, 60d2).   **b3–4 ὅτι τὸν ποιητὴν δέοι κτλ.**
'that the poet, if he [really] was going to be a poet, had to ...'   **μύθους**
ἀλλ᾽ οὐ λόγους: i.e. the sphere of the poet is fiction rather than (true)
accounts of things (or 'rational arguments'). For this view of the poets,
see *Rep.* 376e–377d; cf. also Arist. *Po.* 1, which classifies e.g. the philosopher Empedocles as a φυσιόλογος rather than a ποιητής, despite the
fact that he composed in verse.   **b5 καὶ αὐτὸς οὐκ ἦ μυθολογικός:**
despite the fact that he has just invented a μῦθος on his own account
(60d). He may perhaps mean that he is incapable of composing μῦθοι
of the kind that poets indulge in (i.e. lightweight ones?); for at d10–e3
he declares himself ready μυθολογεῖν (if only on the basis of what he
has heard, 61d) about what awaits us after death. See e1–2n. The
overall effect of S.'s speech is to *devalue* poetry, at least by comparison
with philosophy. Cf. 95a1–2n.   **b5–6 οὓς προχείρους κτλ.:** lit. 'the
stories which I had to hand, and knew by heart, [i.e.] those of Aesop,
of these I made into poems the ones which I came across first'. καί has
an explanatory function, as at 58b6. Aesop's fables have themselves
been described as λόγοι at 60d1; but λόγος has a broader as well as a
narrower meaning: anything written (or spoken), and as opposed to
μῦθος, as here.   **b8 καὶ ἐρρῶσθαι καί κτλ.** 'and to keep well (i.e. say
'ἔρρωσο' to him; a typical formula e.g. for ending a letter, used in
several of the pseudo–Platonic epistles), and if he has any sense, to
come running after me (διώκειν) as soon as possible'. The joke is made
more subtle by the treatment of death as a kind of emigration (c1

ἄπειμι: cf. 61e1, 67c1, 117c2; *Ap.* 40c–41a). Cebes puts it more straight-
forwardly at d5 (τῶι ἀποθνήισκοντι ἐπέσθαι).

c1 ἄπειμι κτλ. 'I shall be going today, it seems; the Athenians say so.'
Socrates thus belittles the court's verdict as much as he does death
itself. **c2–3 οἷον παρακελεύει κτλ.** 'What a thing to urge on Evenus!'
(more literally, 'What a thing this is that you're urging ...'). **c3
πολλά** 'often'. **c4–5 σχεδὸν οὖν κτλ.** 'So I'm pretty sure (σχεδόν),
from what I've seen (ἐξ ὧν = ἐκ τούτων ὧν), that he won't be the
slightest bit (οὐδ' ὁπωστιοῦν, 'not even in any way at all') willing
to listen to you.' **ἑκὼν εἶναι** is a 'limiting' expression: 'so as to be
willing' (cf. ὡς ἔπος εἰπεῖν, 'so to speak'), i.e. 'willingly'. **c6 τί δέ;**
'What?' (expressing surprise). **φιλόσοφος:** Simmias' reply suggests
(c7 'To me he seems so, at any rate') that Evenus may count as a
φιλόσοφος or 'lover of wisdom' in a broad sense (cf. e.g. *Rep.* 475b τὸν
φιλόσοφον σοφίας φήσομεν ἐπιθυμητὴν εἶναι, οὐ τῆς μέν, τῆς δ' οὐ, ἀλλὰ
πάσης); but as S. later argues at length (63e–69e), and as the question
here in itself implies, his attitude towards death already shows him to
be no philosopher in the true sense (cf. c8–9 πᾶς ὅτωι ἀξίως τούτου
τοῦ πράγματος μέτεστιν). **c8 τοίνυν** 'in that case'. **c8–9 τούτου
τοῦ πράγματος:** i.e. philosophy; cf. 61a4 πράττοντος, with n. **c10 οὐ
... φασι θεμιτὸν εἶναι** 'people say it is not right'. The concept of θέμις
relates to the unwritten laws which are felt to govern human con-
duct, based on custom and/or divine sanction (cf. 62b7–9, *Ap.* 30c–d).
c10–d2 καὶ ἅμα λέγων κτλ.: S.'s change of physical position parallels
a shift in the discussion to more serious matters. The use of the verb
διαλέγεσθαι, which for Plato connotes *philosophical* interchange, marks
the same shift. He is no longer the poet, but the philosopher; someone
who himself fits the description in c8–9.

d3 οὖν: see 58b4n. **d3–4 πῶς τοῦτο λέγεις, ὦ Σώκρατες, τό ... ;**
'How can you say this, Socrates – that ...?' τό + acc. and inf. substitutes for the usual ὅτι-clause. **d4–5 ἐθέλειν δ' ἂν κτλ.** 'but that the
philosopher would be willing to follow the man who is dying', i.e. that
he would, if he were a philosopher worthy of the name: cf. c8–9. ἐθέλειν
... ἂν substitutes in the inf. construction for the opt. + ἂν of the apodosis of the implied condition. As the sequel shows, what surprises
Cebes is (*a*) that S. appears to be accepting a universal prohibition on
suicide, while also proposing that philosophers will want to 'follow the

dying'; and (*b*) the latter proposition itself. (*a*) and (*b*) are dealt with separately: Cebes first asks specifically about the ban on suicide (e5–6); the response which he gets on this then leads him to challenge (*b*) (62c9–e7). But until e5, both (*a*) and (*b*) are in play, since in d9–e7 Socrates anticipates a discussion of 'our sojourn there' (i.e. in 'Hades'), which is strictly entailed only by (*b*); on the other hand, Cebes interprets S.'s question at d6–7 ('Haven't you heard about such things from Philolaus?') as applying to the issue of suicide (e5–7). **d6–7 τί δέ κτλ.:** it is now Socrates' turn to be surprised (τί δέ; as at c6): haven't Cebes and Simmias been with Philolaus (a well-known Pythagorean, who as Cebes tells us at e7 had spent some time at Thebes); and if so, haven't they heard about such things from him? The common deduction from this, that the ideas in question were shared by Philolaus (or were more generally 'Pythagorean'), is unsafe, since what Socrates says is in any case explained by the principle enunciated at c8–9 – Philolaus must, surely, have talked about such things, since (or if) he is a philosopher. In fact, Cebes explicitly says that they heard him saying 'nothing at any rate that was clear' (d8); he had heard him say that one shouldn't kill oneself, but he'd also heard the same from others (e5–8). Nor is there any indication elsewhere in the text that P. wished to attribute either the ban on suicide or the idea about the proper philosophical attitude to death specifically to Philolaus: the first is introduced by means of the wholly indefinite 'they say' (c10; see also 62b2–3), the second as a proposition of S.'s own (c8–9). **d8 σαφές** 'clear', i.e. 'well–defined' (as at 57b1). **d9 ἀλλὰ μήν** is strongly adversative (contrast 58d7): 'but [in case you think I am any different] I too (καί) . . . ' **ἐξ ἀκοῆς . . . λέγω:** disingenuous, since at least a large part of what he will have to say about the subjects in hand (περὶ αὐτῶν = περὶ τῶν τοιούτων, d6–7) is not likely to have been said before. There is also probably much in it that is Platonic rather than Socratic – which, if true, would give an extra dimension to the disclaimer. But it is in any case characteristic of P.'s S. to claim no special authority for his statements, as indeed it must be if he is to remain at all recognisable as the man who declares that he knows nothing except his ignorance (see esp. *Ap.* 21d). **d9–10 μὲν οὖν:** μέν may best be treated as the so-called 'solitary' μέν, implying a contrast with a second idea which is not expressed, nor even perhaps clearly defined (*GP* 380); 'what I happen to have heard, . . . [but as for the rest . . .]'. οὖν is loosely inferential: 'so what I [merely] happen to have heard, I don't grudge telling you' (φθόνος οὐδείς, sc. ἐστι, is equivalent to οὐ(δὲν) φθονῶ, and borrows its inf. construction).   **διο καὶ γὰρ ἴσως** 'In fact, it may be that ...'

ει καὶ μάλιστα: καί emphasises μάλιστα.   **μέλλοντα:** sc. τινα.   **ἐκεῖσε** (as often) 'to Hades' (cf. 58e5–6, where the two expressions are used in parallel); or rather, as said by S., 'to the place where the dead go, which people call Hades' (cf. 58e5–6n.).   **ἀποδημεῖν** 'go abroad', 'make a journey': on the significance of this choice of term, see on e4.   **ει–2 διασκοπεῖν τε καὶ μυθολογεῖν:** a virtual oxymoron. μυθολογεῖν here either literally means 'telling stories', or, more likely, compares the business of discussion to story-telling (cf. e.g. διαμυθολόγωμεν, 70b6; διαμυθολογῆσαι πρὸς ἀλλήλους, *Ap.* 39e; and μυθολογεῖν at *Phdr.* 276b). The metaphor is not dead (as suggested e.g. by LSJ), and especially not in connection with a subject like the present one, which may only be describable in imaginative terms (note e2–3 ποιάν τινα αὐτὴν οἰόμεθα εἶναι, 'what sort of [sojourn] we *think* it to be'). This is Socrates' point here: what could a 'detailed examination' of 'Hades', by the living, amount to except a kind of telling of tales? But see further 70b6n.   **ε2 τῆς ἀποδημίας τῆς ἐκεῖ:** ἀποδημία can refer either to the travel itself which takes one abroad, or to the sojourn at the end of it; ἐκεῖ (contrasting with ἐκεῖσε in ε1) shows that the latter is meant. S. here points forward primarily to his 'defence' at 64a–69e, where he explains what he thinks the state of death is like (since he alleges that philosophers practise it).   **ποιὰν τινά** 'what sort of one [i.e. sojourn]'.   **ε3 τί . . . ἄν τις καὶ ποιοῖ ἄλλο . . . ;** 'what else *could* (καί emphasising ποιοῖ: cf. *GP* 313–14) a man do ...?' The position of ἄν (promoted from its natural position after ποιοῖ) contributes to the same effect.   **ε4 ἡλίου δυσμῶν** 'sunset', when (appropriately) the execution would take place. As in his description of death as an ἀποδημία, S.'s language – which in anyone else's mouth might be euphemistic or even sentimental – has the effect of playing down the significance of what is happening to him: this day, he implies, is like any other, when a person has to decide how to occupy the daylight hours (contrast 63d3–e7, where the ordinary man's view of the situation intrudes).   **ε5–6 κατὰ τί δὴ οὖν ποτε οὔ φασι . . . ;** 'Why then (δή, reinforced by οὖν) *do* (ποτε, further intensifying the question) they say ...?' Cebes repeats the question he put at d3–5, which S. has not yet answered. In so far as it repeats that question, it carries the same limitation: 'Why do they say suicide is wrong, if there are circumstances [as you suggest] under which it would appear to be the appropriate thing to do?' **e6–8 ἤδη . . . καὶ Φιλολάου ἤκουσα . . . , ἤδη δὲ καὶ ἄλλων τινῶν, ὡς . . .** 'Actually (ἤδη) I *did* (καί¹, emphatic) hear Philolaus, and actually some others too (καί²), saying that . . .' The second ἤδη gives ἄλλων τινῶν the same weight as Φιλολάου: 'not only did I hear it from Philolaus, but what's more I heard it from others too'. **ἔγωγε** gives still further stress to ἤκουσα. **ὅπερ νυνδὴ σὺ ἤρου** '[to answer] the question which *you* asked me'. **e8–9 περὶ αὐτῶν:** see e5–6. **e9 οὐδένος** '[I have not heard anything clear] from anyone.'

62a1 τάχα . . . ἂν καὶ ἀκούσαις 'perhaps you *may* hear' (sc. something σαφές). **a2 ἴσως . . . 7 εὐεργέτην:** this difficult sentence has been much discussed; for a convenient summary of different interpretations, see Gallop 79–83. The sentence as a whole is best taken as an articulation of Cebes' position, without any implications for S.'s own beliefs. Cebes is supposed to find two propositions surprising ('a matter of wonder', θαυμαστόν: a2, 5): (*a*) that death is never better for any human being than life (a3–5), as a rule which holds, unusually, without exception (a2–3, 4); and (*b*) that for those for whom death is better (if such people exist), it is wrong for them to bring about this result for themselves (a5–7). This generally represents a legitimate working-out of the main part of Cebes' original question (see 61d4–5n.), although S. has slightly modified it, at least in respect to (*a*) (hence his use of the future φανεῖται in a2), in order to take account of the fact that Cebes has not yet accepted the particular claim that death is better for *philosophers*; the issue about suicide is presented instead in terms of the general idea, which Cebes certainly will accept, that death is better for *some* people. The reason why that idea is put in so convoluted a form ('you may find it surprising if it is false that . . .') may be that when beginning the sentence P. already had (*b*) in mind, which contains its real substance, and where the construction θαυμαστόν . . . εἰ is more appropriate. **a2 θαυμαστόν . . . εἰ** is in principle ambiguous between 'surprising if' (i.e. questionable whether) and 'surprising that'; here the first is meant (see preceding n.). **τοῦτο** 'this', looking forward to what immediately follows. Burnet comments 'If we must say what

τοῦτο means, it will be τὸ βέλτιον εἶναι ζῆν ἢ τεθνάναι, but the pronoun is really anticipatory and only acquires a definite meaning as
the sentence proceeds.' **a2–3 μόνον τῶν ἄλλων ἁπάντων:** a regular,
though apparently illogical, use of ἄλλος ('a contamination of "this
alone of all things" and "this as distinct from other things"', Verdenius). **a3 ἁπλοῦν** 'simple', i.e. 'true without qualification' ('this'
will be ἁπλοῦν if death is *never* better than life: a3–5). **a3–5 οὐδέποτε
τυγχάνει κτλ.** 'it never happens, as it does in all other cases, that
sometimes and for some people (ἔστιν ὅτε and [ἔστιν] οἷς are independent expressions, not affecting the syntax) it is better for man [i.e. for
any member of the species] τεθνάναι (see on a5 below) than ζῆν.' 'As it
does in all other cases': literally 'as there does in respect to everything
else' (τἆλλα, acc. 'of respect'), i.e. as in every other case things which
we do not normally choose *will* sometimes turn out to be preferable.
(καί is regularly found after ὥσπερ, as here, but is more intelligible
where a positive comparison is being made, as at c8: cf. *GP* 296.) After
οὐδέποτε, ἔστιν ὅτε καὶ οἷς reads oddly, but is perhaps suggested by the
intervening reference to those cases where the qualifications 'sometimes, for some people' do apply. It is clear enough that S. means
'never, and for no one, is it true that ...' Burnet (following Heindorf)
inserts ὄν after βέλτιον; but the participle of εἶναι is sometimes omitted
with τυγχάνω, and the addition hardly improves the sentence.
a5 τεθνάναι: either (*a*) 'to be dead', or (*b*) 'to die'. In the first
case, the perfect infinitive will be referring to the *state* of being dead
(as in 'Fred's dead', i.e. 'is no more'); in the second, it will refer to
the fact of death, viewed as the completion of the process of dying
('Fred has died'). The sense (*b*) is probably the more appropriate in
the context (as it certainly is at c3): the ordinary sense of 'he'd be
better off dead' would be 'he'd be better off if he ceased living'. But in
the special case of the philosopher, (*a*) will fit as much as (*b*), in so far
as the claim will be that death is preferable for him because of the
benefits he will enjoy after it. **a6 ὅσιον** here functions as a synonym
of θεμιτόν. **αὑτούς** ought logically to agree with τούτοις τοῖς ἀνθρώποις ('... not right for these men themselves to kill themselves'); but
the same factor which explains its juxtaposition to ἑαυτούς – the extra
emphasis achieved by the repetition of the same sound – also naturally
leads to its attraction into the same case **a8 ἠρέμα ἐπιγελάσας ...
ἔφη** 'said with a chuckle'. **ἴττω Ζεύς:** ἴττω is the Boeotian form (τῆι

αὐτοῦ φωνῆι εἰπών) corresponding to Attic ἴστω; cf. Ar. *Ach.* 911 ἴττω Δεύς, said by a Boeotian. The literal meaning of the expression is 'let Zeus be my witness' (Burnet); as a US visitor to Britain might say, 'you better believe it'.

b1 καὶ γάρ 'Yes, [it would certainly seem ...]': cf. *GP* 109. **οὕτω γ'** 'put like that, at least (γε)'. **b2 οὐ μέντοι ἀλλ' ἴσως γ' ἔχει τινὰ λόγον** 'but nevertheless (οὐ μέντοι ἀλλά) it perhaps *does* have ('intensive' γε: cf. *GP* 30, 405, 409) a certain reasonableness about it' (i.e. it is not entirely ἄλογον, if seen in a different way: cf. c6–7). **μὲν οὖν:** μέν signals a contrast (between the idea in b3–5 and that in b7–9), and is answered by οὐ μέντοι ἀλλά in b6; for οὖν, see on 58b4. **b3 ἐν ἀπορρήτοις:** sc. λόγοις, in the sense of 'writings'; by contrast λόγος in ὁ ... λεγόμενος ... λόγος means no more than 'thing said'. To ask which writings are being referred to is useless – and indeed part of the point of saying that they are 'secret' or 'forbidden' may be just to block the question; it is not beyond P. to invent sources for ideas which he needs for his own purposes (as he certainly does at e.g. *Phdr.* 252b). See further on b3–5 ὡς ἔν τινι φρουρᾶι κτλ. **περὶ αὐτῶν:** as at 61d9 and e8–9 ('about the subjects in hand'). **b3–5 ὡς ἔν τινι φρουρᾶι ἐσμεν κτλ.:** the word φρουρά can mean either 'prison' (as at *Gorg.* 525a) or 'guard-duty' (cf. e.g. *Laws* 762b); but given that the scene is set in a prison, that the speaker is a prisoner, and that λύειν has been used of freeing him from his chains (at 59e6 and 60a1), the first sense is more likely. *Crat.* 400c attributes to οἱ ἀμφὶ Ὀρφέα the notion that the body is a kind of prison (δεσμωτήριον) of the soul, and S. makes use of a similar notion later in *Phd.* (see 67d1–2, 81e2, 92a1). Here, because the concept of the opposition between soul and body has not yet come to the surface, he merely hints at it, dismissing it (for the moment) as 'lofty and not easy to see through [i.e. penetrate]' (b5–6). The choice of the slightly unusual word φρουρά may be a way of avoiding the obvious difficulty that he is himself not just in 'a sort of' prison but in a real one; though the parallel with his own case (especially as described in the *Crito*) is certainly intended. If this interpretation is right, then the 'secret' doctrine is an adapted version of something P. elsewhere claims to have discovered in Orphism. On Orphism, and its connections with Pythagoreanism, see Dodds's commentary on *Gorgias*, 297–298, 300, 373–376; and Burkert 1985, 296–304. **b6 οὐ**

μέντοι ἀλλὰ τόδε γε 'but nevertheless this much [seems acceptable]' (for the particles, see on b2). This implies that the idea which S. is now about to introduce bears at least some relation to the one just set aside. From a modern point of view, being in prison is not obviously consistent with the concept of divine providence (b7); but if our imprisonment is divinely ordained (as it presumably is according to 'Orphic' doctrine), and the gods are good, it must be deserved, and deserved punishment, in the view of P.'s S. (see e.g. *Gorg.* 476d–477a), is beneficial (as indeed even undeserved punishment is, in his case). **b7 τὸ θεοὺς εἶναι ἡμῶν τοὺς ἐπιμελουμένους** 'that it is [the] gods (cf. τοῖς θεοῖς in b8) who are the ones who look after us'. For the construction, see 61d3–4n. **b7–8 καὶ ἡμᾶς κτλ.** explains the way in which the gods care for us: as part of their 'possessions' (κτήματα). The sequel (cf. e.g. d7 ἐλεύθερος γενόμενος; d9–e1 φευκτέον ἀπὸ τοῦ δεσπότου) shows that this identifies us as the slaves of the gods. That is not P.'s usual view: cf. e.g. the episode of the dream at 60d–61b.

c1 οὔκουν . . . καὶ σὺ ἄν . . . ; 'Wouldn't you too . . . ?' The MSS read οὐκοῦν ('Well then, you too would . . . ?'), but the sense clearly demands something stronger and livelier ('Well, wouldn't you . . . ?'), which is provided by οὔκουν: see *GP* 432–3. ἄν anticipates (χαλεπαίνοις) ἄν in c3, giving an early indication of the hypothetical nature of the question. **c2 ἀποκτεινύοι** 'were to kill itself'. **μή** gives a conditional sense to the participle ('if you hadn't indicated . . .'). **c3 τεθνάναι** 'to die' (see on a5). **c3–4 εἴ τινα ἔχοις τιμωρίαν:** a truly 'remote' condition; the slave would in fact be beyond the reach of any punishment (as we, if we killed ourselves, would not: the idea of punishment figures, if somewhat fitfully, in the traditional Greek view of Hades: cf. Tantalus, Sisyphus). **c6–8** Since this conclusion (τοίνυν) about suicide is based (*a*) on an analogy, and (*b*) on a description of the relationship between men and gods which P. himself can at best regard as only partially true (see b7–8n.), it is scarcely well supported. But since it is anyway both commonsensical and humane (see c8n.), that hardly matters. **c6 οὐκ ἄλογον:** sc. ἐστί, followed by acc. (τινα is to be supplied) + inf. **c7 πρὶν ἀνάγκην τινα θεὸς ἐπιπέμψηι** 'until [the] god (or 'the gods': the reference is the same as that of θεούς in b7 and τοῖς θεοῖς in b8; cf. d2) sends some necessity', i.e. until he/they bring about circumstances which make it absolutely unavoidable.

(That the gods 'bring about' what happens to us will be true, if we are their slaves.) Some editors insert ἄν before ἀνάγκην, but the construction is sometimes found without ἄν; see LSJ s.v. πρίν II.2.a.   **c8 ὥσπερ καὶ κτλ.:** καί here, according to *GP* (296), implies a reference to 'other, unspecified, examples' – 'like [to name one example *in addition to* others which I might have mentioned] the one which is before us (i.e. me: plural for singular)'. But the only clear sense in which S. is or will be 'killing himself' is that he will willingly take the cup of poison from the prison warder and drink it; and it is hard to think of other cases where quite so strong a 'necessity' would be in question. *Laws* 873c, however, implies that 'killing oneself' should be treated as legitimate in three cases: (*a*) if the penalty has been imposed by the city; (*b*) if someone has met with extreme misfortune; and (*c*) if he has intolerably disgraced himself. Case (*a*) would be a matter of human, not divine, responsibility; but case (*b*) could reasonably be treated as fitting the general description 'necessity sent by god'. S. certainly cannot be referring to the 'divine mission' he describes in *Ap.*, since it was not *forced* on him (cf. especially 28b–d).   **c9 ἀλλ' εἰκός κτλ.** 'This much at least (γε) seems likely' (i.e. what you've just said). ἀλλά here indicates assent (*GP* 19).   **c9 ὃ μέντοι ..., 10 τὸ τοὺς φιλοσόφους ..., d1 ἔοικεν τοῦτο ...** 'But what you said just now, [namely] that ..., this ...'   **c10 τὸ ... ἐθέλειν:** see 61d4–5n.   **ῥαιδίως:** 'easily', i.e. 'lightly', 'without complaint'.

d1 ἀποθνήισκειν: see a5n.   **ἔοικεν ... ἀτόπωι** 'resembles [something] odd', i.e. seems odd.   **d3–6 τὸ ... μὴ ἀγανακτεῖν τοὺς φρονιμωτάτους κτλ.** is the grammatical subject of d6 (οὐκ) ἔχει: 'that the most intelligent people (i.e. the philosophers) should not complain ... is unreasonable'.   **d4 ἀγανακτεῖν** contrasts with ῥαιδίως: 'that [philosophers] should not [rather] complain ...'   **d5–6 ἄριστοι ... τῶν ὄντων:** either 'best of [all the beings] there are', or 'best of [all the overseers] there are'.   **d6 θεοί** is in apposition to the subject of the preceding relative clause: 'those who ..., i.e. [the] gods'.   **d6–7 οὐ γάρ που κτλ.** 'for I don't suppose [sc. anyone] thinks he will look after *himself* (γε emphasising αὐτός) better once he has become free'. που is frequently used to qualify one's assertion of a proposition (as at e3, and at 59b1); here it has an ironic tone ('I don't suppose', i.e. no one could possibly think: 'litotes').   **d8 ἀλλ' ἀνόητος μὲν ἄνθρωπος ...** 'But a

mindless person …', contrasting with ὁ δὲ νοῦν ἔχων … in e3. **d8**
φευκτέον … 9 δεσπότου 'that he must escape from his master', as any
slave might.

e1 λογίζοιτο 'calculate'. **e1–2 ἀπό γε τοῦ ἀγαθοῦ** 'from the *good*
[master]'. **διό** 'and so'. **e3 που:** see d6–7n. **e4 εἶναι παρά** 'be
with'. **καίτοι οὕτως** 'And yet in this way', i.e. 'if this is so'. **e5
τοὐναντίον εἶναι εἰκὸς ἤ** 'it is likely (εἰκός, sc. ἐστι) that it is the opposite of'. **e8 οὖν** is again 'progressive' (58b4n.).

63a1 πραγματεῖαι 'diligence' (cf. πραγματεύομαι at 99d1). **τοι** 'you
see' (see 60c9n.). The tone is well caught by Gallop's 'There goes
Cebes, always …' Cebes' objection is fair, if put in a somewhat long-
winded way, and S. does eventually answer it in b6–7, by suggesting
that death merely means exchanging one set of gods for another. (But
in that case the analogy with the slave ceases to work: the slave who
kills himself is just a corpse, and useless to any master – which is of
course why his master is angry about his dying: 62c1–4.) **a2 λόγους
τινὰς ἀνερευνᾶι** 'sniffs out some argument or other'. **a2–3 οὐ πάνυ
εὐθέως ἐθέλει πείθεσθαι** 'he's not at all (οὐ πάνυ: see 57a7n.) willing
to believe at once …' The same might equally be said of Simmias,
who leaps immediately to Cebes' defence (a4–9). This light charac-
terisation of the two Thebans prepares the way for the important con-
tribution which both will later make to the main discussion which
begins at 69e. **a4 ἀλλὰ μήν … νῦν γε** 'And yet on this occasion, at
least'. (For ἀλλὰ μήν, see 61d9n.) **a4–5 μοι … καὶ αὐτῶι:** i.e. καὶ
ἐμαυτῶι. **a5 τι … λέγειν** 'to be talking sense'. **a5 τί γάρ … 6
φεύγοιεν** 'for why (τί βουλόμενοι, 'wanting what') would men who are
truly wise [i.e. if they are] try to escape masters better than themselves?' For the early placing of ἄν, see 62c1n. **a7 ῥαιδίως:** as at
62c10. **ἀπαλλάττοιντο αὐτῶν** 'rid themselves of them'. **a8 τείνειν**
'aim', as of a weapon.

b2 πρὸς ταῦτα: i.e. against the charge that I am going too lightly, with
too little complaint. **b3 μὲν οὖν:** not as at 61d9–10 or 62b2, but (as
a combination) indicating strong agreement (*GP* 476–7). **b4 φέρε
δή** 'Come then', 'Well then'. **πειραθῶ** 'let me try': 'hortative' subj.
πιθανώτερον: because of course on that occasion his defence failed.
b5 γάρ: see 59d1n. **b6 εἰ … μὴ ὤιμην** 'if I did not [now] think [as

I in fact do]'. **πρῶτον μέν:** in a logical rather than a temporal sense (answered by ἔπειτα καί, 'then too', in b7); virtually equivalent to 'not only [but also]'. **b7 ἄλλους:** they must be 'other', because according to the idea which is currently in play, death means leaving (some) gods behind (those who are our 'masters'); and as it happens the traditional view assigns a separate set of gods to the underworld (the 'chthonian' deities). But P.'s S. is a radical theologian (see esp. *Euth.*), and it is always an open question how much of the traditional views he accepts – which may not be the same as what he assents to for the sake of the argument. See further 81a8–9n. **b8 τετελευτηκότας** 'who are dead' (cf. on 62a5). **ἀμείνους τῶν ἐνθάδε:** this hardly answers Simmias' point, which was about the lightness with which S. seemed to be treating the prospect of leaving his *friends*; but the incident with Xanthippe (60a–b) has already shown that sentiment has little part to play in his attitude. That attitude is perhaps consistent with the arid view of love and friendship which we find in *Symp.*: that we love someone not – as we might say – for himself or herself (as an individual), but rather for what is good about him or her (since only what is good is lovable); and that therefore if we find the latter qualities in greater abundance elsewhere, then the true, philosophical, friend or lover will shift his attentions there. (But at c1 Socrates softens his position: he expects merely to meet good men after death; at 69e1–2, similarly, he thinks that 'there too' he will meet with good masters and companions (ἑταῖροι), *no less* than here.) **b8–9 ἠδίκουν ἂν οὐκ ἀγανακτῶν** 'I would be doing wrong in not complaining' (or 'feeling resentment'). **b9 νῦν δέ** 'but as things are' (contrasting with b6 εἰ μέν). **b9 εὖ ἴστε … c4 καὶ τοῦτο:** having begun as if he were going to say 'be sure that I expect (ἐλπίζω) to arrive to join the company of *both* (τε) good men *and* gods who are good' (cf. b6–8), S. changes his mind, and qualifies his assertion of the first point in comparison with the second (καὶ τοῦτο μέν … οὐκ ἂν διισχυρισαίμην, answered by ὅτι μέντοι …, διισχυρισαίμην ἂν καὶ τοῦτο – incidentally, an almost perfect chiasmus (*AB:BA*), despite the apparently chaotic beginning). Cf. Loriaux. καί in c1 is the simple connective; in c4 it is emphatic ('this I *would* maintain'). οὐχ … πάνυ (c1–2) means 'not absolutely' – but this time (contrast 63a2) in a quite straightforward and literal sense ('I would maintain it, but not without qualification'). In c2, ἐλπίζω is easily understood (from c1) in the ὅτι-clause.

c3 εἴπερ τι ἄλλο τῶν τοιούτων: sc. διισχυρισαίμην ἄν. 'Such things' are perhaps 'things to do with the subject of death' (cf. 61d6–e4). **c4 οὐχ ὁμοίως:** i.e. not as much as he would have done if he had not had the expectations he has just described. That he should after all feel *some* resentment (contrast b9 οὐκ ἀγανακτῶν) is appropriate enough; if he felt none, that would imply certainty on his part about what death means, and what he has just said falls far short of that (as he repeats in c5, it is a matter of ἐλπίς, which differs from 'faith' in that it allows room for doubt). **c5 εἶναί τι τοῖς τετελευτηκόσι:** i.e. that death is not the end (cf. 91b3). **c6 ὥσπερ γε καὶ πάλαι λέγεται:** γε is 'limiting' ('as has long been said – in so far as one can rely on that'), while καί perhaps emphasises πάλαι ('it's a *long*-established idea'). It is a traditional notion that different people suffer different fates after death, some being punished (cf. 62c3–4n.), others being translated to the Isles of the Blest. It is by no means clear that the distinction relates directly to moral worth, as S. suggests (Menelaus, for example, seems to have joined the elect because he married a daughter of Zeus: Hom. *Od.* 4.561–4, Hes. *WD* 166–71); but it is probably sufficient here (*a*) that, traditionally, the fate of outstanding figures was (or could be) determined by their 'worth' (however measured), and (*b*) that S. measures worth exclusively according to one's degree of ἀρετή ('goodness') and κακία. But these terms are ambiguous: if for S. ἀρετή means 'moral excellence', in a non-Platonic context (e.g. in Hom.) it may also have connotations of social status. **c8 τί οὖν . . . ;** 'Well then?' (Are you going to tell us about it, as you promised, or not?) **αὐτὸς ἔχων** 'keeping it to yourself' (see LSJ s.v. ἔχειν A.II.11). **c8–9 τὴν διάνοιαν ταύτην** 'this thought': i.e. about how it is better for the good man to die. The original question (62c–d) related to the philosopher: S. will justify the identification of the two categories (good man and philosopher) only later, at 68c–69d; but since the present context refers to him, and he clearly fits both descriptions, there is no real awkwardness involved. **c9 κἄν** = καὶ ἄν: καί stresses ἡμῖν (or the whole of ἂν ἡμῖν μεταδοίης); and the position of ἄν adds further emphasis (see 61e3n.). The opt. with ἄν expresses what amounts to a polite (though in the context fairly insistent) request.

d1 κοινὸν . . . τοῦτο 'For it seems to me that this is a good which is common to us too' (δή stresses κοινόν, as καί does ἡμῖν). 'This' is either the benefit implicitly referred to in c6–7, or, more likely, S.'s thought, which 'belongs to' everyone in so far as it has universal relevance (if death treats the good more kindly than the bad, that is something all of us should know about). **d1–2 καὶ ἅμα σοι ἡ ἀπολογία ἔσται** 'and at the same time you will have your defence', i.e. the one you have proposed to give. **d2 ἐὰν κτλ.:** cf. a2–5. **d3 Κρίτωνα τόνδε** 'Crito here', 'our friend Crito'. The subject of the relative clause in the following indirect question ('what it is that [Crito] seems . . .') is given prominence by being extracted from its clause and put early in the sentence, as the object (illogically) of σκεψώμεθα; the effect is similar to 'But before that (πρῶτον), what about Crito? Shouldn't we find out what it is . . .?' **d4 βούλεσθαι:** present infinitive, because he has been wanting to say it, and still is. **πάλαι** 'for some time'. **d5 τί δέ . . . ἄλλο γε ἤ . . .** 'And what *else* [would I be trying to say] except [that] . . .', said with more than a hint of exasperation (note πάλαι μοι λέγει, which ironically echoes S.'s πάλαι εἰπεῖν at d4): S. knows perfectly well that the prison official has been trying to intervene and stop him talking. **d7 φράζειν** 'instruct'. **ὡς ἐλάχιστα διαλέγεσθαι:** this, for the Platonic S., would mean 'philosophising as little as possible' (since dialogue or dialectic is the medium of philosophy: cf. 61c10–d2n., and esp. *Phdr.* 276e–278d); his reponse in e3 (ἔα . . . χαίρειν αὐτόν) is therefore hardly surprising. As *Ap.* shows, there are no circumstances under which he will give up philosophical talk; and that is of course the main point of the present interlude in the discussion. **d8 μᾶλλον** qualifies θερμαίνεσθαι: '[people] who talk get overheated'. **προσφέρειν** 'add' (i.e. one shouldn't combine that sort of thing with drinking poison). No medical theory may be involved here, just an empirical observation that the poison has less effect on those who get over-excited for any reason (cf. e2 τούς τι τοιοῦτον ποιοῦντας).

e1 εἰ δὲ μή 'otherwise'. **καὶ δὶς καὶ τρίς** 'two or even three times'. **e3 ἔα . . . χαίρειν αὐτόν** 'Don't mind him' (cf. χαίρειν λέγειν τινά (or τινί), 'say "χαῖρε" ("goodbye") to someone'). **e3–5 ἀλλὰ μόνον κτλ.** 'just let him, for his part (τὸ ἑαυτοῦ, sc. μέρος; used adverbially), prepare [the poison], with a view to (ὡς + future participle) giving [it] . . .' **e6 ἀλλὰ σχεδὸν μέν τι ἤιδη . . . · ἀλλά . . .** 'I pretty well (σχεδόν τι, as at 59a8 etc.) knew [sc. what you would say]; but . . .' The first ἀλλά marks assent (as at 62c9; see also 63d3), the second a contrast (answering to μέν). **e7 παρέχει:** for the present tense, see on d4

βούλεσθαι. **e8 ἔα αὐτόν:** sc. χαίρειν (from e3). **ἀλλ' ὑμῖν δή** . . .
'[Never mind him.] But to *you* . . .' **e9 τὸν λόγον:** i.e. the account
which he has been promising; hence the use of ἀποδοῦναι, in the sense
of giving what is due. **e9–10 ὡς μοι φαίνεται εἰκότως ἀνὴρ** . . .
θαρρεῖν 'how reasonably a man seems to me to have confidence', i.e.
how reasonable it seems to me that he should.

64a1 ἐκεῖ: see on 61e1 ἐκεῖσε. **a2 πῶς ἂν οὖν δή:** for the position of ἄν
cf. 63c9, 61e3. *GP* treats οὖν δή as indistinguishable in meaning from
δὴ οὖν (cf. 61e5–6n.).

64a4–69e5: Socrates' 'defence'

*Socrates defends his proposition that the true philosopher will look forward to his
death, which is a reward rather than a punishment for his way of life.*

64a4–5 κινδυνεύουσι . . . λεληθέναι τοὺς ἄλλους 'Probably the rest of
mankind is unaware': there is of course no 'probably' about it – no one
but (the Platonic) S. would have dreamed of describing philosophy as
he is about to describe it (and if so, he will be the only one who 'fastens
on to philosophy in the right way': cf. 76b). **γάρ:** see 59d1n. **ὅσοι**
'all those who'. **a5–6 αὐτοὶ ἐπιτηδεύουσιν . . . ἀποθνήισκειν τε καὶ
τεθνάναι** 'they deliberately (αὐτοί, 'of their own accord': a playful
reference back to the discussion of suicide?) busy themselves with dying
and being dead': i.e. both the event of death, which will be defined, at
64c, as the separation of soul from body, and the state which ensues on
it, in which the soul will be claimed to subsist apart from the body. But
the provocative use of paradox is as much a part of the method of the
Platonic S. as the irony of a4–5. (If, as Burnet and Gallop suggest,
ἐπιτηδεύω here means 'practise', this is in the sense of 'making it one's
practice' (cf. *Gorg.* 524c), not in the sense that one practises on the
piano; only later does S. begin to talk of '*training* for death' (μελετᾶν,
67e).) **a7 δήπου** 'presumably', 'I suppose'. **a8 τοῦτο:** i.e. dying and
being dead. If this is the philosopher's sole preoccupation, he can reasonably be expected to 'be eager for' it (προθυμεῖσθαι, a7, 9). **δή**
emphasises ἥκοντος: 'but when it actually *comes* . . .'

b1 οὐ πάνυ is used as at 63a2 (the γε which follows is emphatic: 'not *at
all*'). **b1–3 οἶμαι γὰρ ἂν κτλ.** 'I believe most people [i.e. 'ordinary
people'] would think this very thing (αὐτὸ τοῦτο) well said indeed

against those who philosophise, when they heard it.' For the early position of ἄν (promoted, as often, from the infinitive clause to which it belongs), see 62c1n.   **b3–4 τοὺς ... παρ' ἡμῖν ἀνθρώπους:** Boeotians were traditionally seen as stupid and insensitive (Pind. *Ol.* 6.90, Plut. *On the eating of meat* 95e), and ἄνθρωπος often conveys a certain contempt; in this context, perhaps, Simmias counts himself a philosopher first and a Theban/Boeotian second.   **μέν:** see 61d9–10n.   **b5 θανατῶσι** is ambiguous between 'are moribund' (Burnet), i.e. as good as dead, and 'want to die'; both meanings would fit equally well – the first with the idea that philosophers 'practise' death (a6, 9; cf. also 65a6), the second with a7–8 προθυμεῖσθαι ... τοῦτο.   **b5–6 σφᾶς γε κτλ.** 'they ['the many'], at any rate [i.e. if not the philosophers] are quite well aware that [those who philosophise] deserve this [i.e. death]': compare the case of the people of Athens vs. S. σφᾶς ... οὐ λελήθασιν responds to S.'s λεληθέναι τοὺς ἄλλους in a5.   **b7 καὶ ... γ':** see 58d1n.   **b8 λέληθεν κτλ.** 'it escapes them how ...'   **b8–9 ἧι ἄξιοί εἰσιν θανάτου καὶ οἵου θανάτου:** i.e. not as a punishment but as a reward, and not being killed but being separated from the body (cf. on a5–6) – as S. is about to explain.

c1 γάρ logically introduces the explanation, not the sentence εἴπωμεν ... ἐκείνοις (*GP* 62).   **c2 ἡγούμεθά τι τὸν θάνατον εἶναι;** is a typically Socratic way of introducing important items in argumentative passages: cf. 103c11, or *Gorg.* 464a (to Gorgias: 'I suppose you call body a something, and ψυχή?'). Here he is about to ask what death is, and begins by obtaining formal agreement that there is such a thing. As is shown by the definition in c4–5 (or rather its elaboration in c5–8), and by the 'defence' as a whole, 'death' in this context means primarily the state rather than the event. But see following n.   **c4–5 ἆρα μὴ ... ἀπαλλαγήν;** As Cebes in effect points out at 69e–70b, the definition begs the crucial question: is the ψυχή which is 'separated' (ἀπαλλαγή) from the body something which has 'power' and 'directing intelligence' (δύναμις and φρόνησις, 70b3–4), or is it rather something insubstantial like breath or smoke which might be dispersed immediately on its separation (70a2–6)? Both the comparison with breath and smoke, and the idea that the ψυχαί of the dead lack power and intelligence, are traditional (see 70a4–5n.); Cebes refers them to people in general (τοῖς ἀνθρώποις, 70a1). It is untrue, then, to say (as e.g. Gallop says) that the definition itself already presupposes the survival of the ψυχή, in any meaningful sense. What does presuppose it is S.'s retrospective application to the definition of a distinctly non-Homeric view of the ψυχή, of a sort which gained currency in both philosophical and non-philosophical writing from the sixth century on: ψυχή as opposed to σῶμα, the mental (or, in an ethical context, the moral) aspects of human existence as opposed to the physical (cf. the passage from *Gorg.* cited in the previous note; other evidence in Claus 1981). This conception of ψυχή begins to be introduced immediately after c4–9, with the idea of the philosopher as 'turned towards the ψυχή' (e6), away from the 'concerns of the body'. Simmias can accept both this and the definition separately; what Cebes questions (and no doubt Simmias would have concurred) is the unargued combination of them. Anyone – that is, any educated Greek – might accept that something leaves the body at death; and everybody knows that he or she possesses a mind. But what reason do we have for supposing that the two things are the same? In fact, later in the 'defence' S. may himself leave it in principle open whether the 'separated' ψυχή is or is not something intelligent (see 66e6n.); and later still, it turns out that on his view – perhaps – only a few souls are completely separated from the body in death (see esp. 114c2-6, with 114d3n.).   **c5 ἀπαλλαγήν:** the word and its cognates are often used, for example in tragedy (e.g. Aesch. *Ag.* 20), of release from something undesirable, and they certainly acquire this connotation in the later course of S.'s defence (cf. Cebes' summing up at 70a–b); but here the more neutral translation 'separation' is required, since in the following sentence the body is said ἀπαλλαγῆναι from the soul (to revert to the traditional rendering of ψυχή) as well as the soul from the body – and partnership with the soul is hardly an evil for the body, even if its partnership with the body is, in S.'s view, for the soul.   **c5–8 καὶ εἶναι κτλ.** 'And [we think that] being dead is this, the body's having come to be apart, separated from the soul, just by itself, and the soul's being apart, just by itself, separated from the body? Death can't be anything other than this?' χωρὶς μὲν ... γεγονέναι, χωρὶς δὲ ... εἶναι: these are noun clauses, with accusative subjects and infinitives, in apposition to τοῦτο. αὐτὸ καθ' αὑτό, αὐτὴν καθ' αὑτήν: Burnet translates 'alone by itself', comparing μόνην καθ' αὑτήν at 67d1. ἄρα μὴ ... ἦι in c8 is a rare construction, perhaps found only in Plato; *MT* 268 lists two other genuine examples. It seems to be a

combination of two elements, (ἆρα) μή introducing a question which
expects a negative answer, and μή + subjunctive, regularly used for
cautious assertions. The result is a question implying a cautious expectation of a negative answer.   **c10 σκέψαι δὴ κτλ.** 'Now consider [the
points which come next], if, that is (ἐὰν ἄρα: cf. εἰ ἄρα (πολλάκις) at
60e3, 61a6), you too think the same as I do: for it is from these [points],
I believe, that we shall reach a greater understanding of the things we
are inquiring into.' The philosopher distances his soul both (a) from
the pleasures and trappings of the body, more than others do (64d2–
65a2), and (b), in his quest for truth, from the senses, because these
are both deceptive and incapable of giving us access to the objects of
knowledge (65a9–66a10); the remainder of the section (to 69e) then
draws out the conclusions – the desirability of death for the philosopher, and the sense in which he 'deserves' to die.

d2–3 ἐσπουδακέναι περὶ τὰς ἡδονὰς καλουμένας 'to have worked hard
at the so-called pleasures' (cf. 60b4n.). Two things are certainly true:
that no philosopher, *qua* philosopher, has any cause to be interested in
physical indulgence (cf. e4–5), and that excessive indulgence would
interfere with his philosophy. But the same might apply to virtually
any activity; and why should a philosopher not be *moderately* interested
in food, drink, sex and the rest (a possibility S. fails to mention)? So
Simmias ought not to have accepted Socrates' conclusion at 64e8-65a2
– as P. himself perhaps recognises, by making him reply with a rather
grudging φαίνεται ('it seems so') to S.'s 'Is it clear, then, …?' The
'defence' as a whole, appropriately, has a certain rhetorical (or at least
provocative) ring to it (cf. c4–5n.).   **d6 τί δὲ τὰς τῶν ἀφροδισίων;** τί
δέ functions as a kind of shorthand for a longer, implied question which
is easily understood from what has just been said (cf. d8–9, or *HMa.*
288c, where the implied question is then spelt out). The case of the
noun phrase is determined by the role of that phrase in the question in
its full form.

e1 καθ' ὅσον μὴ κτλ. 'to the extent [whatever it may be] to which
there is not great necessity for him to partake in them', i.e. 'except in
so far as it may be absolutely necessary for him to concern himself with
them': μή gives a general or indefinite sense to the clause (similarly in
65a5). αὐτῶν perhaps refers to τὰς περὶ τὸ σῶμα θεραπείας (d8) as a
whole rather than specifically to καλλωπισμοί; would there ever be

'great necessity' καλλωπίζεσθαι, to 'dress up' or 'put on a display'? **e2** ἀτιμάζειν κτλ.: again (as at d5 and d7), Simmias could hardly say that the philosopher favoured *excess*. **e4–5** ἡ τοῦ τοιούτου πραγματεία 'the business of such a person', i.e. what he does (πράττει). **e6** πρὸς δὲ τὴν ψυχὴν τετράφθαι: not a deduction, but – if ψυχή here primarily denotes the category of the mental (cf. c4–5n.) – a plain fact; if philosophy is not concerned with the mind, nothing is. This gives at least some justification for the last part of the conclusion in 64e8–65a2 (διαφερόντως τῶν ἄλλων ἀνθρώπων).

65a4 καὶ δοκεῖ γέ που 'And it *does* seem (καί … γε as at 58d7), presumably (που)': a4–7 points out that the aspect of philosophers just described explains one of the things 'the many' say about them (i.e. ὅτι … θανατῶσι, 64b4–5). The other part of what they say (that philosophers deserve to die) provides the focus of the last, impassioned part of S.'s defence (68c–69e): real virtue issues only from philosophy and wisdom, and will find its reward in death. **a5–6** ὧι μηδὲν … ζῆν 'that [for anyone] to whom none of such things is pleasant and [who] does not share in them it is not worth living'. οὐκ ἄξιον … ζῆν recalls, but is different in meaning from, ἄξιοί εἰσιν (θανεῖν) in 64b5–6. **a6** ἐγγύς τι τείνειν τοῦ τεθνάναι 'comes pretty (τι) close to being dead'. **a7** τῶν ἡδονῶν αἳ διὰ τοῦ σώματός εἰσιν 'the pleasures which have their existence through [their means of realisation in] the body'. Cf. LSJ s.v. διά A.III.b; and d11, where sensations are described in the same way. **a9** τί δὲ δή (also at d4) answers to 64e8 πρῶτον μέν; δή emphasises the second (and third) point(s) in contrast to the first. αὐτήν 'itself': the acquisition of wisdom or understanding (φρόνησις) is the prime or only concern of philosophy (φιλο-σοφία).

b2–4 ἢ τά γε τοιαῦτα … ὁρῶμεν; 'or at least [i.e. whatever more scientific considerations one might adduce] are even the poets [cf. e.g. *Ap.* 22a–c] always repeating such things as this to us, over and over – that nothing we hear nor anything we see is accurate?' Hackforth's suggestion, that the ὅτι-clause echoes a lost iambic line, is attractive. **b4–5** τῶν περὶ τὸ σῶμα αἰσθήσεων 'the sensations which relate to the body' (all sensations do, of course; but their connection with the body is the whole point of the argument). **b5–6** σχολῆι αἵ γε ἄλλαι 'the *others* (emphatic γε) will hardly be [ἀκριβεῖς or σαφεῖς]'. **b10–11** δῆλον ὅτι κτλ.: once again (cf. 64c4–5n., d2–3n.) the argument is

singularly lacking in rigour; we should need more than poetic hyper-
bole (b2–4) to convince us that the evidence of the senses is *always*
deceptive, as S. here implies (cf. 66a5–6). Later, in the argument from
recollection, he in fact suggests a more positive, though very limited,
role for sensation in the acquisition (or reacquisition) of knowledge (see
e.g. 74b4–6); and there are already hints of this position at (65)c8–9,
e2–3, and 68a9–b1.

c2–3 ἆρ' οὖν κτλ.: this and S.'s next speech simply draw out the
consequence of what has just been said – if truth is not acquired
through sensation, or with the help of sensation, then it must be acquired through reasoning (λογίζεσθαι) alone. **τι τῶν ὄντων** could
mean either (*a*) 'any one of the things that are *the case*' (cf. ἔστι in c10,
and see LSJ s.v. εἰμί A.III), or (*b*) 'any one of the things that exist' (LSJ
A.I). While (*a*) at first looks like the obvious choice (the poets, for
instance (b2–4), hardly have much interest in questions about what
exists), within only a few lines (66a3) τὰ ὄντα will be used to refer to
(a kind of) *things*, which favours (*b*). But we may not need to decide,
since 'hunting down' the things that are (as the philosopher is said to
do, 66a3) will certainly include, or lead to, the discovery of truths
(what is the case) about them (cf. 66b7, e1–2). **c5 δέ γε** 'Yes, and
…' (*GP* 154). **c6–7 μήτε ἀλγηδὼν μηδέ τις ἡδονή:** the inclusion
of pain in the list is perhaps partly suggested by the verb παραλυπεῖν
(ἀλγηδών = λύπη), and pleasure is naturally paired with it; μηδέ,
however, makes us pause on this last item – as well we might, since
ἡδονή seems to be the last thing which should (παρα)λυπεῖν us. But S.
says '*some sort of* (τις) pleasure'; the reference is to any of the 'so-called
pleasures' of 64d3, and his description of these would certainly be
consistent with the claim that they 'annoy [the philosopher's soul] by
a diversion' (LSJ's rendering of παραλυπεῖν). **c7 αὐτὴ καθ' αὑτήν**
(also in d1–2) is a deliberate echo of the same phrase in the definition
of death at 64c7–8. **c9 ἁπτομένη** 'in contact [with it]'. **τοῦ ὄντος:**
the collective equivalent of τῶν ὄντων (c3). **c11 καὶ ἐνταῦθα** 'in this
case too', i.e. in addition to the one discussed in 64d–65a.

d4–5 φαμέν τι εἶναι δίκαιον αὐτὸ ἢ οὐδέν; 'Do we say that there
is [exists], by itself (αὐτό: cf. 64c5–8n.), something just (or 'a just
[thing]'), or [do we say that] nothing [of the sort exists]?' d7 καλόν
(γε) τι καὶ ἀγαθόν (i.e. ἀγαθόν τι) seems to confirm that τι and δίκαιον

are to be taken together. The question is 'Do we say that there exists something which is just and nothing else?', i.e. something whose essence is exhausted by justice (cf. d13–e1; and see further 74a9–12n.). We need then to ask what kind of entity this might be. In modern parlance, it might be a *property*: 'Do we say that there is such a property as justice?' This interpretation would certainly fit well with what Socrates goes on to say about his 'something just', and other such things – we do not see (the property of) justice, or of beauty, or of goodness by themselves (d9), whereas we do see instances of them, i.e. just things, beautiful things, etc. (cf. e1–2, with b10–11n.). P., for his part, would technically label them as 'forms' (see Introduction §5). But it is doubtful whether he would have seen himself as so far having introduced anything particularly technical; nor do we need to import any modern philosophical notions to understand his general meaning. All that is so far required is that we should accept the possibility of talking and thinking about justice, or beauty, without reference to specific concrete examples. The Greek which is used here is certainly difficult, but no doubt P. would have expected it to be intelligible to any reasonably reflective reader; anyone, that is, who would distinguish himself from the unphilosophical 'many' of 64b and 65a. True, the 'we' of d4 probably refers in the first instance to a smaller category, i.e. 'S.' and his circle, who have discussed these things before (as Simmias' enthusiastic response suggests). Cf. 74b2n., 75d2–3n. But it is hard to believe that a highly literary and dramatic work like *Phd.*, one of whose chief aims is evidently to persuade its audience of the importance of philosophy, should have been written exclusively for those already on the inside, and in language which would be accessible only to them.   **d6 μέντοι** is clearly affirmative rather than adversative (cf. *GP* 399–404).   **d7 καὶ . . . γε:** as at 58d1.   **d12–e1 λέγω δὲ κτλ.** 'I am speaking about everything, e.g. tallness (or largeness, size: μέγεθος), health, strength, and in a word about the essence of [these and] all the other things, what each actually is.' (For οὐσία in a different sense, see e.g. 76d9, 78d1.)

e1–2 αὐτῶν τὸ ἀληθέστατον: see b10–11n.   **e2–3 μάλιστα . . . καὶ ἀκριβέστατα:** the adverbs qualify διανοηθῆναι, not παρασκευάσηται; their promotion to this early position gives them special emphasis. **αὐτὸ ἕκαστον** 'each by itself'. Here too (cf. 64d2–3n., 65b10–11n.), the argument is less than rigorous: even if we cannot perceive justice, goodness, etc. directly by themselves, it might still be that we would 'come closest to knowing each of them' (e4) by properly *interpreting* the evidence of the senses. But the argument from recollection will purport to close off this alternative.   **e6 οὖν:** this speech by S. brings together the conclusions of a9–d3 and d4–e5.   **τοῦτο:** i.e. αὐτὸ ἕκαστον διανοηθῆναι.   **καθαρώτατα** 'most purely', 'with the least contamination' (cf. 69c–d, where the idea of purification is given a religious sense). The construction is similar to that of a remote future condition, with ἐκεῖνος ... ὅστις substituted for τις ... εἰ.   **e8 παρατιθέμενος** 'adducing in evidence'.

66a1–3 ἀλλ' αὐτῆι καθ' αὑτὴν κτλ. 'but [if] using his intellect (or 'mind': διάνοια) alone by itself, unmixed, he were to undertake to hunt down each of the things that are (τῶν ὄντων: see c2–3n.), [each] alone by itself, unmixed'.   **a3 ἀπαλλαγείς:** cf. 64c4–8.

b1 ἐκ πάντων τούτων: i.e. from the points arrived at in 64d2–65a2 and 65a9–66a10.   **παρίστασθαι** 'be present to', 'occur to', as at 58e5.   **b3 κινδυνεύει ... 5 ὅτι** 'Very likely there brings us and our reason (μετὰ τοῦ λόγου = καὶ τὸν λόγον: Verdenius 201) out in our inquiry, like a path, [the consideration] that ...' The ὅτι-clause is both the logical and (probably) the grammatical subject of κινδυνεύει. For τοι, see 60c9n. We need paths to lead us out of situations in which we are otherwise at a loss: the connection is with ταράττοντος in a5 (the body 'confuses' the philosopher if he tries to use it in his search).   **b5 συμπεφυρμένη** 'contaminated', contrasting with καθαρός (καθαρώτατα) in 65e6.   **b6 μετά** 'in the company of'.   **οὐ μή ... κτησώμεθα:** οὐ μή + aor. subj. expresses a strong denial.

c3 εἰδώλων 'phantoms', 'fantasies', 'illusions'.   **c4–5 ὥστε κτλ.** 'so that really and truly (ὡς ἀληθῶς and τῶι ὄντι are equivalent expressions, used together for emphasis) it is not possible for us (ἐγγίγνεται = ἔξεστι) – as the saying goes (τὸ λεγόμενον) – even to think at any moment about anything'.   **c7 αἱ τούτου ἐπιθυμίαι:** τούτου is shorthand for διὰ τοῦ σώματος (cf. 65a7n., 65d11); there is no suggestion that the body can literally desire (or enjoy, or sense) anything by itself, apart from the soul.   **c7–8:** cf. *Rep.* 373b–e.

d2 τούτου: i.e. the body.   **d3 τὸ δ' ἔσχατον πάντων ὅτι** 'And the worst of all is that'.   **d4 καί** is emphatic ('if we *do* get any rest from it':

GP 327). **d7–8 ἀλλὰ τῶι ὄντι ἡμῖν δέδεικται ὅτι ...** 'But in fact it has been shown to us that ...': shown, that is, by experience, as described in b7–d7. That passage represents a rhetorical version of S.'s points in 64d–66a (cf. b1 ἐκ πάντων τούτων); now, however, an additional conclusion is to be drawn – whereas before it was only that we must separate soul from body 'as far as possible' (65a1, 65c7, 66a4), i.e. in life, the new claim (which is of course the one S. needs for his defence) is that the acquisition of wisdom – if it is possible at all (e6) – depends on complete separation, in death (e2–67a2). But that will follow readily enough, given the assumption that any degree of bodily 'contamination' will prevent us from knowing anything 'purely' (e4–5; cf. 65b10–11n.), together with the definition of death at 64c.

e1–2 αὐτὰ τὰ πράγματα 'things by themselves' (= τὰ ὄντα). **e2 καὶ τότε ... ἡμῖν ἔσται οὗ ἐπιθυμοῦμεν** 'and it is then (τότε, looking forward to e3 ἐπειδὰν ...) that we shall have what we desire'. **e3 καί φαμεν ἐρασταὶ εἶναι:** i.e. in claiming to be philosophers (cf. 65a9n., 66b2, 68a1–2). **e4 ὡς ὁ λόγος σημαίνει:** cf. d7–8n. **e4–5 οἷόν τε:** sc. ἐστι, equivalent to ἔξεστι (similarly ἔστι in e6). **e5 δυοῖν θάτερον** 'the one [or the other] of two things [is the case]'. **e6 ἢ ... τελευτήσασιν** 'either it is not possible [for us] to acquire knowledge anywhere, or [it is possible for us] when we have died'. As yet, then, S. is not claiming actually to prove anything about death (cf. 64c4–5n.). The context as a whole is strongly reminiscent of *Ap.* 40c, where he also manages to combine agnosticism about death with 'much hope' that it is a good thing (cf. 67b8, c1, 63e–64a), though in a different way.

67a2–3 οὕτως ... , ἐὰν 'in this way ..., [i.e.] if'. **a4 ὅτι μὴ πᾶσα ἀνάγκη:** a stronger version of καθ' ὅσον μὴ πολλὴ ἀνάγκη (64e1). **a5 ἀναπιμπλώμεθα:** the verb is used by Thuc. (2.51) of infection by disease. **a6 ὁ θεὸς αὐτός:** cf. 60c2n. **a6–7 καὶ οὕτω μὲν ... ἀφροσύνης** 'and if [we become] pure in this way by being separated from the folly of the body' (μέν contrasts this case with the opposite one, which is referred to in b2). Folly (lack of φρόνησις) 'belongs to' the body in the same sense as desires (66c7). **a8 τοιούτων:** i.e. others who are καθαροί. **a8–b1 δι' ἡμῶν αὐτῶν:** the soul, then, separated from the body (and 'its' pleasures, desires, and folly) represents our real selves.

b1 πᾶν τὸ εἰλικρινές: i.e. αὐτὰ τὰ πράγματα (66e1–2). **τοῦτο δ' ἐστὶν ἴσως τὸ ἀληθές** 'and that, we suppose (ἴσως), is what is true' (cf.

66b7). As well as softening an assertion (as at 61c2), in argumentative contexts ἴσως may also be used, as here, to mark the speaker's own view (cf. 62c6).   **b2 μὴ . . . ἦι** 'For perhaps it is not right (θεμιτόν: cf. 61c10.) for impure (μὴ καθαρῶι: i.e. anyone or anything impure) to lay hold of (ἐφάπτεσθαι, also used of 'attaining to') pure.' The construction (μὴ οὐ + subj.) is the same as that used after verbs of fearing; the effect, like that of ἴσως in the previous sentence, is one of modest assertion (though the modesty may be pretended rather than real: cf. *MT* 265, 266). Similarly at 69a6–7.   **b4 τοὺς ὀρθῶς φιλομαθεῖς:** rhetorical variation for τοῖς γνησίως φιλοσόφοις (66b2).   **b6 παντός γε μᾶλλον** 'Yes (γε: cf. *GP* 130), more than anything.'   **b7–c3** S. now begins to draw out the implications of the conclusions reached by his imaginary philosophers (66b3–67b2) for his own defence.   **b8–9 πολλὴ ἐλπὶς ἀφικομένωι . . . κτήσασθαι** 'there is much hope for [one] who has arrived . . . to obtain': the aor. as well as the fut. inf. is found after expressions of hoping (which after all already imply futurity); cf. also 68a1–2.   **b10 πραγματεία:** as at 64e4.   **ἡμῖν:** i.e. for us philosophers.   **b10–c1 ἥ γε ἀποδημία:** for ἀποδημία, see 61e1n., and *Ap.* 40c–41a; γε limits what is being said to S.'s own case (ἡ νῦν μοι προστεταγμένη), though other philosophers are immediately included (c2–3).

c2–3 ὃς . . . κεκαθαρμένην 'who thinks [i.e. as I do in my case] that his mind (οἱ = αὐτῶι) has been prepared, as it were by having been purified'.   **c5–6** 'And doesn't purification turn out (συμβαίνει) to be this – the very thing that I have been saying for some time in my account, [namely] parting . . . ?' What follows is in fact only a variation of what he has said before; 'habituating [the soul] to assemble and collect itself, by itself, away from every part of the body' (c7–8) is a picturesque way of describing the process by which the philosopher distances himself from sensations – some of which, at least, may be located anywhere in the body.   **c9–d1 ἐν τῶι ἔπειτα** 'in the future', i.e. after death.

d1–2 ὥσπερ δεσμῶν ἐκ τοῦ σώματος 'from the body as [from] fetters'.   **d4–5 οὐκοῦν τοῦτό γε θάνατος ὀνομάζεται κτλ.** 'Then it is *this* (emphatic γε) which we name "death", namely a freeing and parting of soul from body?' S. here asks for formal agreement to an important modification of the original definition of death, for which we have carefully been prepared over the preceding pages: if to die means – for the philosopher – to be *freed* from his body, in order to achieve what he always desired, then clearly it is something which he will face with eagerness (d7–8; cf. 64a7–8); whereas death as it was first described, i.e. merely as the separation of the ψυχή from the body, should attract no one (cf. 64c4–5n.). For S.'s vision of the fate of separated but unpurified souls, see 81b1–82b8, 113d1–114c2. **d7 δέ γε:** see 65c5n. **d7–8 μάλιστα καὶ μόνοι** '[philosophers] especially, or rather they alone': for this use of καί, see *GP* 292 (8). **d8 τὸ μελέτημα** 'what they practise [doing]', as it were in preparation (c2, e1) for the full performance (in life, of course, as we have repeatedly been told, complete freeing of soul from body is impossible). Cf. μελετᾶν + infinitive at e5, which is regularly used of practising an activity requiring effort and attention. The metaphor further develops the original paradox at 64a5–6; and Simmias responds with notably less enthusiasm than he has to Socrates' preceding questions ('It seems so', d11; cf. 64d2–3n.). But it is a natural enough extension of the idea of 'habituation' in c7 (cf. 82b2 ἐξ ἔθους τε καὶ μελέτης). **d12 ἐν ἀρχῆι:** i.e. at 64a4–9. **d12–e2 ἄνδρα παρασκευάζονθ᾽ ἑαυτὸν κτλ.** 'that a man [who is] preparing himself in his life, by being as close as possible to death, to live like that, should then resent it when this [i.e. death] comes to him' (construction as in 64a7–8). The καί (κᾆπειθ᾽ = καὶ ἔπειτα) is redundant, reflecting the logical rather than the grammatical form of the sentence ('that a man *should prepare* himself . . ., *and then* . . .'). Cf. Verdenius, and *GP* 308–9.

e5 ἀποθνήισκειν μελετῶσι 'practise dying', i.e. the event, which is a process of freeing (d4,9); τὸ τεθνάναι, on the other hand, is ambiguous between event and state (cf. 62a5n.). **e6 ἐκ τῶνδε δὲ σκόπει** 'Look at [the matter] from the point of view of these [considerations]', i.e. the ones that follow – although there is in fact little that is new about them except the passionate and rhetorical manner of their expression. **διαβέβληνται** 'are at odds with'.

68a1–2 οἳ . . . τυχεῖν: if they are φιλό-σοφοι (see 65a9n.), it is (and was: 66e2–3) an easy step to say that they 'are in love with' (ἐρᾶν) wisdom; the direct reason for the shift becomes clear when we reach the next point, in a3, but the idea that wisdom and truth are the real and ultimate objects of (what appears as) sexual passion plays a central role in *Symp.* and *Phdr.*   **a3 ἀπηλλάχθαι:** here, plainly, in the sense of 'to be rid of' (cf. 64c4–5n.).   ἤ 'Or [consider this point]'. The point is in the form of another complex question: when human objects of love have died, very many (πολλοὶ δή) have willingly gone to Hades in the hope of seeing them there; will anyone then (a7 ἄρα) who is really in love with wisdom, and has the same hope, be resentful at dying (a3–b2)? Of course not ... (b2–6).   **a6 τε:** with the alternative reading, τι, the sense would be 'the [hope] of catching some sight there of those they desired, and even (? καί: see *GP* 291 (6)) of being with them'. This might fit the traditional idea of Hades, according to which only the insubstantial shape of a person would be there to be seen; but this would hardly be helpful, when a new and different kind of Hades is being proposed (or is S. after all deliberately hinting at the weakness of his argument?).   **a7 καὶ λαβών ... b1 ἐν Ἅιδου** 'and who has firmly grasped this same ἐλπίς, that nowhere else but in Hades will he encounter it in any way worth speaking of': ἐλπίς embraces 'expectation' as well as 'hope'.

b2 οἴεσθαί γε χρή 'One must certainly think so.'   **b3 σφόδρα:** as at a7 – 'he will *firmly* hold this view'.   **b4 μηδαμοῦ:** after δόξει, i.e. in an ordinary acc. + inf. clause, one would expect the negative οὐ; b4 however (with minor variations) repeats a9–b1 μηδαμοῦ ... Ἅιδου, where μή is regular after an expression of hoping (*MT* 685).   **b8 οὐκοῦν ... 9 ὅτι ...** 'Then is this sufficient proof for you of any man whom you see being resentful because he is about to die, that ...', i.e. if you see anyone ..., is this sufficient proof that ... (τοῦτο refers forward to the relative clause).   **b9–c1 οὐκ ἄρ' ἦν φιλόσοφος** 'he is [was] no philosopher [lover of wisdom] after all': for this use of ἄρα + imperfect, see *GP* 36–7.

c1 που is again 'I suppose' (as at 59b1, etc.): S. apologises for introducing without argument a division of humanity into three classes, lovers respectively of wisdom, money, and honour (justified at *Rep.* 580d–581c by reference to the tripartite division of the soul). At 66c–d, φιλοσώματοι were implicitly identified exclusively as φιλοχρήματοι.   **c5–6** 'Then (οὖν) doesn't it follow that what is called by the name of courage, too (καί), belongs (προσήκει) especially to people in the state we have described [i.e. philosophers]?' I.e. given that they have the attitude to death we have attributed to them, the label 'courageous',

as popularly understood (fearlessness: see d11–12n.), must also apply
to them especially. S. here begins the last stage of his defence, against
the charge that philosophers deserve death as a punishment – rather
than as a reward, as he has so far argued (cf. 64b). In fact, they turn
out to instantiate the very qualities which 'the many' themselves ad-
mire, either better than most (c6), or better than anyone (c10).   **c7
πάντως δήπου** 'Of course, absolutely'.   **c8–9 ἣν καὶ οἱ πολλοὶ ὀνομάζουσι σωφροσύνην** 'what even the many call by the name of self-
control' – or, to use the traditional translation, 'temperance': i.e. what
actually is (at least part of) temperance, as even non-philosophers recognise. c5 ἡ ὀνομαζομένη ἀνδρεία is to be taken in the same way (and
is therefore to be distinguished from an expression like τὰς ἡδονὰς
καλουμένας, 'the *so-called* pleasures', at 64d3). What is missing from the
popular descriptions of both virtues is the vital addition of μετὰ φρονήσεως (cf. 69a–c, and e.g. *La.* 196c–197c). But so far the point is just
that even if we take the virtues as (incompletely) described by the
many, philosophers display these (as others do not: d2–69a4).   **c9 τὸ
... μὴ ἐπτοῆσθαι** 'not being excited' (equivalent to κρατεῖν, 69a2).
c10 τούτοις μόνοις: this is a stronger claim than was made in the case
of courage ('belongs to them *especially*', c6); but from d2 S. will treat
both virtues in exactly the same way.

d2 γάρ 'Yes, because ...'   **τῶν ἄλλων** 'everyone else's' (cf. d5 πάντες
οἱ ἄλλοι).   **d8 οὐκοῦν:** οὐκοῦν, in which οὖν is the dominant element,
may indicate anything from strict inference, through the introduction
of new premisses, to mere progression of thought (*GP* 434–5). d8–9
seems meant as one of the premisses, along with d5–6, for the conclusion in d11–13. S. assumes at least two things, (*a*) that it is impossible
to think something a 'great evil' (d5–6) without also fearing it, and
(*b*) that the only motive for withstanding what one fears is to avoid
what one fears more. (*a*) is perhaps reasonable, whereas (*b*) is likely to
appear to us at best ungenerous: is it not possible to fear death more
than anything, and yet choose to die e.g. for the sake of one's family or
friends? This is partly, however, a matter of difference of perspective,
for a fourth-century Greek would probably have seen and felt the fear
of shame as the primary motivating factor in such circumstances (see
Dodds 1963, ch. 2; Dover 1974, 226–42); Simmias' assent (d10) is
neither contrived nor merely mechanical.   **d8–9 αὐτῶν οἱ ἀνδρεῖοι:**

i.e. those of them who exhibit the kind of behaviour (withstanding the prospect of death) which might make it look as if they fit the description 'courageous' (cf. d2–3 τήν ... τῶν ἄλλων ἀνδρείαν).   **d9 ὅταν ὑπομένωσιν:** i.e. on any occasion (cf. Burnet).   **d11–12** 'It is through being afraid, then, and fear that all except philosophers are brave; and yet [it is] quite unreasonable (ἄλογόν γε: cf. 62b1–2, 67e9, 68b6) that anyone should be brave through fear and cowardice' (the opposite of bravery, which they equate with being fear*less*; so they cannot really be brave). Later, however, Socrates offers a different diagnosis of popular 'courage', and a different reason for treating it as spurious – namely that it stems from habit and training (82a10–b3). It is thus legitimate to doubt the seriousness of his conclusion here. He is dealing, once again (as at 64a and 67d–e), in deliberate paradox, though now for polemical rather than constructive purposes. All that he strictly requires for his case is (*a*) that their attitude towards death shows philosophers to be fearless; (*b*) that courage is normally defined as fearlessness; and (*c*) that all, or most, or many, people who allegedly face death 'courageously' in fact fear it (which we ourselves might well want to treat as a necessary condition of courage: cf. Arist. *Nic. eth.* 3.9–12).

e2 οἱ κόσμιοι = οἱ σώφρονες (cf. c8–12).   **e3 ἀκολασίαι τινι** 'a certain sort of licentiousness', or 'intemperance' (ἀκολασία functions as the opposite of σωφροσύνη). For the qualification 'of a certain sort', see 69a3–4n.   **e3–4 καίτοι φαμέν γε ... , ἀλλ' ὅμως** 'Of course we *say* (γε) ..., but all the same': καίτοι ('and yet') introduces an objection, which is then immediately replied to; similarly in e7–69a1 (see *GP* 557–8). 'We' presumably means 'people in general': if 'through intemperance' implies 'through *being* intemperate', S.'s claim will be (apparently) self-contradictory.   **e4–5 τὸ πάθος τὸ περὶ ταύτην τὴν εὐήθη σωφροσύνην** 'what happens in relation to that simple-minded sort of temperance', i.e. to those who possess it.

69a3 ὧι: i.e. τούτωι ὅ. The relative is rarely attracted into the case of the antecedent when it functions as subject of its clause, as here.   **a3–4 τῶι ... σεσωφρονίσθαι** '[that is,] to their having been made temperate in a certain way through intemperance': 'in a certain way' (similarly ἀκολασίαι τινί in 68e3), because the 'pleasures' which 'master' them (ὑπ' ἄλλων κρατούμενοι, 68e7) in this case will turn out to include some which would not normally be associated with intemperance – no one would ordinarily call a person ἀκόλαστος e.g. for abstaining (from pleasures of the usual sort) on grounds of health or reputation. S. is here ascribing an unconscious hedonism to the many, as in *Prot.* (351b–360e): they may think of themselves as employing other criteria of choice (the good, the fine), but in reality they measure everything by the single yardstick of what will maximise pleasure and minimise pain. This analysis applies not only to their 'temperance' ('exchanging pleasures for pleasures and pains for pains', a7), but also to their 'courage' ('fear for fear', a8, where 'fear' means an object of fear, and therefore something painful), and indeed by implication to their 'virtue' in all aspects, which is contrasted with συλλήβδην ἀληθὴς ἀρετή in b3.   **a6 ὦ μακάριε** is a form of address which P. may use especially when S. is introducing a point of special importance (so e.g. at *Rep.* 432d; cf. *Prot.* 309c): 'my *dear* (...)'. Here, it announces the peroration to his defence.   **γάρ** introduces the explanation of the curious state of affairs about whose existence Simmias has just agreed (ἔοικε γάρ, 'Yes, it seems so').   **μὴ ... οὐχ ... ἦι ... a9 ἀλλ' ἦι:** construction as at 67b2 (changing to the positive form in a9, and in b5–c3).   **πρός** 'with a view to' (see Verdenius); in b7 and 8, however, πρός is '[exchange A] *for* [B]' (cf. a10 ἀντὶ οὗ, and Arist. *Nic. eth.* 1117b20).   **a7 ἡδονὰς ... 8 καταλλάττεσθαι:** noun-clause (acc. + inf.) in apposition to ἀλλαγή.   **a8–9 καὶ μείζω πρὸς ἐλάττω:** i.e. in the case of pains and fears (but presumably ἐλάττω πρὸς μείζω in the case of 'pleasures').   **a9 ὥσπερ νομίσματα** 'like coins'. The basis of the comparison is not the exchange of 'greater for less', which is not a feature of normal cash transactions, but rather (*a*) that 'pleasures', pains and fears are exchanged like money (for goods), which implies (*b*) that they are things of value or importance (both as what is exchanged and what is received in exchange). It is (*b*) that provides the starting-point of the next thought: 'but perhaps that, alone, is the true coin, in return for which all these things [i.e. 'pleasures', etc.] must be exchanged, namely wisdom', a9–10. Here the parallel is clearly with selling rather than buying (as in a6–9); but both are introduced side by side in b1–2.

b1 καὶ τούτου μὲν ... 3 φρονήσεως 'and everything being bought and sold for this (μέν is answered by δέ in b6), or rather (καί: see 67d7–8n.)

in the company of this, really is, perhaps (μὴ ... ᾗι), courage and temperance and justice and, in short (σύλλήβδην), true virtue, namely in the company of wisdom': i.e. true virtue is constituted by the buying and selling of everything (only) when the transactions are accompanied by wisdom. This is the crucial omission from the popular descriptions of courage and temperance referred to at 68c5 and c8–10. Buying and selling 'for this' (τούτου, gen. of price), though a natural extension of the notion that wisdom is a kind of coin, wrongly suggests that our store of wisdom will be either decreased (in 'buying') or increased (in 'selling'), and has therefore to be corrected by 'in the company of this'; but then the comparison of wisdom to coinage ceases to hold. When we make choices, we prefer one thing over another; what matters is only that we choose wisely. (Nothing has been said to justify the treatment of justice as a kind of trading transaction, but such a treatment is easily supplied: ordinary justice is a matter of refraining from injustice for fear of becoming the victim of injustice oneself. Cf. e.g. *Rep.* 358e–359a.) **b4 καὶ προσγιγνομένων ... 5 τῶν τοιούτων** 'whether pleasures and fears and everything like that [i.e. 'and pains'?] are added (προσγιγνομένων) or are subtracted'; i.e. such things are irrelevant to the real calculus that is virtue (as was implied in a6–10), even though our choices will themselves relate to things that people think pleasant, or fear. This agrees exactly with what we have been told about the philosopher, who is actually fearless and is unimpressed by ordinary 'pleasures'. (On the whole of a6–b5, which has been much discussed, see especially Bluck 154–6, Verdenius.) **b5–6 χωριζόμενα δὲ ... 8 οὐδ' ἀληθὲς ἔχηι** 'whereas [everything] being parted from wisdom and being exchanged for each other – this kind of virtue is, perhaps, a kind of stage-painting (σκιαγραφία), and in reality [it is] slavish [virtue] and has nothing wholesome [in it], nor [anything] true'. χωριζόμενα ... ἀλλήλων, sc. τὰ τοιαῦτα: this is initially the subject (construction as in b1–2), but is then displaced by ἡ τοιαύτη ἀρετή. The virtue in question is 'slavish' because irrational: for slaves as typically and essentially irrational, see Just 1985. For a discussion of the precise meaning of σκιαγραφία, see Keuls 1978, esp. ch. 4; here Plato is clearly associating it with the production of illusion, as he does elsewhere (e.g. *Rep.* 583b). **b8 τὸ ... ἀληθὲς τῶι ὄντι:** pairing of two equivalent adverbial expressions, for emphasis, as at 66c4.

c1 κάθαρσις is evidently contrasted with c2 καθαρμός: the state of purification – if the virtues are states – as opposed to what brings it about.
Previously it was said that our purification from ordinary desires and
fears was a condition of our acquisition of wisdom (see especially 66c–
67b); now the claim seems to be that such purification is conditional on
wisdom. 'Wisdom' here, however, is not the complete understanding of
things which was talked about earlier (since that was said to be inacces-
sible to the philosopher while still alive), but simply a clear-minded
appreciation of what is truly valuable (which is what will be available to the philosopher, and to him alone).   **c3–4 καὶ κινδυνεύουσι
καὶ οἱ τὰς τελετὰς . . . καταστήσαντες** 'And so (καί[1]: see Verdenius on
63a7) those who established τὰς τελετάς really do (καί[2]: *GP* 321–3)
seem . . .' Despite the mention of βάκχοι in d1, αἱ τελεταί probably
refers to initiatory rites in general, which written evidence from the
fifth century on tends to associate with the name of Orpheus (see
Burkert 1985, 296–7); the idea that the uninitiated 'will lie in the mud'
(c6; cf. *Rep.* 363c–365a, Ar. *Frogs* 145–50) itself probably derives from
an 'Orphic' text, along with the quotation in c8–d1.   **c5 πάλαι αἰνίττεσθαι** 'have long been saying in their riddling fashion', i.e. 'have long
been darkly hinting at the truth in saying'.   **c6 ἐν βορβόρωι κείσεται:**
S. will give his own inventive variation of this idea at 81b–d (cf.
111d–e).   **c8 εἰσὶν γὰρ δή** 'For there really are'.   **οἱ περὶ τὰς τελετάς**
'those concerned with rites'.   **c8 ναρθηκοφόροι ... d1 παῦροι** 'Those
who carry the fennel-stalk [the Dionysiac thyrsus] are many, the [true]
initiates few.' As Burnet suggests, the original line must have been
a hexameter, with πολλοί and ναρθηκοφόροι appearing in reverse
order.

d2 ὧν (with emphatic δή) goes with d4 γενέσθαι: 'It's of these that I
too have omitted nothing . . . but have shown my eagerness to become
[one] . . .'   **d5 ἠνύσαμεν:** the change to the plural perhaps reflects the
Socratic (and Platonic) view of philosophy as a co-operative enter-
prise. By the end of the following main clause, however, 'we' has become virtually equivalent to 'I', since it is natural in the context to take
ὀλίγον ὕστερον as applying at least primarily to S.   **τὸ σαφές** = τὴν
σαφήνειαν: 'the plain truth' (cf. Thuc. 1.22, Antiphon 1.13).   **d6 ἂν
θεὸς ἐθέληι** '[the] god[s] willing': for the use of the singular, and the

lack of the article, cf. 62c7n. **d7–8 ταῦτ' . . . ἀπολογοῦμαι, ὡς εἰκότως . . .** 'I offer this as my defence, [to show] how reasonable it is (ὡς εἰκότως: cf. 63e9–10n.) . . .' ταῦτα is internal accusative after the intransitive ἀπολογοῦμαι. **d8–e1 ὑμᾶς τε ἀπολείπων καὶ τοὺς ἐνθάδε δεσπότας οὐ χαλεπῶς φέρω:** cf. 63a8–9.

e3 τοῖς . . . παρέχει has been doubted by editors as an interpolation from 70a1. But it seems just about defensible: '[this is my defence;] but it is quite unbelievable to the many. So if I am in any respect (τι) more credible to you than [I was] to the Athenian judges, it will be well.' Cebes then replies (70a1): what really *does* seem unbelievable to people is what you claim about the soul . . .

69e6–70c3: an objection from Cebes

Cebes objects that Socrates' whole defence has presupposed two points, about which people generally are likely to be sceptical: that when a person dies, his soul continues to exist; and that it also continues to possess 'power and intelligence'. Socrates proposes further discussion of these two points (which turns out to include the first three of the four central arguments of the dialogue: the 'cyclical' argument, the argument from recollection, and the 'affinity' argument: 70c–72e; 72e–77d; 77d–84b).

69e6 δή here merely marks the next step in the narrative (*GP* 238); cf. e.g. 58c6. **ὑπολαβών:** see 60c8n.

70a1 πολλὴν ἀπιστίαν παρέχει τοῖς ἀνθρώποις 'causes much disbelief among people' (followed by the construction used after verbs of fearing). **a2 οὐδαμοῦ ἔτι ἦι** 'is no longer anywhere' (repeated in a6 with the addition of adverbial οὐδέν): accordingly what Socrates first sets out to show in the sequel is that the souls of the dead ἐν Ἅιδου εἰσίν (c4). As the whole context shows, not being *somewhere*, for the soul, is regarded as equivalent to its not being (i.e. existing) at all; so most clearly in the next sentence, where ἔστι . . . ψυχή (b2–3) answers to εἴη που (a6). **a4 εὐθὺς ἀπαλλαττομένη** 'just as it is becoming separated from the body'. **a4–5 καὶ ἐκβαίνουσα . . . διαπτομένη** 'and as it emerges, flies off in different directions, dispersed like breath or smoke'. The description 'flies off . . . like . . . smoke' is a reminiscence of Hom.

Il. 23.100–1 ψυχὴ δὲ κατὰ χθονὸς ἠΰτε κάπνος | ὤιχετο (cf. 16.856, 22.362 ψυχὴ δ᾽ ἐκ ῥεθέων πταμένη Ἄιδοσδε βεβήκει: both lines are already quoted in this connection by Olympiodorus); and the notion that the ψυχαί of the dead lack 'power and intelligence' (δύναμις and φρόνησις, b3–4) derives from the continuation of the same context: ὦ πόποι, ἦ ῥά τις ἔστι καὶ εἰν Ἀΐδαο δόμοισιν | ψυχὴ καὶ εἴδωλον, ἀτὰρ φρένες οὐκ ἔνι πάμπαν (23.103–4). All these Homeric lines are cited verbatim at *Rep.* 386d–387a. Whether Homer makes any connection between ψυχή and breath is disputed (cf. e.g. LSJ s.v. ψυχή), but such a connection would be suggested by expressions like *Il.* 22.467 ἀπὸ δὲ ψυχὴν ἐκάπυσσε, and was certainly made by others (cf. e.g. Eur. *Or.* 1163; (P.) *Crat.* 399d–e). **a6 ἐπεί, εἴπερ εἴη που** 'For if indeed it *were* somewhere'.

b2–4 The first point will be directly addressed in the 'cyclical' argument, the second in the argument from recollection (see 76c12–13); the 'affinity' argument in effect relates to both. **b2 πίστεως:** here of what produces conviction: 'proof', 'argument'. **b3 τοῦ ἀνθρώπου** 'the man', i.e. the composite of body and soul. **τινα δύναμιν** 'some power', 'some capacity' (but the only relevant capacity will in fact be that for understanding). **b6 βούλει διαμυθολογῶμεν** 'would you like us to talk' (for an explanation of the construction, see *MT* 288). For the combination διαμυθολογεῖν ... διασκοπεῖσθαι (c3), cf. 61e1–2n. Here, the effect of the combination may be to allow S. to eat his cake and have it. What they will talk about ('spin tales about') is merely 'whether it is *likely* to be like that or not' (b6–7) – to which Cebes replies that he will be delighted to hear what Socrates *thinks* about the subjects in question (b8–9); on the other hand, says S. (b10–c2), it will not be a matter of idle chatter (ἀδολεσχεῖν), about things that don't concern me (οὐ περὶ προσηκόντων): 'And so, if you agree, we must look into [the questions in hand]' (c2–3). (Cf. Loriaux.) Thus, perhaps, we are warned simultaneously not to place too much weight on the arguments, and to regard Socrates as being in deadly earnest: they are simply the best arguments which are presently available to him, without claiming to be the last word on the matter (cf. 106e–107b). **b8 ἐγὼ γοῦν** 'I, at all events' (i.e. whatever might hold for anyone else: *GP* 454). **b10 οὔκουν γ᾽ ἂν οἶμαι** 'I certainly *don't* think';

both the οὖν in οὔκουν and the γε strengthen the negative (cf. *GP* 422–5). As at 64b2, the ἄν strictly belongs to the following infinitive clause.

c1 οὐδ' εἰ κωμῳδοποιὸς εἴη: at *Ap.* 19b–c Socrates attributes such a charge against him specifically to Ar. *Clouds* (Σωκράτης ... περιεργάζε-ται ζητῶν τά τε ὑπὸ γῆς κτλ.; and the term ἀδολέσχης is in fact used in connection with Socrates at *Clouds* 1485). Olympiodorus cites some lines from Eupolis (= fr. 352 Kock), which complain about Socrates as a πτωχὸς ἀδολέσχης, concerned about everything except about where he will get his next meal from; but the treatment of science later in *Phd.* (96a–99c) would give rather more point to a reference to the *Clouds*.

70c4–72e2: the 'cyclical' argument

The souls of the dead must continue in existence; for from what other source could those souls come which animate the living?

70c4–5 σκεψώμεθα δὲ αὐτὸ κτλ. 'Let us consider it [i.e. the matter] in some such way as this, [by asking] whether in fact (ἄρα), when the men [i.e. the combinations of body and soul] have died, their souls are in Hades, or whether they are not' (ἄρα and καί seem merely to give equal weight to both alternatives – making the question a genuinely open one: cf. *GP* 42, 305). There is a gentle irony in this opening to the argument, in so far as the Homeric view to which Cebes has referred *does* suppose the presence of ψυχαί in Hades (and ἐν Ἅιδου εἰσὶν αἱ ψυχαί may itself be intended to recall *Il.* 23.103–4 ἦ ῥά τις ἔστι καὶ εἰν Ἀΐδαο δόμοισιν | ψυχή: cf. a4–5n.). But S. cannot lay much weight on that, since Cebes' objection relied on the point (also Homeric) about the insubstantiality of the ψυχαί of the dead (so insubstantial that they might be blown away on their exit from the body).   **c5–6 παλαιὸς μὲν οὖν ἔστι τις λόγος οὗ μεμνήμεθα** 'Well then, there is an ancient doctrine, which we [i.e. I: cf. 69d5n.] remember.' μέν and οὖν function here as at 62b2; μέν contrasts the παλαιὸς λόγος with the more general principle which will supersede it in d7–e6. S.'s present speech states what is to be proved, namely that the living in some sense 'come to be again from' the dead (c8–9), from which it will allegedly follow that 'our souls are there', i.e. in Hades (c9–d1). Cf. d2. On the sources of the doctrine of *palingenesia* or *metempsychosis* (the 'transmigration' of souls from one body to another – an idea which is not necessarily entailed by those mentioned in 69c–d, although it too has strong 'Orphic' connections), see Burkert 1985, 298–301; P. himself, at *Meno* 81a–c, refers it to certain priests and priestesses, and to Pindar 'and many other inspired poets' (cf. Pind. *Ol.* 2.56–80, and frr. 129–31, 133 Snell, the last of which is quoted in the *Meno* passage).   **c6 ὡς εἰσὶν ... 8 ἐκ τῶν τεθνεώτων** 'that they are there having come from here, and moreover (καὶ ... γε as at 58d1, etc.) that they come back here again and ('explanatory' καί: cf. 58b6n.) are born (γίγνεσθαι, sc. again) from those [persons] who have died': i.e. that the surviving residue of the dead person, his soul, migrates 'there', and then enters a new body 'here', which constitutes the coming into being or birth of a new living person. That it is the latter, rather than the soul, which strictly γίγνεται in this sense (but see d9n.) is confirmed by c8–9 πάλιν ... ζῶντας (on the other hand, the new person cannot himself strictly be said to be born *again*). But see d1–2n.   **c9 ἄλλο τι ἤ:** lit. 'is anything else the case than that' (i.e. 'surely ... ?'); further abbreviated as ἄλλο τι at 79b1.

d1–2 οὐ γὰρ ἄν που πάλιν ἐγίγνοντο μὴ οὖσαι 'For I suppose (που, with litotes) they could hardly be born again [enter a new body], if they did not exist [i.e. if they had ceased to exist].' As before (cf. a2n.), not being anywhere is assumed to be equivalent to not being *tout court*. **d2 τοῦ ταῦτ' εἶναι** 'of the fact that this [i.e. that our souls are in Hades after our death] is the case'.   **d7 τοίνυν** 'Well then' (like οὖν in c6). **κατ' ἀνθρώπων** 'in relation to human beings' (cf. περί in 9).   **d9 ὅσαπερ ἔχει γένεσιν περὶ πάντων** 'about everything that admits of coming-into-being', i.e. coming to be something, coming to acquire a new property – as, according to the implication of the 'ancient doctrine', those who are dead come to be alive. S. has two ways of describing this process, which are entirely compatible: he talks either (*a*) of one property itself 'coming to be' from another (as e.g. in e1–2), or (*b*) (as in e.g. e6–8) of something coming to be *F* (i.e. to possess property *F*) from being *G* (possessing property *G*).

e1 ἆρ': for this (relatively rare) use of ἆρα to introduce an indirect question (also in e4), cf. *GP* 50.   **e1 οὑτωσὶ ... 2 οἷον** 'everything comes to be like this, [i.e.] opposites from nowhere else except their opposites – everything, that is, which actually has such a thing [i.e. an 'opposite'], as for example ...' For the use of ἐκ here, compare e.g. Soph. *OT* 454 τυφλὸς ἐκ δεδορκότος (what was previously qualified by one attribute comes to be qualified by another). S. does not say what he means by 'opposites': the examples he gives (beautiful/ugly, just/unjust) suggest that he means pairs of simple contraries; but he establishes the principle exclusively by means of comparatives (e6–71a7: if a thing becomes larger, i.e. than it was, it must previously have been smaller, etc.). See e6–8n. As Gallop points out (108), this strategy makes the principle look more plausible than it is: if something becomes larger (than it was before), it must previously have been smaller, and vice versa; but while the ugly duckling turned into a beautiful swan, as a cygnet it might have been either ugly or beautiful, or neither. Similarly with the crucial pair 'living' and 'dead' (see 71d5–e3). If something comes to be alive, it need not previously have been dead, since it might simply not (yet) have been alive. Only if 'opposites' are defined as contradictories (beautiful / not beautiful, living / not living, etc.) will the principle 'opposites from opposites' begin to hold any water; but since 'living' and 'dead' are contraries rather than contradictories, it will then no longer help S.'s case. There is also a problem about what it is that 'comes to be alive' when a new person is born. S.'s argument will generally presuppose that it is the soul, which was previously 'dead' (by virtue of being the residue of someone or something now dead), but now comes to acquire the attribute of 'living' by virtue of coming to be the soul of the new living person. Yet Cebes' suggestion at 69e–70b, that the separation of soul from body at death would be consistent with its perishing, implicitly rejects that kind of description of the coming into being of the living (since there would be no soul left to 'come to be alive' in this way). Nevertheless, there will still be something which comes to be alive, namely the new person himself or herself, or, alternatively, their matter or body – from not having been alive before. **e3–4 καὶ ἄλλα δὴ μυρία οὕτως ἔχει** 'and indeed (καὶ ... δή, marking an important addition: *GP* 253–4) countless other things are like this'. **e5 αὐτό:** after ὅσοις we might have expected a plural; but the sense is clear enough. **e6–8 οἷον ὅταν κτλ.:** for the move from simple adjectives to comparatives (e1–2n.), cf. 102b–c, where 'Simmias is larger than S. but smaller than Phaedo' is treated as interchangeable with 'Simmias is both large [in relation to S,] and small [in relation to Phaedo]'.

71a3 καὶ μὴν ... γε: καὶ μήν is 'progressive', while γε gives emphasis to the new example (*GP* 351–2, 119–20). **a9–10 ἱκανῶς οὖν ... τὰ ἐναντία πράγματα;** 'Then are we satisfied about this, [namely] that all come to be in this way, namely opposite things from opposites?' πάντα must have the same reference as at 70e1 (all *opposites*); there is no attempt to translate all change into change between opposites. Nor is there any suggestion either that everything that is *F* must previously have been the opposite of *F*, or that it must later become the opposite of *F*. The point (to judge from the examples given) is only that *if* something comes to be *F*, it must do so from having been the opposite of *F*. In one way, since there is indubitably something which comes to be alive when someone or something is born (cf. 70e1–2n.), this hypothetical aspect of the principle does not affect the argument. In another way, however, it is crucial: S. is setting out to establish that any and all souls survive death, and even if it were true that any soul which 'comes to be alive' must previously have been 'dead', i.e. have survived the death of an earlier living thing, there might be other souls which did not. This gap in the argument is closed in the last section, beginning at 72a11. **a12 τί δ' αὖ; ἔστι τι καὶ τοιόνδε ἐν αὐτοῖς, οἷον ... 13 δύο γενέσεις** 'And what [of this point], in its turn (αὖ)? Is there some such thing, too (καί), in them [i.e. in the case of opposites] as two processes of coming into being (γενέσεις), between all opposites, taken as pairs (ἀμφοτέρων), [these] being two [in each case] ...?' On the basis of a new (and slightly less peremptory) survey of instances, S. now claims that between any pair of opposites there are two balancing processes, one in one direction, one in the other: not, again (see previous n.), that anything which changes from *F* to the opposite *G* must sooner or later change back to *F*, but only that changes in both directions do in fact occur with any pair of opposites, either in relation to the same subject or to different ones. The purpose of this move is to add new weight to the idea that the living 'come from' the dead. If there are always counterbalancing pairs of changes between opposites, then since the living undoubtedly change into the dead, the dead must at least sometimes change (back) into the living ('In this way too, then, we are agreed that the living come from the dead no less than the dead from the living', 72a4–6). The existence of both these types of change would of course already be given by the application of the opposites-from-opposites principle to the pair 'living' and 'dead' (in so far as things do in fact come to be alive as well as dead). But this application has yet to take place, and the opposites-from-opposites principle does not by itself imply that changes in both directions actually occur in the case of all pairs of opposites. Unfortunately they do not (things grow old, but it is hard to think of anything that grows young); but if they did, that would indeed offer further confirmation of S.'s conclusion.

b1–2 αὖ . . . πάλιν: not 'back again' (which would imply that everything which changes in one direction subsequently changes in the reverse direction: see a9n.), but 'conversely' (cf. e.g. *Ap.* 27d). **b3–4 καὶ καλοῦμεν κτλ.** 'and accordingly (οὕτω) we call the one (τὸ μέν) "increasing" and the other (τὸ δέ) "decreasing"'. **b6 οὐκοῦν καὶ διακρίνεσθαι καὶ συγκρίνεσθαι** 'Then (οὐκοῦν) too [we recognise] separating and combining . . .' οὐκοῦν is 'progressive' (cf. 68d8n.), introducing further examples. What the 'opposites' are in the case of separation and combination is unclear (unless they are respectively 'dead' and 'alive': cf. 70e1–2n.); but special use will be made of this pair of processes in the last stage of the argument (see 72c3–5). **b7 καὶ πάντα οὕτω . . . 8 ἀλλ' ἔργωι γοῦν** 'and all of them like this [i.e. in pairs] – even if (κἂν εἰ) we sometimes do not use their names [i.e. have no names for them], still in actual fact' (ἀλλά . . . γοῦν introduces the apodosis of the concessive conditional clause: *GP* 458–9). κἂν εἰ logically ought to be used in cases where the main clause requires ἄν (as in e.g. 'even if he were dead, he would still be – εἴη ἄν – happy'); but it can also be used in other cases, as here. **b9 αὐτά** 'they', i.e. opposites. γίγνεσθαι . . . εἰς ἄλληλα states the two principles together: '[still . . . it must be like this in all cases, namely] both that they come to be from each other, and that there is a process of coming into being of either [member of a pair] into each other [i.e. the other, in every case]'.

c1–2 Having established his two principles, S. now begins to apply them to the key pair, alive and dead. His first move is to introduce an allegedly parallel pair (awake and asleep), where both principles apply with particular transparency (c6–8); he then invites Cebes to identify the relevant features of the first pair on the model of this one (c9–d2). For the purposes of the argument, the infinitive expressions τὸ ζῆν, τὸ ἐγρηγορέναι etc. refer to the states themselves (being alive, awake; cf. c11–d1), while τὸ ζῶν and τὸ τεθνηκός (d10, 11) refer to things as possessing them (what is alive, dead; cf. 70d9n.). **c6 εἴπερ** 'if indeed'. **c9 συζυγίαν** 'pair', originally of horses or oxen. **c10 καὶ αὐτὴν καὶ τὰς γενέσεις** 'both itself and its processes'.

d2–3 ἱκανῶς σοι: sc. ἔχει. **d5 καί¹** is emphatic: 'Well then (δή), *you* tell me ...' **d8 γίγνεσθαι ... ἐξ ἀλλήλων:** i.e. on the basis of the principle of a9–10 (cf. c6–7). **d13** This reply of Cebes' perhaps suggests some reluctance, as do his following two (φαίνεται, e1, ἔοικεν, e3; contrast e.g. πῶς γὰρ οὔ; at c8, and d4, e7 πάνυ μὲν οὖν); that the living come from the dead is something about which he remains sceptical, although – as he says – he is bound to accept the conclusion, after having swallowed the premisses offered. But this in turn seems to imply at least some awareness on P.'s part of the weakness of the argument he has attributed to S. See further e8n. **d14–15 τὰ ζῶντά τε καὶ οἱ ζῶντες:** with οἱ ζῶντες, we return specifically to the central case of human beings.

e2 εἰσὶν ἄρα ... αἱ ψυχαὶ ἡμῶν ἐν Ἅιδου: cf. 70c9–d1. This conclusion, if it implies that all souls 'are in Hades', is premature: see a9n., e13n., 72d1–3n. 'Our souls', here as before, must mean primarily human souls (70c9–d1 varies 70c4–5 ἐν Ἅιδου εἰσὶν αἱ ψυχαὶ ... τῶν ἀνθρώπων); but that will also entail that each individual soul 'is in Hades' after death, which is what matters to S. and Cebes. Whether it will retain its individuality in the next stage, i.e. when it enters a new body, is another question; cf. Crombie 1963, I 295–7. **e4 οὐκοῦν καί:** cf. b6. **e5 σαφὴς οὖσα τυγχάνει** 'is actually obvious'. **δήπου** 'presumably'. **e8 οὐκ ἀνταποδώσομεν κτλ.:** lit. 'Shall we not assign the opposite process as a balance (ἀνταποδιδόναι, whose primary sense is of repaying a debt), but will nature be lame in this respect?'; i.e. 'Shall we refuse to restore balance to nature by assigning her the opposite process, but leave her lame ...?' Or, simply, is there a second and complementary γένεσις in this case as in every other? S. is not content to allow the argument to speak for itself, but couches the question in a highly charged rhetorical form. But at the same time these three lines form part of a context which, unlike the 'defence' which preceded it (cf. 64d2–3n., etc.), could not as a whole be described as 'rhetorical', in so far as it gives a greater priority to precision – or apparent precision – of argument than to the use of persuasive language. The result is that we cannot draw any hard and fast distinction between the two sections – indeed the second is formally an extension of the first (see 69e–70b); both represent a combination of logic and rhetoric, and the only real difference is in the proportions in the mix. Cf. Introduction §1. **e11 πάντως που** 'Absolutely, I suppose' (cf. *GP* 492). Cebes takes with one hand what he gives with the other (cf. d13n.). **e13 ἀνα-βιώσκεσθαι** 'coming to life again (ἀνα-)'. It is one of the agreed premisses of the whole argument (agreed, that is, by implication; S. presupposes it, and Cebes does not object) that 'the dead' are souls which have become separated from bodies; if so, then 'living' will apply primarily to embodied souls (see 70e1–2n.), and only by extension to composites of soul and body, οἱ ζῶντες. If it is granted that whatever admits of γένεσις in one direction must be of the same type as what admits of the corresponding γένεσις in the other (only the sorts of things which can be combined can be separated, and only the sorts of things that can become hotter can become cooler), then it must be souls which come to be alive; and these must be (previously) 'dead' souls, i.e. ones which have had at least one earlier sojourn in a body. Having come this far, then, Cebes is right to offer coming to life *again* as the opposite of the process of dying. However, despite his summing up in 72a4–8, S. has still shown no reason for supposing that all souls survive to be reborn (see 71a9–10n.). **e14–72a2 ἐκ τῶν τεθνεώτων κτλ.** 'won't this [sc. γένεσις], coming to life again, be a process of coming to be from dead to living people?'

72a4 ὁμολογεῖται ἄρα ἡμῖν καὶ ταύτηι 'It is agreed for us (ἡμῖν, dative of relation), then, in this way too' (see 71a12–13n.). **a6 ἱκανόν που ἐδόκει τεκμήριον εἶναι:** 70d2. (που here = 'I think'; που in a8 is of course 'somewhere'.) **a7–8 ὅθεν δὴ πάλιν γίγνεσθαι** '– the place, that is (δή, after ὅθεν, emphasises the antecedent που: *GP* 219), from which they come to be [are born] again'. The inf. is used in place of the expected indicative (γίγνονται), by assimilation to the preceding clause (cf. *MT* 755). **a11 ἰδὲ τοίνυν οὕτως . . . ὅτι οὐδ' ἀδίκως ὡμο-λογήκαμεν** 'Now (τοίνυν: cf. 70d7n.) observe in this way that we are not wrong, either (οὐδέ), to have agreed . . .', i.e. 'look at it in this way, and you will see that . . .' S. now does supply a reason for supposing that death will always be followed by rebirth (see 71e13n., 71a9–10n.): it is not merely that changes take place in both directions between opposites, but that change in one direction must always be balanced by change in the other, because otherwise the difference and change on which the world-order depends would ultimately be eliminated.   **a12 εἰ γὰρ μὴ ... b1 περιιόντα** 'For if one set [of opposites] did not balance (ἀνταποδιδόναι, here used in an intransitive sense, as in b8) the other by coming into being, going round as it were in a circle' (i.e. so as to come back to their starting-point: cf. Hdt. 1.159).

b2 εὐθεῖά τις εἴη ἡ γένεσις 'the process were to be one in a straight line' (i.e. from A to B).   **b4 οἶσθ' ὅτι ... σχοίη** 'do you realise that everything would finally (τελευτῶντα) have the same character'.   **b7 οὐδέν** 'not at all'.   **οἷον** 'as for example'.   **b9 τελευτῶντα ... c2 φαίνοιτο** 'in the end everything would make [the case of] Endymion seem a trifle, and he would be nowhere to be seen'; Endymion (sometimes associated with Elis), condemned – or, according to another version of his story, privileged – to sleep for ever, would be indistinguishable from anyone or anything else. For ἀποδείκνυμι in the sense of 'make seem', Burnet compares e.g. *Phdr.* 278c.

c4–5 ταχὺ κτλ. 'soon what Anaxagoras describes would be realised – "all things together"'. The reference is to Anaxagoras DK 59 B 1, which describes the original state of things, before the formation of the world we know, when all its constituents were jumbled together, and 'none was patent (ἔνδηλον) because of its smallness ...' (Barnes's translation). Anaxagoras, fifth-century philosopher-scientist (and associate of Pericles), figures again later in the dialogue (97b–99d).   **γεγονὸς εἴη:** the periphrastic form of the perfect optative is more common than the simple form.   **c5 καὶ εἰ** 'if, too'.   **c6 ὅσα ... μεταλάβοι, ἐπειδὴ δὲ ἀποθάνοι:** we might expect ὅσα ... μεταλαμβάνει, ἐπειδὰν δὲ ἀποθάνηι; the optatives result from assimilation to the optative of the conditional clause (ἀποθνήισκοι).

d1–3 εἰ γὰρ ἐκ μὲν τῶν ἄλλων κτλ. 'For if living things came from the other things [i.e. things other than the dead], and living things died [sc. and did not come back to life], what escape could there be from everything's being used up [spent] on dying?' (μὴ οὐ + inf. is used as after negatived verbs of preventing, with οὐ strengthening the negative implied in the rhetorical τίς: cf. *MT* 815, 749.) Suppose (1) that the living (i.e., presumably, the souls of the living) did not come from the dead: then (2) they would have to come from a different source; but since (3) (from (1)) no material could be reused, therefore (4) (given that the universe is finite, as S.'s/P.'s evidently is) everything would end up dead – which is taken to be inconceivable. (The universe, S. might reasonably have said, shows no visible signs of running down.) True, any individual soul might still perish, or fail to be reincarnated (see 71a9–10n.); but either possibility might appear to threaten the assumed stability and eternity of the world-order. (Another alternative might be to suppose that the living were animated by new souls, not previously incarnated. But in this case too life would ultimately cease, unless the stock of new souls were infinite; and an infinite stock of items which could not survive outside a body seems inherently implausible.)   **d4 οὐδὲ μία μοι δοκεῖ:** sc. εἶναι. οὐδὲ μία is more emphatic than the familiar οὐδεμία ('none whatever'). Cebes' enthusiasm here – if that is what it is – contrasts strongly with his response to the earlier sections of the argument (see 71d13n.). Whether any enthusiasm on his part would be justified is another matter (and it appears in any case to have evaporated by 77c–e, where he not only has to be reminded of his acceptance of the argument, but asks for another argument for the same conclusion). The best that can be said for this last section is that it has a slightly greater superficial plausibility (and ingenuity) than the earlier ones. But we should notice in any case that accepting the proposition in d1–3 does not in itself entail accepting S.'s position: (*a*) everything *might* end up dead (though Cebes shows no signs of wanting to embrace that possibility); (*b*) even if souls themselves perished, the stuff out of which they were formed might be reused in the creation of new souls, just as, presumably, the matter of any body may be reused in the formation of new bodies; and (*c*) Simmias will later introduce a theory (at 86b–d) which would in a sense allow the soul to 'come from the other things' without entailing universal death.   **d8 ἔστι τῶι ὄντι** 'really are facts'.   **καὶ ἐκ τῶν τεθνεώτων … εἰ εἶναι:** τό is easily supplied after καί in both cases (thus giving three subjects for ἔστι).

e1–2 καὶ ταῖς μέν γε κτλ. makes no sense in this context, and is clearly an interpolation from 63c6–7.

72e3–77a5: the argument from recollection

The previous argument claims to have shown that our souls survive death; this new argument sets out to provide a separate proof that they existed, and possessed intelligence (76c12–13; cf. 70b2–4) before our birth, reasoning that 'learning' in the most important cases is really a matter of our being reminded of items of knowledge which we can only have acquired in a previous (discarnate) existence.

e3 καὶ μήν ... γε: cf. 71a3b. **ὑπολαβών:** cf. 60c8n. **e3–4 καὶ κατ' ἐκεῖνον ... τὸν λόγον** is repeated in different forms, first in e6 (καὶ κατὰ τοῦτον), then in 73a2 (καὶ ταύτηι); only the last context tells us what really follows (or seems to follow) from the λόγος in question 'too' (καί, i.e. as well as from the previous argument). e6–7 itself merely states part of the new argument, not its conclusion. λόγος here = 'statement', 'thing said'. **e4–5 ὃν σὺ εἴωθας θαμὰ λέγειν:** the theory of learning as recollection was probably an invention of P.'s; and 73a7–b2 strongly suggests an intended reference to *Meno*, where a slave-boy is shown allegedly discovering (or rather rediscovering) a mathematical truth for himself, prompted by questioning from Socrates (ἐάν τις καλῶς ἐρωτᾶι, 73a8) and by the use of diagrams (ἐάν τις ἐπὶ τὰ διαγράμματα ἄγηι, b1). The effect of the fiction that the theory is already well known – at least to Cebes, and to Simmias (though he has forgotten the arguments for it: 73a4–6) – is both to allow this covert reference to *Meno* (so adding its argument to the present one: cf. 73b8–9) and to avoid the necessity for a long explanation of what is after all a strange-sounding thesis. Its strangeness then provides an excuse for a new demonstration (73b3–10). **e5 ἡμῖν** 'for us' (dative of relation), i.e. for human beings; when we learnt our knowledge 'in some previous time' (e6–7), learning presumably was not like this. **e6 τυγχάνει οὖσα** 'actually is'. **e7 ἃ νῦν ἀναμιμνηισκόμεθα** '[the things] which we now [i.e., as 73a1–2 confirms, in our bodily existence] recollect', or 'of which we are now reminded' (with ἃ as internal accusative): one can ἀναμιμνήισκεσθαι in Greek, just as one can 'recollect' (i.e. recover a lost item of memory) in English, without being reminded (i.e. by something or someone else: cf. e.g. *Rep.* 329a). The latter notion will be crucial to the argument of *Phd.*, but was less important to that of *Meno*; thus if there is a covert allusion to *Meno* here (see e4–5n.), that might be a reason for opting for the first translation in this case – and after all the core of the doctrine in general is just that learning is the recovery (recollection) of knowledge once possessed. But no doubt S.'s prompting in *Meno* could be represented as 'reminding' (cf. 73a10n.); and the way in which Simmias is made to play on the notion of reminding in the following interjection (a5–6) probably clinches the case.

73a1 εἰ μὴ ἦν που ἡμῖν ἡ ψυχή 'unless our (ἡμῖν: dative as in e5) soul[s] were somewhere'. **a2–3 ὥστε καὶ ταύτηι κτλ.:** cf. *Meno* 86a–b. Strictly speaking, however, as Cebes himself later says (77c, following Simmias' lead), that our souls pre-existed our birth does not entail that they will survive death, which is presumably what being ἀθάνατος ('deathless') primarily means. In this respect, *Phd.* appears as correcting *Meno*. **a7 ἑνὶ μὲν λόγωι ... καλλίστωι** 'By one outstanding argument' (ἀποδέδεικται is easily understood from a4–5 ποῖαι ... ἀποδείξεις). For εἷς with superlative, see e.g. LSJ s.v. 1b; for μέν, see 61d9–10n. (ἔπειτα in a10 does not introduce a contrast.) **a8–9 αὐτοὶ λέγουσιν πάντα ἧι ἔχει** 'say for themselves everything as it is', i.e. the truth about everything (about which they are questioned). **a9 καίτοι** 'and yet'. **a9–10 καὶ ὀρθὸς λόγος:** S. later suggests (76b5–6) that one of the conditions of possessing knowledge of something is the ability to 'give an account' (δοῦναι λόγον) of it; and presumably that account must be ὀρθός ('correct'). **a10 ἔπειτα** 'In that case', referring back to the conditional clause ἐάν τις καλῶς ἐρωτᾶι; Cebes then in effect repeats that clause in a different form (ἐάν τις ... τῶν τοιούτων, b1), and completes the sentence in b2 with a variant of a9–10, which explained the implication of the original apodosis (αὐτοὶ ... ἔχει, a8–9). (For a nearly identical use of εἶτα, see *Phdr.* 229c.) Tr. 'In that case – if one takes them to diagrams or something else of that sort – it proves (κατηγορεῖ, used intransitively) most clearly that it is like this [i.e. that the knowledge was already in them].' The process of 'taking them to diagrams' is illustrated by the case of the slave-boy in *Meno* (cf. 72e4–5n.), while 'or something else of that sort' might include any examples which would enable the person being questioned to see (for himself) what was true or false; both cases will fall under that referred to in a8 ἐάν τις καλῶς ἐρωτᾶι, if they are not equivalent to it. σαφέστατα κατηγορεῖ in b2 and ἑνὶ ... λόγωι ... καλλίστωι in a7 will then refer to

the same proof, as logic seems to demand. a10–b2 as a whole is confused in expression, and deliberately so: see b8–9n.

b5 ἡ καλουμένη μάθησις: cf. 64d3 τὰς ἡδονὰς καλουμένας. (Real learning, of course, must be the acquisition of new knowledge.) **b6 ἀπιστῶ
... οὔ** 'Disbelieve I do not ...' **b8 καὶ σχεδόν γε ... 9 καὶ πείθομαι**
'And I *almost* (γε emphasising σχεδόν) remember already, from the
things Cebes attempted to say [sc. however badly he said them], and
I'm *almost* convinced.' **b9 οὐδὲν ... ἧττον** 'no less'. **σὺ ἐπεχεί-
ρησας:** ἐπιχειρεῖν (lit. 'take in hand') is here more 'undertake' than
'try', which is what it is in b8; the play on the word ('how *you* ἐπεχεί-
ρησας') removes any sting that Cebes might have felt from b8.

c1 δήπου: cf. 64a7n. **c4 παραγίγνηται** 'comes to [someone]'. **c5–6
λέγω δέ τινα τρόπον τόνδε** 'I mean in some such way as this': the
elaborate way in which S. introduces his description of ἀνάμνησις
marks its fundamental importance to the argument. **c6 ἐάν τις ... d1
ἔλαβεν;** 'If on seeing some one thing (τι ἕτερον), or hearing it, or
perceiving it in some other way, someone not only recognises that
thing, but also comes to have in mind (ἐννοεῖν) a second thing (καὶ
ἕτερον), of which [lit.] there is not the same knowledge but another
[i.e. knowledge of which is not entailed by knowledge of the other
thing: see d3n.], are we not right in saying that he was reminded of this
thing, of which he came to have the thought [which he came to have
in mind]?' Three further alleged features of ἀνάμνησις will shortly be
added: (*a*) that it occurs especially (μάλιστα) in relation to things
which have been forgotten 'through lapse of time and lack of attention'
(e1–3); (*b*) that what one is reminded of may be either like or unlike
the thing which does the reminding (e5–74a3); and (*c*) that where it is
like, one necessarily has in mind whether the resemblance is lacking in
any respect or not (74a5–7). The main part of the argument, which
relates cases of 'learning' to this account of ἀνάμνησις, then begins at
74a9.

d2 πῶς λέγεις; As the sequel shows, Simmias' inability to understand
relates to the complexity of the description rather than to any particular item in it. **d3 οἷον τὰ τοιάδε** 'I mean something like the following'; οἷον, as often, introduces an explanation, which continues until

e1. **ἄλλη που ἐπιστήμη ἀνθρώπου καὶ λύρας:** i.e. from the fact that
one knows who a particular man is, it does not follow that one knows
(is able to recognise) his lyre; nor vice versa (one can know that this is
x's lyre, without knowing *x*). **d5 οὐκοῦν:** moving on to the next point
(cf. 68d8n.) **d6 τὰ παιδικά** is probably a true plural, corresponding
to οἱ ἐρασταί (cf. *Symp.* 178e). **d7 ἔγνωσάν τε . . . καὶ . . . ἔλαβον:**
gnomic aorists, indicating what generally happens (similarly ἀνεμνήσθη in d9). **d9 ὥσπερ γε καί:** both γε and καί give added weight to
the new, and more immediate, example. **d10 καὶ ἄλλα κτλ.** 'and
there will, I suppose (που) be countless other cases of this sort'. **d11
μέντοι:** affirmative, as e.g. at 65d6; similarly at 74a1.

e1 οὐκοῦν . . . τὸ τοιοῦτον ἀνάμνησίς τίς ἐστι; 'Then is this sort of
thing a kind of ἀνάμνησις?' 'This sort of thing' is illustrated by the two
examples just given, i.e. seeing one thing and coming to think of some
different thing as well; but it is only 'a kind of ἀνάμνησις', because as
S. immediately goes on to say, there is a further important condition that attaches to ἀνάμνησις in the primary sense. **e1–3 μάλιστα
μέντοι . . . ἃ ὑπὸ χρόνου καὶ τοῦ μὴ ἐπισκοπεῖν ἤδη ἐπελέληστο:** 'by
[the passage of] time' and '[by] not paying attention [to them]' go
together; the reference is to things which the person forgot at some past
time – ἐπελέληστο, pluperfect, itself representing an action as completed in the past (*MT* 43), and reinforced by ἤδη (cf. LSJ s.v. 11) –
because of long inattention. One could be 'reminded' of something
which happened to be merely temporarily out of one's mind, as probably in the examples so far given: it would be a poor lover who had
actually forgotten his beloved, and part of the point about Simmias
and Cebes is presumably that they are close associates who are often
found together. This, S. now suggests, is not ἀνάμνησις in the primary
sense (and if it were, it would clearly bring his argument to an abrupt
halt: if learning were like *that*, it would not in the least help to establish
the case for our existence before birth). **e5 ἔστιν . . . ὁ ἀναμνησθῆναι**
'Is there [such a case as] [someone's] being reminded of a man on
seeing a painted horse or (καί: cf. *GP* 292) a painted lyre?'

74a2 ἆρ' οὖν οὐ . . . συμβαίνει 'Then doesn't it turn out [that . . .]?'
The significance for the argument of the feature of ἀνάμνησις in question (to which S. later refers twice: see c11–d2, 76a3–4) turns out to
have to do with the peculiar nature of the things which are claimed to

do the reminding in the crucial case of 'learning': that they are seen as *both* like *and* unlike what they remind us of. See b7–9n., c11n. **a5 ἀλλ' ὅταν γε . . . ἀναμιμνήισκηταί τίς τι** 'But whenever someone is reminded of something from things that are *like* ('determinative' γε, stressing this case to the exclusion of the other: *GP* 119). **a6 προσπάσχειν** 'experience in addition'. **a6–7 ἐννοεῖν εἴτε τι ἐλλείπει κτλ.** '[namely] having it in mind whether this [i.e. the thing from which the process of ἀνάμνησις starts] is lacking at all (τι) or not in its likeness to the thing of which he was reminded'. Whether in such cases (that of paintings, say – which is the only relevant example we have been given) we always, and necessarily, think consciously 'is this a good likeness?' seems doubtful. But all that the argument will require is that we *can* do so: S.'s sole purpose here is to prepare the way for the (independent) introduction of a similar claim about cases of 'learning' in d4–7; and even if the claim turned out to hold universally of these, but only sometimes of (recognised) cases of ἀνάμνησις, that would not count against the former being included among the latter. **a9 σκόπει δή** 'Well then, consider . . .' **a9–10 φαμέν πού τι εἶναι ἴσον . . . 11–12 αὐτὸ τὸ ἴσον** 'We say, I suppose, that there is [exists] something equal – I don't mean a stick [which is equal] to a stick, or a stone to a stone, or anything else of that sort, but some further thing over and above all of these, [i.e.] the equal by itself: *are* we to say that there is something [of the sort], or nothing?' This is in essence a variant of the question in 65d4–5 (φαμέν τι εἶναι δίκαιον αὐτὸ ἢ οὐδέν;), applied to a new example; see n. The new formulation strongly suggests that ἔστι τι ἴσον/ δίκαιον (αὐτό); is a way of applying the standard 'is *x* something?' question (see 64c2n.) to items like τὸ ἴσον (αὐτό), τὸ δίκαιον (αὐτό); and the neuter singular of an adjective with the definite article is regularly used in Greek as an abstract noun (cf. c1 ἡ ἰσότης, which appears to be equivalent to τὸ ἴσον here). S.'s question will then be 'is there such a thing as equality by itself, which is different from the equality of one stick, or one stone, to another?' Simmias agrees enthusiastically that there is (b1). Exactly what it means to say that 'equality by itself is [exists]' is still unclear; but one new piece of information has been added, in the shape of the suggestion that this equality is separate from ('something further, over and above') all perceptible instances of equality. S. will provide an argument for this suggestion in b6–c6.

b1 Having already answered φαμὲν μέντοι νὴ Δία to the same sort of question at 65d6, Simmias now adds even more weight to his assent (θαυμαστῶς γε). **b2** ἦ καὶ ἐπιστάμεθα αὐτὸ ὃ ἔστιν ;: lit. 'Do we also (καί) know it (αὐτό is here an ordinary pronoun: cf. b4 αὐτοῦ), what it is?' Cf. 75b5–6 ἐπιστήμην αὐτοῦ τοῦ ἴσου ὅτι ἔστιν. For other examples of the relative introducing an indirect question, see LSJ s.v. ὅς ιν.6. 'We' here, as in 65d4 and 6, means (at least) primarily 'we members of the Socratic [Platonic] circle' (see 75d2–3n.); clearly not everyone could be said to know 'the equal by itself', especially if that had to include 'giving an account' of it (cf. 73a9–10n.). Some less restricted conception of knowledge could in principle be involved here; and indeed Simmias will shortly suggest (76b10–12) that if it comes to giving a proper account of things, S. is the *only* person capable of doing it. However, this remark is made after the introduction of other 'forms', like 'the beautiful', 'the good', 'the just', or 'the pious' (75c7–d3), and makes more sense in relation to these than in relation to 'the equal'; it surely requires little ingenuity to construct an adequate account of the latter (e.g. 'that which is commensurable with something else, and neither larger nor smaller': cf. 75c8–9, which juxtaposes knowledge of 'the equal' with knowledge of 'the greater' and 'the smaller'), whereas the difficulty of giving an account of the moral 'forms' is a recurrent theme of the Platonic dialogues (cf. e.g. *Phdr.* 263a–b, *Pol.* 285d–286a). Its relative straightforwardness may be part of the explanation for the choice of equality as the central example in the present argument; certainly it would not help to choose a case in which the very possibility of 'learning', i.e. getting knowledge, was in doubt. **b4** πόθεν λαβόντες αὐτοῦ τὴν ἐπιστήμην; ἆρ' οὐκ ἐξ ὧν ... 6 ἕτερον ὂν τούτων; lit. 'Having got the knowledge of it from where? Is it not the case that from the things we were mentioning just now, [that is] from seeing sticks or stones or some other equal things, from these we came to have that thing [i.e. the equal] in mind (ἐννοεῖν), [it] being different (ἕτερον) from these?' The first question is ambiguous: it may relate to either the immediate or the ultimate source of the knowledge in question (see respectively c7–9 ἐκ τούτων ... τῶν ἴσων – i.e. equal sticks, stones, etc. – αὐτοῦ τὴν ἐπιστήμην ἐννενόηκάς τε καὶ εἴληφας, and 76c6–9 πότε λαβοῦσαι αἱ ψυχαὶ ἡμῶν τὴν ἐπιστήμην αὐτῶν; οὐ γὰρ δὴ ἀφ' οὗ γε ἄνθρωποι γεγόναμεν. ... πρότερον ἄρα). Taken in the second sense, it introduces the whole of the main part of the argument;

taken in the first, it merely introduces the next step (in the shape of the question ἆρ' οὐκ ἐξ ὧν κτλ.). **b7 καί:** i.e. in addition to whatever reasons you have for thinking so already (cf. a11–b1, and especially *Symp.* 210e–211b). **b7–9 ἆρ' οὐ λίθοι μὲν ἴσοι κτλ.** 'Don't equal stones and sticks, while being the same [i.e. staying the same], some-times appear equal to one, but not to another?' This sentence has been much discussed; the main issues are whether we should read (*a*) τῶι μὲν ... τῶι δέ or (*b*) τοτὲ μὲν ... τοτὲ δέ (for which the evidence of the MSS is about equally balanced), and if the first, what is meant: τῶι μὲν ... τῶι δέ could mean either (*a.1*) '[seem] to one person ... [not] to an-other', or (*a.2*) '[equal] to one thing ... [not] to another'. The require-ments of the argument, however, seem to tip the balance decisively in favour of (*a*) over (*b*), and of (*a.2*) over (*a.1*). (*a.1*) and (*b*) would both reduce the point to one about how the ordinary equal things *appear* (equal sticks and stones are capable of appearing to this person here as equal, to that person there as unequal, or now, under one set of condi-tions, as equal, now under another as unequal); and while that may be sufficient for S.'s immediate needs (since the same will not hold of 'the equal by itself', c1–2), it is not enough to support the further claim which he will introduce at d5–7 (see n.), without further justification, that the equal sticks and stones are somehow *in themselves* deficient in respect of equality, when compared with 'the equal by itself'. Only (*a.2*) seems to come anywhere near meeting this requirement: a stone or stick which is equal to another (S. will be saying) is capable simulta-neously of appearing as (i.e. being seen as: φαίνεσθαι) equal to its pair (cf. a10 ξύλον ... ξύλωι) and as unequal to some further stone or stick; if so, it will evidently *be* both equal and unequal, while remaining the same (ταὐτὰ ὄντα). Of course, we might reply that in relation to the first thing it is a perfectly good example of equality; but it would still be true to say that its membership of the class of equals is qualified and conditional (as that of 'the equal by itself' allegedly is not).

c1–2 αὐτὰ τὰ ἴσα ἔστιν ὅτε ἄνισά σοι ἐφάνη, ἢ ἡ ἰσότης ἀνισότης; lit. 'Did the equals by themselves [or 'equals by themselves', referring to a class of such things: see below] sometimes (ἔστιν ὅτε = b8 ἐνίοτε: cf. 62a3–5n.) appear to you [to be] unequal, or equality [to be] in-equality?' The usual interpretation of this line takes 'the equals by themselves' and 'equality' simply as alternative names for 'the equal by itself': the point is (since a negative answer is clearly expected) that it, unlike equal stones and sticks, never appears to be the opposite of what it is (and so must be something different from them, c4–5). There are difficulties about taking at least αὐτὰ τὰ ἴσα in this way: most importantly, it would appear to imply that the 'form' of equality is to be conceived of as a set of two or more equal things, which apart from anything else would be at least superficially inconsistent with S.'s later claim that forms are among the things most likely to be 'incomposite' (ἀσύνθετα, 78c–d). The phrase might be no more than a loose form of expression, in which the plural is suggested by the preceding reference to perceptible equals (cf. Owen 1968, 114–15). An alternative solution is to suppose that the set of things describable as 'equal and nothing else' contains other members besides the form: specifically, the many instances of equality 'in' particular things (see esp. 102b5–6n., 103b4–5n., and Bluck 1959). In this case, S. will be establishing a truth about one member of the class (the form) by referring to something which is true of the class as a whole. For a related explanation, see Loriaux. (*Parm.* 129b αὐτὰ τὰ ὅμοια gives no help with the present passage, since it raises identical problems of interpretation.) That 'equals by themselves' do not φαίνεται unequal (or equality inequality) will be true in both possible senses of φαίνεσθαι: neither are they *seen as* (cf. b7–9n.) unequal (we do not see such things at all: cf. 65d9–10), nor do they *seem* so. **c3 οὐδεπώποτέ γε** 'Never yet, at any rate'. **c4 ταῦτα . . . τὰ ἴσα:** i.e., obviously, the equal stones and sticks of b7–9, not αὐτὰ τὰ ἴσα. **c7–9 ἀλλὰ μὴν ἐκ τούτων γ' κτλ.** 'And yet (ἀλλὰ μήν: *GP* 341), it is from *these* (γε: see a5n.) . . . equals, which are different from that equal [as has just been shown], that you nevertheless have come to have in mind, and got, your knowledge of it?' In that case, Simmias' acquisition of his knowledge of the equal matches the initial (and incomplete) description of ἀνάμνησις in 73c4–9. **c11** 'Then (οὐκοῦν) [sc. you got your knowledge of it from them, it] being either like them or unlike [them]?' In other words, the (immediate) 'getting of the knowledge of the equal' fulfils another of the conditions of ἀνάμνησις, the one laid down at a2–3. This follows from b6-c6: the equal will be on the one hand like equal stones and sticks, in so far as they are equal, but on the other unlike them (and so different from them), in so far as they are unequal. S. appears deliberately to leave it open under which guise they cause the equal to come to mind (we are said ἐννοεῖν it merely from seeing them, b5–6). Although in d4–7 their relationship to the equal seems at bottom to be treated as a case of likes to like (which would accord with one of P.'s ways of treating the relationship between forms and particulars: cf. 100a1–3n.), what is stressed is the limited nature of the likeness – they 'fall short' of the equal (d6–7); and the respect in which they fall short, on the interpretation to be adopted, is their capacity to be seen as, and be, unequal as well as equal, which makes them unlike it. Thus when we get knowledge of the equal from them, we can legitimately be said to be getting knowledge either of like from likes, or of unlike from unlikes (and both options are still left open in 76a). But the only point relevant to the argument, as S. suggests (c13–d2), is that on either alternative the case will still fit the relevant part of the description of ἀνάμνησις (74a2–3). **c13 διαφέρει δέ γε ... οὐδέν** 'But in any case (δέ γε, 'pick[ing] up the thread' after Simmias' reply: *GP* 154) it makes no difference.' **c13–d2 ἕως ἂν κτλ.** 'so long as, on seeing one thing, you come [i.e. one comes], from this sight, to have another in mind, whether like or unlike, it must have been [a case of] being reminded'. In fact, another important condition needs to be fulfilled, at least if there is to be ἀνάμνησις in the primary sense: what one is reminded of must have been *forgotten* (see 73e1–3n.). S. will return to this condition at a later stage (75c–d). Meanwhile, he attempts to demonstrate that our knowledge of the equal must originally have been acquired before birth (d4–75c5).

d4 τί δέ; The point from which the demonstration begins is the one prepared for at a5–7: our awareness, when we are being put in mind of one thing by another like it, of the degree of the likeness. **d4–5 περὶ τὰ ἐν τοῖς ξύλοις τε καὶ οἷς νυνδὴ ἐλέγομεν τοῖς ἴσοις:** lit. 'in relation to the [things] in the sticks and the equals which we were mentioning just now', i.e. 'in relation to what we perceive [or what happens] in the case of the sticks and in general (καί: see 58b6n.) the pairs of equal things ...' **d5 ἆρα φαίνεται:** sc. the sticks, etc. **d6 αὐτὸ τὸ ὃ ἔστιν ἴσον:** lit. 'the what is equal by itself'; i.e., as before, what is just equal, equal and nothing else. **d6–7 ἢ ἐνδεῖ κτλ.** 'or do they fall short of that (ἐνδεῖν used like a6 ἐλλείπειν; cf. 75b2 αὐτοῦ ἐνδεέστερα) at all (τι) in respect of being such a thing (τοιοῦτον) as the equal, or [do they] not [fall short] at all?' Simmias replies emphatically that they do. So (*a*) these things are equal, or at least can be referred to as such; (*b*) they are not equal in the same way that *the* equal is; rather (*c*) they fall short of being such as it is (τοιοῦτον εἶναι οἷον is apparently identical in meaning to τοιαῦτ' εἶναι οἷον, which is substituted for it in a variation of the same formula at 75b7). (*b*) and (*c*) have frequently been interpreted in terms of a claim that perceptible equals are never *perfectly* equal; but such a claim is nowhere argued for (certainly not in 65a–66a: cf. 65b10–11n., e2–3n.), and could hardly be derived directly from ordinary experience (why, for example, should one bronze casting not be exactly equal in size to another from the same mould – or ten cows exactly equal in number to ten more?). Given the proposed interpretation of b6–c6, however (b7–9n., c1–2n.), the importation of any large new premiss is in any case unnecessary: perceptible equals are not 'equal in the same way as the equal' just in so far as they are capable also of being unequal, as the equal is not; they 'fall short' of it, therefore, just in not being simply *equal*, as it is. (This, of course, will leave as an open question what it means to say that the form of equal 'is equal': that is, whether 'is' here is the copula, so that 'equal' is being predicated of the form, or whether it is rather the 'is' of identity, so that all that is being said, as Gallop puts it (128), is that 'the Form Equal *is* [identical with] Equal'. The first alternative certainly raises the more difficult questions; in particular, about what it is equal *to*. Cf. c1–2n.; and see further 106d5–7n.) **d9 οὐκοῦν:** again used to introduce a new point (as at 71b6, 73d5, etc.). **d9–10 βούλεται . . . εἶναι** 'aims to be', i.e. 'tends towards being'. Aristotelian parallels (e.g. *Nic. eth.* 1119b34) suggest that the metaphor is as good as dead.

e3–4 ἐνδεεστέρως δὲ ἔχειν: sc. αὐτοῦ (a variation on d6–7 ἐνδεῖ . . . ἐκείνου). **e6 τί οὖν; κτλ.** 'Well then? Have we or have we not ourselves (καὶ ἡμεῖς, 'we too') had this sort of experience [i.e. the one referred to in d4–7] in relation to equals and the equal by itself?'

75a1–2 ὅτε τὸ πρῶτον ἰδόντες τὰ ἴσα ἐνενοήσαμεν ὅτι ὀρέγεται κτλ. 'when we first came to have it in mind on seeing equals, that they strive . . .' There is no implication that we came to have this complex idea as soon as we began seeing equal things, or seeing them as equal. **a5 ἀλλὰ μήν:** as at 74c7, ἀλλὰ μήν announces one of the central premisses of the argument; similarly ἀλλὰ μὲν δή (used as a variant of ἀλλὰ μήν: *GP* 394–5) in all. If we can only come to have the equal in mind from seeing or from perceiving in general (a5–8, cf. 74b4–6), and if it is from (the same) acts of perception that we must come to have in mind that what we perceive falls short of the equal (a11–b2, cf. 74d4–8), then, given that we must have known the equal prior to our first having the experience in question (i.e. recognising that perceptible equals fall short, 74d9–e8), we must have got the knowledge of it before we began to use our senses; otherwise we should never have been able to compare perceptible equals to it (b4–9). If we did get it after that time, it must have come from the senses – but that is impossible, since at any time that sense-experience put us in mind of the equal, it must also have put us in mind of the difference between it and the equals we perceive, which will imply that we knew it even before that.   **a7 ἔκ τινος ἄλλης τῶν αἰσθήσεων** 'from some other of the kinds of perceiving'. The argument from 73d onwards has been couched exclusively in terms of seeing; S. now reintroduces the other senses, which were included in the original account of ἀνάμνησις at 73c4–d1. **a7–8 ταὐτὸν δὲ κτλ.** 'I count all these [as] the same'. **a9 ταὐτὸν γὰρ ἔστιν** 'Yes, they are the same.' **βούλεται:** cf. 74d9–10n. **a11 ἀλλὰ μὲν δὴ ἔκ γε τῶν αἰσθήσεων:** ἀλλὰ μὲν δή introduces a new step (*GP* 394), while γε functions as at 74a5, 74c7 – 'Again, it is from our acts of sensing and from nowhere else' (contrast γε in a9, which is 'limitative': 'at least').

b1 τὰ ἐν ταῖς αἰσθήσεσιν: sc. ἴσα.   **b1–2 τοῦ ὃ ἔστιν ἴσον:** see 74d6n. **b4–6 πρὸ τοῦ ἄρα ... αὐτοῦ τοῦ ἴσου ὅτι ἔστιν** 'Then it must, I imagine (που), have been before we began seeing and hearing and having the other sorts of sensations (τἄλλα is internal accusative after αἰσθάνεσθαι) that we actually got knowledge of what the equal by itself is' (lit. 'of the equal by itself, what it is': cf. 74b2).   **b6 εἰ ἐμέλλομεν ... 7 ὅτι** 'if we were going to refer the equals from our acts of sensing to it (ἐκεῖσε), [and to come to have in mind] that'. ('Perhaps ... ἐκεῖσε ἀνοίσειν is felt as equivalent to ἐκεῖσε ἀναφέροντες ἐννοήσειν', Hackforth, comparing 75a1–2 ἐνενοήσαμεν ὅτι ὀρέγεται.)   **b7 προθυμεῖται:** like a2 ὀρέγεται, a variation on 74d9 βούλεται, playing on its literal meaning of 'want'.   **b10–11** 'Well then (οὐκοῦν), it was as soon as we were born (γενόμενοι εὐθύς) that we were seeing, hearing, and in possession of the other senses?'

c1 ἔδει δέ γε ... ; 'And (δέ γε: cf. 74c13n.) must we have ...?''   **c4 πρὶν γενέσθαι κτλ.:** it would apparently have been possible for S. to move directly from here to his conclusion at 76c11–13 ('Then our souls did exist even before they were in human form ...'). Instead, he gives Simmias a choice: either we have retained our pre-natal knowledge of the equal and the other 'forms' all along, in which case we all actually know, now, the most important philosophical truths, or we lost it at birth, and have to recover it through 'learning'. This strategy is intelligible, however, given that the original project was to demonstrate the pre-existence of the soul by way of the theory of learning as ἀνάμνησις. Even if it has been established that our knowledge was originally acquired before birth (and Simmias himself will briefly raise an objection at 76c14–15), the theory of ἀνάμνησις itself requires it to be shown that that knowledge is somehow lost (see 73e1–3, 74c13–d2n.) – and in the specific case of equality, it is perhaps not obvious that it is (for example, having some workable sort of knowledge of equality is implied in the very ability to use the word 'equal', which will take one back, if not as far as birth, then close to it). Hence the fact that our attention is immediately switched, in c9–d5, to more problematic cases: cf. 74b2n. But the strategy also has rhetorical and dramatic advantages: it gives P. the opportunity to relax the somewhat constricted style forced on him by the complex argument of the preceding pages, and at the same time to reintroduce S. in his key role as the dying philosopher (76b10–12).   **c7 οὐκοῦν εἰ μὲν ... 10 σύμπαντα τὰ τοιαῦτα;** 'Now if, having got it before being born, we were born with it (ἔχοντες, sc. αὐτήν), did we know both before we were born and as soon as we were born not only the equal and the larger and the smaller [cf. 74b2n.] but also absolutely all such things?' This question begins by putting the first of the two options (see preceding n.) exclusively in terms of the equal, but ends by extending the scope of the discussion to all 'forms'. The following two sentences (c10–d5) constitute a kind of parenthesis justifying this extension; d7 εἰ μέν γε ... ἐπιλελήσμεθα then repeats c7–8 εἰ μὲν ... ἔχοντες ἐγενόμεθα, while applying it to the newly extended field, and both occurrences of μέν (since they now attach essentially to the same case) are answered by δέ in e2.   **c10–11 οὐ ... μᾶλλόν τι** 'not ... more at all'.

d2 οἷς ἐπισφραγιζόμεθα ... 3 ἀποκρινόμενοι: lit. 'on which we set this seal, "what is", both in our questions, when we ask questions, and in our answers, when we give answers'; i.e. which we label 'what is [equal, beautiful, good, etc.]' (cf. 74d6n., 75b1–2) in our dialectical (philosophical) exchanges (cf. 61c10–d2n., 63d7n.). There could be no

clearer way of indicating that ὃ ἔστι is a technical term (or of confirming the scope of 'we' in this context: cf. 74b2n., 65d4–5n.). Three
other interpretations of ὃ ἔστι are in principle possible: (*a*) 'that which
is [exists]'; (*b*) 'that which [e.g. the equal, the beautiful, or the good]
is'; (*c*) 'that which is', where this somehow combines (*a*) and (*b*). (*b*) is
Gallop's choice, (*c*) apparently that of Loriaux. (*a*) and (*c*) face the
objection that they are irreconcilable with the two immediately preceding passages in *Phd.* itself in which ὃ ἔστι appears to be used in the
kind of technical way suggested by the present passage, i.e. 74d6 and
75b1–2 (cf. also 78d4, 5n., and 92d8–9n.). (*b*), on the other hand, will
fit both 74d6 and 75b1–2, if ἴσον can be taken as subject of the phrase
(thus Gallop translates, in the second case, 'what equal is'). But given
that the emphasis of the surrounding context is on the difference between the ways in which particular equals and the form *are equal* (see
74c1–2 and esp. d5–6), and given also the position of ἴσον in 74d6 (if
it is to be read there at all) and 75b1–2, it seems easier and more
natural to take it as predicate rather than subject. What sense 'is'
has will still remain uncertain: see 74d6–7n. **d4 τούτων πάντων τὰς
ἐ.·ιστήμας:** lit. 'our knowledges of all these', i.e. our knowledge of the
beautiful, our knowledge of the good, etc. For related uses of the plural
of ἐπιστήμη, see *Theaet.* 197e–200c, *Phdr.* 276c. **d7 καὶ εἰ μέν γε …
8 εἰδέναι** '[It is] also [necessary], if having got [our knowledge of the
beautiful, the good, etc.] we did not forget [it] in each case [or 'on
each occasion', ἑκάστοτε], that we should be born knowing always [or
'should always be born knowing'] and should know throughout life.'
The alternative translations of ἑκάστοτε and ἀεί[1] (in brackets) represent the normal way of taking the sentence, and would import a reference to the idea of rebirth. But that is irrelevant to the argument,
and would anticipate both its conclusion and its formal combination
with the argument from opposites at 77c–d. The translations adopted
(suggested by Jowett and Hackforth respectively) give the points required: that if we did not forget *any part of* our knowledge, we must
always possess every part (so that everyone ought to know about the
things just mentioned, the beautiful, the good, etc., whereas in fact
they do not: 76b5–c3). The second point is in any case contained in ἀεὶ
διὰ βίου εἰδέναι: for a similar repetition, see 72b3–4. μέν γε (d7): γε
here, and in e2, gives extra weight to the clause as a whole ('determinative' γε again, as at 74a5, etc.; similarly at 76a1, 5: *GP* 159,
115). **d9 λαβόντα:** sc. τινά.

e2 οἶμαι is parenthetical, and does not affect the syntax of the sentence. **γιγνόμενοι ἀπωλέσαμεν** 'we lost [our knowledge] on being born'. **e3–4 περὶ αὐτὰ ἐκείνας . . . τὰς ἐπιστήμας** = d4 τούτων πάντων τὰς ἐπιστήμας. **e4 ποτε καὶ πρίν** 'at some earlier time too'. **e5–6 ἆρ' οὐχ . . . εἴη** 'wouldn't what we call learning be recovering knowledge which is our own (οἰκείαν)?'

76a1 δυνατὸν γὰρ δὴ τοῦτό γε ἐφάνη 'Yes, because (γάρ, reinforced by δή) this (τοῦτό γε: 'determinative' γε again, as at 74a5, etc.) seemed possible, [namely that . . .].' **a1–2 αἰσθόμενόν τι ἢ ἰδόντα ἢ ἀκού-σαντα ἤ . . . λαβόντα** 'on perceiving something – whether seeing it or hearing it or getting some other kind of [sense-perception] of it'. **a3 ἐπλησίαζεν** 'was close'. **a4 δυοῖν θάτερον** 'one of two things [sc. is the case]'. **a5 αὐτά:** cf. 75e2–3n. **a6–7 οὐδὲν ἀλλ' ἢ ἀναμιμνήισκονται οὗτοι** 'these [are doing] nothing except being reminded'.

b3 οὐκ ἔχω κτλ.: this is not slowness on Simmias' part, but a reaction to two more or less equally unpalatable alternatives – since in different ways both would do away with the apparently familiar process of learning. **b5 δοῦναι λόγον:** 'giving an account' here seems to mean giving a definition which can be rationally defended; see 78d1–2, and *Rep.* 534b–c. **b8 ἦ καὶ δοκοῦσί σοι πάντες ἔχειν** 'Does everyone really (καί) seem to you able . . .?' **b8–9 τούτων ὧν νυνδὴ ἐλέγομεν:** i.e. the things mentioned in 75c11–d2, the beautiful, the good, the just, the pious (and so on). The Platonic dialogues are full of people failing to 'give an account' of such things: so Hippias fails with beauty in *HMa.* (if that is genuinely Platonic), Thrasymachus with justice in *Rep.* i, Euthyphro with piety in *Euth.* **b10 βουλοίμην μεντἄν** 'I should certainly *like* [sc. that to be the case].' 'In potential statements, [μέν-τοι] with ἄν and optative, by crasis, μεντἄν, expressing lively surprise or indignation', *GP* 402. **b10–12 ἀλλὰ πολὺ μᾶλλον κτλ.:** in what are probably the earlier dialogues, like *Euth.*, S. is found acting out the role he attributes to himself in *Ap.*, of the person who only differs from others in knowing his ignorance; and in *Rep.* vi (506b–507a) he openly declares himself ignorant of the good. In Book iv, however, he has advanced at least to provisional definitions of some of the virtues, and perhaps the ability to do that would count as giving an account ἀξίως (b12).

c6–7 οὐ γὰρ δὴ κτλ. 'Certainly not (οὐ γὰρ δή … γε: *GP* 243) since we were born as human beings.' **c12–13 καὶ φρόνησιν εἶχον:** cf. 70b3–4. **c14 εἰ μὴ ἄρα** 'unless after all'. **ἅμα γιγνόμενοι** 'at the same time as we were being born'. Simmias attempts to go back a step: given that we must have had the relevant pieces of knowledge once, and must have acquired them before we began using our senses (74d4–75c3), why should that not have happened at the very moment of birth, rather than being pushed back into some previous period? The proper place for the objection, then, would have been in 75c; P. delays it, however, because its refutation (d1–4) depends on the point introduced in the intervening section, namely that the knowledge originally acquired must have been lost.

d1 εἶεν, ὦ ἑταῖρε κτλ. 'Very well, dear boy; but at what other time, may I ask, do we lose them?' ποῖος suggests a note of scorn (cf. Burnet). **d2 οὐ γὰρ δή … γε:** see c6–7n. **d3 ἢ ἐν τούτωι ἀπόλλυμεν ἐν ὧιπερ καὶ λαμβάνομεν;** 'Or we lose them at the very time at which we also get them?', where the 'also' (καί) logically belongs in the main clause rather than the relative clause: cf. *GP* 295–6. **d5 οὐδὲν εἰπών** 'talking nonsense'. **d8 ἃ θρυλοῦμεν ἀεί** 'which we are always talking about', i.e. in our discussions (see 75d1–3), including the present one. (For θρυλεῖν, see also 65b3.) **d8–9 πᾶσα ἡ τοιαύτη οὐσία:** lit. 'all being of that sort': οὐσία, a noun originally derived from the verb εἶναι, is here applied collectively to a group of things in virtue of their 'being', i.e. existing (hence 'existents of this sort'). **d9 τὰ ἐκ τῶν αἰσθήσεων πάντα ἀναφέρομεν:** cf. 75b6–7.

e1–2 What 'was there before' (ὑπάρχουσαν πρότερον), is 'rediscovered' (ἀνευρίσκοντες), and 'is ours' (ἡμετέραν οὖσαν) is clearly not the οὐσία in question, as the text literally says, but our knowledge of it. **e2 ἀπεικάζομεν** 'we compare'. **e2 ἀναγκαῖον … 5 εἰρημένος εἴη** 'it is necessary that just as *these* (καὶ ταῦτα, with emphatic καί: i.e. the things referred to in d8–9, not the ταῦτα of e2) exist, just so too (καί²) does our soul even (καί³) before we were born; but if these do not exist, this argument of ours will have been gone through [lit. 'said'] in vain'. As e5–7 confirms, S.'s point is no more than that the force of the preceding argument will depend on the truth of the claim that things like 'the beautiful' and 'the good' (i.e. 'forms') exist. In so far as that claim (and even its meaning: cf. 74a9–12n.) remains unestablished, so too then will the pre-existence of the soul. **e5 ἴση ἀνάγκη:** i.e. whatever degree of necessity is involved in the first case (which might be none at all) will carry over to the second. **e6 πρὶν καὶ ἡμᾶς γεγονέναι** 'before we were actually born'. **e7 καὶ εἰ μὴ ταῦτα, οὐδὲ τάδε** 'and if not these, not τάδε either', where τάδε refers to τὰς ἡμετέρας ψυχὰς (εἶναι) ... (i.e. 'if it is not the case that these exist, neither is it the case that our souls ...'). **e8 ὑπερφυῶς ... δοκεῖ μοι ... 77a2 ἣν σὺ νῦν λέγεις** 'There appears to me to be emphatically (ὑπερφυῶς, lit. 'extraordinarily') the same necessity [sc. in both cases], and it is opportune indeed ('intensive' γε, as at 60c9, etc.) that the argument takes refuge in [lit.] the like existence of both our soul before birth and the being of which you now speak' (referring to e2–4 οὕτως ὥσπερ ... πρὶν γεγονέναι ἡμᾶς). For εἰς καλόν, used adverbially ('opportunely'), see *Meno* 89e, *Symp.* 174e; for the metaphor καταφεύγει ὁ λόγος (which makes the argument the prey, and Socrates and Simmias the hunters), cf. 63a2 and 88d9, with Burnet's nn.

77a2 οὐ γὰρ ἔχω ... 3 ὡς τοῦτο, τὸ ... 'For I for my part (ἔγωγε) have nothing which is as plain to me as this, [namely] that ...' This explains εἰς καλὸν ... καταφεύγει ὁ λόγος: if the argument depends on accepting *this*, Simmias at least has no qualms. **a3–4 εἶναι ὡς οἷόν τε μάλιστα:** either (*a*) 'are [exist] as certainly as anything could' (cf. Hackforth), or (*b*) 'are [exist] to the highest possible degree' (cf. e.g. Gallop). The idea of degrees of being is undoubtedly Platonic (see e.g. *Rep.* 585b–c), but probably could not be introduced in so casual a way; and (*a*) is in fact all that the context requires. **a5 ἔμοιγε** 'for me, at least'.

77a6–78b3: Cebes asks for further reassurance

This short section links the first two arguments (the cyclical argument and the argument from recollection), and introduces the third, the 'affinity' argument.

77a6 τί δὲ δὴ Κέβητι; is equivalent to τί δέ δή; ἱκανῶς ἀποδέδεικται Κέβητι; (For τί δὲ δή, cf. 65a9, d4.) **a8 καίτοι** 'and yet'. **a9 ἀλλ'** 'Still' (i.e. despite the fact that he is an obstinate sceptic about arguments). **a10 οὐκ ἐνδεῶς τοῦτο πεπεῖσθαι αὐτόν, ὅτι** 'that he has been fully (οὐκ ἐνδεῶς: cf. the use of ἐνδεῖ, ἐνδεεστέρως, ἐνδεέστερος in the preceding argument) persuaded of this, [namely] that'.

b1 εἰ 'whether'.   **b2 οὐδὲ αὐτῶι μοι δοκεῖ . . . ἀποδεδεῖχθαι** 'doesn't seem even to me to have been demonstrated'.   **b3 ἐνέστηκεν** 'is blocking the way' (a military metaphor: cf. Thuc. 3.23).   **νυνδή:** 70a.
b3–5 τὸ τῶν πολλῶν, ὅπως μὴ . . . τέλος ἦι 'the [fear] of the many, that at the same time as the person is dying his soul is scattered, and that this is its end'. For ὅπως μή instead of plain μή after expressions of fearing (here easily supplied from the context, supported by 70a), see *MT* 370. διασκεδάννυται is to be taken as a form of the subjunctive, in place of διασκεδαννύηται (similarly ε1 διασκεδάννυσιν, for διασκεδαννύηι; cf. also the optative form πήγνυτο at 118a2, for πηγνύοιτο): the normal way of expressing fears about what may be the case (or may turn out to be the case) is with the subjunctive, as also in (ὅπως μὴ) αὐτῆι τοῦ εἶναι τέλος ἦι, the present indicative being reserved for cases where what is feared is something actually occurring now (so e.g. at 84e2–3 φοβεῖσθε μὴ . . . νῦν διάκειμαι: cf. *MT* 92, 369.1).   **b6 γίγνεσθαι** 'come into being'.   **b6–7 ἄλλοθέν ποθεν:** i.e. from some source other than itself. The possibility Simmias raises here is not quite the one that S. raised and rejected at 72d, since that did not include pre-existence (καὶ εἶναι πρὶν κτλ.); but it will be covered by his argument there, as he proceeds to point out (c–d).   **b8 καὶ αὐτὴν** 'it too'.

c1–2 φαίνεται . . . ὥσπερ 'it seems as if' (cf. *Phdr.* 270d, Ar. *Clouds* 1276).   **c2 οὗ δεῖ:** i.e. τούτου ὃ δεῖ ἀποδεδεῖχθαι.   **c6 μέν:** as d4–5 shows, the μέν is answered by d5 ὅμως δέ, and in effect signals in advance that a concession is going to be made: 'It has actually been shown even now (c7 καὶ νῦν) . . . All the same . . .'

d2–3 τοῦ τεθνάναι 'being dead'.   **d4 ἐπειδή γε** 'given only that' (see *GP* 143).   **d4–5 ἀποδέδεικται κτλ.** 'Well then (οὖν), the point in question (ὅπερ λέγεται, lit. 'what is being said') has been shown even now' (picking up the beginning of the speech at c6–7).   **d5 δοκεῖς . . . 7 ἔτι μᾶλλον** 'I think you and Simmias would like to work through this point (τοῦτον . . . τὸν λόγον = d5 ὅπερ λέγετε = d3–4 (τὴν ψυχὴν) καὶ ἐπειδὰν ἀποθάνηι εἶναι) too (καί), still further' (i.e. even though it has already been covered).   **d7 τὸ τῶν παίδων:** cf. b3–4 τὸ τῶν πολλῶν (tr. 'like children').   **d7–8 ὡς ἀληθῶς** 'literally': S. plays on Cebes' language at 70a, which Simmias has here recalled in 77b.   **d8–e1 διαφυσᾶι καὶ διασκεδάννυσιν:** both subjunctives (see b3–5n.).

e3 ὡς δεδιότων: sc. ἡμῶν: 'as though we were afraid' (i.e. of what you say we are afraid of); the gen. abs. is used despite the fact that the accusative ἡμᾶς has to be supplied after ἀναπείθειν.   **e4 μᾶλλον δὲ ...
5 φοβεῖται** 'or rather, not as though *we* were afraid [of it], but [lit.] perhaps there is even in us [sc. adults] a child who fears such things', i.e. 'but as though there were a child in us ...'   **e6 μεταπείθειν:** if the simple form πείθειν (a7, 9) denotes persuading in general, μεταπείθειν means to persuade someone to change (μετα-) his or her opinion; similarly perhaps ἀναπείθειν (e4).   **e9 ἕως ἂν ἐξεπάισητε** 'until you succeed in charming it out of him'. The reading ἐξεπάισητε seems on balance preferable to ἐξεπάισηται (and to ἐξιάσηται): the middle ἐξεπάισηται seems difficult to justify, and even if Cebes does not respond immediately to the suggestion that he and his friends are the ones to do the 'charming' (cf. Verdenius), S. means it seriously (78a7–9). (ἐπάιδειν also appears at 114d7, in an interestingly different role.)

78a2 ἐπειδὴ σύ ... ἡμᾶς ἀπολείπεις: good arguments are similarly represented as ἐπωιδαί at *Charm.* 157a.   **a4 πολλὰ δὲ καὶ τὰ τῶν βαρβάρων γένη** 'and there are many races of non-Greeks too', sc. ἐν οἷς ἔνεισί που ἀγαθοὶ ἄνδρες. Characteristically, S. declines to accept Cebes' praise: presumably (που) the human race as a whole (= Greeks + non-Greeks) is large enough to contain good men ... But the seriousness of this suggestion (and so also the tone of the 'presumably') is immediately put in doubt by the reference to money in a5–7; S. has little regard for those who expect payment in return for their wisdom (i.e. the 'sophists' and rhetoricians: see e.g. *Ap.* 19d–20c). Cebes may actually find better resources closer to hand (a7–9).   **a5 διερευνᾶσθαι** 'track down'.   **a6–7 οὐκ ἔστιν εἰς ὅτι κτλ.** 'there is nothing on which you could more opportunely spend money'.   **a7–8 ζητεῖν δὲ χρὴ καὶ αὐτοὺς μετ' ἀλλήλων** 'But you must also search by yourselves along with one another': as Socrates' next words confirm ('for neither perhaps would you easily find people able *to do this* more than you'), the implied object of ζητεῖν is ἐπωιδάς, i.e. ways of charming away the fears of the 'child' (arguments), rather than ἐπωιδόν (cf. Verdenius).   **a10–b1 ἀλλὰ ταῦτα μὲν δή κτλ:** ἀλλὰ ... δή prepares us for the main point, given in ὅθεν δὲ κτλ. (see *GP* 241, on 95b7): 'That will certainly be done; but let us return [to the point] from where we left [the argument] behind, if that meets with your approval.'   **ἀπελίπομεν:** Cebes' repetition of the same verb that he used in a2, but with a different object, perhaps signals his acceptance of S.'s implied rebuke – what matters is the argument, not the effect on him and his friends of S.'s imminent departure.

b2 ἀλλὰ μὴν . . . γε: cf. 58d7n., d4n. ('I certainly *am* happy').   **πῶς γὰρ οὐ μέλλει;** lit. 'how is it likely that it should not [meet with my approval]', i.e. 'of course' (cf. LSJ s.v. μέλλω i.f).

78b4–84b8: the argument from 'affinity'

Socrates next argues that soul is immortal by reference to its affinity to the un-changing and incomposite 'forms'. In the course of the argument, especially in its later stages, he reintroduces and expands the central themes of his 'defence', which initially gave rise to the discussion of immortality, so renewing his plea for the life of philosophy.

78b4–5 δεῖ ἡμᾶς ἀνερέσθαι ἑαυτούς: what follows will thus be an example of what S. proposed at a7–8, ζητεῖν . . . αὐτοὺς μετ' ἀλλήλων.   **b5 τῶι ποίωι τινὶ ἄρα προσήκει** 'to what sort of thing it actually belongs' ('actually' is meant to render ἄρα, which in such cases 'in effect . . . does little more than add liveliness to the question': *GP* 39). προσήκει = 'belongs to', indicating a somewhat loose relation: if prop-erty *F* is said to 'belong to' item *G* in this sense, no more may be meant than that *F* may reasonably be expected to attach to *G* (but see 68c5–6). Cf. 80b9, where what is said to 'belong to' body (to be quickly dissolved into its parts) turns out either not to be true of it at all, or only usually and in most respects.   **b7 οὐ** is indispensable for the sense, but, curiously, absent from all MSS.   αὖ 'in turn'.   **b8 πότερον** 'which of the two'.

c1 τῶι μὲν συντεθέντι τε καὶ συνθέτωι ὄντι φύσει 'what has been compounded [i.e. put together] and is composite by nature': what is 'composite by nature' can evidently still be said συντεθῆναι (c2); this second description does not therefore introduce something in addition to τὸ συντεθέν, but merely makes it clear that that description includes natural entities as well as artificial ones (which have literally been 'put together').   **c2 τοῦτο** simultaneously refers backwards, to b6 τὸ διασκεδάννυσθαι, and forwards, to διαιρεθῆναι ταύτηι ἧιπερ συνετέθη ('being divided in the way in which it was compounded', i.e., presumably, into the parts from which it was compounded), which is S.'s interpretation of διασκεδάννυσθαι. On προσήκει, see b5n.: S. is not proposing that if something has parts, it must necessarily undergo division, but only that it is this sort of thing that we should expect to be divided. The relationship between incompositeness and indivisibility, on the other hand (c3–4), is clearly meant to be a necessary one. But that προσήκει should be made to cover this case too is both stylistically convenient and logically unobjectionable: if the incomposite is necessarily indivisible, it will also be true that indivisibility 'belongs to' it in some weaker sense. **c3–4 τούτωι μόνωι . . . εἴπερ τωι ἄλλωι:** for the apparent illogicality, cf. 62a2–3n. **c6–8 οὐκοῦν ἅπερ ἀεὶ κτλ.** 'Well then, isn't it most likely that the things that always remain in exactly the same state (κατὰ ταὐτά and ὡσαύτως are here equivalent expressions, paired for emphasis: cf. 78e2–5, Gallop 137, and Verdenius) are the things that are incomposite [sc. and therefore indivisible], whereas [it is most likely, isn't it, that] the things that are now like this, now like that, and never the same (τὰ . . . κατὰ ταὐτά, sc. ἔχοντα), are composite?' All that can strictly be derived from c1–4 is that *if* something is divided, it must be composite (see b5n. and c2n., and b6–7 ὑπὲρ τοῦ ποίου τινὸς (προσήκει) δεδιέναι μὴ πάθηι αὐτό), and that only in the case of the incomposite is division ruled out. This will leave it open that what is composite might nevertheless not be divided (so for example 72a–d assumed the permanence of the universe itself, which is certainly a composite thing). It will then follow that if there are any things that are actually unchanging (where change includes being divided), they will be the most likely candidates for membership of the class of the incomposite; while at the same time there will be no certainty that they belong to it. (Similarly, things which are always changing are only the most likely candidates for compositeness, so that there might be things that were incomposite, and so not subject to division, but which were nevertheless permanently changing in other respects. There seem to be no grounds for Gallop's suggestion (138) that change of any kind is understood to depend on the rearrangement of parts.) The next step (c10–d7) will be to identify a group of things which fit the description 'unchanging': the forms. For the double δέ in c7–8 (τὰ δέ ... ταῦτα δέ) see *GP* 183–4; the second reinforces the contrast marked by the first ('whereas . . .'). **c10 δή:** cf. 71d5n. **ἐφ' ἅπερ:** sc. ἦιμεν. **c10–d1 ἐν τῶι ἔμπροσθεν λόγωι:** 74a–77a.

d1–2 αὐτὴ ἡ οὐσία ἧς λόγον δίδομεν τοῦ εἶναι καὶ ἐρωτῶντες καὶ ἀποκρινόμενοι 'The very set of existents of whose essence we give an account in our dialectical exchanges': οὐσία is used as at 76d8–9 (see n.), while τὸ εἶναι substitutes for οὐσία in the sense of 'essence' (see 65d13). εἶναι is taken by Verdenius to 'refer to . . . existence'; but in the previous argument, to which we have just been referred, 'giving an account' in relation to the forms was connected with knowing what each of them is, rather than merely that it is (exists): see 74b2n., 75b5–6n. καὶ ἐρωτῶντες καὶ ἀποκρινόμενοι also takes us back to the same argument: see 75d2–3n. **d2–3 ὡσαύτως ἀεὶ ἔχει κατὰ ταὐτά:** ὡσαύτως in this case strictly qualifies ἔχει κατὰ ταὐτά ('is it always identically in the same state . . . ?'); but the effect is scarcely different from c6 κατὰ ταὐτά καὶ ὡσαύτως. **d3 αὐτὸ τὸ ἴσον . . . 4 τὸ ὄν** 'the equal by itself, the beautiful by itself, each "what is [F]" by itself, that which [just] is [F]'. ὃ ἔστιν in ἕκαστον ὃ ἔστιν must be taken as the technical formula which was introduced in 75d1–3, in a virtually identical context (extending a point from particular forms to forms in general); see 75d2–3n. τὸ ὄν is the participial version of ὃ ἔστι, and seems merely to serve to give the sentence a more manageable subject: on the interpretation adopted, it is shorthand for the whole of αὐτὸ ἕκαστον ὃ ἔστι, to which it stands in apposition. (Gallop, e.g., appears to take ὄν here in an existential sense; but that P. should here be using the description 'that which exists' to pick out the forms is made unlikely by 79a6 τῶν ὄντων, in which εἶναι must be used existentially, and which refers indiscriminately both to forms and to particular things in the physical world.) **d4–5 μή . . . ἐνδέχεται** 'do they ever admit of any change whatever?' The μή suggests that a negative answer is expected, as indeed it is; but a translation which emphasises this will make nonsense of the next question ('Or do they always remain the same?'). Cf. *Gorg.* 488b. **d5 αὐτῶν ἕκαστον ὃ ἔστι:** lit. 'each "what is" of them', i.e. each member of the class in question (forms), to which we attach the label 'what is [F]'. ἕκαστον ὃ ἔστι needs plainly to be taken in the same way as in the line before. **d5–6 μονοειδὲς ὄν αὐτὸ καθ' αὑτό** 'being uniform in and by itself', i.e. when considered in and by itself, apart

from its counterparts in the world of the senses (cf. Loriaux). Particular beautiful things, for example, have a habit of changing (d10–e4);
but there is only one way of being 'the beautiful by itself'. For αὐτὸ
καθ' αὐτό, see 64c5–8n.   **d10 τί δὲ τῶν πολλῶν καλῶν . . . ;** 'And
what [sc. do you say] about the many beautiful [things] . . . ?' Cf. τί δὲ
. . . περί at 65a9; for verbs of speaking and thinking (unusually) with
plain genitives, see e.g. Soph. *El.* 317, (P.) *Rep.* 459b.

e1 [ἢ καλῶν]: editors are divided about whether to delete ἢ καλῶν
here or καλῶν in d10 (the text hardly makes sense with both); but
the decisive consideration seems to be that ἢ πάντων τῶν κτλ. (e2)
makes it necessary to take ἴσων as substantive (= τῶν πολλῶν ἴσων)
rather than as adjective, as it would be if καλῶν (d10) were removed
('. . . the many things, such as men, etc., [i.e.] either equal men, etc.,
or . . .').   **e2 πάντων τῶν ἐκείνοις ὁμωνύμων** 'all the things that share
the same names as those things', i.e. all the types of things that share
the same names as the corresponding forms (as e.g. equal things share
the name 'equal' with 'the equal by itself').   **e2–3 πᾶν τοὐναντίον
ἐκείνοις** 'in complete contrast with those things'.   **e3–4 οὔτε αὐτὰ
αὑτοῖς . . . κατὰ ταὐτά;** '[are they] practically (ὡς ἔπος εἰπεῖν) never
in any way the same (κατὰ ταὐτά) either as themselves or as each
other?' Particular equal and beautiful things are almost always changing, in every respect, and so vary both in relation to what they previously were themselves, and in relation to other things (cf. Gallop).
With ὡς ἔπος εἰπεῖν, S. recognises the exaggeration, which corresponds
to the emphatic contrary claim claim in d6–7 in relation to forms.   **e5
οὕτως αὖ . . . ταῦτα** 'I agree with your description in this case too
(αὖ).'

79a1 κἂν . . . κἂν . . . κἂν: the καὶ in κἂν is emphatic (cf. 63c9n.), but
at least in the second and third cases also connective.   **a3 ἄλλωι** logically belongs outside the relative clause ('there is nothing else with
which . . .').   **a4 ἀιδῆ . . . οὐχ ὁρατά:** οὐχ ὁρατόν explains the unusual
and poetic ἀιδές, required for the pun (ἀιδής/Ἅιδης) which surfaces
explicitly at 80d5–6. 'Unseen'/'invisible' here is clearly shorthand for
'imperceptible by any of the senses', which in turn seems to imply
'non-bodily', ἀσώματος: see 85e5. (For a defence of the reading ἀιδῆ,
in preference to ἀειδῆ, see Burnet.)   **a6 θῶμεν οὖν . . . ὄντων** 'So do
you want us to posit two kinds of existent things . . . ?'

b1 φέρε δή introduces a crucial stage in the argument (the application of the results so far obtained to the case of soul and body); cf. 63b4. **ἄλλο τι:** see 70c9n. That 'part of ourselves is body, part soul' has of course been assumed at least since 64c (the definition of death as the separation of soul from body). **b4–5 φαμὲν ἂν εἶναι ... τὸ σῶμα** 'do we say that the body would be' (cf. 70b10n.). The body can hardly fail to be 'more like' and 'more akin to' the class of the visible, sc. than that of the invisible (as Cebes' answer implies), since it is itself patently a member of the class. Cf. b12–17, where S. moves from 'soul is unseen/invisible' to 'soul is more like the invisible [than the body]'. A claim of this kind is needed to prepare the way for the desired conclusion (80a–b) that soul shares other features which have been attributed to the visible (via the forms: permanence (i.e. lack of change), and therefore (most likely) incompositeness), in turn entailing indivisibility or indissolubility. **b8 οὐχ ὑπ' ἀνθρώπων γε:** ἄνθρωποι are here probably being contrasted not so much with gods as with disembodied souls (see esp. 76c7 ἀφ' οὗ ... ἄνθρωποι γεγόναμεν, 76c11–12, 77b7). According to the traditional/Homeric view of death, which Cebes is still in effect representing (see 70a, 77d–e), ψυχαί (i.e. the shades of the dead) are in fact visible – though not to the living, unless, *per impossibile*, they emulated Odysseus in *Od.* 11. **b9–10 ἀλλὰ μὴν ἡμεῖς γε** 'But (adversative ἀλλὰ μήν) we at any rate [sc. whatever anyone else may choose to do] were talking about what was visible and invisible with reference to human nature.' S.'s reponse here is slightly sharp in tone. **b12–17** The expected pair to b4–5 would be 'soul is then more like the invisible [than the visible]'; on the other hand, as c2–8 will admit, the soul obviously does have something in common with the visible, namely that – under some conditions – it is subject to change, of a quite violent kind. Thus the most that it is so far prudent to assert is that the soul is more like the invisible *than the body* (in so far as it is itself invisible). Once a limit has been set to the changeability of soul in d1–7, S. can be less circumspect: d8–9 'To which category ... does soul seem to you to be more alike and akin?', to which Cebes responds '... soul is completely and absolutely more like the unchanging than the changing' (but again only 'more like', in the light of c2–8).

c2 καὶ τόδε: another consideration which will allow the same conclusion, that the soul is more akin to the unchanging (the forms), the body to the changing.   **πάλαι ἐλέγομεν:** 65a–67b. As in that earlier context, soul is again understood exclusively in terms of the intellect. **c4–5 τοῦτο γάρ . . . σκοπεῖν τι:** the explanation seems hardly necessary; but it is rhetorically useful, in returning our attention to the leading concept of σῶμα.   **c6 μέν:** repeated from c2.   **c6–8 ἕλκεται . . . πλανᾶται . . . ταράττεται . . . εἰλιγγιᾶι ὥσπερ μεθύουσα:** for the first and third ideas, see esp. 66a5–6; the second and fourth are picturesque developments of these.   **c8 τοιούτων** = πλανωμένων, i.e. μηδέποτε κατὰ ταὐτὰ ἐχόντων.

d1–2 ἐκεῖσε οἴχεται εἰς τὸ καθαρόν: see 65c–67b. The forms are 'pure' in that they are 'unmixed' with anything else (εἰλικρινής, 66a2, 67b1); each is whatever it is just by itself. The further epithets added in d2 are justified by the preceding stage of the present argument: that forms remain the same (ὡσαύτως ἔχον), and admit no change of any kind, was agreed at 78d; but what admits no change must always exist (ἀεὶ ὄν), and therefore be 'deathless' (ἀθάνατος), in the extended sense of not perishing (which in turn is understood in the argument as a whole in terms of a thing's not being divided into parts: see 78b4–c4, and cf. 80b2 ἀδιαλύτωι, 4 διαλυτῶι).   **d3 καὶ ὡς συγγενὴς οὖσα** primarily explains ἀεὶ μετ' ἐκείνου . . . γίγνεται, and only secondarily d4–6 πέπαυταί . . . ἐφαπτομένη, which describes the consequences of that. S. is implicitly referring to the idea that 'like is drawn to like', which is at least as old as Homer (*Od.* 17.218). (For a more direct exploitation of the same idea, see *Lysis* 214a–d, which quotes – or slightly misquotes – the Homeric line.) But S.'s argument should probably not be regarded as depending on this idea, which would involve an obvious *petitio principii*; soul is 'akin' to the forms in so far as they constitute its proper objects.   **d4 πέπαυταί . . . ὃ ἐφαπτομένη** 'has ceased from its wandering and in relation to those things always stays identically in the same state, because laying hold of such things', i.e. other things which stay in the same state. If the soul (*qua* intellect) only 'wanders about' when in company with the body, and achieves stability without it, then there will be grounds for saying that the latter rather than the former state reveals its true nature.   **d6–7 καὶ τοῦτο αὐτῆς τὸ πάθημα φρόνησις κέκληται** adds further confirmation of the same point: wisdom rather than drunken confusion is surely the soul's natural and proper condition (τοῦτο . . . τὸ πάθημα = τὸ πεπαῦσθαι, etc.).

e3 μεθόδου 'line of inquiry'; originally, and perhaps to some degree still, 'pursuit', as in hunting.   **e3–4 ὅλωι καὶ παντί** 'completely and absolutely'.   **e8 ὅρα δὴ καὶ τῆιδε, ὅτι . . .** 'Now look [at the matter] in this way too, that . . .' On this new μέθοδος (e8–80a9), see 80a2–3n. **ἐν τῶι αὐτῶι ὦσι:** lit. 'are in the same [place]', i.e. are together.

80a1 ἡ φύσις προστάττει: '. . . the conception of "nature" here, as elsewhere in P., is normative. What "nature ordains" . . . is what ought to happen, not what usually does' (Gallop 141, explaining the apparent contradiction e.g. with 66b–d, 83c–e).   **a2 καὶ κατὰ ταῦτα αὖ . . . 3 τῶι θνητῶι;** 'in this way too, in its turn, which of the two seems to you to be like the divine [i.e. the immortal], and which like the mortal?' (That 'the divine' is equivalent to 'the immortal' is shown both by its opposition to τὸ θνητόν, and by 80b1, where the function of καὶ ἀθανάτωι is primarily to explain θείωι: cf. Loriaux.) The way in which this question is introduced (καὶ κατὰ ταῦτα αὖ) implies that the previous μέθοδος too (which according to the implications of 79d9–e5 comprised the whole of 79a1–e7) was about the same question; and that entails that the real point of the conclusion in 79e2–7 – as we might expect – was about soul and body in relation to one particular kind of change, i.e. perishing: cf. 79d1–2n., 78c6–8n. S. can now use the simple adjective ('like') rather than the comparative, because no qualification attaches to the point of resemblance now being introduced (see 79b12–17n.).   **a3–4 ἢ οὐ δοκεῖ σοι . . . ἄρχειν** 'Or doesn't the divine seem to you [to be] such as to rule . . .?' 'The divine', *qua* ruling, can hardly refer to the forms; presumably the gods are meant. These will constitute a new category of things which are 'very likely' to fall into the class of the incomposite, (*a*) in so far as they are immortal (if dying or perishing is assumed always to be a matter of a thing's being divided into its constituent parts: see 79d1–2n.), but also (*b*) in so far as they are unchanging. While being capable – like the soul – of thought, action and movement, they do not change in their essence: cf. esp. *Rep.* 380d–381e.   **a8 δῆλα δή** 'It is quite clear'.   **a10–b5** collects together the threads of 78d1–80a9 as a whole: soul is (very) like the divine and immortal (80a8; cf. 79d2), intelligible (νοητόν, referring both to what is an object of thought and knowledge, and to what is unseen: 79d1–7, 79b16), uniform (μονοειδές: 78d5), undissolved (ἀδιάλυτον: see b2n.) and unchanging (79d9–e5), while body is (very) like the human and mortal, multiform (πολυειδές: cf. 78d5–6n.), unintelligible (ἀνόητον), meeting with dissolution (διαλυτόν: see b4n.) and always changing. The most important items in both lists are the second, fifth and sixth (immortal/mortal, undissolved/dissoluble, unchanging/changing), the others being included in so far as they have been held to imply these. Since he and Cebes have discovered a number of different grounds for connecting soul with the divine, immortal, etc. (i.e., primarily, the forms), and body with the human, mortal, etc. (particular things), S. now feels able to strengthen his claim: soul and body are now not merely 'like' (80a3) or 'more like' (79b16, e1, 4) the immortal and the mortal respectively, but 'most like' them (ὁμοιότατον, 80b3, 5). The implication is clear: that there are good grounds for supposing soul itself to be unchanging, unperishing and undivided, and body to be the opposite.

b1 τάδε ἡμῖν συμβαίνει 'we reach the following results'. **b2 ἀδιαλύ-τωι:** what is ἀδιάλυτον is either (a) what is incapable of being dissolved (divided), or (b) what is not actually dissolved, although it is capable of it. (b) is to be preferred here, since (a) would be unjustified by the argument (see 78c6–8n.). (a) will, however, be introduced in the next stage of the argument, in b8–10 (= τὸ παράπαν ἀδιάλυτον). **b4 ἀνόητωι** 'unintelligible': i.e., primarily, not the object of intellect (b1 νοητῶι), though as Burnet suggests, the normal meaning of ἀνόητος ('mindless', 'foolish') is probably also meant to be present: what is merely visible does not allow the growth of intelligence. **διαλυτῶι** 'meeting with dissolution' (as implied by θνητῶι); but that, of course, will entail dissolubility. **b6 ἧι οὐχ οὕτως ἔχει** '[to show] how it is not like this'. **b8 τί οὖν;** 'Well then?' ('What do you say about the next step?') Cf. 63c8, 74e6. **b8–9 σώματι μὲν ταχὺ διαλύεσθαι προσήκει:** i.e. on death. προσήκει = 'belongs': see 78b5n., c2n., and the following n. **b9–10 ψυχῆι δὲ αὖ τὸ παράπαν ἀδιαλύτωι εἶναι ἢ ἐγγύς τι τού-του;** 'while [it belongs] to soul, for its part (αὖ) to be completely ἀδιάλυτον, or something close to that?' The addition of 'completely' is Plato's way of overcoming the ambiguity of ἀδιάλυτον, and of distin-guishing actual indissolubility from what merely happens never to be dissolved (see b2n.). He here makes use of the argument of 78c1–9: that it 'belongs to' the incomposite not to be divided into parts, and that what is unchanging is 'most likely' to be the incomposite. If soul is

indeed itself describable as unchanging (see a10–b5n.), it will thereby
be a good candidate for membership of the class of the incomposite,
which would make it absolutely indissoluble; alternatively, since we
cannot be sure of its incompositeness (which is only the 'most likely'
option), it will be composite but nevertheless everlasting. (An interesting outcome of this interpretation of the argument is that – contrary to
the usual view – it will contain no clear commitment to the view that
the soul is partless; indeed it might be said deliberately to avoid the
issue. *Rep.* is similarly indecisive, arguing for a tripartite view in Book
IV, but then essentially rejecting it in Book X; *Phdr.* and *Tim.*, by contrast, seem to be firmly in favour of tripartition.) Even this result –
either incomposite, or composite but everlasting – is insecure, given the
doubtful use made of the idea of likeness: that one thing shares even
several features with another is no guarantee that it is like it in some
further respect. But the verb προσήκει makes no claim to certainty in
any case: what is said προσήκειν the body in the first half of the sentence does not in fact hold of it, as c2–d2 admits (cf. 78b5n.), and there
is no justification for taking προσήκειν in any stronger sense in the
second half. It is, perhaps, P.'s/S.'s own way of acknowledging the
insecurity of the argument. b8–10 as a whole begins the statement –
completed in c2–e1 – of the conclusion of 77c–80b, which constitutes
the first and main part of the 'affinity' argument: contrary to the fears
of the imaginary child in Cebes and Simmias (77d–e), it is only the
body, not the soul, which is the sort of thing that is liable to be scattered and blown apart (διασκεδάννυσθαι, διαφυσᾶσθαι; cf. c4 διαπνεῖσ-
θαι) on death. Even in the case of the body, the process takes some time
(c2–d4); how much less likely is it to affect the soul, given what we
have agreed about it (d5–e1).

c2 ἐννοεῖς οὖν ... ἐπειδὰν κτλ. 'You are aware, then, [that] when
...' The οὖν is 'progressive', as at 58b4 (see n.) and elsewhere.   **c2–3
τὸ μὲν ὁρατὸν αὐτοῦ ... καὶ ἐν ὁρατῶι κείμενον** 'the [part] of him
that is visible, and situated in [the] visible [realm]': the article is felt to
be dispensable on the second occurrence of ὁρατός. ἐν ὁρατῶι κείμενον
re-emphasises the body's connection with the world of change; contrast
d5–6 (τὸ ἀιδές,) τὸ εἰς τοιοῦτον τόπον ἕτερον οἰχόμενον.   **c3–4 ὃ δὴ
νεκρὸν καλοῦμεν** 'the very thing we call a corpse' (to which διαλύεσθαι, etc. seem especially to 'belong').   **c5–6 ἐπιεικῶς συχνὸν ...**

χρόνον 'a fairly long time': time being relative, this might be meant
still to be consistent with b9 ταχὺ διαλύεσθαι προσήκει; but the theme
of the whole speech seems to be the surprisingly long time that does, or
can, elapse before decay sets in.   **c6 ἐὰν μέν τις ... 7 καὶ πάνυ μάλα:**
lit. 'if someone dies with his body in an attractive condition (καί emphasising χαριέντως), and at such an age [sc. as to have his body in this
condition], very much so': i.e. what has been claimed is especially true
in such a case. The usual objection to an interpretation of this kind is
that in terms of pathology a young, healthy body will actually decom-
pose more quickly than an old one, and ἐὰν ... καί is accordingly read
as 'even if'; but the emphatic καὶ πάνυ μάλα (in which καί and μάλα
both intensify πάνυ) makes that difficult, and it cannot in any case be
assumed that P. knew the relevant (and somewhat surprising) clinical
fact – or that, if he did, he would necessarily have felt bound by it (cf.
117e5n.). μέν is 'solitary' (see 61d9–10n.); the implied contrast in this
case is with the body of an old man, and presumably most of all with
that of the seventy-year-old S. The syntax of the Greek as a whole
is precisely paralleled by *Crat.* 400b–c (πολλαχῆι μοι δοκεῖ τοῦτο γε·)
ἄν (= ἐάν) μὲν καὶ σμικρόν τις παρακλίνηι, καὶ πάνυ.   **c7 συμπεσὸν
γὰρ τὸ σῶμα καὶ ταριχευθέν ... 9 ταριχευθέντες** 'For when the body
has shrunk and been embalmed, as in the case of those who have
been embalmed in Egypt'. γάρ is used somewhat loosely, introducing further support for the general idea contained in the preceding
sentence.   **c9 ὀλίγου ... χρόνον** 'remains practically whole for an
extraordinarily long time'.

d1 καὶ ἂν σαπῆι 'even if (ἂν = ἐάν) it [i.e. the rest of the body] de-
cays'.   **d5 ἡ δὲ ψυχὴ ἄρα** 'Are we to suppose, in that case (ἄρα), that
the soul ...'   **d5 τὸ εἰς τοιοῦτον τόπον ἕτερον ... 8 τῆι ἐμῆι ψυχῆι
ἰτέον:** this exploits 79d ἐκεῖσε οἴχεται κτλ., which described the philosophical soul's metaphorical 'departure' from the body, in life, to 'join
the company of' the forms; but after all S. has earlier argued (64a–
69e) that for the philosopher death is simply the full realisation of that
process. τοιοῦτον: i.e., in the first instance, ἀιδῆ; but c6 adds γενναῖον
(recalling the opposition ἄρχειν/δουλεύειν in 80a) and καθαρόν (recalling 79d: all three parts of the preceding argument are thus again
brought to mind). Whether P. would have wanted to claim that the
forms were literally located anywhere is doubtful; but at least it is clear

that the soul changes its place on death. **εἰς Ἅιδου ὡς ἀληθῶς:** lit. 'to [the place] of Hades in the true sense'; Hades here becomes the unseen god (or god of the unseen), and good and wise besides (παρὰ τὸν ἀγαθὸν καὶ φρόνιμον θεόν: cf. 63b–c, 69d–e). For the play on ἀιδής/ Ἅιδης, cf. Hom. *Il.* 5.844–5, where Athena puts on the 'cap of Hades' to make herself invisible to Ares.   **d7–8 ἂν θεὸς θέληι:** as at 69d6.   **d8 αὕτη δὲ δή** 'does *this* . . . ?', with δή emphasising αὕτη; αὕτη itself stands in apposition to d5 ἡ . . . ψυχή. For the duplicated δέ (ἡ δὲ ψυχὴ . . . , αὕτη δέ), see 78c6–8n.   **d8–9 ἡ τοιαύτη καὶ οὕτω πεφυκυῖα** refers back to d5–6. οὕτω adds nothing to τοιαύτη except emphasis (cf. e.g. 78c6); οὕτω πεφυκυῖα means exactly the same as τοιαύτη πεφυκυῖα.   **d10–e1 εὐθὺς . . . οἱ πολλοὶ ἄνθρωποι:** cf. 77b3–5, 70a1–6.

e1 πολλοῦ γε δεῖ 'Far from it' – not because the soul would have to survive to go anywhere (cf. 70c4–5), but because of its (essential) nature and the destination for which that nature fits it (d8–9, 5–6).   **e2 ἐὰν μὲν καθαρὰ ἀπαλλάττηται:** answered by b1–2 ἐὰν δέ γε οἶμαι μεμιασμένη καὶ ἀκάθαρτος . . . ἀπαλλάττηται. All souls will be immortal, if all share the same essential nature; but not all, of course, will in fact go off to join the forms (or the gods). e2 marks the beginning of the last stage of the 'affinity' argument, which relies on a vivid description of the contrasting lives and destinies of philosophical and unphilosophical souls: the first, at the highest level, achieving assimilation to the divine, to which the soul in itself has been shown to be akin, the second tied irrevocably to the body.   **e3 ἅτε οὐδὲν κοινωνοῦσα** 'because it had no commerce with it'.   **e4 ἑκοῦσα εἶναι:** cf. 61c4–5n.   **e4–5 καὶ συνηθροισμένη αὐτὴ εἰς ἑαυτήν:** cf. 67c–d.   **e5 τοῦτο:** i.e. τὸ συναθροίζεσθαι κτλ., which is then explained in e6 τὸ δὲ οὐδὲν ἄλλο ἐστὶν κτλ.   **e6 τὸ δὲ οὐδὲν ἄλλο ἐστὶν . . . 81a1 ῥαιδίως** 'and this is nothing other than philosophising in the right way, and, in reality, practising dying without complaint': a telescoped version of the main claim of S.'s 'defence', that philosophers will not complain about death because that is what they have been preparing for all along (see esp. 67e4 τῶι ὄντι . . . ὁ φοβερόν, which shows that καί in the present passage is explanatory: cf. 58b6n.). τῶι ὄντι – as in 67e4 – underlines the (still) paradoxical nature of the idea of 'practising dying' (cf. d5–6 εἰς Ἅιδου ὡς ἀληθῶς), as does the way in which S. immediately pauses to ask for Cebes' assent to it. For ῥαιδίως in the sense of 'without complaint', see e.g. 62c10–d1 ῥαιδίως ... ἐθέλειν ἀποθνήισκειν (contrasting with e6 ἀγανακτεῖν ἀποθνήισκοντας).

81a1–2 ἢ οὐ τοῦτ' ἂν κτλ.: Socrates here finally abandons the sentence he began in 80e2 (ἐὰν μὲν κτλ.); a4 makes a new start (with a second μέν, reintroducing the original contrast: cf. *GP* 384–5). τοῦτο = τὸ ὀρθῶς φιλοσοφεῖν (see preceding n.). **a3 παντάπασί γε** 'Yes, absolutely.' Cebes remains an enthusiast for Socrates' views – if the case for immortality can be established (69e–70b, 86e–88b). **a4 τὸ ἀιδές** is in apposition to τὸ ὅμοιον αὐτῆι (as is a5 τὸ θεῖόν τε καὶ ἀθάνατον καὶ φρόνιμον). **a5 φρόνιμον:** what has been said to be like the soul is, of course, the forms; and they are 'wise' in so far as they are the source of wisdom (cf. 79d1–7, and n. on 80b4 ἀνοήτωι). But at the same time the 'place' of the forms is also equated with the place of gods (see further a8–9n.), who are wise in a more straightforward sense (80d5–8n.). **a6 ὑπάρχει αὐτῆι εὐδαίμονι εἶναι** 'it is its lot to be εὐδαίμων', i.e. to have what in S.'s eyes is truly desirable (as described in the remainder of the sentence). **a6 πλάνης ... 8 ἀπηλλαγμένηι:** cf. esp. 66b–67b. **a8 ὥσπερ δὲ λέγεται ... 9 διάγουσα** 'and as is said of the initiated, in the true sense passing the rest of time with [the] gods'. Cf. 69c–d. ὡς ἀληθῶς is used in the same way as at 80d5–6 (cf. 80e6–81a1n.): what is promised to the initiated is that they will dwell with the gods (or at least, according to other sources, some kind of better fate than will be granted to the uninitiated: Burkert 1985, 289); the true sense of that, for S. (i.e. P.), is communion with τὸ θεῖον, the forms. Yet he will shortly suggest also that the philosopher who has been completely 'purified' will actually join the 'race of [the] gods' (εἰς ... θεῶν γένος ... ἀφικνεῖσθαι, 82b10–c1), an idea which is partly explained by 114c2–4 ... οἱ φιλοσοφίαι ἱκανῶς κεκαθαρμένοι <u>ἄνευ</u> ... <u>σωμάτων ζῶσι τὸ παράπαν εἰς τὸν ἔπειτα χρόνον</u>: Platonic gods are perhaps usually (*Phdr.* 256b–d, *Laws* 897bff.), though not always (*Tim.* 41a–b), seen as souls permanently without bodies. S. will stop short of suggesting that this will be *his* fate (see 114b7–c1n.; the 'true, pure' Hades to which he hopes he will go (80d) turns out to have two levels). διάγουσα: we should strictly expect the participle to be in the dative, in agreement with a6 αὐτῆι (i.e. τῆι ψυχῆι); but 'the soul' is the actual subject of the first part of the sentence, and the logical subject of the rest.

b2–3 ἅτε τῶι σώματι . . . καὶ ἐρῶσα 'because it was constantly with the body, and paying court to this and in love [with it]'; but since συνεῖναι is itself a regular term for sexual intercourse, συνοῦσα too will have erotic connotations.   **b3–4 ὑπ' αὐτοῦ ὑπό τε τῶν ἐπιθυμιῶν καὶ ἡδονῶν** 'by it and by [its] desires and pleasures' (cf. 66c7).   **b4 ἀληθές:** here 'real' rather than 'true', as applied to objects (b5–6).   **b6 τὸ δὲ τοῖς ὄμμασι σκοτῶδες . . . 8 καὶ φεύγειν:** lit. 'but what is obscure to the eyes and unseen, but intelligible and grasped through philosophy, accustomed to hate and tremble at and shun this': construction as at 80d5–8, with τοῦτο in apposition to τὸ . . . τοῖς ὄμμασι κτλ., and duplicated δέ (τὸ δὲ τοῖς ὄμμασι . . . τοῦτο δέ); the intervening δέ (νοητὸν δέ) marks a contrast by itself, without a preceding μέν (cf. GP 165). εἰθισμένη balances, and has the same syntactical role as, b3 γεγοητευμένη ('because it was always with the body, . . . and is bewitched by it . . . so as to . . . , while it has been accustomed to hate . . .').   **b8–c1 οὕτω δὴ ἔχουσαν οἴει ψυχήν** 'do you think that a soul in *this* condition . . . ?' The οἶμαι in b1 is forgotten after the long and complex conditional clause.

c4 ἀλλὰ διειλημμένην γε οἶμαι ὑπὸ τοῦ σωματοειδοῦς 'Rather, I think (sc. αὐτὴν ἀπαλλάξεσθαι, that it will depart from the body) interspersed with what belongs to the category of the body.' (The καί found after ἀλλά in part of the textual tradition looks obtrusive, spoiling the effect of the emphatic ἀλλά . . . γε: 'it will not be εἰλικρινής when it departs; what it will be is . . .' Cf. 74a5n.)   **c6 τὴν πολλὴν μελέτην:** contrasting with 81a1–2 μελέτη θανάτου.   **ἐνεποίησε σύμφυτον:** lit. 'made grown together in [the soul]', like e.g. a stone grown into the root of a tree.   **c9 βαρὺ καὶ γεῶδες καὶ ὁρατόν:** 'what belongs to the category of the body' (τὸ σωματοειδές, c4), at least in the obvious sense, will also belong to the category of earth, τὸ γεῶδες (because solid: cf. *Tim.* 31b), which is heavy and visible.   **c11 φόβωι τοῦ ἀιδοῦς τε καὶ Ἅιδου:** cf. b4–8, 80d6–7.   **ὥσπερ λέγεται:** what 'is said' is presumably that ghostly shapes roam around tombs (c11–d2), a phenomenon which S. purports to take as evidence for his thesis about the fate of the non-philosophical soul – these shapes are 'some sort of shadow-like phantasms of souls, wraiths of the kind that such souls afford, [i.e. such souls as] those that have not been released in a pure state but have a share of the visible, and that is why they are seen' (d2–4). See Bremmer 1983, 108–23; and Burkert 1985, 195: 'Among the Greeks, as among all peoples, there are ghost experiences, and here too, there are tales of the dead who can find no repose and who wander near their graves menacing passers-by' (referring to the present context, and to Rohde 1894, II 362–4).

d1 περὶ ἃ δή: cf. 72a7–8n., 80c3. **d1–2 καὶ ὤφθη** 'have actually been seen'. The evident irony of the whole context (see esp. e4n., 82b6–8n.) prevents us from telling even whether S. is really meant to believe in ghosts. The category of souls being described here is the same as the one in the myth which finds itself on the shores of the Acherusian lake: see 113a5n., d6–e1n., and 108a6–b3, which serves as a bridging passage between the two contexts. **d2 ἄττα ψυχῶν σκιοειδῆ φαντάσματα:** a φάντασμα is an 'apparition' or 'appearance'; what we see (or would be seeing, if the thesis were true) is not souls themselves but their 'bodily accretions' (c8–9). The point is reinforced by the indefinite ἄττα (= τινα: 'some sort of apparitions of souls'), and also perhaps by σκιοειδῆ, which suggests a comparison both with shadows in the ordinary sense and with the 'shades' (σκιαί) of the dead in Homer – which Homer also calls ψυχαί. **d3 εἴδωλα** is logically the antecedent of οἷα, and in apposition to φαντάσματα. εἴδωλον, which was used at 66c3 merely of insubstantial form, here clearly carries the extra connotation of likeness (to the dead person). **d4 διὸ καί:** cf. *GP* 295 (and 307–8 on 58c4). **d5 εἰκός γε** 'Yes (γε: cf. 67b6n.), [it is] likely [to be as you say]'; a markedly qualified response (contrast Socrates' οἴεσθαι χρή in c8). Cf. 71d13n. **d6 εἰκὸς μέντοι** 'Indeed it is likely' (similar uses of μέντοι at 65d6, 73d11). **d6 καὶ οὔ τί γε ... 7 εἶναι** 'and what is more (καί ... γε: cf. e.g. 58d1), that they (αὐτάς, i.e. the ones mentioned in d3–4) are not at all (οὔ τι) the [souls] of the good'.

e2 ὥσπερ εἰκός: once again, S. rests his case on what is 'likely' (if re-imprisonment is caused by the desire for the body felt by the bodily element, then it is likely – i.e. reasonable to suppose? – that particular types of bodily desire will lead to imprisonment in bodies which exhibit the corresponding traits, ἤθη). **e4 τὰ ποῖα δὴ ταῦτα λέγεις, ὦ Σώκρατες;** 'Whatever do you mean by these, Socrates?' (δή emphasises the interrogative: *GP* 210–11). The idea of the transmigration of human souls into animal bodies, to which e2–3 ἐνδοῦνται ... ἐν τῶι βίωι leads (e5–82b8), is well-attested as a Pythagorean doctrine (D. L.

8.36, Hdt. 2.123, etc.); Cebes' apparently incredulous question will
then imply either that what is contained in e2–3 was not part of the
Pythagorean doctrine, or that he was not a Pythagorean (see 59c1n.).
His replies at 82a2, 6, 9, and b9 hardly suggest enthusiasm for the idea
– or at least for Socrates' half-playful use of it: see 82a2n. It is incorpor-
ated into the myth at the end of the dialogue (113a5), on whose truth
in all details S. is unwilling to commit himself (114d). In the present
context its chief role is to suggest the affinity of certain types of human
beings to animals (an old idea – cf. e.g. Semonides fr. 7 Bergk); see
82a7–8.   **e5 οἷον** 'For example'.   **γαστριμαργίας τε καὶ ὕβρεις καὶ
φιλοποσίας:** *Phdr.* 238a–b treats ὕβρις as the genus of which γασ-
τριμαργία and φιλοποσία are species; hence 'excess'. The plurals refer,
strictly speaking, to instances (of gluttony, etc.); one trains to be a
glutton by being gluttonous.   **e6 καὶ μὴ διευλαβουμένους** 'and who
were not on their guard' (present participle with imperfect sense, as
at 80e3, etc.).   **e6–82a1 εἰς τὰ τῶν ὄνων γένη καὶ τῶν τοιούτων
θηρίων** 'into the class ('family': γένος) of asses, or those of wild animals
of the same character'.

82a2 πάνυ μὲν οὖν εἰκὸς λέγεις 'What you say is absolutely likely.'
This response could by itself be taken as entirely serious; but read in
conjunction with those that follow, and with the context (unless we
suppose Cebes to be oblivious to Socrates' tone), it is surely ironic.   **a3
δέ γε** 'Yes, and', as at 65c5, etc.   **a5 ἢ ποῖ κτλ.** 'or where else do we
say such [souls] would go?'   **a6 ἀμέλει:** frequently, though not necessarily, used ironically (cf. English 'doubtless'). See LSJ.   **a7 δῆλα δή:**
cf. 80a8.   **a7–8 ἧι ἂν ἕκαστα κτλ.:** lit. 'where each group (ἕκαστα)
would go, in accordance with the resemblances of their training', i.e.
according to what their training made them resemble.   **a10 εὐδαιμονέστατοι ... b1 ἐπιτετηδευκότες** 'happiest even of these, and [the
ones] going to [the] best place, are those who have practised the common or civic virtue'. 'Even of these' (καὶ τούτων): in their case too, it
is virtue which makes the difference – even if it is not genuine virtue,
because it is lacking in 'philosophy or intelligence' (b2–3; cf. 81d6–7,
68c–69c). καί², as b4–6 shows, is explanatory (as at 58b6, 80e6); καί³
links alternatives (as at 73e5).

b1–3 On the repeated τε καί (similarly in c5–7), see *GP* lxii.   **ἣν δὴ
καλοῦσι σωφροσύνην τε καὶ δικαιοσύνην:** cf. 68c–69c.   **b4 πῆι δή**

'How, exactly' (cf. 81e4n.).   **b5 τοιοῦτον** is explained by ὁ πολιτικὸν καὶ ἥμερον. There is a particular edge to ἥμερον: it is after all a citizen court of justice that has just sentenced Socrates to death. (Yet, as he claims, that is really the mildest of sentences.)   **b6 ἢ που μελιττῶν ... 8 ἄνδρας μετρίους** 'either, I imagine, [the γένος] of bees, or of wasps, or of ants, or else back into the very same one (emphatic γε) again, the human race, and that respectable men are born from them'. What at first seems like a concession to this category of people (εἰς τοιοῦτον πάλιν ..., which suggests the human γένος) is immediately withdrawn (ἢ που ..., i.e. other socially organised but unreflecting γένη), but then reinstated (καὶ εἰς ταὐτόν ...). ἄνδρας μετρίους ('respectable men') may also suggest 'men of a normal size', contrasting with the bees, wasps and ants that some of them become (cf. Hdt. 2.32, where μέτριοι ἄνδρες are contrasted with pygmies); the pun would be consistent with the lightness of tone which characterises the context as a whole.   **b10–c1 εἰς δέ γε θεῶν γένος κτλ.:** see 81a8–9n. (δέ γε here is strongly adversative).   **c1 ἀλλ' ἢ τῶι φιλομαθεῖ** 'except to the lover of learning' (written as if οὐδενί had preceded). φιλομαθής is a synonym of φιλόσοφος: see 66b2, 67b4.

c6–7 ἀτιμίαν τε καὶ ἀδοξίαν μοχθηρίας '[the] loss of esteem and repute which goes with depravity'.   **c8 ἔπειτα** 'for that reason'.   **c9 οὐ γὰρ ἂν πρέποι** 'No, because it would not be fitting.'

d1 οὐ μέντοι μὰ Δία: for μέντοι, see 81d6n.; μὰ Δία increases the emphasis still further.   **d1 τοιγάρτοι ... 4 ὅπηι ἔρχονται** 'That is why, Cebes, saying goodbye to all these people, those who care at all about their own soul and do not live moulding [their] bodies into shape, do not follow the same path as they (d1 τούτοις) do, aware that they [i.e. the ones to whom they 'say goodbye'] do not know where they are going.' σώματα πλάττοντες is a bold metaphor for caring for the body (rather than the soul); cf. Tim. 88c τὸν ... σῶμα ἐπιμελῶς πλάττοντα (with specific reference to athletic training), contrasted with the man who is absorbed in some intellectual pursuit. (Attempts to defend the alternative and more difficult reading σώματι πλάττοντες have not succeeded.)   **d6 ἐκείνης:** for the gen., cf. c7 μοχθηρίας.   **καθαρμῶι:** cf. 69c2.   **d6–7 ταύτηι δὴ τρέπονται κτλ.** 'they turn along *this* road (emphatic δή), following it [i.e. philosophy], [the one] along which it leads'. The relative clause explains ταύτηι; but its reference is already clear.   **d9 γάρ:** cf. 59d1n.

e1 παραλαβοῦσα ... ἡ φιλοσοφία 'when philosophy takes their soul in hand' (παραλαμβάνειν: 'esp. of persons succeeding to an office, etc.', LSJ).   **e1–2 ἀτεχνῶς διαδεδεμένην** 'absolutely bound fast'.   **e3 ὥσπερ διὰ εἱργμοῦ διὰ τούτου:** lit. 'through this [i.e. the body] as through a prison'.   **e5 ὅτι δι' ἐπιθυμίας ... 83a1 τοῦ δεδέσθαι** '[namely] that it is [i.e. works its effect] through desire, in such a way that the prisoner will especially himself be an accomplice in his imprisonment'. For this use of (relative) ὡς, introducing what is in effect a final clause, see *MT* 400–1.

83a1 οὖν: resumptive, as at 58b1.   **a2–3 οὕτω παραλαβοῦσα ... ἔχουσαν αὐτῶν τὴν ψυχήν** 'when philosophy takes in hand their soul in this condition (οὕτω ... ἔχουσαν)'.

b1–2 ὅτι ἄν ... τῶν ὄντων: lit. '[in relation to] whichever of the things that are (cf. 65c2–3n.) it apprehends alone by itself, [when it is] alone by itself': see esp. 66a1–3.   **b2 ὅτι δ' ἄν δι' ἄλλων ... 3 μηδὲν ἡγεῖσθαι ἀληθές** 'but to consider nothing real which it investigates through other means, in other things, it [i.e. the object of investigation] being other'. The 'other means' are, of course, the senses: if the soul sets out to investigate something, e.g. beauty, by these means, it will be investigating it, not as it is in itself, but 'in other things', i.e. in its perceptible instances ('the many beautifuls' of 78d10–e2: people, horses, cloaks, etc.); but in that case the object of the investigation will in fact turn out itself to be something 'other' (than 'beauty by itself'), i.e. the beauty of the particular things being surveyed. All of this is consistent with the position which S. has maintained throughout, that in his search for truth the philosopher will reject the use of the senses, even if they may have a positive role in (initially) reminding us of the forms. It is not said here that nothing on the level of the sense is real, only that it is the key to the freeing of the soul to think that to be so: an antidote, presumably, to the kind of attitude of mind described in 81b, according to which only what can be touched or seen or otherwise perceived is real. At the same time, in so far as they are 'other' than the true objects of the philosopher's search, there is a clear sense in which perceptible beauty and the rest will fail to be truly, genuinely and really what they claim to be.   **b6 οὕτως** 'for this reason', i.e. οὐκ οἰομένη κτλ.   **b7 καὶ φόβων** should probably be retained: in the context, the philosopher's attitude towards fears is especially relevant (cf. e5–6, with note on e5).   **b9 οὐδὲν τοσοῦτον κακὸν ... c3 καὶ οὐ**

λογίζεται αὐτό: lit. 'one suffers (ἔπαθεν, gnomic aorist) no evil so great from them [i.e. the passions mentioned], of the ones which (ὧν = τούτων ἅ) one might think [sc. that one suffers in such circumstances], such as by falling ill or by incurring some expenditure because of one's desires, but what is the greatest and most extreme of evils, this one suffers, and does not take it into account': that is, the harmful consequences one expects from intense pleasure, pain, etc. are not so great as the one which is not taken into account, but which is actually the greatest evil of all. The construction begun in οὐδὲν τοσοῦτον κακὸν ἔπαθεν ἀπ' αὐτῶν, which would naturally be completed by ὅσον ἀπό . . . , is broken off and replaced by ἀλλ' ὃ κτλ.

c8 ταῦτα δὲ μάλιστα ὁρατά 'and these [i.e. the things in relation to which extremes of pleasure and pain occur] are especially visible things'.

d4 ὥσπερ ἧλον ἔχουσα 'as if with a nail'.   **d5 ποιεῖ σωματοειδῆ:** cf. 81c4–6.   **d6 καί:** cf. 76d3n.   **d8 ὁμότροπός τε καὶ ὁμότροφος** 'of like character and nurture' (Gallop).   **d9 ἀφικέσθαι** is a consecutive infinitive after οἵα ('such as [never] to . . .').   **ἀεί** 'on each occasion'.

e1 καὶ ὥσπερ σπειρομένη ἐμφύεσθαι 'and as if it were a seed, grow in [it]'. This kind of soul, in other words, will actually flourish in the prison of the body.   **e2–3 τῆς τοῦ θείου κτλ.** 'communion with the divine and pure and uniform', to which it is akin.   **e5 τούτων . . . ἕνεκα . . . 6 φασιν:** the explanation that has now been given of the self-control (κόσμιος = σώφρων: see 68c8, 10, d3, e2) and courage of the philosopher is essentially the same as the one that S. gave in his 'defence', which it is clearly intended to recall; namely that the philosopher is self-controlled and brave because he makes the right choices in relation to pleasures, pains and fears on the basis of wisdom (69a6–c3), or, more specifically, of an understanding of the true ends of life and of the soul. In the earlier context, he was said to reject (bodily) pleasures because he saw them as a distraction from those ends (64c10–d4, 66c2–d3, 68c11–12), and to lack fear of death because he saw it as promising their fulfilment; in both cases he will be refusing to allow his soul to become identified with ('nailed to') the body and its concerns, which distort our view of reality.   **e5 οἱ δικαίως φιλομαθεῖς** = 82c2–3 οἱ ὀρθῶς φιλόσοφοι (cf. 67b4 οἱ ὀρθῶς φιλομαθεῖς, 66b2 οἱ γνησίως φιλόσοφοι). **e6 οὐχ ὧν οἱ πολλοὶ ἕνεκά φασιν** 'not for the reasons that the many say', sc. that one should be κόσμιος and ἀνδρεῖος: cf. 82c. That passage in fact only refers to σωφροσύνη (= ἀπέχεσθαι τῶν κατὰ τὸ σῶμα ἐπιθυμιῶν: cf. 68c8–10); but a parallel account of common-or-garden courage is easily supplied from 68c–69a, with which 82c is closely linked. **e7 ἢ σὺ οἴει;** 'or do you think [sc. it is ὧν οἱ πολλοὶ κτλ.]?'

84a2 οὐ γάρ 'No indeed' ('assentient' γάρ, as e.g. at 69a5). **οὕτω** 'in the way said'. **a3 ἑαυτήν** 'itself', i.e. the philosopher's soul (the subject of the sentence). **a4 λυούσης δὲ ἐκείνης** 'but while it [philosophy] is working its [the soul's] release'. **a4 αὐτὴν παραδιδόναι ... 6 μεταχειριζομένης** 'it should (χρῆναι is supplied from the preceding line) of its own accord (αὐτήν) surrender itself to pleasures and pains, to bind it back in again [sc. to the body], and should perform an unending task of a Penelope, working at some web of hers in a reverse fashion' (the real Penelope unpicked during the night what she had woven during the day (Hom. *Od.* 2.92–105, etc.), whereas in this case it would be the other way round: cf. Loriaux). **a8 ἀεὶ ἐν τούτωι οὖσα** 'always being occupied in this' (i.e. reasoning). **ἀδόξαστον** 'not the subject of δοξάζειν'. The contrast is with the case described in 83d6, δοξάζουσαν ταῦτα ἀληθῆ κτλ. – the soul does not merely *think* the forms to be real; they *are* real. ἀδόξαστος appears nowhere else in this sense; compare the similarly unusual use of ἀνόητος ('not the object of νοῦς') at 80b4, as a pair to νοητός.

b2 ἕως ἂν ζῆι, καὶ ἐπειδὰν τελευτήσηι: i.e. while it is associated with a body, and when it leaves it (cf. 'living' and 'dead' as applied in the cyclical argument). **b2 εἰς τὸ συγγενὲς ... 3 ἀπηλλάχθαι** 'when it has arrived at what is akin [to it] and (or 'i.e.': explanatory καί?) what is such [as we have described, in a8], [it thinks] that it is released from human ills'. **b4–8 οὐδὲν δεινὸν μὴ φοβηθῆι ... ὅπως μὴ κτλ.** 'there is no danger that it will fear ... that (ὅπως μή: see 77b3–5n.), torn apart on its separation from the body, blown to pieces by winds and flying in different directions, it may depart and be no longer anywhere at all' (b5 ταῦτα δ' ἐπιτηδεύσασα appears to have originated as a later gloss on ἐκ δὴ τῆς τοιαύτης τροφῆς). διασπασθεῖσα ... ἔτι οὐδαμοῦ ἦι combines elements both from Cebes' original statement of his fears at 70a and from S.'s parody of it at 77d–e. No philosopher, then, S.

claims, will entertain such fears (as he himself does not). But he has hardly added anything to his argument since 80e. If there is any argument at all in this section, it is the old one he first advanced in his 'defence', about the alleged parallelism between the philosopher's rejection of bodily concerns and the separation of soul and body in death – although that has acquired some new substance through the idea of the natural affinity of soul to the forms. When this fact is added to the openly inconclusive nature of the argument in 78b–80e, it comes as no surprise that Cebes and Simmias remain sceptical, and weigh in with new objections. See further 92d4n.

84c1–85e2: interlude

After a long silence, Simmias says that he and Cebes have some questions to ask Socrates, but feel hesitant about asking them in the present circumstances; then, when Socrates replies once more that their concern for him is misplaced, Simmias explains the importance they attach to continuing the argument. This interlude, together with the one that will follow the statement of their objections (88c–91c), has the effect of underlining the significance of Simmias' and Cebes' new intervention: instead of responding to Socrates from the point of view of the ordinary man, as for the most part they have done up till now (see especially 70a, 77c–e), they now pose a more philosophical, and accordingly more serious, challenge – the equivalent of a reversal of fortune, or peripeteia *(Aristotle,* Poetics *ch. 6 etc.), in a tragedy: see 88c.*

84c1 οὖν: progressive (Phaedo moves on to the next stage in his story). **c2 πρὸς τῶι εἰρημένωι λόγωι ἦν** 'was absorbed in the preceding argument'. **c3 ὡς ἰδεῖν ἐφαίνετο:** lit. 'as he appeared, to look at' (ἰδεῖν, explanatory infinitive). **c4 σμικρὸν ... διελεγέσθην** 'were talking ... in a low voice' (cf. e.g. *Lysis* 211a). **c5–6 ὑμῖν τὰ λεχθέντα ... λέγεσθαι;** 'Surely you don't think there was anything lacking in what was said?' μῶν μή can hardly be taken except as expecting a negative answer (cf. *Rep.* 505c); in view of what S. says next, the question must therefore be ironic. He would be the last person to claim to have said the last word on a subject (contrast e.g. the peroration of the speech attributed to the orator Lysias at *Phdr.* 234b–c). **c6–7 πολλὰς ... δὴ ἔτι ἔχει ὑποψίας καὶ ἀντιλαβάς** 'there are still very many ways in which it leaves room for misgiving and for counter-attack'. **c7 εἴ γε**

δή 'at any rate, if': they could, of course, choose not to 'explore properly' (ἱκανῶς διεξιέναι) what has been said. **c8 οὐδὲν λέγω** 'I am
speaking to no purpose'.

d1 εἴ πηι . . . λεχθῆναι 'if it seems to you that it would have been
better said in some [other] way'; the ἄν is indispensable to the sense.
d4 καὶ μήν: cf. 58e1n. **d6–7 διὰ τὸ ἐπιθυμεῖν κτλ.** explains the hesitation implied in ἑκάτερος . . . τὸν ἕτερον κτλ. **ἀκοῦσαι:** sc. answers to
his questions. μὴ ἦι = 'in case it may be'. **d9 ἦ που χαλεπῶς ἂν τοὺς
ἄλλους . . . πείσαιμι . . . e1–2 ὅτε γε μηδ' ὑμᾶς δύναμαι πείθειν** 'I
would certainly find it difficult to persuade the rest of mankind . . .
when (virtually equivalent to 'if', and so followed by μή) I cannot even
persuade you': for ἦ που . . . γε, see *GP* 281–2. 'Even you', because
they ought to know that he is not so peevish (δύσκολος, e2). Once
again, the closeness of Simmias and Cebes to S. is underlined: cf.
59c1n., 75d2–3n., etc.

e2–3 μὴ . . . διάκειμαι: for the present indicative, see 77b3–5n. **e4
φαυλότερος . . . τὴν μαντικήν:** the seer is able to foresee the future by
irrational means, whereas S. has been investigating it through argument. For another, equally unserious, claim to μαντική by S., see *Phdr.*
242c.

85a1 μάλιστα: either 'loudest' (Verdenius compares Hom. *Il.* 12.51),
or simply 'most of all' (and therefore more or less equivalent to πλεῖστα); the emendation κάλλιστα is unnecessary. For the truth about
'swan-songs', see Arnott 1977. **a2 παρὰ τὸν θεόν:** i.e. Apollo (see b1–
2n.). **a3–5 οἱ δ' ἄνθρωποι . . . καταψεύδονται, καί φασιν αὐτοὺς
θρηνοῦντας τὸν θάνατον . . . ἐξάιδειν:** as so often, P. adapts a traditional idea to his own purposes (cf. 81c–d). Cf. Aesch. *Ag.* 1444–5,
Arist. *Hist. an.* 615b2–5. **a3–4 διὰ τὸ αὐτῶν δέος . . . καὶ τῶν κύκνων καταψεύδονται** 'because of their own fear of death tell lies about
the swans too': i.e. attribute their own mistaken attitude to death to
swans as well. **a5 ἐξάιδειν** 'sing their last song'. **a7 ἥ τε ἀηδὼν καὶ
χελιδὼν καὶ ὁ ἔποψ:** an allusion to the story of Procne, Philomela, and
Tereus, who after a series of violent events were turned respectively
into a nightingale, a swallow, and a hoopoe; these are birds which one
would expect to sing from pain and grief, because of their history. **ἃ
δή** 'the very [ὄρνεα] which'.

b1–2 ἅτε . . . Ἀπόλλωνος ὄντες: as they will already be, in virtue of being singers. Swans are traditionally sacred to Apollo: cf. e.g. Sappho fr. 208 L–P. **b5 ὁμόδουλός τε . . . τῶν κύκνων καὶ ἱερὸς τοῦ αὐτοῦ θεοῦ:** cf. 60c–61b, *Ap.* 23c. ἱερὸς τοῦ αὐτοῦ θεοῦ extends the idea of ὁμόδουλος κτλ.: in so far as he is devoted to the service of Apollo, he may also be said to be 'sacred to' him. **b7–8 ἀλλὰ τούτου γ' ἕνεκα** 'No; so far as that goes' (Gallop). **b9 Ἀθηναίων . . . ἄνδρες ἕνδεκα** 'eleven Athenian men': cf. 59e6n.

c2 περὶ τῶν τοιούτων 'about such things', i.e. as the fate of the soul after death, on which S. has just restated his view. What else Simmias might be thinking of, as possessing the same degree of uncertainty, is not clear; but cf. 96a–102a. The principles which Simmias is about to suggest appear to be identical to S.'s (cf. 75d2–3n., 78d1–2; 100a3–7, 85d1n.). **c2–3 ἴσως ὥσπερ καὶ σοί** 'as perhaps to you too'. **c3 τὸ . . . σαφὲς εἰδέναι** 'to know the plain truth': the τό is here probably to be taken with σαφές, whereas in the answering τὸ . . . μὴ οὐχὶ . . . ἐλέγχειν κτλ. in 4–5 it must be taken with the infinitives. **c4 αὖ** 'on the other hand', strengthening μέντοι. **c4–5 τὸ . . . μὴ οὐχὶ παντὶ τρόπωι ἐλέγχειν καὶ μὴ προαφίστασθαι:** μὴ οὐ is the regular way of negativing infinitive with τό after a negatived verb or an expression implying a negative (here c6 πάνυ μαλθακοῦ εἶναι ἀνδρός, lit. '[seems] to belong to a quite feeble person'), οὐ merely serving to strengthen this original negative idea. Cf. *MT* 815.2. The second μή is clearly not parallel to the first, but is said from the point of view of the positive necessity ἐλέγχειν: one must not not ἐλέγχειν, i.e. one must ἐλέγχειν, and not προαφίστασθαι. **c5–6 πρὶν ἂν πανταχῆι σκοπῶν ἀπείπηι τις** 'until one becomes exhausted from examining [τὰ λεγόμενα] in every way'. **c7 γε** is emphatic: '[it seems to me] that one must certainly achieve one of these things, . . .' **c7–8 ἢ μαθεῖν ὅπηι ἔχει ἢ εὑρεῖν** 'either to learn how [the things in question] are [from someone else], or to discover it [for oneself]. **c8 εἰ ταῦτα ἀδύνατον:** sc. διαπράξασθαι. **γοῦν** 'at least'. **c9 τῶν ἀνθρωπίνων λόγων:** λόγοι here = λεγόμενα (c4), 'things said'; ἀνθρώπινοι contrasts with d3 θείου 'from a divine source'. **καὶ δυσεξελεγκτότατον** explains βέλτιστον (καί as at 80e6 etc.).

d1 ὥσπερ ἐπὶ σχεδίας: like Odysseus in *Od.* S. seems to echo the whole idea at 100d8–e3. **d2 εἰ μή τις δύναιτο:** the optative shows that

Simmias thinks this a remote possibility – as indeed the whole context implies. **d3 [ἤ]:** even if ἤ might on occasions come close to 'or, in other words' (Verdenius), here it would be extremely harsh. **d4 καὶ δὴ καὶ νῦν** 'And so now' (cf. 59d7–8n.). **d5 ταῦτα:** i.e. that he need not hesitate, which is implied in ἐπαισχυνθήσομαι ἐρέσθαι. **d5–6 οὐδ' ἐμαυτὸν αἰτιάσομαι** 'and I shall not [then] blame myself'. **d9 οὐ πάνυ:** presumably, in the context, 'not quite' rather than 'altogether not' (cf. 57a7n.).

e1–2 ἴσως γάρ ... ἀληθῆ σοι φαίνεται 'Yes, and perhaps your view is correct' (lit. 'true things appear to you', picking up Simmias' φαίνεται: cf. *GP* 89).

85e3–88b8: objections from Simmias and Cebes

Simmias' objection consists in pointing out that the same sorts of things that Socrates has said about the soul – that it is invisible, incorporeal, and divine – could also be said about the attunement, or state of being in tune (ἁρμονία: see below), of a lyre and its strings, which clearly cannot outlast the lyre itself; and as a matter of fact he and others are inclined to hold that the soul is a kind of 'attunement' of the constituents of the body. Cebes, for his part, compares the soul to a weaver, who although more long-lived than a cloak, will nevertheless perish before the last one he weaves: just so, a soul might wear out many bodies, and yet itself be worn out and perish before the last.

85e3 ταύτηι ἔμοιγε ... ἧι δή: lit. 'In this way [it seems] to me, at least [that what has been said is not adequate], in that ...' **e3–4 καὶ περὶ ἁρμονίας ἄν τις ... εἴποι** 'one might say the same thing also about an attunement and a lyre and its strings'. The ἁρμονία of a lyre is perhaps first its attunement, the state resulting from the relative adjustment of the strings to produce the required range of notes, and then by extension that range of notes itself. These two meanings, however, are not really distinct, since the state of being in tune will be defined by reference to the notes to be produced – this state being the capacity to produce that particular set of notes, and no other. It is in this way that the term ἁρμονία appears to be used in the present passage: it is the capacity to produce concordant music which would naturally be said both to be 'in' the tuned lyre, and to be πάγκαλόν τι καὶ θεῖον (e5–86a1). **e5 ἀσώματον:** see 79a4n. **τι** belongs with all four adjectives in the list, of which πάγκαλον ... καὶ θεῖον represents the climax.

86a2 σύνθετα: ἀσύνθετον is noticeably absent from the opposing list in 85e5–86a1. Simmias will in fact go on to treat ἁρμονίαι as σύνθετα (92a7–8, which is based on (86)b6–d4). **a4–5 εἴ τις διισχυρίζοιτο:** the protasis introduced here is first interrupted by a parenthesis in a6–b2 (οὐδεμία γὰρ ... ἀπολομένην), then resumed (ἀλλὰ φαίη ἀνάγκη ...), then interrupted again by b5–c2 (καὶ γὰρ οὖν ... πρὸς ἄλληλα); but b5–c2 now causes the substitution of a new protasis (c2–3 εἰ οὖν ... ἁρμονία τις), answered by the apodosis in c3–d1 (δῆλον ὅτι ... κατασαπῇι). **a5 τῶι αὐτῶι λόγωι:** 'argument' is clearly appropriate for λόγος here (as opposed to the vaguer 'thing said' in 85e4); the argument is stated, *mutatis mutandis*, in the parenthesis in a6–b2. **a6–7 οὐδεμία γὰρ μηχανὴ ἂν εἴη** 'there would be no way that', followed by acc. + inf. (cf. 72d2–3). **a8 καὶ τὰς χορδάς:** sc. εἶναι.

b2–3 ἀλλά, φαίη, ἀνάγκη ἔτι που εἶναι αὐτὴν τὴν ἁρμονίαν repeats a5–6 ἀνάγκη ἔτι εἶναι τὴν ἁρμονίαν ἐκείνην, but now in direct speech, with parenthetical φαίη (= the regular φησί, adapted to the conditional construction) substituting for διισχυρίζοιτο ... ὥς. που εἶναι = 'be somewhere': cf. 70a2n. **b5 καὶ γὰρ οὖν** 'And in point of fact' (Hackforth): an intensified form of καὶ γάρ as used at e.g. 57a6–7. The reference to 'tuning', Simmias explains, is even more appropriate than might have appeared. **b5–7 καὶ αὐτόν σε ... τὴν ψυχὴν εἶναι** 'that you yourself (καί seems to be purely emphatic) have noticed that we suppose the soul to be most of all (μάλιστα) something like this ...' The fact that S. is supposed to have 'noticed' 'our' endorsement of the theory in question suggests that it has come up before, in previous discussions. 'We', then, will be either Simmias on his own (cf. 92c11–d1 ὅδε ... μοι γέγονεν), or else Simmias and others in his and S.'s circle – though apparently not Cebes, unless 87a1–7 marks a complete conversion on his part. (But as before, the real reference is likely to be to discussions in the *Platonic* circle: cf. esp. 74b2n., 65d4–5n.) Cf. Arist. *De an.* 407b27–30, where the ἁρμονία theory of the soul is introduced as 'no less persuasive, to many people, than any of those we have mentioned, and one that has given an account of itself, as if to public assessors, in open discussions'. Alternatively, 'we' are to be seen as Pythagoreans (so e.g. Echecrates, who is represented by D. L. 8.46

as a Pythagorean, declares himself an enthusiastic supporter of the ἁρμονία theory at 88d), or the reference is to people in general who might be expected to have a theory on the subject at all (cf. 92d2n.). But the idea of the soul as a ἁρμονία is incompatible with any other known Pythagorean belief about the soul; and even if the theory was widely accepted (92d2), we need not assume Simmias to be referring to that fact here – what matters in this context is that *he* accepts it.　**b7 ὥσπερ ἐντεταμένου ... c1 τὴν ψυχὴν ἡμῶν** '[i.e.], given that our body is in tension, as it were, and held together by hot and cold and dry and wet and such things as these, that our soul is a blending and attunement of these very things'. ὥσπερ ἐντεταμένου (the same verb is used of the string of a lyre in [Arist.] *Probl.* 921b27) is explained by συνεχομένου ... καὶ τοιούτων τινῶν, in combination with c1–2 ἐπειδὰν ταῦτα καλῶς καὶ μετρίως κραθῆι πρὸς ἄλληλα: what holds the body together, and so keeps it 'in tension', is the right mixture, or ἁρμονία, of hot, cold, etc. – and this right mixture or ἁρμονία is the soul. What Simmias seems to mean here is that 'having a soul' (being ensouled or alive, ἔμψυχος) is merely another way of describing the state of the bodily constituents when mixed and 'in tension': the set of capacities which we associate with 'soul' *is* just this state. We will then have a precise parallel to the case of the lyre: there, as here, the relevant state arises simply as a result of the adjustment of physical elements (cf. 85e3–4n.). The core of Simmias' position is that soul is not an entity in itself, distinct from the body and added to it at birth, as the case for immortality presupposes; his challenge, then, will be a crucial one for S. to meet. For ancient criticisms of the theory of soul as ἁρμονία, see Arist. *De an.* 1.4, and Lucr. *DRN* 3.94–135. A very similar theory, but using a political rather than a musical metaphor, was advanced by the fifth-century medical thinker Alcmaeon (DK 24 b 4) as an explanation of health (cf. *Symp.* 186d), but he evidently did not take the short step to treating it also as an explanation of life, and so of 'soul' (see Arist. *De an.* 405a29–b1). Who first did so, and who first introduced the specific conception of ψυχή as a ἁρμονία, is unknown; but see preceding n.

c1–2 καλῶς καὶ μετρίως 'well and in due proportion'.　**c2 οὖν** is clearly resumptive; contrast a3, where it is progressive (so probably also at d1).　**c3–4 χαλασθῆι ... ἢ ἐπιταθῆι:** cf. b7 ἐντεταμένου.　**c6**

ὥσπερ καὶ αἱ ἄλλαι ἁρμονίαι ... 7 πᾶσι: lit. 'like the other attunements too, the ones in sounds and in all the products of the craftsmen': i.e. like real attunements (compared with which the soul is only ἁρμονία τις, c3), the ones found in the sphere of (musical) sound, and in all the instruments which produce it (cf. a1 ἐν τῆι ἡρμοσμένηι λύραι). Cf. 85e3–4n. ἐν τοῖς τῶν δημιουργῶν ἔργοις πᾶσι is usually taken as referring to artificial products generally; but a new metaphorical extension of ἁρμονία here would be an unnecessary distraction from the argument.

d5 διαβλέψας 'with a broad stare' (Burnet). Burnet connects the phrase with the peculiar and well-known (cf. ὥσπερ τὰ πολλὰ εἰώθει) prominence of S.'s eyes: *Theaet.* 143e, Xen. *Symp.* 5.5. Cf. 117b5 ὥσπερ εἰώθει ταυρηδὸν ὑποβλέψας, a different kind of look, but one which such startling eyes would make similarly striking.   **d7 τί οὐκ ἀπεκρίνατο;** 'In questions with τί οὐ, expressing surprise that something is not already done, and implying an exhortation to do it, the aorist is sometimes used strangely like a future' (*MT* 62).   **d7–8 καὶ γὰρ ... τοῦ λόγου:** lit. 'For he really (καὶ γάρ) resembles [someone] getting a grip on the argument [i.e. mine: cf. e1] in no mean way.'   **d9 χρῆναι:** sc. ἡμᾶς.

e1 τί αὖ ὅδε ἐγκαλεῖ τῶι λόγωι 'what charge he in his turn will bring against the argument'.   **e3 προσάιδειν** 'strike the proper note' (Fowler).   **e4 ἀλλ' ἄγε:** ἀλλά marks the change of pace which occurs with the imperative (cf. *GP* 13–14).   **e5 τί ἦν τὸ σὲ αὖ θρᾶττον** 'what it was that was troubling you, now that Simmias has had his say' (αὖ as in e1). ἀπιστίαν παρέχει can only be explained as an interpolated gloss.   **e6–87a1 ἐμοὶ γὰρ φαίνεται κτλ.** 'The argument seems to me still to be in the same place, and to be liable to the same charge as we were making against it before.'

87a2 εἰς τόδε τὸ εἶδος ἐλθεῖν: cf. 76c12 εἶναι ἐν ἀνθρώπου εἴδει.   **a2 οὐκ ἀνατίθεμαι μὴ οὐχὶ ... 4 ἀποδεδεῖχθαι** 'I do not retract [my admission] that it has been demonstrated ...': the metaphor of ἀνατίθεσθαι is from taking back a move in a board game. μὴ οὐ + inf. is the usual construction after a negatived verb of denial (implied in οὐκ ἀνατίθεμαι); cf. 72d1–3n., and *MT* 815.2. The difference between this construction and one like that at 85c4–6 is that the μή does not here negative the following infinitive, but merely continues the negative idea in the main verb. **a3 ἐπαχθές** 'lacking in taste': Burnet compares Dem. *Cor.* 10 ἵνα μηδὲν ἐπαχθὲς λέγω, where what is in question is overdone *self*-praise. **a5 οὔ μοι δοκεῖ τῆιδε:** sc. ἱκανῶς ἀποδεδεῖχθαι (with τῆιδε referring to the preceding ὡς-clause). **ἰσχυρότερον καὶ πολυχρονιώτερον:** as already implied by his acceptance of the argument from ἀνάμνησις (a1–4). a1–7 as a whole shows Cebes' position to be much closer to S.'s than to Simmias'; in particular, he accepts that the soul is an entity in itself, capable of subsisting independently of the body. **a9 τό γε ἀσθενέστερον** 'what is actually the weaker part' (emphatic γε).

b3 γάρ perhaps explains the hesitation implied in ἐπίσκεψαι εἴ τι λέγω. **b4 ἐμοὶ γὰρ δοκεῖ ... 5–6 τοῦτον τὸν λόγον:** lit. 'For these things [referring to S.'s last argument] seem to me to be said in the same way as if one were to say this [i.e. what follows] about an old weaver who has died.' ἄνθρωπος is regularly combined with other nouns, especially those denoting occupations, but after a9 τοῦ ἀνθρώπου (= combination of body + soul; cf. a2) it has additional point. **b6–7 ἔστι που σῶς** 'exists intact somewhere'. σῶς is a necessary correction found in a secondary MS (cf. b8 ἐστὶ σῶν, c5 σῶς ἐστιν). **b7–8 τεκμήριον δὲ παρέχοιτο θοιμάτιον ... ὅτι ἐστὶ σῶν** 'and were to produce as evidence the cloak ..., that it is intact'; i.e. were to produce as evidence the fact that his cloak is intact. **αὐτὸς ὑφηνάμενος:** for the point of this addition, see esp. d7–e1.

c2 γένος 'class'. **c3–4 ἀποκριναμένου δή ... οἴοιτο** '[and] then (δή) when someone answered ..., were to think ...': οἴοιτο, like b7 παρέχοιτο and c1 ἀνερωτώιη, continues the construction begun by ὥσπερ ἄν ... λέγοι in b4–5. δέ for the better attested δή in c3 looks right (connective δή does not usually occur in mid-sentence); as does Burnet's bracketing of τινος (the person answering must be the same as the τις of b8), but there is a certain awkwardness in Cebes' speech as a whole. Cf. 88b6n. **c3 ὅτι πολὺ τὸ τοῦ ἀνθρώπου** 'that the [class] to which the man belongs [is] by far [the more long-lived]'. **c6 τὸ δ' οἶμαι ... οὐχ οὕτως ἔχει** 'But in fact (τὸ δέ, used absolutely: cf. 109d8, and LSJ s.v. ὁ VIII.3) it is not like that'. **c6–7 σκόπει γὰρ καὶ σὺ ἃ λέγω:** by including Simmias at this point, Cebes mitigates the implied rudeness to S. in what he is about to say (c7–8 'Anyone would retort that this is a simple-minded thing to say'). **c7 γάρ** refers back to οὐχ οὕτως ἔχει.

d3–4 τὴν αὐτὴν δὲ ταύτην οἶμαι εἰκόνα δέξαιτ' ἂν ψυχὴ πρὸς σῶμα: lit. 'Soul in relation to body would, I think, admit this same image', i.e. the relationship of soul and body can itself be described in terms of a weaver and his products (d5–e5). Cebes' objection follows a similar pattern to Simmias': what begins as a counter-example to S.'s argument (the ἁρμονία of a lyre, a weaver and his cloaks) turns out itself to provide a metaphorical way of thinking directly about soul and body (soul as a ἁρμονία of bodily constituents, soul as a weaver). **d4 αὐτὰ ταῦτα** 'these very things', sc., *mutatis mutandis*, as described in d5–e5. **d5–6 ἡ μὲν ψυχὴ πολυχρόνιόν ἐστι, τὸ δὲ σῶμα ἀσθενέστερον ...:** i.e. in the light of the relationship which is about to be ascribed to them. **d7 ἀλλὰ γάρ** introduces a qualification to what has just been said ('But all the same': cf. *GP* 104–5, 100-1). The qualification consists in the complex proposition 'each soul wears out many bodies in the course of a lifetime (d7–8; sc. and hence is more long-lived), but nevertheless (e2 μέντοι, sc. on the analogy of the weaver) it will perish before the last one it "weaves"'. **d8 εἰ γὰρ ... ει ἀνυφαίνοι** 'for if the the body is in flux, and is perishing even while the person (ἄνθρωπος, as before, denoting the combination of soul and body) is alive, still (ἀλλά: see *GP* 11) the soul always weaves again what is being worn out': a parenthesis which explains the idea underlying d7–8. Cebes here combines the general idea of the soul as what brings life to the body (implied e.g. in the 'cyclical' argument) with an obvious fact of experience, that the tissue of the living body is continually dying off and being replaced (cf. e.g. Arist. *Pol.* 1276a34–b1); though the verb ῥεῖν probably also contains an allusion to the 'flux' theory of Heraclitus (cf. e.g. *Theaet.* 182c, with 181a). The optative ἀνυφαίνοι (similarly e5 ἐπιδεικνύοι, διοίχοιτο) resembles the independent optatives which can follow ὡς- or ὅτι-clauses with optative after a past main verb (as e.g. in Thuc. 2.72), and are sometimes even found where no such clause precedes (but still someone's views are being reported; cf. 95d3–4). See *MT* 675. We certainly need to suppose an implied construction with ὡς (cf. d5); but the main verb in this case, d7 ἂν φαίη (cf. d5 ἂν ... φαίνοιτο λέγειν), refers to the future rather than the past, and it may therefore be better to explain the optative in terms of assimilation to the potential idea which introduces it (ἂν φαίη), and which surfaces in its full-blown form in e2 (ἀναγκαῖον) ἂν εἴη. Cf. Dem. 16 (*For the Megalopolitans*) 5 οὐ γὰρ ἐκεῖνό γ' ἂν εἴποιμεν, ὡς ... βουλοίμεθα. ῥέοι (the theory is that the body is in flux, not that it might be: cf. d8 κατατρίβειν) and e2 ἀπολλύοιτο are certainly to be explained in terms of assimilation; for at least these optatives, cf. 72c5–6.

e4–5 τὴν φύσιν τῆς ἀσθενείας 'its natural weakness' (cf. Burnet). **e6 πιστεύσαντα:** sc. τινα.

88a2 τῶι λέγοντι [ἢ] ἃ σὺ λέγεις: Cebes again shows tact towards S. (cf. 87c6–7n.). ἢ (bracketed by several editors) would entail (*a*) that the same imaginary critic was speaking, and (*b*) that σύ refers to Cebes; but (*a*) is unlikely in view of τις; and (*b*) would involve a singular harshness. The introduction of the word probably resulted from a misunderstanding of καὶ πλέον ('even more', i.e. than what I originally conceded at 87a1–4: (88)a3–4 δοὺς αὐτῶι μὴ μόνον κτλ.). **a5 ἐνίων** '[the souls] of some [of us]', because it will be the consequence of the scenario now being advanced that not all souls will survive (every) death. **a6 αὐτό** 'the thing in question', i.e. the soul. **a8–9 ἐκεῖνο μηκέτι συγχωροῖ, μὴ οὐ πονεῖν αὐτήν** 'were not to concede the further point, that it does not suffer': construction much as in 85c4–6, with (τὸ) μὴ οὐ πονεῖν κτλ. as a noun-clause in apposition to ἐκεῖνο. **a9 τελευτῶσάν γε** 'finally', with γε marking the beginning of the climax of the sentence. (But the other sense of τελευτᾶν, 'die', must also be present.)

b1 διάλυσιν τοῦ σώματος 'separation from the body' (referring back to the original definition of death in 64c), not 'dissolution of the body': the latter process may be quick (87e5), but does not coincide with death. Cf. Gallop. **b2–3 ἀδύνατον γὰρ εἶναι ὁτωιοῦν αἰσθέσθαι ἡμῶν** 'for [sc. he would say] that it was impossible for any of us to perceive [sc. that he was undergoing his final death and separation from body]'. **b3 εἰ δὲ τοῦτο οὕτως ἔχει** 'but if this [i.e. what has been suggested in a8–b3] is the case': Cebes finally breaks off the long conditional clause begun in a1, and replaces it with a new one; he also ceases to talk for an anonymous 'someone' (88a2, etc.), and puts his point directly (οὐδενὶ προσήκει κτλ.). It was of course precisely the opposite of this that S. originally set out to show (63e9–64a2; cf.

84b4–8).   **b3–4 οὐδενὶ ... θαρρεῖν:** lit. 'it does not belong to anyone who is confident about death not to be foolishly confident', i.e. anyone confident about death must be foolish to be so (μὴ οὐ as in a8–9). **b4–5 ὃς ἂν μὴ ἔχηι ἀποδεῖξαι** 'whoever is not able to demonstrate', i.e. unless he is able to demonstrate.   **b5–6 παντάπασιν ἀθάνατόν τε καὶ ἀνώλεθρον:** to show that the soul is 'altogether deathless' will be to show that it survives every death, i.e. every separation from the body in every successive life; but given Cebes' assumption, that if it perishes it will do so 'in one of its deaths' (a9–10), this will be equivalent to showing that it is 'altogether imperishable'. (The force of παντάπασιν will then be quite different from that of παράπαν (ἀδιαλύτωι) at 80b9.)   **b6 ἀνάγκην εἶναι:** explained by Hackforth as 'depend[ing] on something like πᾶσι προσήκει ἡγεῖσθαι felt as the opposite of οὐδενὶ ... προσήκει ... θαρρεῖν'. The whole speech is less than fluent, though its content is sound enough; is Cebes perhaps less successful than Simmias in overcoming his embarrassment at putting his objection? (See 84d4–7; and cf. b3n.)   **b7–8 ἐν τῆι νῦν τοῦ σώματος διαζεύξει** 'in its present disjunction from the body' (Gallop); i.e. in the one that is about to occur (b6–7 τὸν μέλλοντα ἀποθανεῖσθαι).

88c1–91c5: further interlude

Before he recounts Socrates' reply to the objections just mounted, Phaedo describes the dismay at them felt by all those present, and how Socrates rallied them: just because some arguments may turn out to be weak, that is no reason to reject argument altogether.

88c1 ἀηδῶς διετέθημεν 'were disagreeably affected' (Gallop).   **c2 ὅτι** 'because'.   **c2–3 τοῦ ἔμπροσθεν λόγου:** i.e. the 'affinity' argument, against which both Simmias' and Cebes' objections were directed; c4–5 τοῖς προειρημένοις λόγοις, however, must refer to all the preceding arguments.   **c3 ἐδόκουν:** i.e. Simmias and Cebes.   **c4 εἰς ἀπιστίαν καταβαλεῖν:** followed first by a dative, by analogy with ἀπιστεῖν/πιστεύειν, then by εἰς ('towards').   **c6–7 μὴ ... ἦι** 'for fear that we would turn out to be worthless (οὐδενὸς ἄξιοι) judges or the things themselves to be untrustworthy as well' (ἢ καί: see *GP* 306). Fears referring to the future, in secondary time (ἐδόκουν ... εἰς ἀπιστίαν καταβαλεῖν), are expressed by μή (μὴ οὐ 'that ... *not*') and optative or, less frequently, subjunctive (cf. *MT* 365; here Plato uses first one and then the other, for variation). 'The things themselves': either the things S. set out to establish, or the subject of the arguments in a more general sense, i.e. the nature and fate of the soul (in which case ἄπιστα = 'doubtful', 'not admitting of certainty'). **c8 συγγνώμην γε ἔχω ὑμῖν** 'I really (γε) have sympathy for you.' **c9 καὶ γάρ:** the καί stresses αὐτόν με (cf. *GP* 108).

d1 ἐπέρχεται 'it occurs [to *me*, too, to say …]'. **d2–3 ὡς γὰρ … καταπέπτωκεν:** lit. 'For being how [exclamatory] emphatically persuasive, which argument [the argument which] S. was uttering, has now fallen into distrust', i.e. how very persuasive S.'s argument was, and yet now it has been discredited. Echecrates speaks as if he were himself present at the conversation, so demonstrating his full involvement in it: for him, as of course for us, as readers, the arguments are of more than historical concern. (But in any case the 'history' is invented.) **d3–4 ὁ λόγος οὗτος:** Simmias' theory (τὸ ἁρμονίαν κτλ., d4–5). **d4 ἀντιλαμβάνεται** 'has a hold on'. **d5 ὥσπερ ὑπέμνησέν με** 'reminded me, so to speak' (he had not actually forgotten, if the theory has a hold on him καὶ νῦν καὶ ἀεί). This reminiscence of the argument from ἀνάμνησις anticipates S.'s first move against Simmias' theory in 91e. **d8 συναποθνήισκει** 'die with [him]'. According to the definition of death originally agreed on by the protagonists (64c4–8; cf. 88b6–8), the soul cannot strictly be said to 'die'; but (*a*) what Echecrates says is rhetorically effective (ἀποθανόντος … συναποθνήι-σκει), and (*b*) in any case a supporter of the ἁρμονία theory of soul ought not to accept that definition of death. **d9 μετῆλθε τὸν λόγον:** for the metaphor, cf. 63a2, 76e9. e2, by contrast, has Socrates 'coming to the aid of' his λόγος (in both cases, λόγος is perhaps 'argument' in a broad sense).

e1 ὑμᾶς φήις: sc. ἐνδήλους γενέσθαι ἀχθομένους. **τι** 'at all'. **e2 ἐβοήθει τῶι λόγωι:** Szlezák 1985 attributes a special importance to this notion in the Platonic dialogues; cf. *Phdr.* 275e, 276a, 278c–d. **ἢ καί** 'Did he also …?' See *GP* 285, and cf. 94a12. **e4 καὶ μήν** as at 84d1, 58e1.

89a1 ὅτι λέγοι: deliberative subjunctive (τί λέγω;) becomes optative in indirect speech after a secondary main verb. **a2 αὐτοῦ … τοῦτο**

'this [feature] of him', i.e. of his behaviour. **a4–5 ἔπειτα . . . τῶν λόγων** 'next, how sharply he observed us, what effect their speeches had had on us'.

b1–2 ἐπὶ πολὺ ὑψηλοτέρου: not 'on a much higher [stool]', since he is still sitting on the bed (see 60b, 61c–d), but simply 'in a much higher position', loosely echoing the preceding construction. **b3 συμπιέσας** 'squeezing'. **b3–4 εἰώθει γάρ . . . τὰς τρίχας** 'for he had a habit now and then (ὁπότε τύχοι: lit. 'at whatever time he happened', sc. to do it), of making fun of my hair'; perhaps because Phaedo was past the age at which it would be usual for an Athenian man to wear his hair long (Robin). **b4–10** Phaedo should not cut his hair tomorrow (as a sign of mourning), but rather today, if they cannot breathe new life into the argument (10 ἀναβιώσασθαι; cf. ἀναβιώσκεσθαι in 71e–72a). In any case, S. does not think of his death as anything to grieve about. **b8 ἀλλὰ τί;** 'What then?'

c2 ἔνορκον ἂν ποιησαίμην 'I would swear an oath'. **ὥσπερ Ἀργεῖοι:** see Hdt. 1.82.7 ('the Argives . . . swore that none of them would grow their hair long [again] . . . until they recovered Thyreae'). **c3 ἀναμαχόμενος** 'fighting back' (ἀνα-). **c5–6** While fighting the hydra, Heracles was attacked by a giant crab, and was aided by his nephew Iolaus (cf. *Euthd.* 297c). οἷός τε εἶναι: sc. μάχεσθαι. **c7–8 ἀλλὰ καὶ ἐμέ . . . παρακάλει** 'then summon me as your Iolaus' (with καί emphasising ἐμέ): another piece of characteristic 'irony' on S.'s part (Iolaus played only a supporting role to the much stronger Heracles (as c5 implies). ἕως ἔτι φῶς ἐστιν: cf. 61e3–4. **c11 οὐδὲν διοίσει** 'it will make no difference', i.e. whichever of us has the greater resources, let's fight together.

d1 μισόλογοι 'misologists', i.e. haters of arguments (d3). **d1–2 ὥσπερ οἱ μισάνθρωποι γιγνόμενοι** 'in the way that those who become misanthropists [become like that]': cf. d4–5. **d2–3** 'since there is no greater evil that could befall anyone than this, [namely] than coming to hate arguments'. **d3–4 ἐκ τοῦ αὐτοῦ τρόπου** 'in the same way' (cf. e.g. Lys. 31.30 μηδὲ ἐξ ἑνὸς τρόπου). **d5 ἄνευ τέχνης** 'without expert knowledge'. **d6 ἡγήσασθαι ... 7 εὑρεῖν:** continuing the infinitive construction begun in d5 (ἐκ τοῦ πιστεῦσαι). **d8 καὶ αὖθις ἕτερον** 'and then [finding] a second person [similarly untrustworthy, instead of the reliable person he thought he was]'. We thus have the sequence one, then two, then many (καὶ ὅταν τοῦτο πολλάκις πάθηι τις, d8–9).

e1 προσκρούων: lit. 'stumbling', so 'making mistakes'. **e2 οὐδενὸς οὐδέν** 'no one in any respect' (lit. 'nothing of anyone'). **e5 αἰσχρόν** 'not a pretty thing'. **e7–90a1 εἰ γάρ . . . ἡγήσατο** 'For presumably (που) if he handled [people] on the basis of a proper understanding, he would have thought [things to be] as they [really] are' (ὥσπερ ἔχει οὕτως = οὕτως ἔχειν ὥσπερ ἔχει).

90a1–2 τοὺς μὲν χρηστοὺς κτλ.: the parallels in a4 and 5 suggest that σφόδρα qualifies χρηστοὺς καὶ πονηρούς rather than ὀλίγους (or as well as: so Verdenius). The general thought seems to be that there is some bad in everyone good, and vice versa. This suggests that 'good' and 'bad' are regarded as forming a continuum, like hot and cold. **a5–6 οἴει τι κτλ.** 'do you think there is anything rarer than (ἤ[1]) to find an extremely large or extremely small man, or dog, or anything else?' **a7 λευκὸν ἢ μέλανα** 'pale or dark'. **a8 τὰ . . . ἄκρα τῶν ἐσχάτων** 'the ends of the extremes', i.e. the most extreme instances at either end of every spectrum.

b1–2 ἄν . . . φανῆναι represents ἄν . . . φανεῖεν in direct speech. **b4–5 ταύτηι . . . οὐχ ὅμοιοι οἱ λόγοι τοῖς ἀνθρώποις:** i.e. there is no lack of extremely bad arguments; the reference is perhaps especially to those produced by the category of people to be introduced in b9–c1, οἱ περὶ τοὺς ἀντιλογικοὺς λόγους διατρίψαντες. **b6–8 ἀλλ' ἐκείνηι ἧι, ἐπειδάν τις πιστεύσηι . . . , κἄπειτα . . . δόξηι** 'but in the way in which, when someone trusts . . . , and then . . . it seems . . .': S. then breaks off the sentence without providing the expected apodosis, in order to insert a new subject (οἱ . . . διατρίψαντες, b9–c1). **b6 ἀληθεῖ:** an ἀληθής argument is perhaps one that we – or rather one who possesses the relevant τέχνη (b7) – can safely accept as establishing a given conclusion (cf. 85b–d). **b8 ὤν:** sc. ψευδής. **b9–c6** On 'antilogic', see esp. Kerferd 1981, ch. 6: '[it] consists in causing the same thing to be seen by the same people now as possessing one predicate and now as possessing the opposite or contradictory predicate' (61, with reference to *Phdr.* 261c–e, and the discussion there of Zeno of Elea, the antilogician *par excellence*); '. . . it constitutes a specific and fairly definite technique, namely that of proceeding from a given logos, say the position adopted by an opponent, to the establishment of a contrary or contradictory logos in such a way that the opponent must either accept both logoi, or at least abandon his first position' (63). The typical result of the 'antilogical' procedure is 'two statements which are mutually contradictory' (65). This makes good sense of the present passage: in so far as the contradictory statements claim to be statements about how things are, and the procedure can be applied to any subject whatever, the consequence will be that 'no aspect of reality' (c3 τὰ πράγματα = c4 τὰ ὄντα, 'the things that are', 'what is the case') is sound or secure; and the same will hold of arguments (c4 οὔτε τῶν λόγων), since the method supposes that any argument can be matched by one for the opposite conclusion. c2–3: 'they think that they have become very wise, because they have understood, unlike anyone else, that ...' S. goes on to question both halves of the anti-logicians' claim (the second immediately, and the first in his reply to Cebes, which reintroduces the forms – objects which are in his view undoubtedly 'secure').

c5 ἐν Εὐρίπωι: the narrow strait between the island of Euboea and the mainland, in which the strong currents frequently change direction (hence ἄνω κάτω στρέφεται 'are turned this way and that'). There is a clear reference here to the 'flux' doctrine of the Heracliteans (cf. e.g. *Crat.* 440a–c; and see *Theaet.* 152–60, where extreme Protagorean relativism – 'man is the measure of all things' – is combined with Heracliteanism). **c5–6 ἐν οὐδενί** 'in no [place]'. **c8** We here return from the special and extreme case of the antilogicians to the τις (d3, cf. b6) we are to beware of becoming. **c9 ὄντος δή** 'when there really existed'. Whether S.'s arguments so far are meant to be capable of fitting the description 'true' and 'secure' is left unclear (b8–9 ὕστερον ... δόξηι ψευδὴς εἶναι, ἐνίοτε μὲν ὤν, ἐνίοτε δ' οὐκ ὤν), and appropriately so, since Simmias' and Cebes' objections have thrown the company into confusion (88c). On balance, however, it seems unlikely that P. wants us to think of them as sufficient: see 91e1n.

d1 ἔπειτα 'even then', 'despite that'. **παραγίγνεσθαι** 'associating with'. **d4–5 ἀλλὰ τελευτῶν ... ἀπώσαιτο** 'but instead, because of the pain [of the experience] were happily (ἄσμενος) to shift the blame from himself to arguments'. **d6–7 τῶν δὲ ὄντων ... στερηθείη:** lit. 'and were to be deprived of the truth and knowledge of the [things] that

are': i.e. of knowledge of the truth about things.   **d9 πρῶτον μὲν . . .
εὐλαβηθῶμεν:** cf. 91c3n.   **d9–e2 μὴ παρίωμεν . . . ὑγιὲς εἶναι** 'let us
not admit into our soul [the thought] that there is likely to be nothing
sound in arguments'.

e2 οὔπω ὑγιῶς ἔχομεν: i.e. we do not yet possess the necessary τέχνη
περὶ τοὺς λόγους (b7).   **e3 σοὶ μὲν οὖν:** οὖν 'emphasis[es] . . . prospec-
tive μέν' (*GP* 473), heightening our expectation of the answering ἐμοὶ
δέ in the following line.

91a1 αὐτοῦ ἕνεκα τοῦ θανάτου 'for the sake of my death itself', i.e., as
the sequel shows, in order that he may encounter death with the right
(philosophical) attitude.   **a2–3 ὥσπερ οἱ πάνυ ἀπαίδευτοι φιλονίκως:** these are the 'eristics', people who – like the sophists Euthydemus
and Dionysodorus portrayed in *Euthd.* – show their complete lack of
'education' in the science of argument by caring only about appearing
to their audience to win their case, by whatever means are available
(a3–6). The 'antilogicians' of 90b–c evidently form a separate class,
since they allegedly have a particular view about the nature of reality
(90c2–6), whereas the eristics simply do not care how things really are
(a4). S.'s suggestion that he is presently (ἐν τῶι παρόντι, a1) in danger
of emulating the eristics must be a reflection on his performance until
now – and perhaps especially in the affinity argument, the larger part
of which contains more persuasive description than hard reasoning (cf.
84b4–8n.). But in a6 he switches into the future: 'it seems to me that I
shall on the present occasion (again, ἐν τῶι παρόντι) differ from them
. . .' However close he may have come to them, his attitude from now
on will be clear. This change in (or clarification of) his approach corresponds to the change in the roles of Simmias and Cebes: see introductory note to 84c1–85e2, and further a7n.   **a4 ὅπηι . . . ὁ λόγος:** lit.
'how [the things] are in relation to which the argument may be', i.e.
the truth of the matter under discussion.   **a5 ἃ αὐτοὶ ἔθεντο** 'their
own theses'.   **a7 τοσοῦτον μόνον:** the difference in question (that he
will try to persuade himself rather than his audience) will be a small
one only if S. is on the same level as the eristics, and πάνυ ἀπαίδευτος
like them; and of course he is not, although with his usual 'irony' he
pretends to be. Rather, he is as complete a philosopher (see esp. 76b–
c), and therefore as skilled in argument, as anyone living. Something
which appears true to him will therefore have passed the most exacting

test available – although even that may not be sufficient, as Simmias'
speech at 85b–d has warned us (see esp. c1–4 ἐμοὶ γὰρ δοκεῖ ... περὶ
τῶν τοιούτων ἴσως ὥσπερ καὶ σοὶ τὸ μὲν σαφὲς εἰδέναι ἐν τῶι νῦν βίωι
ἢ ἀδύνατον εἶναι ἢ παγχάλεπόν τι). b1–c5 then has a double meaning,
one as spoken by S. the ignoramus, the other as spoken by S. the
philosopher. **a8–9 εἰ μὴ εἴη πάρεργον** 'except incidentally'.

b1–2 θέασαι ὡς πλεονεκτικῶς: lit. 'watch how graspingly' (cf. a3
φιλονίκως), i.e. because either way he will win. **b3 εἰ δὲ μηδέν ἐστι
τελευτήσαντι** 'whereas if there is nothing for one who has died'. **b3–
4 ἀλλ' οὖν ... γε** 'still, at least' (*GP* 444); cf. ἀλλὰ ... γοῦν at 71b8.
b5–6 ἡ δὲ ἄνοιά μοι αὕτη οὐ συνδιατελεῖ 'this silliness [i.e. the one
which would be involved in wrongly believing that there is something
for the dead] will not persist with me', i.e. it will shortly perish with me
(ὀλίγον ὕστερον ἀπολεῖται). With the reading διάνοια, what would be
perishing, less colourfully, would be 'this thought [that there is something ...]'; cf. 63c9. **b7–8 παρεσκευασμένος δὴ ... ἐπὶ τὸν λόγον**
'Prepared, then (δή: cf. 71d5), Simmias and Cebes, in this way, I
advance against the argument' (i.e. your arguments).

c1 σμικρόν: adverbial. **c3 εὐλαβούμενοι:** we thus at last find a pair
to 90d9 πρῶτον μὲν ... εὐλαβηθῶμεν – although the groundwork for it
began as far back as 90e4 (ἐμοὶ δὲ κτλ.). **c4 ὑπὸ προθυμίας** 'through
zeal' (i.e. my zeal to convince myself, a7–b1).

91c6–95a3: Socrates' reply to Simmias

*After a short recapitulation of both Simmias' and Cebes' objections, Socrates turns
to the former, first pointing out that the view of the soul Simmias has proposed is
incompatible with the argument from ἀνάμνησις (which he accepts), and then
mounting two independent arguments against it.*

91c6 ἀλλ': marking the transition from reflection to action (see *GP*
14). **c6–7 ἐὰν ... μεμνημένος** 'in case I prove not to remember'.
c8–d2 φοβεῖται μὴ ... οὖσα 'is afraid that despite being (ὅμως ... ὄν:
see LSJ s.v. ὅμως II.2) something both more divine and more beautiful
than the body, the soul may perish before it, being a kind of attunement' (ἐν ἁρμονίας εἴδει οὖσα: cf. 86c3, 92a8, and *Rep.* 389b4 (ψεῦδος)
ἀνθρώποις ... χρήσιμον ὡς ἐν φαρμάκου εἴδει, 'useful for human beings
as a kind of medicine').

d3–4 τόδε ἄδηλον παντί: φάναι is easily supplied from συγχωρεῖν. For the following construction (μή + subj.), cf. e.g. 67b2n.; the idea of fearing is clearly implicit in τόδε ἄδηλον παντί. **d4 πολλὰ . . . σώματα καὶ πολλάκις:** i.e. many bodies in many separate lifetimes (87d–88a). **d5 νῦν:** i.e. τὸ τελευταῖον σῶμα καταλιποῦσα. **d6 καὶ ἦι αὐτὸ τοῦτο θάνατος, ψυχῆς ὄλεθρος** 'and whether death might not be this very thing, [the] perishing of [the] soul', i.e. under the circumstances described in d4–5 πολλὰ . . . καταλιποῦσα; but since we could not predict when these might hold (88b), any death might mean just this. (As d7 adds, the body will of course also perish; but that is neither here nor there, since on Cebes' hypothesis it is continually perishing, even during life.) d5 (ψυχὴ) τὸ . . . σῶμα καταλιποῦσα shows that the definition of death as the separation of soul from body, agreed at 64c, is still in force; it was temporarily abandoned by Cebes in 87e1–5, but then implicitly reinstated by his concession to S. of the idea of multiple reincarnations (88a–b; cf. 91d4 καὶ πολλάκις, which seems to confirm that S.'s summary here refers to this latter, more generous, version of Cebes' objection). For other interpretations of d6, see O'Brien 1968, 98–100, and Gallop 155–6. **d7 ἀεὶ ἀπολλύμενον οὐδὲν παύεται** 'does not stop at all (οὐδέν is used adverbially) from a process of incessant change'. **d7–9 ἆρα ἄλλ' ἢ ταῦτ' ἐστίν . . . ἃ δεῖ ἡμᾶς ἐπισκοπεῖσθαι;** 'Are [the points] we have to consider other than these?'

e1 δή 'Well, . . .' (*GP* 238). **e4** All that is certain is that they accept the argument from ἀνάμνησις (e5–92a5); 77c–e, at least, suggests no great enthusiasm on their part for the cyclical argument (cf. 72d4n., and 87a4–5), and not only were their present objections mounted directly against the affinity argument, but they in fact present powerful challenges to it – Simmias', by offering an example of something else which is unseen and incorporeal, like the soul, yet perishable, and Cebes' by pointing out, in effect, that likeness may be only relative ('I concede that the soul may be longer-lived than the body, but . . .'). Nor, in the event, does Socrates attempt to rebut these specific criticisms of the affinity argument (which he himself in any case admitted was open to attack: 84c6–7), preferring instead to attack Simmias' positive proposal to regard soul itself as 'a kind of ἁρμονία', and to respond to Cebes by inventing an entirely new argument for immortality. Given that 77c–e has also suggested the inadequacy of the ἀνάμνησις argument by itself to prove the case (a point which is

underlined by e6 τούτου ... 92a1 ἐνδεθῆναι; see also 87a1–5), his strategy is at least consistent with supposing that that is the only complete
argument that is to count as accepted.

92a2 θαυμαστῶς ὡς ἐπείσθην 'I was wonderfully convinced'. **a4 καὶ
μήν . . . καὶ αὐτός** 'Yes (καὶ μήν: cf. *GP* 353), and I myself too.' **a7
οἴησις = δόξα.** **a8–9 ἐκ τῶν κατὰ τὸ σῶμα ἐντεταμένων συγκεῖσθαι**
'is composed out of the [things] held in tension in the body', or 'out of
the constituents of the body, when these are held in tension'. If the soul
is 'composed out of' these, that would on the face of it imply that they
are its constituent parts; and S. does go on to treat ταῦτα ἐξ ὧν ἂν
(ἁρμονία) συντεθῆι as equivalent to τὰ αὐτῆς μέρη (93a6–7, 9). Simmias ought to be unhappy about accepting this, (*a*) because he started
off by suggesting that the ἁρμονία of the lyre, at least, was ἀσώματον
(85e5), and (*b*) because in any case states (if ἁρμονίαι are states: cf.
85e3–4n., 86b7–c1n.) cannot obviously be said to have parts. (The
strings, in the case of the lyre, will be parts of what is in a tuned state;
in the same way the constituents of the body will be parts of the living
(ensouled) body.) Nevertheless, there is a sense in which the soul (as
ἁρμονία) will be something 'put together' from the constituents of the
body, namely that it results from the putting together of these parts
(see 86b7–c1n.); and perhaps that is all that is meant. The point S. is
preparing to make, about the incompatibility of the ἁρμονία theory
with the theory of learning as ἀνάμνησις, will be unaffected. **a9–b1
οὐ γάρ που ἀποδέξηι γε σαυτοῦ λέγοντος** 'for I don't suppose you'll
allow yourself to say'; γε emphasises the negative statement.

b1 ἦν . . . συγκειμένη 'was there already composed' (similarly εἶναι
... συγκειμένην at b6). **b4 συμβαίνει:** cf. 74a2. **b5 εἰς ἀνθρώπου
εἶδος:** cf. 73a1–2, 76c12. **b7 οὐ γάρ ... 8 ὧι ἀπεικάζεις** 'An *attunement*
certainly isn't (οὐ γὰρ δή ... γε: cf. 76c6–7n.) the sort of thing with
which you're comparing it', i.e. a composite thing which pre-exists the
elements out of which it is compounded. Simmias will be bound to
regard an attunement in the same way, in so far as he wants to call the
soul a kind of attunement.

c1 οἱ φθόγγοι: even an untuned instrument will produce sounds; but
these will of course be different from the sounds it can produce when
tuned. **c2–3 οὗτος ... ἐκείνωι:** respectively, soul-as-ἁρμονία and
learning-as-ἀνάμνησις (c9–10). **c5 καὶ μήν ... 6 ἁρμονίας** 'Yet if

there is any other theory which *ought* to be in tune, it's certainly (καί²)
the one about attunement' (for adversative καὶ μήν ... γε, see *GP*
357). **c8 οὗτος κτλ.** 'Well (τοίνυν), you'll find (σοι, ethic dative) this
one isn't.' **c11 ὅδε μὲν γάρ ... d1 εὐπρεπείας** 'For I have acquired
the latter without proof, on the basis of a certain likelihood and [super-
ficial] plausibility' (μετά, 'with', is the natural pair of ἄνευ).

d2 τοῖς πολλοῖς ... ἀνθρώποις: presumably an exaggeration; most
people, literally, would be unlikely to hold any reasoned theory about
the soul. There is, however, some good evidence that the soul-as-
ἁρμονία theory was in one form or another quite widespread: see esp.
Laws 891b–c, and Arist. *De an.* 407b27–30 (quoted above at 86b5–
7n.). **d4 ἀλαζόσιν** 'impostors', claiming to have achieved more than
they really have. Interestingly, Simmias' description seems to fit at
least part of one of S.'s own arguments: the latter part of the affinity
argument (from 80e) is almost completely based on what is εἰκός (from
81c8 to 82b8, explicitly so), and yet ends by stating its conclusion in a
completely unqualified form (84b4–8: 'there is no danger that [the
philosophical soul] will fear' its dissolution). But after pondering on
the argument, Socrates quickly recognised its weaknesses (84c), just as
Simmias now recognises his mistake in relation to the ἁρμονία theory:
as before (see 85c2n.), the two march wholly in step in methodological
matters. **d5 ἐξαπατῶσι:** participle, continuing the construction begun in d2–4 (τοῖς ... λόγοις σύνοιδα οὖσιν ἀλαζόσιν). **καὶ ἐν γεωμετρίαι κτλ.:** i.e. in other spheres as much as in geometry. Skilled
geometers don't accept proofs based on τὰ εἰκότα, and neither should
anyone else. **d6–7 δι' ὑποθέσεως ἀξίας ἀποδέξασθαι:** quite why the
hypothesis in question (the existence of forms, d8–9) is 'worthy of
acceptance' Simmias does not say. He presumably cannot *prove* it, or it
would not count as a hypothesis or postulate (cf. d6 καὶ ἐν γεωμετρίαι
κτλ.), but on the other hand he has some sort of independent reason or
reasons – beyond what is merely εἰκός – for accepting it (see e1 'I have
accepted it, I am convinced, ἱκανῶς τε καὶ ὀρθῶς'; i.e. I think I am
sufficiently justified in accepting it). He might perhaps begin from an
optimistic belief in the possibility of ethical knowledge (see esp. 76b),
supposing this to depend on the existence of stable objects ('the beautiful', 'the good', etc.). S. will later introduce a much longer account of
hypothetical method (100a–102a), in the context of a discussion of
explanation; but that throws no new light on the present question. One

of the effects of what Simmias says here is to give a concrete illustration of the procedure he proposed at 85c–d, of taking the best available λόγος and depending on that, in the absence of anything more secure; it also exemplifies an important part of S.'s method of hypothesis, according to which, after 'hypothesising' (ὑποτίθεσθαι) whichever λόγος appears strongest, he goes on to posit whatever harmonises with this as true, and whatever does not as not true (100a3–7). But 85c–d is already closely connected in thought and language with this later context: cf. 85d1n. **d7–8 οὕτως . . . ὥσπερ:** cf. 76e8–77a2 (ἡ αὐτὴ ἀνάγκη . . . τὸ ὁμοίως εἶναι). **d8 αὐτή** seems a necessary replacement for the far better attested αὐτῆς. Tr. '[as] the being (ἡ οὐσία, as at 76d8–9, of a collection of existents) itself (αὐτή) exists, bearing the name of "what is [F]"'. For this interpretation of ὃ ἔστιν, see 75d2–3n. The reading αὐτῆς, 'belonging to it' (in the sense of being the object of the soul's understanding: see Loriaux I 155), although literally in accord with 76e1–2 (ταύτην τὴν οὐσίαν) ὑπάρχουσαν . . . ἡμετέραν οὖσαν, and accepted by most recent editors, is impossibly harsh.

e4 τί δέ . . . τῆιδε; 'And what [if we look at the matter] like this?' S. here begins his two arguments against Simmias' theory (the previous section being, of course, purely *ad hominem*: it would not affect anyone who rejected the theory of ἀνάμνησις). He begins by asking for Simmias' agreement to some of the premisses he will need for one of the two arguments (92e4–93a10); then follows the other argument, in full (93a11–94b3), and finally the completion of the first (94b4–95a3). The reason for this apparently curious arrangement seems to be rhetorical rather than logical. There is no logical connection between the premisses agreed in 92e4–93a10 and those of the second argument (see Gallop 158); on the other hand, it clearly adds to the psychological effect of S.'s refutation to have the conclusions of the arguments follow each other in quick succession. **e4–93a1 ἢ ἄλληι τινὶ συνθέσει:** see 92a8–9n.

93a1 προσήκειν: cf. 78b5n. In this case, however, what is in question is clearly a necessary truth (whether any ἁρμονία *is* a state of the underlying physical elements). **a4 οὐδὲ μήν** 'Nor again' (sc. δοκεῖ σοι προσήκειν); cf. *GP* 338–40. As Gallop points out (167), there is one thing that the ἁρμονία of a lyre can πάσχειν without its 'components' being affected in the same way, namely being destroyed (the strings and frame may well survive its destruction). It remains true, however, that what the ἁρμονία 'does' (if it does anything) and has happen to it depends on what the strings do and have happen to them, and not vice versa; and that is all S. requires.   **a6 οὐκ ἄρα ἡγεῖσθαί γε προσήκει ἁρμονίαν** 'We should certainly not in that case expect an attunement to *direct*.' Given what was agreed about the soul's function in relation to the body at 79e–80a, the general trend of the argument is already clear enough.   **a8 ἐναντία . . . κινηθῆναι** 'to move in contrary directions'.   **a11–12 τί δέ; οὐχ οὕτως . . . ὡς ἄν ἁρμοσθῆι;** S. now begins his second argument (see 92e4n.): 'Another thing: isn't it natural for each attunement to be an attunement in whatever way it has been tuned?' This question becomes intelligible only in the more specific version which follows (a14–b2, prompted by Simmias' οὐ μανθάνω): if it is tuned more, will it be more of a harmony, and if less, less? S.'s point is that any difference in the tuning of an attunement (that is, any difference between the results when an instrument like a lyre is tuned on different occasions – except, presumably, when the musician is actually aiming at different sets of notes) will affect the degree to which it can be called, and is, an attunement. The results of any fully successful tunings, on the other hand, will presumably be identical. 'Tuning an attunement' sounds odd in English, but ἁρμόζειν ἁρμονίαν is less so in Greek, which likes to group together words with the same root. Without qualification, it amounts to no more than '*producing* an attunement'; and ἁρμόζειν ἁρμονίαν 'more' or 'less' will mean producing a result which approximates to a greater or lesser degree to the one desired.   **a14 ἐπὶ πλέον** seems here to function simply as a variant of μᾶλλον; similarly b2 ἐπ' ἔλαττον and ἧττον (but see further d9–10n.); if so, b2 πλείων will add nothing – except rhetorical force – after b1 μᾶλλον, nor ἐλάττων after ἧττον.

b1 εἴπερ . . . γίγνεσθαι: strictly speaking, of course, there will be no degrees of attunement – an instrument will either be in or out of tune; but in so far as one tuning may be more nearly right than another, we may speak of its being 'more of an attunement'.   **b4 ἦ οὖν ἔστι τοῦτο περὶ ψυχήν, ὥστε** 'Well ('progressive' οὖν, as at 58b4, etc.), is this the case in relation to soul, with the consequence that . . .?' The question clearly expects a negative answer, which it duly gets. No soul can be more or less of a soul than another. (But there are differences between souls (b8–c1); if soul is a kind of harmony, how then do we explain these (c3–5)?) **b5** The first μᾶλλον is of course strictly unnecessary. **b8–9 νοῦν τε ἔχειν καὶ ἀρετὴν καὶ εἶναι ἀγαθή:** according to S., as we know from 69a–c, true virtue presupposes wisdom or φρόνησις; and sound sense (νοῦν ἔχειν) will be a part of wisdom.

c3 τῶν οὖν θεμένων ... 4 ἐν ταῖς ψυχαῖς: lit. 'Then of those who have posited that soul is attunement [of whom, of course, Simmias used to be one, but is no longer: cf. his perhaps ruefully ironic reply at c9–10], what will any one say that these things which are in the soul are?' **c5 πότερον ... ἀναρμοστίαν;** If (a) soul is (an) attunement, and (b) attunements differ, if at all, only in the degree to which they are attunements (see a11–12n.), then the difference between good and bad souls must be explicable in similar terms (full attunement in the case of the good, and the absence of it altogether in the opposite case); but since (c) both types are already attunements, this must be by reference to some further attunement. Whether it is possible to attach any sense to the idea of such a further attunement is a problem for the upholder of the ἁρμονία theory himself; in any case S. does not try to analyse it, but instead ends by treating it, reasonably enough, as another instance of an attunement's being tuned 'to a greater extent', and its absence as an instance of tuning to a lesser extent (see d1n.). In the final part of the argument (93d–94b), he sets out to show on this basis that such a way of accounting for virtue and vice in the soul is incompatible with what has already been agreed in 93a11–c1; if there is no other account available to the proponents of the ἁρμονία theory, that theory must then fall, since virtue and vice are a reality. In simplified form, the argument as a whole seems to run something like this: there are differences between souls; if there are differences between attunements (of the same type), this will be because some of these attunements are attunements to a lesser degree than others; all souls are equally souls, and – on the theory – equally attunements; the theory cannot therefore account for differences between souls. The ἁρμονία-theorist might, perhaps, respond by attributing such differences to differences in the 'mix' of bodily constituents, so that the comparison would be with different tunings of the lyre (i.e. ones resulting in different, but all equally concordant, sets of notes); but then people would apparently be born either virtuous and vicious, which among other things would

raise serious problems about moral responsibility. In any case, Simmias'
original account suggested a single formula for the mix (86c1–2
ἐπειδὰν ταῦτα καλῶς καὶ μετρίως κραθῆι πρὸς ἄλληλα). **c6 τὴν μὲν
ἡρμόσθαι** is explained by καὶ ἔχειν ... ἄλλην ἁρμονίαν. **c7–8 τὴν δὲ
ἀνάρμοστον αὐτήν τε εἶναι** 'while the other [sc. the bad soul] is itself
[i.e. despite being an attunement?] untuned'. That, at least, is the sort
of thing we should expect to be said, balancing τὴν μὲν ἡρμόσθαι; the
difficulty, apart from the precise function of αὐτήν, is the surprising
(but by no means unique: see *GP* 517) postponement of τε, linking the
clause with the (explanatory?) καὶ ἔχειν ... But if αὐτήν can be taken
as suggested, the postponed τε could be said to add emphasis to it, and
the alternatives ('the untuned soul is just itself', Bluck; or supplying
ἁρμονίαν as complement of εἶναι) are even more unappealing. **c10 ὁ
ἐκεῖνο ὑποθέμενος:** cf. c3n.

d1 προωμολόγηται: b4–7 (μηδέν 'in no way': we might have expected
οὐδέν, but see *MT* 269–70). S. commences his demolition of the idea
just proposed (c5–8). It has previously been agreed that no soul is any
more or less a soul than any other (d1–2), and this will amount to an
agreement that (?) no attunement is any more or less an attunement
than any other (d2–4, substituting 'attunement' for 'soul' in 1–2); but
it has also been agreed that what is neither more nor less an attunement
is neither more nor less tuned (d6–8: a valid inference, by 'contraposi-
tion', from a14–b2), and what is neither more nor less tuned has
an equal share in attunement, not more or less (d9–11, where the new
formula 'sharing more/less in attunement' covers the proposed second attunement/non-attunement of c5–8: cf. the substitution of πλέον
ἀναρμοστίας/ἁρμονίας μετέχειν for πλέον ἢ ἔλαττον ἁρμονίας μετέχειν
in e4–5); therefore, since (again) no soul is more of a soul than any
other (d12–e1 = d1–2), and is therefore neither more nor less tuned
(e1–3 = d2–8, but with the resubstitution of 'soul' for 'attunement'),
it will not share more in non-attunement or in attunement (as on the
hypothesis of c5–8: e4–5). **d2 τοῦτο ... 4 ἁρμονίας εἶναι** is probably
the only problematical move in the sequence: it will not follow from
the available premisses (that no soul is more or less a soul than any
other, and that soul is an attunement) that no attunement whatever
may be more or less an attunement than any other; and after he has
earlier (b1) left open the general possibility of degrees of attunement,

it would be strange for S. to discard it so carelessly. What does follow is that the type of attunement soul allegedly is will always equally be an attunement; and, especially given the way in which the proposition is reached (see previous n.), this is probably what is meant. (But in d6–10, the reference is certainly to attunements in general.)   **d4 εἶναι:** sc. ἁρμονίαν (similarly ψυχήν has to be supplied as complement of εἶναι in d2).   **ἤ γάρ;** 'Isn't that so?' (cf. *GP* 284–5).   **d6 τὴν δέ γε:** sc. ἁρμονίαν (for δέ γε, see 65c5n.).   **d6–7 μηδὲ μᾶλλον μηδὲ ἧττον ἡρμόσθαι:** the first μηδέ is adverbial (cf. *GP* 193–4). Tr. 'and has not been tuned more or less either'; similarly οὐδέ ... οὐδέ in e1–2. See Verdenius.   **d9–10** 'And is there a way in which what has been neither more nor less tuned shares to a greater or lesser degree in attunement, or [does it share in it] to an equal degree?' This important proposition seems, reasonably, to be treated as intuitively obvious; on its function in the argument, see d1n. For the adverbial use of ὅτι (acc. neut. sing. of ὅστις), cf. e4 οὐδὲν πλέον, 7 τι πλέον. That S. switches here from μᾶλλον and ἧττον to the pair πλέον and ἔλαττον (= ἐπὶ πλέον, a14, b5; ἐπ' ἔλαττον, b2, b6) is perhaps designed to help underline the fact that he is now moving to the second, allegedly different way of distinguishing between attunements (c5–8, cf. e4, 7; see d1n.); at the same moment, however, he is in the process of reducing it to the first (cf. c5n.) – so that ultimately as in a14–b6 and d3–4, the two pairs will turn out to be equivalent.

ei δή 'in that case' (cf. *GP* 224–5).   **e4–5 πλέον ἀναρμοστίας κτλ.:** see d1n. (τοῦτο ... πεπονθυῖα 'in this condition'.)   **e6 οὐ γὰρ οὖν** 'Certainly not' (with οὖν strengthening 'assentient' γάρ, *GP* 447).   **e7–94b3** Conclusion. No soul, in that case, will have a greater share in vice or virtue than another (e7–9) – or rather, no soul will share in vice (94a1–7), so that all souls will be equally virtuous (94a8–11); since that is plainly untrue, the hypothesis which led to it, that soul is an attunement, must be incorrect (94a12–b3).   **e8–9 εἴπερ ἡ μὲν κακία κτλ.:** 'if indeed ...', i.e. as the proponent of the soul-as-attunement theory has been portrayed as holding.

94a1 μᾶλλον δέ γε ... 'Or rather, I suppose (που: as at 70d1, scarcely indicating real doubt), to follow the correct reasoning', i.e. the reasoning to be given in a2–7 (cf. a8 ἐκ τούτου τοῦ λόγου). If an attunement is completely an attunement (i.e. unqualifiedly, contrasting with the cases first introduced in 93a14–b2), it will never share in non-attunement (a2–5); in the same way (a6–7), if (a) soul is – as agreed at 93b4–7 – always completely soul (and therefore, being an attunement (a2), always completely an attunement: 93d1–4), it will never share in vice (given the identification of κακία with non-attunement: 93c5–8, e8). **a3 δήπου** 'presumably' (as at e.g. 64a7); indistinguishable, in practical terms, from a1 που. Cf. *GP* 267. **a6 οὐδέ γε** 'And neither …' (the 'negative counterpart' of δέ γε, *GP* 156). **a7 ἐκ … τῶν προειρημένων:** see a1n. **a8 ἡμῖν:** ethic dative (tr. 'Our conclusion will be that …'). **a9 ὁμοίως ἀγαθαί** 'equally good', i.e. identical in their goodness. **a12 ἢ καί:** the καί seems to emphasise καλῶς ('Do you think this is an *acceptable* conclusion?'). **a12–b2 καὶ πάσχειν ἂν κτλ.** 'and that the argument would have this happen to it [i.e. would end in so absurd a conclusion], if the hypothesis that soul is an attunement were correct?' The present argument thus appears as a further practical lesson in the application of hypothetical method, in advance of S.'s sketch of such a method in 100–1; see 92d6–7n. What we were taught earlier was about the requirement for a secure hypothesis, to serve as a basis for accepting or rejecting other λόγοι; as we have now learned, not all hypotheses will be secure, since they may turn out to conflict with things that are independently known to be true – in which case the hypothesis itself will have to be rejected. There is nothing in S.'s account which corresponds exactly to this idea, but cf. 101d3–5, where he recommends examining the consequences of one's hypothesis (τὰ ἀπ' ἐκείνης ὁρμηθέντα), to see 'whether they are in accord or discord with each other'. On the analysis proposed in the preceding nn., S.'s demolition of the soul-as-attunement hypothesis has been fairly conducted; but see next n. For a different, and comparatively ungenerous, analysis see Gallop, who includes judicious comments on some of the many other treatments of the argument, from Philoponus to W. Hicken.

b4 τί δέ; S. now completes the first argument, begun in 92e4–93a10. Of all the things that make up a human being, it is the soul that rules (b4–5), sometimes going along with, but also sometimes opposing, the bodily passions (b7–c1, c9–e1); but it was agreed that an attunement is dependent on what happens to its constituent elements, and cannot control or oppose them (c3–8); it cannot therefore be right to say that soul is an attunement (e2–95a2). One might ask why the passions in question (τὰ κατὰ τὸ σῶμα πάθη, b7) should be treated as belonging to the body and not to the soul, as they are in S.'s own account in *Rep*.: if, on the theory being considered, they are states of the body (cf. c4–6n.), then so too is what S. here calls ψυχή, i.e., presumably, reason (cf. b5 ἄλλως τε καὶ φρόνιμον). Granted, if soul is an attunement, the result would then be an attunement in discord with itself – a kind of idea which quite reasonably ruled out in the course of the preceding argument. A subtle attunement-theorist, however, could respond that what was intended was only an *analogy* with the attunement of a musical instrument, and that 'soul' of course represents a much more complex set of phenomena than an attunement. If there are difficulties in explaining these phenomena in terms of the relative 'adjustment' of physical elements, these are in principle no greater than those involved in explaining them on S.'s conception of soul as a separable incorporeal entity (and indeed, in *Rep*., we find S. himself wrestling with the question how such a thing could be subject to internal conflict of the kind he describes here). However effective the present argument may be against the simple version of the theory (i.e. that soul is a kind of attunement, and nothing more – which is, admittedly, how Simmias has presented it), it will have no force against other, more interesting versions; and the same limitation will attach to the argument of 93a–94b. **b4 τῶν ἐν ἀνθρώπωι … 5 ἄρχειν** is (perhaps deliberately) ambiguous between 'of all the [things] in a human being, is there any other which you say rules …?' and 'is there anything else which you say rules over all the [things] in a human being?' **5 ἄλλως τε καὶ φρόνιμον:** according to S.'s account in 68d–69c, anyone who lacks φρόνησις will in fact be ruled by 'the bodily passions'. **b8 λέγω … τὸ τοιόνδε, οἷον … 9 ἕλκειν** 'I mean this sort of thing, such as that [it] draws …': ἕλκειν seems to continue the acc. and inf. construction begun in b4–5, like b7–8 συγχωροῦσαν κτλ. But the construction is broken off in b10–11 καὶ ἄλλα μυρία … ὁρῶμεν … **b10 που** softens μυρία (as we should say, 'in thousands of ways').

c4 ἁρμονίαν γε οὖσαν 'if it were an attunement' (and not something else: γε). **c4 οἷς ἐπιτείνοιτο … 6 οὖσα** '[contrary] to the tightenings, relaxations, pluckings, or any other affections (πάθη, 'passions') of the things out of which it happens to be composed': see 93a4–5. (ᾄδειν, in c4, will presumably be an (or the only) example of what an attunement 'does'.) **c9 νῦν** 'as things are'.   **c10 τις:** i.e. anyone who says it is an attunement.

d1 ὀλίγου πάντα 'in almost everything'.   **d3–4 τά τε κατὰ τὴν γυμναστικὴν καὶ τὴν ἰατρικήν:** a second τὰ κατά is easily supplied after καί (cf. *GP* 518–19). The whole stands in apposition to, and explains, τὰ μὲν χαλεπώτερον ... καὶ μετ᾿ ἀλγηδόνων (as d4–6 καὶ τὰ μὲν κτλ. explains τὰ δὲ πραιότερον).   **d5–6 ὡς ἄλλη οὖσα:** i.e. in a way that betrays it as being something separate from them.   **d6–7 οἷόν που ... πεποίηκεν:** lit. 'Which sort of thing Homer too (cf. 95a1–2), surely, has composed (πεποίηκεν) in the *Odyssey*' (20.17–18).   **d7 λέγει τὸν Ὀδυσσέα:** the expected infinitive is displaced by the construction of the quoted lines.

e2–3 διανοούμενον ὡς ... αὐτῆς οὔσης 'in the belief that it was' (for ὡς with participles in indirect statements see *MT* 916).   **e5–6 θειοτέρου ... ἢ καθ᾿ ἁρμονίαν:** lit. 'greater than to be compared with an attunement' (cf. LSJ s.v. κατά B.IV. 3).

95a1 οὔτε γὰρ ἄν ... 2 ὁμολογοῖμεν: elsewhere, Plato's Socrates is scathing about poetic 'authority' (see esp. *Rep.* x, where he begins by attacking the 'divine' Homer; and cf. 61b5n); nor is he necessarily entirely serious in appealing to it here, although Simmias certainly accepts it.   **a2 οὔτε αὐτοὶ ἡμῖν αὐτοῖς:** sc. because internal dialogue and conflict is a matter of our common experience (c8–d6); but cf. also 92a–e.

95a4–102a9: preliminaries to the final argument

Socrates now prepares to deal with Cebes' objection, first giving a longer recapitulation of it, and then setting out and justifying the hypotheses he will use in his attempt to show what Cebes has demanded at 88b: that 'soul is altogether deathless and indestructible'. In the course of fulfilling the latter task, he claims to tell us something of his own intellectual history, and outlines both a type of philosophical method and a theory of explanation which are (and are intended to be) of interest in their own right.

95a4–6 τὰ μὲν Ἁρμονίας κτλ. 'the matter of Harmonia [wife of Cadmus, mythical founder-hero of Thebes, Simmias' and Cebes' home city] could be said (πως, acknowledging the metaphor) to have turned out to be moderately propitious for us [i.e. the attunement-theory has been shown moderately well not to be the stumbling-block it purported to be]; what, then, about the matter of Cadmus [i.e. Cebes' objection] – how, and with what argument, shall we propitiate it [make it similarly 'propitious']?' For the abbreviated question τί δὲ ... Κάδμου, cf. 64d7n., d8–9; and for τί δὲ δή, see 65a9n. **a8–9 θαυμασ-τῶς ... ὡς παρὰ δόξαν** 'wonderfully unexpectedly'. **a9 Σιμμίου ... ἠπόρει** 'when Simmias was saying what he was in difficulty about'. The ὅτε of the vast majority of the MSS, even if it can be taken in a partially causal sense (Verdenius), is hard to accept. **a9 πάνυ ἐθαύ-μαζον ... b1 αὐτοῦ** 'I was very much wondering whether anyone would be able at all to handle his argument' (Gallop).

b2 μοι ἀτόπως ἔδοξεν ... οὐ δέξασθαι 'seemed to me extraordinarily not to have withstood', i.e. it seemed to me extraordinary that it did not. **b7 ἀλλὰ δή:** the combination is used as at 78a10. **b7–8 Ὁμη-ρικῶς ἐγγὺς ἰόντες:** ἐγγὺς ἰόντες both has the form of the end of an epic hexameter, and recalls a typical action of a Homeric warrior (see e.g. Il. 22.92 ἆσσον ἰόντα, of Achilles advancing on Hector). **b8 πει-ρώμεθα ... λέγεις** 'let us test whether there really (ἄρα: cf. 78b5n.) is anything in what you say'.

c1 ἀνώλεθρόν τε καὶ ἀθάνατον: see 88b5–6n. **c2 θαρρῶν τε καὶ ἡγούμενος κτλ.:** sc. like me. **c3 εἰ ... ἐτελεύτα** 'if he were dying after having lived a different [i.e. non-philosophical] life'. **c4–5 τὸ δὲ ἀποφαίνειν ὅτι ... 6–7 οὐδὲν κωλύειν φῂς πάντα ταῦτα μηνύειν** 'Showing that ... – you say that nothing prevents all of this from indicating.' Whether or not 'all this' has actually been shown is left open, as it was in Cebes' original statement. **c9 ᾔδει τε καὶ ἔπραττεν πολλὰ ἄττα:** the first, given the theory of ἀνάμνησις; the second, perhaps, given that it has undergone multiple births, lives and deaths. ἀλλὰ γάρ 'but in any case' (see GP 101–2).

d1 ἦν 'was [as you said]'. **d3–4** The optatives ζώιη ... ἀπολλύοιτο are written as if the sentence had been introduced by an ἔλεγες ὅτι. τελευτῶσά γε: see 88a9n. On the final occasion, the event we label as 'death' (ὁ καλούμενος θάνατος) turns out, on Cebes' account, to involve the perishing of the soul itself (cf. 91d6 ... καὶ ἧι αὐτὸ τοῦτο θάνατος, ψυχῆς ὄλεθρος). **d4 δὲ δή:** cf. e.g. 65a9, 65d4. **d5–6 πρός**

γε τὸ . . . φοβεῖσθαι 'so far at least as the fears of each one of us are concerned'. **d7 μηδὲ ἔχοντι λόγον διδόναι** 'and does not have a proof to give'.

e1 ἀθάνατον here seems to be shorthand for ἀνώλεθρόν τε καὶ ἀθάνατον (c1), which is itself a shortened version of 88b5–6 παντάπασιν ἀθάνατόν τε καὶ ἀνώλεθρον. **e2 πολλάκις:** more than once, at least (see 91d2–7). **e7–8 συχνὸν χρόνον . . . σκεψάμενος:** cf. 84c1–3. **e9 ὅλως . . . περὶ γενέσεως καὶ φθορᾶς τὴν αἰτίαν διαπραγματεύσασθαι** 'to investigate thoroughly the αἰτία in relation to coming-into-being and ceasing-to-be in general'. As the sequel will show, S. has in mind the coming-into-being and ceasing-to-be or destruction (φθορά = ὄλεθρος: cf. e.g. 96a9–10) of attributes as well as of the bearers of attributes (in fact more particularly of attributes: Hackforth 144–6); in other words, he will be concerned with the explanation of why x comes to be or ceases to be F (or indeed is: 96a10, 97c7), as well as why x comes to be or ceases to be (or is). αἰτία was once traditionally rendered as 'cause', but this is misleading. If A is the cause of B, then (roughly speaking) A will be an event or state of affairs which brings about another event or state of affairs B; and not only are many of the things S. will mention incapable of being explained in this way, but the types of αἰτία he will ultimately prefer seem to be of quite a different kind (97b–99c, 99c–102a). What he is after is the best available answer to the question 'Why does this or that come to be / cease to be as it is?' or 'Why is this or that as it is?', without any restriction in principle as to the kinds of explanation which may be considered. (See esp. Vlastos 1969 (1973).) S.'s suggestion, then, is that Cebes' demand necessitates an inquiry into the explanation of coming-to-be and destruction in general. A single-word translation of αἰτία is probably not available; but '"reason" is perhaps the least unsuitable' (Gallop 170).

96a2 πάθη: here 'experiences'. To the extent that the theory of 99c–102a rests on Platonic rather than Socratic ideas (see Introduction §5), the following account certainly cannot be wholly historical. Some of it might be; or else P. might be describing his own intellectual development. But it is also possible that it is wholly invented, as a conveniently dramatic way of presenting a collection of problems and solutions ('I was once a devotee of natural science, but . . .'; 'I was at first attracted by what Anaxagoras has to say, until . . .', etc.). **a3–4 πρὸς τὴν**

πειθώ κτλ.: lit. 'you will use [it] towards conviction in relation to what you say', i.e. you will use it to help you convince us (i.e. of whatever you have come to think: cf. Loriaux) about what you say. **a5 ἀλλὰ μήν ... γε:** cf. 78b2. **a6 ἄκουε τοίνυν ὡς ἐροῦντος** 'Then I'll tell you; so listen.' **a8 δή:** cf. 72a7–8n. **περὶ φύσεως ἱστορίαν** 'inquiry about nature'.

b1 ἐμαυτὸν ... μετέβαλλον 'I used to shift back and forth.' **b2 ἆρ' ἐπειδὰν ... 3 συντρέφεται;** 'Is it when the hot and the cold are affected by a sort of putrefaction, as some say, that living things grow up, [?] by combination [sc. of the hot and cold: cf. LSJ s.v. συντρέφω II.4]?' σηπεδών can apparently be used of the decay of any substance (or of the cause of it: so at 110e4, in connection with stones); here, it might refer, first, to the breaking down of the separate elements when in combination. Its primary association, however, is probably with *rotting*, particularly of flesh, in which case there would be, from S.'s point of view, an appropriate irony in its use here. The basic question is whether the coming-into-being of living things (growth will be considered at b7–d5) can be explained in terms of the combination of elements. S.'s 'mature' view, as we know from his response to Simmias' attunement theory, is that it cannot – mere combinations of inanimate elements, without the superaddition of soul, will themselves be inanimate, and so indistinguishable from corpses. But he is about to raise an objection of quite a different kind: see c1–2n. Scholars have traditionally seen a reference in b2–3 to what seems to be a theory about the *first* animals, attributed to the fifth-century philosopher Archelaus (said to have been a pupil of Anaxagoras): see e.g. Burnet. But the question is about how animals do in general come to be, not how they originally did. On the interpretation suggested, the τινές in question will be anyone who (a) thought of matter as composed of elements, and (b) held a materialist theory of 'soul'. The ideas referred to in b3–8 come from the same materialist stable. **b4 ὧι φρονοῦμεν** 'what we think with', which is equivalent to 'what it is in us that thinks'. For the identification of this with blood, cf. Empedocles' αἷμα γὰρ ἀνθρώποις περικάρδιόν ἐστι νόημα (DK 31 b 105); air is the seat of thought according to Diogenes of Apollonia (2nd half of fifth century: DK 64 b 4, 5), and probably also to the earlier Anaximenes (DK 13 b 2), while Heraclitus 'the Obscure' says some things which suggest an identification of the rational soul with fire (e.g. DK 22 B 36). **b4–8 ἢ τούτων μὲν οὐδέν, ὁ δ' ἐγκέφαλός ἐστιν κτλ.:** if, as this next theory holds, the brain is the locus of sensations, and memory and opinion (or judgement: δόξα, b7) come from these, while knowledge in its turn arises from memory and judgement, the latter three things, which are aspects of 'thought' in general, must be states of the brain as much as sensations are. The idea that the brain is responsible for sensations is attributable to Alcmaeon (DK 24 A 5; cf. *HGP* I 347–9); the rest either belongs to Alcmaeon, or is P.'s reconstruction of the account of the coming-to-be of memory, judgement and knowledge which might have been given by a materialist of Alcmaeon's sort, who (unlike e.g. Empedocles) distinguished thought from sensation (ibid.). That knowledge can be derived exclusively from sensation has of course already been ruled out in the course of the argument from ἀνάμνησις. **b7 γίγνοιτο:** as in 95d3–4 (see n.), the construction switches to the optative of past reported speech; in b8, we find acc. + inf. (γίγνεσθαι ἐπιστήμην). **b7 ἐκ δὲ μνήμης ... 8 ἐπιστήμην** 'and from memory and judgement, when these acquire stability, [is it the case, as they say] that knowledge comes to be in this way (κατὰ ταῦτα)?' **b9 αὖ** 'in turn'. **τούτων:** i.e., in the first instance, knowledge, memory, and judgement; but these are after all only examples of the things into which he (first) inquired (b1 σκοπῶν πρῶτον τὰ τοιάδε). **b9–c1 τὰ περὶ τὸν οὐρανόν τε καὶ τὴν γῆν πάθη** 'what happens in the heavens and on the earth'.

c1–2 οὕτως ... πρὸς ταύτην τὴν σκέψιν ἀφυὴς ... ὡς οὐδὲν χρῆμα: lit. 'as naturally ungifted for this inquiry as no [other] creature'. The reason why he reached this view of himself, as it emerges in what follows, seems to be that he is unable to see how the coming-to-be of anything (or its being, i.e. what it is: cf. a10) can ever be explained by reference to the addition of other things to each other, as the natural scientists purport to explain it (so that, for example, according to them, living things result from the combination of hot and cold, knowledge etc. from a succession of sensations, and so on: see b2–3n., 4–8n.). There are some instances where such an analysis seems wholly unobjectionable: for example, a person surely does come to be larger by getting extra flesh and bone (c7–d7); and there is surely nothing wrong with saying that someone is taller than someone else 'by a head', or that ten is greater than eight because it has an extra two, or two cubits larger than one cubit because it exceeds it by half (d8–e4). So, at any rate, S. used to think; the problem is that when he tries to apply the same sort of analysis to bare numerical addition (which ought to provide a fair test of the powers attributed to combination), he finds that it does not work, and this makes him doubt whether it is really the right way of dealing even with the cases that had seemed so unproblematical (96e6–97b3; sc. let alone with the ones mentioned in 96b). He will return to these at 100e8–101b7.   **c3–5 ἃ καὶ πρότερον σαφῶς ἠπιστάμην . . . ἐτυφλώθην:** lit. 'I was blinded as to those things which I *did* (καί) know clearly before [at least, as I and others thought: ὥς γε κτλ.]'; i.e. they no longer appeared clear to me (καί does not emphasise πρότερον, but is used much as at 66d4: cf. *GP* 325–7, Verdenius). 'This inquiry' (αὕτη ἡ σκέψις, c5, i.e. the sort encouraged by the scientists) induced the state in question in that it led to the discovery of problems when he tried to apply the same approach elsewhere: see preceding n., and cf. 97b3–7 ('I can no longer convince myself that I know . . . why anything comes to be . . ., if I follow this method of inquiry').

d1–5 This elaboration of the simple idea that a person grows through eating and drinking strongly recalls Anaxagoras (see esp. DK 59 B 10 πῶς γὰρ ἄν . . . ἐκ μὴ τριχὸς γένοιτο θρὶξ καὶ σὰρξ ἐκ μὴ σαρκός;). Whether or not we suppose an intended reference to him will depend on whether we take c3 πρότερον, and πρὸ τοῦ in c6 and 8, as meaning the time before S. found himself blinded by his scientific studies, or before he had even embarked on them; in the latter case, the reference will be to a common-sense version of Anaxagoras' idea. But perhaps a decision is unnecessary, since in any case the scientists' theories will have seemed to him to accord with common sense.   **d8 ᾤμην . . . εἰ αὐτῆι τῆι κεφαλῆι** 'I used to think it was a sufficient view, whenever a large person standing beside a small one appeared to be taller just by his head', i.e. I thought that was a sufficient explanation of his being taller: cf. c1–2n., and e2–3 τὰ δέκα . . . προσεῖναι. In normal Greek, the dative '[taller] by a head' would merely indicate the degree of difference; but if, as on the scientists' method of explanation, a thing x or a property F is to be explained just by reference to addition or combination (see c1–2n.), then – or so S. suggests – the head should be the αἰτία of the taller man's being taller. See further 101a5–6n.

e1–2 ἔτι . . . τούτων ἐναργέστερα is loosely in apposition to what follows. **e3 τὸ δίπηχυ** 'two cubits' rather than 'what is two cubits long', just as e2 τὰ δέκα means 'ten' rather than 'ten things' (although it might be held, and P. might hold, that even such expressions – 'two cubits', 'ten' – carry an implicit reference to things measured and numbered; that is, they do not commit either us or him to the separate existence of numbers and measures). **e7 ὅς γε οὐκ ἀποδέχομαι** 'seeing that I don't accept' (with γε adding weight to the causal ὅς). **e8 οὐδὲ ὡς ... 97a1 δύο ἐγένετο** '[not] even that when someone adds one to one, either the one to which [the other one] was added has become two, or that the [one] that was added and [the one] to which it was added become (ἐγένετο, gnomic aorist) two because of the addition of the one [one] to the other [one]'. If one tries to explain the coming into being of x through the addition of y to z (as the scientists propose: c1–2n.), then it will be true to say of y and z that they have become x through the process of addition. But try adding one and one: we cannot say that the addition has made either the first one, the one to which the second was added, or both (separately), into two (for the reason to be given in 97a2–5). If I get into such difficulties even here (e8 οὐδέ), says S., i.e. even with the most basic case of addition, then clearly I can't claim to know the αἰτία in the other cases (e6–7). The thing that most puzzles him is how one thing can become another at all; and invoking simple addition (or, for that matter, division: 97a5–b3) does not seem to help.

97a2–5 'for I am astonished if [it really is the case that] when each of them apart from the other, each was actually (ἄρα) one and they were not then two, but when they came close to each other, it was actually this that was responsible (αἰτία) for their becoming two, [i.e.] the coming together which consists in their being placed close to one another' (for θαυμάζω . . . εἰ, cf. 62a2–7n.; on ἄρα, see *GP* 38–9). If two 'came into being', then the ones cannot previously have been two; but – Socrates wonders – why not? Why should bringing them together make any difference? (Are they not countable even when apart?) Cf. Gallop 173. **a5–6 οὐδέ γε ὡς ἐάν τις . . . , δύναμαι ἔτι πείθεσθαι ὡς:** S. seems to begin as if he is going to continue with another ὡς-clause governed by 96e7 οὐκ ἀποδέχομαι ἐμαυτοῦ (ὡς ἐάν τις . . . clearly echoes 96e8 ὡς ἐπειδὰν . . . τις . . .), but then to change his mind, and introduce a new verbal idea to govern the indirect statement, which calls for a second ὡς. **a7 τοῦ δύο γεγονέναι** 'of the coming to be of two', not 'of its coming to be two' (cf. b3–4 οὐδέ γε δι' ὅτι ἓν γίγνεται . . . : i.e. 'if I'm not clear why two comes into being, I'm not clear either about why one does either'). The general sense is as follows. If in the first case (ἐπειδὰν ἑνί τις προσθῆι ἕν) the explanation of the coming-into-being of two is addition, in this second case it ought to be division; but S. can 'no longer persuade himself' that this is right, since the second explanation is the opposite of the first (a7–b3). How can he think he knows why two comes about, if he has two opposing accounts of the matter? On the role of a5–b3 in the argument, see 96e8–97a1n. We must in any case still be dealing with the method of explanation suggested by the scientists, as b4–6 shows: 'Nor again do I persuade myself that I know why one comes into being, nor, in short, why anything else comes into being . . . , *if I follow this method of inquiry*' (κατὰ τοῦτον τὸν τρόπον τῆς μεθόδου): cf. 96c3–5n. **a7–b1 ἐναντία γὰρ . . . γίγνεσθαι** 'for [in that case] there turns out to be an opposite reason (αἰτία) of two's coming to be'. This is not intended to be a knock-down argument; it is after all only part of an explanation of why S. lost his previous confidence that he knew the answers. **b1 ἤ**: the MSS reading ἤ produces a sentence which is close to being non-sense, and at best is an awkward way of saying the same as the emended version.

b2 ἕτερον ἑτέρωι 'one thing to a second'. **b6–7 ἀλλά τιν' ἄλλον κτλ**. 'but I make up some other confused jumble of a method of my own, and in no way incline to this one'. More will be heard about this 'jumble' shortly. **b8 ἀλλ':** we return to the past. S. had thought once that he had discovered Anaxagoras suggesting an explanation of a kind that pleased him . . . **μέν** seems to be 'solitary': see 61d9–10n.

c1 ἄρα 'actually', as at a3 and 4, but without the note of scepticism. For the thesis here attributed to Anaxagoras, see DK 59 B 12. **c2 ταύτηι δή:** cf. 82d6–7n. **c3 τρόπον τινά:** i.e. he liked the general idea, without necessarily wanting to commit himself to the specific idea of a cosmic mind. **c4–6 ἡγησάμην . . . ὅπηι ἂν βέλτιστα ἔχηι** 'I supposed, if that is the case, that *mind* (τόν γε νοῦν), in doing the ordering, orders everything and places each thing in whatever way is best.' Reason by itself, for S., always aims at the good (cf. esp. 69a–c).

d1 ἄλλο: we should probably not hold Plato to the implication that 'being' is an instance of 'being acted on or acting' (πάσχειν ἢ ποιεῖν). **d2 περὶ αὐτοῦ ἐκείνου** = περὶ αὐτοῦ τοῦ ἀνθρώπου (Burnet), i.e. in relation to himself. 'Knowing oneself', then (the kind of knowledge that P.'s S. normally most desires: see e.g. *Phdr.* 230a), becomes a matter of knowing what is best for oneself. **d3 (οὐδὲν ἄλλο ...) ἀλλ' ἤ:** cf. 81b4–5. **d4–5 ἀναγκαῖον δὲ εἶναι κτλ.:** for the underlying principle, that opposites are subjects of a single science, cf. e.g. *Ion* 531d–532a. The aside may be meant to correct any impression that he thinks the universe good in all respects; man, at least, as we know, has the capacity for evil. **d7 κατὰ νοῦν ἐμαυτῶι:** if there is no pun here, there is certainly one at 98b8–9 (see n.). **d8–e1 πλατεῖα ... ἢ στρογγύλη:** flat-earthers are plentiful among the Presocratics; definite round-earthers are harder to come by (cf. Loriaux).

e1 ἐπεκδιηγήσεσθαι ... 3 τοιαύτην εἶναι 'that he would go on to explain the reason why it must be so (τὴν αἰτίαν καὶ τὴν ἀνάγκην: hendiadys), by saying what was better [i.e. which of the two alternatives was better], that is (καί: cf. 58b6n.), that it was better that it should be like that'.

98a2–3 οὕτω παρεσκευάσμην ὡσαύτως πευσόμενος 'I was similarly prepared to find out in the same way.' **a3–4 τῶν ἄλλων ἄστρων:** either 'the other stars', or 'the stars besides': the planets are sometimes also called ἄστρα (e.g. *Tim.* 38c), but are usually distinguished from them. **a5 ποτε** intensifies the interrogative ('exactly how ...'?). **a6 ἄν** belongs with 8 ἐπενεγκεῖν ('I never thought that he would ...'). **a7 φάσκοντά γε** 'seeing that he was claiming' (for the γε, cf. 94c4n.).

b1 ἑκάστωι οὖν ... 3 ἐπεκδιηγήσεσθαι ἀγαθόν 'so I thought that, in assigning the αἰτία to each thing [i.e. the one which belongs to each], and to everything in common [since each thing would in a sense share the same αἰτία, i.e what was best], he would explain in addition what was best for each and what was the good common to all' (cf. 99c, which introduces the notion of good as somehow binding the cosmos together). P. himself fulfils something like the programme outlined here in *Tim.* **b7 ἀπὸ δὴ ... φερόμενος** 'It was from astonishingly high hope, then, my friend, that I came hurtling down.' **b8–9 τῶι ... νῶι οὐδὲν χρώμενον** 'not using his mind', in both senses: cosmic mind, and his own (in not making the use he should have of cosmic mind). **b9 οὐδέ τινας αἰτίας ἐπαιτιώμενον** 'nor charging [it] with any αἰτίαι', i.e. giving it any role in explanation. Probably a further pun: ἐπαιτιᾶσθαι τινα αἰτίαν would normally be used of bringing a legal charge against someone (with αἰτίαν as internal acc.). It will then be a nice question whether the pun is continued in c2 αἰτιώμενον: if the primary meaning of αἰτιᾶσθαι is 'blaming' (cf. 85d6), the general sense of 'giving as a reason' is already well established.

c1 ἀέρας ... καὶ αἰθέρας καὶ ὕδατα 'things like air and aether and water' (for 'aether', see 109b7–c1n.). **c3 ὁμοιότατον πεπονθέναι** 'to be in exactly the same position' (Gallop). **c3 ὥσπερ ἂν εἰ ... 5 λέγοι** 'as if someone, despite saying that everything S. does is to be attributed to mind, should then in attempting to give the reasons for all the things I do, were to say ...' ὥσπερ ἂν εἰ is indistinguishable in meaning from ὥσπερ εἰ; for κἄπειτα, after a participial clause, see 67e2 with 67d12–e2n. **c5 πρῶτον μέν** is answered by d6 καὶ αὖ (... λέγοι). **c8 διαφυὰς ἔχει χωρὶς ἀπ' ἀλλήλων:** lit. 'have joints [are jointed] separately from each other', i.e. are separated from each other by joints. **οἷα** '[are] such as to'.

d2 αἰωρουμένων οὖν ... 5 μέλη 'so, with the bones suspended in their sockets, the muscles, I suppose (που), by slackening and tightening, make me capable now of bending my limbs'. **d5 συγκαμφθείς** 'bent', referring to the action (κάμπτεσθαι τὰ μέλη) that got him into his sitting position. **d6 περὶ τοῦ διαλέγεσθαι ὑμῖν** 'in relation to [my] conversing with you'. **d7 λέγοι** continues the construction begun in c3–5 (ὥσπερ ἂν εἴ τις ... λέγοι).

e3–5 S. seems to offer the city's decision as an explanation both of his thinking it 'better' to stay where he is and not run away, and of his thinking it 'more just' (which in turn explain his staying). For him, in fact, the two types of consideration run together: the justice of an action is in itself sufficient to make it 'better' for the agent (thus accepting the city's decision on the grounds that doing so is 'more just and fine', 99a2–3, is equated with 'the choice of what is best', 99b1). In taking this attitude, he of course dismisses ordinary prudential considerations (e5–99a2). For a reconstruction of the ethical case for compliance, see *Cr.* 50a–53a. (On whether or not justice played any part in the Athenians' verdict, he is noticeably silent.) **e5 νὴ τὸν κύνα:** an oath particularly favoured by Socrates, but – as Ar. *Wasps* suggests (83) – not peculiar to him (Dodds 1959, 262–3, sees it as jocular).

99a2 ὑπὸ δόξης ... τοῦ βελτίστου: the muscles and bones, were it left to them, would naturally opt to save their own skin. **a2–3 δικαιό-τερον ... κάλλιον:** τὸ καλόν ('the fine', 'the admirable') is the genus, τὸ δίκαιον the species. **a4 ὑπέχειν τῆι πόλει δίκην:** for the dat., cf. διδόναι δίκην (τινι). **a4–7 ἀλλ' αἴτια μὲν κτλ.:** the hot and the cold will similarly be necessary conditions of the coming-to-be of animals (96b2–3), sensations necessary conditions of that of (some kinds of) memory, judgement and knowledge (96b5–8), and the units of that of two (96e8–97a5). The general effect of the present section (97b8–99d2) is to extend the case begun in 96a against the scientists' type of 'explanation', while introducing the type that S. would prefer (but cannot discover, c8–9). **a7–8 ὡς μέντοι ... b2 τοῦ λόγου** 'but [to say] that I do what I do because of these things, and I perform these actions by the use of my mind [cf. 98c3–4], but not by my choice of what is best, would be an extremely careless way of talking'.

b2 τὸ γὰρ μὴ ... 4 οὐκ ἄν ποτ' εἴη αἴτιον '[How absurd] not to be able to (exclamatory inf. with τό: cf. *MT* 787, 805) discern that in reality the reason (τὸ αἴτιον) is one thing, and that without which the reason would never be a reason [i.e. without which there would be nothing to be explained], another!' **b4 ὃ δὴ ... 6 προσαγορεύειν:** lit. 'the very [thing] which the many seem to me, groping about [for it] as if in darkness, using a name that belongs to something else, to address as if itself a reason'. The language is from a game like blind man's buff: the blindfolded player gropes around, finds someone, and then misidentifies him. S. has once before associated the views of the scientists with those of the ordinary man ('the many'): see 96c7–8, with 96d1–5n. Here, however, his point is not, as before, about the apparent coincidence of their insights with common sense, but rather that their absurd muddling of reason and necessary condition makes them no different from the non-philosophical many. The effect is heightened by the following lines: 'Hence it is that one person, whoever it may be (τις: in fact Empedocles, if Arist. *DC* 300b2–3 can be trusted), puts a whirl round the earth and makes it stay in place (δή stresses μένειν, perhaps pointing to the (superficial?) oddity of making lack of movement

dependent on movement) under the influence of the heavens, while
someone else [Anaximenes, Anaxagoras, Democritus: *DC* 294b13–17]
puts air under it as a base, as if it [i.e. the earth] were a flat kneading-
trough.' The latter comparison suggests the parodies of scientific ideas
found e.g. in Ar. *Clouds* (the word κάρδοπος is itself found at *Frogs*
1159, though not with reference to cosmology), while the nonchalant
ὁ μέν τις ..., ὁ δὲ ... itself reduces Empedocles and the rest to mere
faces in the crowd.

c1–2 τὴν δὲ ... οὕτω νῦν κεῖσθαι: lit. 'But their capacity to be now
located in the way in which it is possible for them (αὐτά, loosely
generalising from the case of the earth) to be placed best', i.e. their
capacity to be situated in the best way possible.   **c3–5 ἡγοῦνται ...
ἐξευρεῖν** 'they think they might at some time find an Atlas stronger
and more immortal (ἀθάνατος, probably a variant on c2 δαιμόνιος,
'divine', 'superhuman') and holding all things together more than this
one'. Atlas, in myth, is a Titan (and so a god) who holds up the sky;
the real Atlas, S. suggests, is the δύναμις just mentioned, which holds
everything together – but the people in question go searching (hope-
lessly) for a stronger one.   **c5–6 καὶ ὡς ἀληθῶς κτλ.:** lit. 'and that
what is good and binding really (ὡς ἀληθῶς) binds and holds together,
they don't believe at all'. τὸ δέον is both what is necessary and what is
literally binding (i.e. binds one thing to another); according to the
kind of theory S. wishes (but is unable: c8–9) to discover, the good
would meet both descriptions, in being what will explain why things
must be (cf. 97e1–2 τὴν αἰτίαν καὶ τὴν ἀνάγκην) as they are both in
themselves and in relation to each other, and therefore what binds
them together.   **c7 ποτέ:** cf. 98a5n.   **c8–9** Cf. 85c7–8.   **c9–d2 τὸν
δεύτερον πλοῦν ἐπὶ τὴν τῆς αἰτίας ζήτησιν ἧι πεπραγμάτευμαι βούλει σοι ... ἐπίδειξιν ποιήσωμαι ...;** 'do you wish me to give you
(ποιήσωμαι is deliberative subj., i.e. 'am I to ...?', introduced, as
often, by βούλει) a display of how I have engaged in my second voyage
in search of the αἰτία?' According to an ancient interpretation (see e.g.
Eust. *in Od.* 1453.20), the phrase δεύτερος πλοῦς refers to the use of
oars in the absence of a fair wind, suggesting the use of a slower and
more laborious, but more reliable, method of getting to the same destination, or at least achieving the same objective. Since S. has just said,
at c8, that he was 'deprived' of the sort of αἰτία which he had hoped

for (A*), either (*a*) his new journey ἐπὶ τὴν τῆς αἰτίας ζήτησιν has
resulted in the discovery of a different αἰτία, or (*b*) the journey has not
yet been completed. In the latter case, either (*b.1*) he has so far discovered nothing, or (*b.2*) he has discovered something (or thinks he
may have), which either (*b.2.i*) has – as yet – no determinable relation
to A*; or (*b.2.ii*) is not incompatible with it; or (*b.2.iii*) positively
points the way towards it; or (*b.2.iv*) points in a different direction
altogether. The sequel strictly only rules out (*b.1*) (the new method has
had *some* results), but the space that has been devoted to the description of A* also makes (*a*) and (*b.2.iv*) unlikely. We are therefore left,
theoretically, with (*b.2.i*), (*ii*) and (*iii*). But since S. himself makes no
explicit attempt to link up his new ideas with A*, we should clearly
prefer (*b.2.i*) or (*ii*), and probably (*i*) to (*ii*). His main hypothesis, of
the existence of the forms (100b), is in fact combined with an application of A* in *Tim.* (and perhaps in *Rep.*), but so far as concerns him,
here and now, in *Phd.*, that kind of project belongs to the future. The
relevant facts are that he knows what sort of αἰτία he would like to
discover, that he has not in fact discovered it, but that he has nevertheless found *a* way of explaining things which at least avoids the sorts of
problems raised by the scientists' 'explanations' (100c–101d).

d3 ὑπερφυῶς μὲν οὖν . . . ὡς βούλομαι 'Yes ('assentient' μὲν οὖν), I'd
like that enormously.' **d4–5 μετὰ ταῦτα, ἐπειδὴ ἀπειρήκη τὰ ὄντα
σκοπῶν** 'when I had failed in my inquiry into things', i.e. the sort of
inquiry introduced in 96a6–b1, using the methods of the natural scientists. Anaxagoras had initially seemed to offer something different, but
in the end turned out to employ the same approach as the others, that
things can be explained in terms of the combination of underlying
material factors (98c1–2, etc.) – an approach which, S. said, 'blinded'
him (96c5). He now proceeds to build on this metaphor (d5–100a3).
d5 ὅπερ ... 6 σκοπούμενοι 'what [sc. happens to] those who observe
and examine the sun in eclipse', i.e. who examine it by gazing at it.
(πάσχουσιν is easily supplied; its presence in the majority of MSS is
probably due to copyist's over-correction: Verdenius.)

e2 μὴ παντάπασι τὴν ψυχὴν τυφλωθείην: i.e. that the state described
in 96c5 might become permanent (and he might become no longer
able to 'see' anything at all). **e3 τὰ πράγματα = d5 τὰ ὄντα. e3 καὶ
ἑκάστηι ... 4 ἅπτεσθαι αὐτῶν:** his problems were not, of course,

caused through trying to 'grasp' things by looking at them (as the
metaphor of 'blinding' could suggest), but by the use of sensory observation in general.   **e5 τοὺς λόγους** 'things said', i.e. 'statements', or
'propositions', of the form given in 100b5–7: 'there is τι καλὸν αὐτό',
etc. (cf. 100a3–4 ὑποθέμενος ἑκάστοτε λόγον ..., b5 ὑποθέμενος; and
100a3–7n.). If he is going to study the truth of things 'in' propositions
(ἐν ἐκείνοις), as eclipse-watchers study the sun in water etc., propositions must contain 'images' ('likenesses', εἰκόνες, 100a2) of things as
they are. But 'in' must here also have the sense of 'among', unless all
the propositions chosen happen to be true; and the method to be outlined allows that this may not be the case (some are 'stronger', or
'safer', than others: 100a4, d8, e1). Of course the scientists too, in a
sense, deal in λόγοι (how else would they frame their theories?). The
difference seems to be that their λόγοι derive (or purport to derive)
from observation, whereas for S. λόγοι will themselves be the starting-
point (see further 100a3–7n.).   **e6–100a1 ἴσως μὲν οὖν ... οὐκ ἔοικεν:** lit. 'Perhaps [this method] in a way is not like what I am likening
it to.' For μὲν οὖν, cf. 90e3n.; μέν is answered by 100a3 ἀλλ' οὖν δὴ ...
γε ... ('Still, ... at least ...': ἀλλ' οὖν ... γε as at 91b3–4, but with
ἀλλ' οὖν reinforced by δή).

100a1–3 οὐ γὰρ πάνυ συγχωρῶ κτλ. 'for I do not at all (οὐ πάνυ as
at e.g. 63a2) admit that ...' This cryptic point is most naturally taken
as referring to an idea which is common in dialogues other than the
Phaedo, that particular things are themselves 'images' or 'likenesses'
(εἰκόνες, ὁμοιώματα, εἴδωλα, μιμήματα) of the forms (see e.g. *Phdr.*
250b3, 4; *Rep.* 520c4-6, *Tim.* 48e–49a). Cf. Patterson 1985, 28–9. For
S. to have explained the reference would no doubt have interrupted
the flow of his exposition; it would also cause a slight embarrassment
to the argument from ἀνάμνησις (see esp. 74c11n.).   **a3–7** This brief
account needs to be taken closely with b1–9, in which Socrates claims
to 'say more clearly what I mean' (a7–8). What he is talking about is
what he has never stopped talking about (b1–3): he is undertaking the
promised exposition of 'the kind of αἰτία I have been engaged with'
(b3–4, cf. 99c9–d2) by going back to 'those much harped-on things
and beginning from them, hypothesising that there is something beautiful itself by itself, and good, and large, and all the rest' (b4–7), and
if Cebes grants him that, he will 'demonstrate the αἰτία, and find out

that the soul is immortal from these' (b7–9). This clearly suggests two things: firstly, that if the general principle is to hypothesise 'whatever λόγος I judge to be strongest' (i.e., probably, least open to objection: cf. 85c8–9 βέλτιστον (λόγον) καὶ δυσεξελεγκτότατον), the hypothesis chosen will in fact always be of the form 'there is something beautiful [good, etc.] by itself', or at least will always include a proposition of such a form (cf. c3n.); and secondly that both the following excursus on explanation (c3–102a2) and the final argument for immortality will be based on the new method (cf. 95e8–96a4), so that it should in principle be possible to get further information about it from them. But the form-hypothesis has already been applied in the recommended way, since it was used as the basis for accepting the theory of ἀνάμνησις and for rejecting the attunement theory (in so far as that was 'out of tune' with the theory of ἀνάμνησις: 92c2–10); see esp. 92d6–7n. As S. tells us, the method is also applicable to other subjects, not only to that of explanation (100a5–6 καὶ περὶ αἰτίας καὶ περὶ τῶν ἄλλων ἁπάν-των).   **a3 ἀλλ' οὖν δὴ ταύτηι γε ὥρμησα** 'In any case (ἀλλ' οὖν δή) I started out like this', i.e. this was my starting-point; what follows tells us where he went from there (and is still going: a5 τίθημι, pres.). ἀλλ' οὖν δή (. . . γε) is a reinforced version of ἀλλ' οὖν (. . . γε) as at 91b3–4: *GP* 445.   **a6** With ὄντων (see apparatus), the meaning would be either 'and about all the other things that *are*' or 'and about all the things that *are* as well', neither of which makes any sense (the αἰτία is αἰτία of 'the things that are').

b1–2 ἀεί τε ἄλλοτε καὶ ἐν τῶι παρεληλυθότι λόγωι 'both on every other occasion and in the preceding argument', i.e. both before the present conversation and during it. The forms – which must be what S. is referring to: see a3–7n. – have certainly not been far from the surface of the discussion ever since 65d.   **b3 ἔρχομαι . . . ἐπιδείξασ-θαι** 'I am setting about trying to show you' (γὰρ δή as at e.g. 59d1). 'I am going to . . .', as it is usually translated, suggests an unambiguous reference to the future; but (*a*) in that case we should expect a future participle, and (*b*) while one of the two following verbs in the sentence (b4 εἶμι) probably has to be treated as future, the second (b5 ἄρχομαι) is indubitably present.   **b4 εἶδος** 'kind', 'type'.   **b5–6 εἶναί τι καλὸν αὐτὸ καθ' αὑτό:** cf. 65d4–5n., 66a1–3n., 74a9–12n., 78d5–6n.   **b7 ἅ . . . ταῦτα** 'if you grant me these and agree that they exist'.

c1–2 'Well, ..., I certainly (ἀλλὰ μήν as at e.g. 58d7) do grant them to you, so you could not be too quick in finishing the task.'   **c3 τὰ ἐξῆς ἐκείνοις** 'the [things] next to those', i.e. what I want to say next, once given the hypothesis of the existence of forms. It is best to take this new proposition (that x is F through nothing else than its 'partaking in' the form of F, c4–5), with Gallop, as an extension of the hypothesis, since S. will go on to set aside the type of explanation he used to favour at least partly (see d3n.) on the grounds that it disagrees with this new one (c9–10 οὐ τοίνυν ... ἔτι μανθάνω κτλ., e8–101a1, etc.), and the method as stated is to 'treat as true whatever seems to be in accord with [the hypothesis], and whatever does not as not true' (a4–7). What will be 'in accord with' the hypothesis, on this interpretation, will be any particular application of it. Cf. also 102a10–b2.   **c4–5 εἴ τί ἐστιν ... αὐτὸ τὸ καλόν** 'if there is something beautiful apart from the beautiful by itself' (construction as in b5–6 εἶναι τι κτλ.), i.e. if there are any such things as particular 'beautifuls'.   **c5 οὐδὲ δι' ἕν:** a stronger version of δι' οὐδέν.   **μετέχει** 'shares in', 'participates in': one of the standard expressions used for the relationship between particulars and forms (another being 'imitation' or 'resemblance': cf. 100a1–3n.). It is not explained or justified (though Cebes is evidently familiar enough with it, c8), and when in d5–6 S. describes the relationship from the other side, he is careful not to commit himself to any particular way of putting it; all that matters is that there is such a relationship, and that it seems to him to offer the 'safest' kind of explanation (d8–e3; on why he thinks of it as having explanatory force, see d4–6n.). As at 100a1–3, he goes no further into the form-hypothesis than is necessary for the immediate context. See further 101c9–102a1n.   **c9 οὐ τοίνυν ... ἔτι μανθάνω ... 10 γιγνώσκειν** 'Then ... I no longer understand nor am I able to recognise these other wise reasons [sc. as reasons].' 'These other wise reasons' are those of the type represented in 96a–97b, some of the original examples of which will recur in e8–101c2; but they are introduced by a new example, the case where the beauty of something is 'explained' by reference e.g. to its bright colour, or shape. This is like the other cases in that one thing (property) is reduced to, or alleged to arise from, something quite different.   **c10 ἀλλ' ἐάν τίς μοι λέγηι ... d1 σχῆμα** 'but if anyone tells me why something is beautiful, [saying that it is beautiful] either because it has a bright colour or [because it has] a shape [of a particular kind]'.

COMMENTARY: 100d2–100d9

d2 τὰ ... ἄλλα = c9–10 τὰς ἄλλας αἰτίας ... ταύτας, of which the alleged αἰτίαι just given are examples (see preceding n.). **d3 ταράτ-τομαι γὰρ ἐν τοῖς ἄλλοις πᾶσι:** the perplexity with the old type of explanation which caused him to look for something else is of course still with him, and constitutes another separate reason for discarding it, besides the fact that it is 'not in accord' with his hypothesis (cf. c3n.). **d3 τοῦτο δὲ ... 4 παρ' ἐμαυτῶι** 'in my plain, artless and perhaps simple-minded way I hold this close to myself'. But ἁπλῶς and ἀτεχ-νῶς can both also mean 'simply' in the sense of 'without qualification'; and 'perhaps simple-minded' is itself no more to be taken at face value than the contrasting description of the other alleged αἰτίαι in c10 as 'wise'. **d4 οὐκ ἄλλο ... 6 προσγενομένου** 'nothing else makes it beautiful except the presence of that beautiful, or its [?] being associated with it (κοινωνία), or in whatever way and manner [it makes it beautiful] by having come to be added to it'. How the metaphor of κοινωνία ('association', 'partnership') is to be understood is left unclear; but if the particular 'shares in' the form (c5–6), the latter must somehow be 'associated' with the former (if it is not actually 'present' in it) – or somehow 'added to' it. προσγενομένου (agreeing with ἐκείνου τοῦ καλοῦ, with a continuation into the elliptical clause ὅπηι ... of the preceding construction) is on balance the most likely reading; προσγενομένη (or προσγι(γ)νομένη), found in the majority of primary MSS, involves an illogical and probably unacceptable assimilation to παρουσία and κοινωνία. But it is in any case 'that beautiful' which is 'added'; and even if we read προσαγορευομένη (an unsupported conjecture made by Wyttenbach), the point would be the same, namely that the partic-ular thing's being beautiful comes from the form's being somehow 'in' or 'with' it (which would be brought out rather more clearly by προσ-γενομένου/η). In other words, beauty is there in the beautiful thing (somehow, but in any case in virtue of the latter's 'sharing in' the form) as a separate item, and is not reduced to other factors, as it is, puzzlingly, with the other form of explanation. **d6 οὐ γὰρ ἔτι ... 8 γίγνεται καλά** 'I no longer affirm this with confidence, but [only] that it is by the beautiful that all [particular] beautifuls come to be beautiful', i.e. I do not want to commit myself on this point in the way I do on the main one (ἀλλ' ὅτι κτλ.). 'By the beautiful', i.e. because of it: cf. c5–6 οὐδὲ δι' ἓν ἄλλο ἢ διότι κτλ. **d8 ἀσφαλέστατον** 'safest': see 101a5–6n. **d9 καὶ ἐμαυτῶι ... καὶ ἄλλωι:** i.e. if I ask myself, or anyone else asks me, why the beautiful comes to be (d8), or is (c5), beautiful.

e5 ἄρα: i.e. by the principle (hypothesis) agreed at c3–8.

101a1 διαμαρτύροιο ἄν 'you would solemnly protest'. **a2 τὸ μεῖζον πᾶν ἕτερον ἑτέρου** 'everything that is larger than something else'. **a3 καὶ διὰ τοῦτο μεῖζον, διὰ τὸ μέγεθος:** perhaps added largely for emphasis, but partly also because of the ambiguity of the dative in the case of comparatives (cf. 96d8–e1n.). **a5–6 τις . . . ἐναντίος λόγος** 'some opposing argument'. If Cebes says that someone is larger and (someone else: 100e8–101a1) smaller because of the (first man's) head (a6–7), then what makes the larger one larger and the smaller one smaller is the same thing (a7–8), and the larger will be larger because of something small, which is incredible (a8–b2). Cebes' amusement at this (b3 γελάσας) suggests that these objections are not to be taken wholly seriously, and they can in fact be easily answered. If two individuals are involved, as they are (though this is obscured by the shorthand of a6–7), there is nothing to prevent the same αἰτία having an effect on the second which is opposite to the one it has on the first; and there is nothing more problematical about a small addition than about a large one 'making something larger'. The objections nevertheless illustrate the sources of S.'s 'confusion' about the 'wise' sort of αἰτία being considered (100c9–d3). Firstly, it will still be true that the alleged αἰτία is no more associated with one outcome than with its opposite (the head still 'makes' something smaller at the same time as 'making' something larger), and if it is *the* explanation of something that is being looked for (cf. 100c5–6), it is reasonable to demand that the account given should be exclusive to the thing being explained, just as it is reasonable to demand that the same thing should not be 'explained' by reference to two different αἰτίαι (97a5–b3). Secondly, there remains the general problem about how a thing can be of a certain character (in this case, larger, or large: b2), or acquire it, when none of the alleged factors (the man and his head) has any necessary connection with that character (cf. esp. 96e8–97a1n.). The 'safer' thing to say, S. suggests, is that the man is large(r) because he has a (greater) share in size. If 'man + head = large(r) man' seems a formulation that no one would sensibly adopt, it is in fact the one that is implied by the scientists' general approach to explanation (see 96d8–e1n.); the context as a whole represents a complex *reductio ad absurdum* of that approach, but with a new type of explanation – which is at least 'safe' from the objections and difficulties affecting the other – thrown up in the process.

b5 ὑπερβάλλειν = πλείω εἶναι. **b9–c2** ἑνὶ ἑνὸς προστεθέντος κτλ.: see 96e7–97b3. (τοῦ δύο γενέσθαι = 'of the coming-into-being of two': cf. 97a7, b1.)

c2 οὐκ οἶσθα ... 4 οὗ ἂν μετάσχηι 'you know of no other way in which each thing comes to be except by having come to share in the appropriate essence (οὐσία) of each [thing] in which it comes to share'. For 'the οὐσία of each thing' (i.e. largeness, beauty, etc.), as a way of referring to forms, cf. 65d13–e1, where οὐσία is filled out as 'what each thing actually is'. **c4** ἐν τούτοις 'in these cases', bringing us back from the general principle to the cases raised in b9–c2. **c5** τὴν τῆς δυάδος μετάσχεσιν 'having come to share in the two', i.e. the form of two, which by analogy with 'the just' and 'the equal' (see 65d4–5n., 74a9–12n.) will be what is two and nothing else – whatever that might turn out to be; it will at any rate be what we are implicitly referring to when we say of anything, or any pair of things, that it 'has come to be two' (if the latter case is possible: see 97a2–5n.), in so far as this can be reformulated, according to the hypothesis proposed, as 'has come to share in the two'. μετάσχεσις, found only here (in place of the usual μέθεξις), corresponds to the aorist μετασχεῖν (μετασχόν, 'by having come to share in', c3; etc.). **c6** μονάδος '[the] one'. **c8–9** παρεὶς ... σοφωτέροις 'leaving [them] to those wiser than you to give as answers'. **c9–102a1** Hardly any two scholars agree completely about most aspects of this passage; yet the outsider Echecrates immediately comments, apparently without irony, that S. has spoken 'with a wonderful transparency, even for someone of small intelligence' (102a3–5). The simplest interpretation might be as follows. If asked for the αἰτία of two's, or one's, coming-into-being, Cebes would give the reply indicated in c2–7, fearing for his inexperience (by contrast with the 'wisdom' of others' 'subtleties', c8–9), and 'holding on to' (ἔχεσθαι, as at 100d9) the safety which was found in the hypothesis, as Socrates himself does (100d7–e3). This 'safety' of the hypothesis (ἐκείνου τοῦ ἀσφαλοῦς τῆς ὑποθέσεως, d2) lay in its capacity for avoiding counter-arguments. But 'if anyone were to hold on to the hypothesis itself' (d3), i.e. propose its acceptance in itself, without reference to its usefulness for dealing with particular problems, Cebes would keep silent until he had examined whether 'the things that came from it' (τὰ ἀπ' ἐκείνης ὁρμη-θέντα) are in harmony with each other, or whether (sc. like the principle of explanation which is being rejected) it leads to contradictory results (d3–5). When the time came for 'giving an account' of the hypothesis itself (i.e. answering for or defending it in itself, which would be a separate matter from merely making sure that it did not lead to any impossible consequences), Cebes would proceed by the same method, 'by hypothesising another hypothesis, whichever seemed best of those above, until you reached something adequate' (d5–e1). The extra hypotheses in question are, I suggest, of the form 'the F makes particulars F by being present in them', or '... by being associated with them', or '... [by having come to be added to them in some other way]' (100d4–6). These would be 'above' the original hypothesis – i.e. 'x comes to be (or is) F by coming to share (or sharing) in the F' – in two ways: first, in that they would be ways of explaining (and so 'defending') it, and second in that they would describe the form–particular relationship from the side of the forms rather than that of particulars, forms being themselves 'higher' because they are supposed to explain particulars. The hypothesis which at first 'seemed best' might then turn out not to be serviceable (after examination of its consequences?), in which case another would be taken, until at last one emerged which was satisfactory (i.e. to which there seemed to be no objections). Finally (e1–102a1), in following this procedure, Cebes would not jumble things up together, like the antilogicians, by talking simultaneously about the starting-point (the hypothesis) and its consequences. Read in this way, the whole passage is a justification of S.'s own procedure in applying his hypothesis about the αἰτία of coming-into-being without settling the question about what 'participation' actually implies. It is not only possible but necessary, if we are to discover anything (e3), to separate questions about the hypothesis in itself from the examination of its consequences; it has after all been proposed for the sake of its explanatory force (see esp. 100a3–7), which simultaneous discussion about how to explain *it* would only obscure. *Parm.* 131–5 gives several examples of how the hypothesis runs into difficulties on particular readings of 'participation': they will count as reasons for looking for a different reading, not for abandoning the hypothesis, to which

S., here at least, is firmly committed. The clause 'until you found something adequate' (e1) suggests confidence that a workable way of understanding 'participation' can ultimately be found – which is the least we should demand, if we are to be expected to entertain the hypothesis at all. Some references to other interpretations of the passage (which despite what Echecrates says remains exceptionally difficult) are included in the following nn.; for other Platonic essays in hypothetical method, see *Meno* 86e–89a, *Rep.* 510b–511d, *Parm.* 135d–166c (though how far these are relevant to the present context is itself a matter of dispute).   **c9–d2** For the repeated ἄν (δεδιὼς ἄν ... ἀποκρίναιο ἄν), see e.g. 62c1n. (τὸ λεγόμενον = 'as the saying goes'.)

d1–2 ἐχόμενος ἐκείνου τοῦ ἀσφαλοῦς τῆς ὑποθέσεως 'holding on to that safety (τὸ ἀσφαλές = ἡ ἀσφάλεια) of the hypothesis', not 'that safe [part] of the hypothesis' (cf. Anscombe 1981, 15–16), since no part of the hypothesis has been identified (ἐκείνου) as 'safer' than any other.   **d3 εἰ δέ τις αὐτῆς τῆς ὑποθέσεως ἔχοιτο** 'if anyone were to hold on to the hypothesis itself': scholars have generally supposed the reference to be to an objector, and have therefore either taken ἔχεσθαι here in the sense of 'attack' (cf. Dem. *Cor.* 79), or – since the change in meaning from d2 ἐχόμενος would be harsh – accepted the emendation ἔφοιτο, but without enthusiasm. For the interpretation adopted above, cf. Burnet.   **d4 ἕως ἄν ... σκέψαιο:** the conditional construction (ἐῴης ἄν καὶ οὐκ ἀποκρίναιο) is extended into the ἕως-clause (cf. LSJ s.v. ἕως I.3); the temporal clause in d5–6 acquires opt. in a similar way ('if..., you would..., until you had...; and when the time came..., you would...').   **τὰ ἀπ' ἐκείνης ὁρμηθέντα** 'the things that came from it', 'its results' or 'consequences': what turns out when one applies it.   **d5 διαφωνεῖ:** as has been shown at length to be the case with the 'consequences' of the sort of αἰτία proposed by the scientists; S. is sure that there is no such διαφωνεῖν in the case of *his* (cf. 100a3–7n., 100d8–e3, 101a5–6n.).   **d6 διδόναι λόγον:** usually taken as 'providing a proof', as at 95d7 (contrast 76b5, 78d1–2, where it is 'giving a reasoned definition'). The method of διδόναι λόγον which S. outlines (d6–e1) is then supposed to consist in hypothesising a series of ever 'higher' propositions, and perhaps ending in an 'unhypothetical starting-point' (ἀνυπόθετος ἀρχή) of the type *Rep.* discovers in the form of the good (510b, 511b). Cf. Gallop 187–92. But (*a*) the good was casually introduced as one form among others in the original hypothesis (100b6); (*b*) teleology is not mentioned; (*c*) if ει ἕως ἐπί τι ἱκανὸν ἔλθοις suggests a series of successive operations, there is no indication that these concern propositions on more than one level; and (*d*) little of the method supposedly discovered, on this interpretation, in d6–e1 could be described as 'said ἐναργῶς' (102a4) in these lines themselves, or in the surrounding context. For an alternative way of taking διδόναι λόγον, see c9–102a1n. While we might in principle have expected some sort of reference to a procedure for establishing the hypothesis, there are strong indications that S. is taking it as itself the ἀρχή (e2): it will be the λόγος which he judges to be ἐρρωμενέστατος (100a4), and the basis of the 'safest' response, which he thinks will prevent him from falling if he holds on to it (100d8–e3) – language which recalls Simmias' suggestion at 85c–d that we must *either* discover the truth about things, *or* take the best available λόγος and rely on that. There will of course be reasons for 'taking' this λόγος (cf. 100a3–7n., 92d6-7), but these will fall short of a full proof.

e1–2 οἱ ἀντιλογικοί: see 90b9–c6n. Mixing talk about the ἀρχή and its 'consequences' (e2–3 τῶν ἐξ ἐκείνης ὡρμημένων = d4 τὰ ἀπ' ἐκείνης ὁρμηθέντα) is doing the same sort of thing as the antilogicians in that they mix *everything* up together (e5), and as in their case it will not lead to the discovery of the truth about anything – but of course they haven't the slightest interest in that (e4–5). Their 'mixing up everything together' probably refers just to their lack of any systematic method of inquiry (which, if they're not interested in the truth, they don't need). On the interpretation proposed (see c9–102a1n.), 'talking about the ἀρχή' refers to the process described in d5–e1, i.e. 'giving an account' of the original hypothesis (with ἀρχή substituted for ὑπόθεσις to avoid confusion with d6–7 ἄλλην ... ὑπόθεσιν). **e3 εἴπερ βούλοιό τι τῶν ὄντων εὑρεῖν** 'if you wanted to discover any of the things that are [the case]'. **e4 ἴσως** reinforces the statement rather than qualifying it (cf. 67b1n.), as the emphatic οὐδὲ εἷς shows. **λόγος** 'reasoned reflection'. **e5 ἱκανοὶ γὰρ ... 6 ἀρέσκειν** 'for their wisdom enables them to mix everything up together and still be pleased with themselves'.

102a3–5 This brief new interruption by Echecrates marks another important turning-point in the dialogue, the transition to the long-awaited final proof of immortality.   **a8 καὶ γάρ** 'And [to us] too' (cf. *GP* 109–10).

102a10–107b10: the final argument

Armed with his hypothesis, that forms exist, and that the corresponding particulars have the character they have by coming to 'share in' them (or, as it is put in 102b1–2, 'that the other things, by coming to share in these, have the names of these very things'), Socrates can now embark on the main task, to show that the soul is 'altogether deathless and imperishable' (see 88b5–6n.).

102a10 μέν: see 61d9–10n.

b1 εἶναί τι: cf. 64c2n., 74a9–12n.   **εἰδῶν:** P. here unobtrusively brings in one of his standard terms for 'form'.   **b2 αὐτῶν τούτων τὴν ἐπωνυμίαν ἴσχειν:** cf. 78e2. So e.g. a particular beautiful thing will share the name 'beautiful' with the beautiful (the form); but it will of course also *be* beautiful, even if not in the same way as the form (see 74d4–7, with nn.).   **b5–6 εἶναι ἐν τῶι Σιμμίαι ἀμφότερα, καὶ μέγεθος καὶ σμικρότητα:** if Simmias is larger than S. and smaller than Phaedo (and so also large in relation to S., small in relation to Phaedo: cf. 96d8–e4), then he is so by virtue of 'sharing in' the large and the small (the forms) respectively (100c); but this in turn means that the large and the small are somehow 'in' him (see 100d4–6n.), and it becomes possible to talk of 'the large in us' and 'the small in us'. καὶ μέγεθος καὶ σμικρότητα is a first reference to these. They are simultaneously distinguished from the forms (see esp. 103b5 οὔτε τὸ ἐν ἡμῖν (ἐναντίον) οὔτε τὸ ἐν φύσει) and identified with them ('now I am talking about forms', says S. barely two lines later, referring to a passage which has been primarily about the opposites 'in us': see 103b7–c2n.). A similar ambiguity might arise, under similar circumstances, in the case of what we call properties and their instances (cf. 65d4–5n.) But whether forms *are* properties still remains as open as before; and we can hardly ask for greater precision from S. about the status of 'the large in us' and 'the small in us', since that would require him to settle the proper description of the form–particular relationship, which he has deliberately left aside (100d5–6; cf. Loriaux II 114). 'The large/small (largeness/smallness) in us' stands simply for what *x* (any particular thing, like Simmias, or S.) has by virtue of sharing in the *F* (the form of F). It may be because even the form of words in b5–6 might raise this issue that S. begins his next sentence, in b8, 'But in any case …' (ἀλλὰ γάρ as at 95c9). **b8–c1 τὸ τὸν Σιμμίαν κτλ.** 'as to Simmias' overtopping of S., the truth is not as it [Simmias' overtopping of S.] is expressed in the words ["Simmias overtops S."]'; an awkward clause, in which τὸ … Σωκράτους starts off as subject, but is then replaced by τὸ ἀληθές.

c1 οὐ γάρ που … 4 τὸ ἐκείνου μέγεθος 'For [you don't think], surely, that Simmias is naturally such as to overtop, through his being Simmias, but rather that it is through the largeness that he happens to have; nor again that he overtops S. because S. is S., but rather because S. has smallness in relation to his largeness?' If we say 'Simmias overtops – i.e. is larger than – S.', that implies (or might be taken as implying) that the overtopping is because of attributes that are essential to Simmias and S., i.e. largeness and smallness respectively; whereas in fact largeness is merely something Simmias 'happens to' have in relation to S.'s smallness, which in turn will be something he 'happens to' have in relation to Simmias' largeness ('happens to', marking the contingency of their having the attributes on the relevant relation). **c6–8** Similarly, Simmias will be overtopped by Phaedo 'not because Phaedo is Phaedo [i.e. because he is large in himself], but because Phaedo has largeness in relation to Simmias' smallness'. **c10–d2** 'So it is in this way that Simmias is called both small and large, namely because he is in the middle of both [Phaedo and S.], submitting his smallness to the largeness of the one to [be] overtop [ped], and offering his largeness to the other, which overtops his smallness.' This summarises b8–c8. The immediate function of that passage is to explain the proposition at b5–6, that 'both largeness and smallness are in Simmias', which is S.'s version, in the light of his hypothesis, of 'Simmias is both small and large' (c10–11). But it also has a further purpose, which S. reveals in d5–103a2. The description in c11–d2, 'submitting his smallness', etc., suggests that the smallness of Simmias is itself small, and the largeness large – since only what is (relatively) small can be 'overtopped', and only what is (relatively) large can do any overtopping. But since the description is at least partly metaphorical, the point could not be established from this passage alone. See further d9–e2n.

d2–3 ἔοικα . . . καὶ συγγραφικῶς ἐρεῖν 'I look as if I am about to speak συγγραφικῶς' (with the adverb stressed by καί). συγγραφικῶς: 'like a book, i.e. with great precision' (LSJ); 'in the manner of a legal contract' (Archer-Hind and others, referring to συγγραφή in another sense); 'like a prose-writer' (συγγραφεύς), referring to the sophisticated style e.g. of a Gorgias (Burnet). 'Like a book' seems right, but with reference to the greater opportunity writing gives for stylistic artifice (what S. has just said is certainly more remarkable for its studied structure than for its precision: cf. preceding n.). **ἀλλ' οὖν . . . γε:** cf. 91b3–4n. **d5 λέγω δή κτλ.** 'It's for the sake of what follows that I'm speaking, because I want what [seems] to me [on the subject] to seem to you.' **d6–8** If αὐτὸ τὸ μέγεθος is the form (as it must be), the content of the 'not only' clause is directly comparable to that of at least the second half of 74c1–2 ('does equality ever seem to you to be inequality?'), and like it seems to be treated as intuitively obvious. Only something which 'happens to have' largeness, like Simmias, can also be small; the form cannot, and b8–c8 is meant to have helped Cebes somehow to see that the largeness in us cannot either. On how it is meant to do this, see e3–6n. **d6 ἐθέλειν:** of inanimate things, with neg., close in meaning to δύναμαι (cf. LSJ s.v. 1.2). **d8 προσδέχεσθαι τὸ σμικρόν** 'admit the small in addition', i.e. become small as well as large. **d9 ἀλλὰ δυοῖν τὸ ἕτερον** 'but [it seems to me] that one or the other of two things [must happen]'. **d9 ἢ φεύγειν . . . e2 ἀπολωλέναι** 'either that it retreats and gets out of the way, when the opposite, the small, advances on it, or that when that has completed its advance, it has perished'. 'When the small advances' must be when e.g. Simmias starts being compared with the larger Phaedo instead of the smaller S. (cf. 96d9 παραστὰς μέγας σμικρῶι). He will of course not stop being larger than S. (unless he somehow actually loses some height), but that is not the point: what matters, for S.'s argument, is that there are, logically, only two alternatives – at the onset of smallness, Simmias' largeness must either get out of the way (so that it is still there, but without any role in the action), or perish. The one thing it cannot do is to 'stand its ground and admit smallness', because that would mean its being 'other than it was', i.e. largeness (e2–3) – largeness being something which is essentially large. Like the form of largeness, 'the largeness in us' will itself be describable as 'something large', μέγα τι, and can be referred to by the use of the neuter of the def. art. + adj.:

see e5 ἐκεῖνο (the largeness in us) ... μέγα ὄν κτλ., and e6 τὸ σμικρὸν τὸ
ἐν ἡμῖν. But 'the large in us is large' no more implies, by itself, that it is
something large in the sense of *having a large size* than 'equality [the
form] is equal' implies that the form is equal to something else, or
consists of a pair of equal things (cf. 74d6–7n.); and unless and until
such an idea is required by the argument (as it is not by the argument
here: see following n.), the attribution of it to P. is unjustified, especially when he has allowed S. to be so imprecise about the whole
question about how particulars come to have *F*-ness 'in' them at all:
see 100d4–6n. 'The small' in e1 (like 'smallness' in e2, 4) will be ambiguous between the form and 'the small in us' (cf. 102b5–6n.).

e3 ὥσπερ ἐγὼ ... 6 σμικρὸν εἶναι: it now becomes clear how b8–c8 is
supposed to have helped Cebes to see the relevant point, that the
largeness in us cannot be both large and small (but must either retreat
or perish at the onset of smallness); that is, by suggesting that a large
thing can only be small as well if its acquisition of smallness does not
change its essential nature. So, for example (e3 ὥσπερ), S. can become
small – through standing beside, or being compared with, Simmias –
while still being S. (just as Simmias is Simmias whether he is standing
beside Phaedo or S., and so whether he is large or small); but the
largeness in us cannot, because that would mean its having come to be
something different, indeed its opposite. How (and it seems a reasonable question) could one of a pair of opposites become the opposite of
itself? The difference between this case and a thing's acquiring opposite attributes will be driven home in 103a4–c2. **e8 ἔτι ὄν ὅπερ ἦν:**
again, as in the sort of case where τὸ ἐναντίον *can* 'be or become' its
opposite, i.e. where τὸ ἐναντίον is (not the opposite itself but) something characterised by an opposite.

103a1–2 ἐν τούτωι τῶι παθήματι 'when this happens to it', i.e. what
was previously envisaged, the advance of the opposite (102d9–e1 ὅταν
προσίηι τὸ ἐναντίον). **a4–10** A confused objection from a suitably
anonymous member of the audience. Wasn't S.'s own first argument
based on opposites 'coming from' opposites? This elementary confusion
(too elementary, it seems, for the philosophically more experienced
Cebes; c3–6, with c5–6n.) gives S. an opportunity for further clarification (a11–c2): to say that one of a pair of opposites cannot become the
other is of course quite consistent with saying that an opposite *thing*

(something qualified by one of a pair of opposites) can become the opposite of that (come to be qualified by the other). **a8 ἀτεχνῶς ... τοῖς ἐναντίοις** 'that coming-to-be for opposites was simply this'.

b1 ἀνδρικῶς ... ἀπεμνημόνευκας 'Manfully recalled'. **b4–5** When we refer either to 'the *F* in us' (where *F* is one of a pair of opposites), or to 'the *F* in nature', i.e. the form of *F* (cf. e.g. *Rep.* 597b), we will be referring to the *F* 'itself', or 'by itself' (αὐτὸ τὸ ἐναντίον; cf. 74c1–2n). **b7 ἐπονομάζοντες ... ἐπωνυμίαι:** cf. 102b1–2. **b7 νῦν δὲ ... c2 δέξασθαι:** lit. 'whereas now [we are talking] about those very things of which, being in [them], the things which are named have the names; and those things themselves we say would never be able to admit coming-to-be of one another'. The first part is explained by 102b1–2 (if a thing's 'coming to share in' the *F* means that the *F* somehow comes to be 'in' it); and the second part must mean the same as b4–5 αὐτὸ τὸ ἐναντίον ... γένοιτο. We were in fact talking about the opposites 'in us' rather than directly about the forms; but see 102b5–6n. The important thing, in any case, is that we were not talking about opposites in the sense of the things that are qualified by them.

c3–4 ἆρα μή που ... καὶ σέ κτλ. 'I don't suppose any of the things this person said troubled you as well?' If ἆρα μή invites a negative reply (but see *GP* 47–8), the που here serves to make the question more open. **c5 οὐδ' αὖ ... οὕτως ἔχω** 'Nor do I feel like this again', i.e. I am not objecting now as I have done before (?). This is the best that can be done with οὐδ' αὖ, the only defensible MS reading. **c5–6 καίτοι οὔτι κτλ.:** cf. S.'s ταράττομαι at 100d3; Cebes' 'perplexities' are perhaps, like S.'s, of a more sophisticated kind. Real questions, it seems, remain to be raised (which is no doubt the point of Cebes' reply); the nature of the mysterious '*F* in us' might be one. **c7 ἁπλῶς** 'without qualification'. **c11 θερμόν τι καλεῖς καὶ ψυχρόν;** 'Do you call something hot and cold?', i.e. 'Is there something you call "hot" and [something else you call] "cold"?' For the form of the question, see 64c2n., 65d4–5n., 74a9–12n. The reference is to 'the hot' and 'the cold' (d2–3); not, as the sequel shows, hot things and cold things, but the hot itself (by itself) and the cold itself, which may be either the forms of hot and cold or the instances of them 'in us' (b5). **c13** Sc. καλεῖς.

d5 ἀλλὰ . . . γ': cf. 74a5n. **d5 οὐδέποτε χιόνα οὖσαν . . . 8 ἢ ἀπολεῖσ-θαι** 'that [snow], being snow, after admitting the hot, as we were saying in what went before, will never still be what it was, snow and [be also] hot, but when the hot advances on it, it will either get out of its way or perish'. 'As we were saying . . .' recalls the working principle introduced in 102b–103a, that what is *F* can only 'admit' the opposite of *F* if that does not change what it is (see 102e3–6n.). The cold thing which is snow can no more admit the hot while still being snow than 'the *F* in us' can admit the opposite of *F* (102d–103a); but if so, then the same two alternatives must apply as in that sort of case – when the hot advances on it, snow must itself either get out of the way or perish. **d10 καὶ τὸ πῦρ γε αὖ** 'And fire too, for its part'. **d11 τολμήσειν:** the idea of 'submitting' clearly goes with δεξάμενον rather than ἔτι εἶναι ὅπερ ἦν.

e2 ἔστιν ἄρα . . . περὶ ἔνια τῶν τοιούτων, ὥστε 'So the position with respect to some things like this [i.e. cases where a thing has / shares in an opposite] is such that'. **e3 αὐτὸ τὸ εἶδος** 'the form itself' (nothing can be true of 'the *F* in us' εἰς τὸν ἀεὶ χρόνον, but only ὅτανπερ ἦι, 'whenever it exists', as in the case of the category about to be mentioned: e4–5). **ἀξιοῦσθαι** 'is entitled to'. **e4–5 ἀλλὰ καὶ κτλ.** 'but also something else which is not that [the form itself], but which always has its character, whenever it exists'. μορφή, like εἶδος, is used in a special meaning, but one that is clearly deducible from the immediate context (both terms usually range between 'visible form' and 'class'). At the last moment, ὅτανπερ ἦι introduces a difference between the things being compared: the form of hot (e.g.) is always hot (in whatever sense), and similarly fire – or at any rate whenever it is there in the world. Forms, of course, exist permanently. **e5 ἐν τῷδε** 'in the following example'. **e9 ἄρα μόνον τῶν ὄντων:** sc. ἀεὶ δεῖ τούτου τοῦ ὀνόματος τυγχάνειν.

104a1–3 ὅμως δὲ δεῖ κτλ. 'but nevertheless one must always call it this too [i.e. odd] along with its own name because it is naturally such as never to be separated from the odd'. **a3–4 λέγω δὲ κτλ.** 'I say that it [the feature just mentioned] is the sort of thing that happens to three, and to many other things.' If this case is to throw light on what was said in 103e2–4, as it was introduced to do (e5–6), then 'the odd' must be the form, and ἡ τριάς something which 'shares in' the form, i.e. a particular (hence 'three', not 'the three'). A particular three (corresponding to a lump of snow, or an actual instance of fire) will be any group of three things – including, perhaps, the groups of three units used by mathematicians in their operations. (According to Arist., e.g. *Met.* 1028b19–21, P. proposed to treat the objects of mathematics as a special class of entities, intermediate between forms and particulars; but there is little evidence of such a view in the dialogues.)   **a6–7 ὄντος οὐχ ὅπερ τῆς τριάδος** 'although it [the odd] is not what three is'. We should expect ὅπερ ἡ τριάς (ἐστι); cf. καθάπερ (= καθ' ἅπερ) without a verb.

b6 ὃ . . . βούλομαι δηλῶσαι: this, explained in b6–c1, must be broadly the same as what was contained in 103e2–5, since the intervening passage set out only to say that 'more clearly' (103e5–6). The difference, however, is that b6–c1 refers back more directly than 103e2–5 to what has preceded: b7–8 φαίνεται οὐ μόνον ἐκεῖνα τὰ ἐναντία ἄλληλα οὐ δεχόμενα takes us back to 103b4–5 αὐτὸ τὸ ἐναντίον ἑαυτῶι ἐναντίον οὐκ ἄν ποτε γένοιτο, where 'the opposite' is either the form or the opposite 'in us' (cf. also 103c7–8), while 103e3–4 restricted the point to the form; and the passage generally reintroduces the more detailed account of what it means for *x* to be *F* which was given in 102b–103c, in terms of *x*'s 'having *F*-ness in' it. But now this formula is replaced by the one brought in at 103e4–5, 'has the character of the *F* [in it]' (see b9–c1n.).   **b7–8 φαίνεται . . . οὐ δεχόμενα** 'clearly do not admit'.   **b8–9 ὅσα . . . τἀναντία:** as e.g. three and two are not opposites (c5), but always 'have' the opposites oddness and evenness.   **b9 οὐδὲ ταῦτα . . . c1 ὑπεκχωροῦντα** 'neither do these resemble things which admit [i.e. neither do these seem to admit] that character (ἰδέα), whichever it is that is opposite to the character which is in them, but when it advances, they [clearly] either perish or get out of the way' (with ἀπολλύμενα and ὑπεκχωροῦντα continuing the construction after b7 φαίνεται). ἰδέα is here synonymous with 103e5 μορφή (see d9–10 ἡ ἐναντία ἰδέα ἐκείνηι τῆι μορφῆι); in other dialogues it is used, like εἶδος, in the sense of (Platonic) 'form'.

c1 τὰ τρία: evidently synonymous with ἡ τριάς, in the light of the juxtaposition of the latter with τὰ δύο and τὰ τέτταρα in a8–b2. **c1–2 καὶ ἀπολεῖσθαι πρότερον καὶ ἄλλο ὁτιοῦν πείσεσθαι:** a variation on the formula 'perishes or gets out of the way', which trades on the language of human choice ('I would rather die, or do anything, than ...'). **c5** 'Nor again (οὐδὲ μήν as at 93a4) is two *opposite* (γε) to three', confirming that these (and by implication the other numerical examples) do in fact illustrate the type in question. **c6 οὐ γὰρ οὖν:** see 93e6n. **c7–9 οὐκ ἄρα μόνον κτλ.** 'In that case it is not only the opposite forms which do not withstand each other's advance, but also some other things do not withstand the advance of the opposites.' Strictly speaking, it is the opposites in us, rather than the opposite forms, which 'do not withstand each other's advance' (cf. 102d–103a), since forms themselves cannot 'advance' on each other, or indeed do anything. But see 102b5–6n.

d1–3 ἃ ὅτι ἂν κτλ. '[things] which, whatever occupies [them], compels [them] not only to have its own character by itself, but also [compels them] always [to have the character] of something opposite to something', or '[things] which not only compel whatever they occupy to have its own character ...' The first is preferable, especially because it fits better with the form of d5–7, which is supposed to explain the definition by giving an application of it: 'You recognise, presumably, that whatever [things] the character of the three occupies [i.e. any group of three things, *qua* three], it is necessary for them to be not only three but odd.' If 'being occupied by the character of the three' describes the same state of affairs as 'having the character of the three' (103e4–5, 104b10), and that in turn describes the same state of affairs as 'having threeness' (see b6n.), then threeness ('the threeness in us') will be an example of what 'occupies' the things in question in d1; it will 'compel' each set of things it occupies to 'have its own character' by making them three; and it will compel them to have 'the character of something opposite to something' by making them odd. (So with snow and fire: whatever snowiness occupies must be both snow and cold; whatever fieriness occupies must be both fire and hot?) For αὐτό (neuter, 'by itself', d2) associated with a noun of a different gender, cf. *Rep.* 363a1–2 οὐκ αὐτὸ δικαιοσύνην ἐπαινοῦντες (but the credit that comes from it). The MS reading αὐτῶι (d3) is impossible; Robin's τωι (= τινί) is the best available solution ('but also, always, of some opposite paired to some other'?), with simple deletion of αὐτῶι the next best (see Verdenius). **d9–10 ἐπὶ τὸ τοιοῦτον κτλ.** 'Well then (δή as at e.g. 91b7), we're saying, the character opposite to the one which has this effect would never come to a thing of this kind.' 'We're saying': the reference is to b9–10, 'the character which has this effect' (i.e. of making three odd: d12) corresponding to τῆι ἐν αὐτοῖς οὔσηι. A character's 'coming to' a thing in this sense will then be equivalent to the thing's 'admitting' it (δέχεσθαι), and coming to have it (cf. 102e3–4).   **d12** 'And it was the odd character [the character of the odd] that had this effect?' εἰργάζετο is a 'philosophical imperfect' ('x was the case' = 'as we agreed, x is the case'): S. is recurring to his old principle that the particular F 'is F by the F' (100c–e), but in its latest form (see b6n.).

e3 'Three, then, has no share in the even.'   **e5** See 105d13–15.   **e7 ὃ τοίνυν ἔλεγον ὁρίσασθαι** 'What I said we should define' (see LSJ s.v. λέγω III.5). The sentence, if completed, would have run 'What I said …, ὅρα δὴ εἰ οὕτως ὁρίζηι …' (105a1–2); as it is, it is interrupted by the rehearsal of examples (e8–105a1), which necessitates a new beginning with ἀλλά (105a1 ἀλλ' ὅρα …). d1–3 itself was a first shot at a definition, and in fact says much the same as the new one in 105a2–5 (see n.), except in different language; but Cebes' failure to understand what was said there necessitated an explanation which took S. away from the job of definition, which he now resumes.   **e9 οὐδέν τι μᾶλλον** 'none the more [for that]'.

105a2 μὴ μόνον … 5 μηδέποτε δέξασθαι '[by saying that] not only does the opposite not admit the opposite, but also that which brings (ἐπιφέρειν) some opposite to that to which it comes itself, [i.e.] the thing itself which does the bringing, never admits the opposite of the thing conferred' (τὴν τοῦ ἐπιφερομένου ἐναντιότητα = the cumbersome τὸ τοῦ ἐπιφερομένου ἐναντίου ἐναντίον). 'Coming to' here must be interpreted in the same way as in 104d9–10 (see n.) and e1 (contrast 106b3, and 104b10 ἐπιούσης); a3 ἐκεῖνο must then be something which is 'in' ἐκείνωι ἐφ' ὅτι ἂν ἴηι, as threeness 'occupies' (104d6) and is in three. ('Occupying' itself seems to be equivalent to 'coming to': see 105d3–4.) This is initially puzzling, since we seemed to be setting out to define a class of things (which 'have opposites', 104b8–9) rather than of characters. But the shift is immediately intelligible if we understand S. to be performing the same sort of operation as at 102b–d, namely rewording statements about things in terms of the F-ness, G-ness, etc. 'in' them. There we were encouraged to understand a relation between x and y (two 'things') in terms of the relations between opposites (largeness, smallness, etc., which are themselves 'characters') which they 'have'; now, similarly, S. is urging us to analyse statements of the form 'three will not admit evenness, because it always brings with it the opposite of that' (the formulation used in 104e8–105a1) exclusively in terms of characters – it is, strictly, not three itself but the threeness which it has (or which 'occupies' it, 104d1, 5–6), which always 'brings' oddness with it, and which will not 'admit' evenness. He has already partly prepared us for this move at 104d1–7, when he identified the class of things in question as those things that 'are compelled by whatever occupies them to have both its own character and that of some opposite', since this attributes the presence of the opposite, which is the source of the things' resistance to its pair, to their 'occupying' character rather than directly to them. Nevertheless, because we are dealing here with *essential* characters, the original formulation still remains the natural one: three will not become even, any more than fire will become cold. And the definition itself is framed in terms which will not restrict its application exclusively to characters (see further b5n.). S. now has the formula which he will use in the next stage of the argument: what always brings one of a pair of opposites to whatever it comes to (or 'occupies') will never admit the other. **a6–b3** gives further applications of the general principle, and deals with a case which seems to break it in one respect: 'five [i.e. whatever fiveness occupies] will not admit the [character] of the even, nor ten, the double [of five], the [character] of the odd (while this [i.e. the double: μὲν οὖν as at 90e3] is itself too opposite to something else, nevertheless it will not admit the (character) of the odd); and neither will the one-and-a-half, nor the other things of that kind, the half [i.e. the series of halves?], [admit] the [character] of the whole, and again [the] third and all such things [i.e. the series of thirds] ...' This way of taking 'the half' is difficult, however, and it may be that it should be bracketed as a gloss. The sense is probably in any case as given; though why does the first series begin with one and a half rather than half? See O'Brien 1967, 221–3.

b5 πάλιν δή μοι . . . ἐξ ἀρχῆς λέγε: S. now goes back to the original discussion of explanation. He now says (b7–c6) that the preceding analysis shows him another kind of 'safety' (cf. 100c–e): if asked what it is that, when it comes to be in a body, makes that body hot, or ill, he will not answer 'hotness', or 'illness', as he proposed to do before, but 'fire' and 'fever'; if asked the same sort of question in relation to the oddness of a number (of things), he will answer 'the unit', not 'oddness'. These answers are 'safe' in that fire always 'brings' hotness with it to whatever it comes to be in, fever illness, and the unit oddness. The purpose of the passage is to suggest that the principle of a2–5 applies not only to 'characters' but to other items which come to be in, or come to, things: fire, fever and the unit ('and so on', τἄλλα οὕτως: c6), like some characters, when they come to be in things, always bring certain characters/opposites with them. In these cases, there will then seem to be an αἰτία of the sort preferred by the scientists (who like to explain F-ness by reference to factors other than F-ness); hence the description of the new kind of answer as κομψοτέραν (c2), which recalls 101c8 κομψείας, and contains an identical irony – if S. happens, here, to find some limited aspect in which the scientists' method of explanation seems to work, still his general unhappiness with that method remains. Although he might seem to suggest, at least in b8–c6, that the old 'safe' answer is now generally to be replaced by the new one, it is hard to believe that this is seriously meant, since there is no obvious way in which the latter will fit in those cases which originally led to the introduction of the former (what is it that, when it comes to be in something, that something will be beautiful/large/small – if not beauty/largeness/smallness?); and if he really is pointing the way to a revised general theory of explanation, it would be a strange theory that attempted to explain a genus (illness) by reference to one of its species (fever). Two further points: (a) if S. is actually abandoning his original answer, he went to a surprising amount of trouble to set it up; (b) his remarks at the end of the argument in fact imply a continuing commitment to it (see 107b4–9, with nn.). What matters here in 105 for the argument is just that sometimes a more particular explanation than the original 'safe' one is available, as it will be in the case of living creatures (which are alive by virtue of having souls in them: cf. 96b2n.). Cf. Hackforth 161–2. **b5–6 καὶ μή μοι κτλ.** 'And do not give as an answer whatever I ask about, but by imitating me'; i.e., when I ask about the F-ness of anything (what in it makes it F, the question to which we are implicitly returned by ἐξ ἀρχῆς λέγε), don't reply 'F-ness', but instead something on the following model (b8–c6). **b6 λέγω δὲ … 8 ἀσφάλειαν** 'I say [that], because, over and above the

answer I was talking about first, that safe one, I see from what is now
being said [i.e. the definition of a2–5, and the discussion leading up to
it] a different [kind of] safety.' **b9 ὧι ἄν . . . ἔσται:** lit. 'in whichever
[thing], in the [i.e. its?] body, what comes to be, it [the thing] will be
hot'. The reference seems to be to living creatures; cf. 96b2–3.

c1 ἀμαθῆ: cf. 100d4 ἴσως εὐήθως.   **c4 πυρετός:** the example is perhaps
suggested by the previous one, fever being a particular form of hotness
in a body (overheating).   **c6 μονάς:** the reference is probably to the
sort of definition of τὸ περιττόν criticised by Arist. at *Top.* 142b7–10,
'that which is greater by one (μονάς) than the even'; the word περιττός
itself has connotations of 'what is left over' (cf. *OED* s.v. 'odd': 'Of a
number: having one left over as remainder when divided by two'). The
passage only commits S. to saying that if (the extra) unit is present in
an ἀριθμός, that ἀριθμός will be odd; not to saying that this is the
proper way of accounting for oddness (any more than c2–4 commits
him to explaining illness by reference to fever). See b5n. The two
previous examples, of things which bring opposites to a *body*, are especially important, as preparing the way directly for the question in
c9–10 ('What is it that by its presence in a body makes it alive?'); the
present one maintains the analogy with the case of ἀριθμοί, which has
been central to the argument throughout.   **καὶ τἄλλα οὕτως** 'and [I
shall deal with] the other things in the same way'. By 'the other things'
S. does not mean literally everything, except to the extent that he is
ironically suggesting a renewal of his old allegiance to the αἰτίαι of the
scientists, but all the other cases where an item always brings one of a
pair of opposites to what it occupies.   **c9–10** S. now begins the application of his results, which will lead to the conclusion that soul is
ἀθάνατος (e6). The idea that soul makes bodies alive by being present
in them is consistent with the original definition of death at 64c4–5
(see n.).

d1 οὐκοῦν should probably be treated here as inferential (cf. 68d8n.):
if *whatever* body soul comes to be in is alive, then it will always be
the case that if soul is in a body, that body will be alive (ἔμψυχος).
The next step is to agree that aliveness has an opposite, i.e. deadness
(d6–9). Soul, then, will be one of those items which, though not being
opposites themselves, always bring one of a pair of opposites with them
to whatever they occupy, and since it has previously been agreed that

such items will never admit the other member of the pair, soul will never admit the opposite of what it brings to the body (d10–12). Given that what does not admit the character of the even is called ἀνάρτιον, and what does not admit the just and the musical respectively ἄδικον and ἄμουσον, we shall call what does not admit deadness ἀθάνατον (d13–e3); soul is therefore ἀθάνατον (e6). This stretch of the argument turns on treating the relationship between soul and body as like that between threeness (the character) and three: as threeness 'occupies' three (104d5–6), so soul 'occupies' body (105d3); and as threeness brings oddness to three, and refuses to admit evenness, so soul brings aliveness to body, and refuses to admit deadness. (Both 'soul' and 'threeness' here refer to sets of particulars: 'soul' refers to each and every soul, 'threeness' to the threeness, or the three, in each and every three.) But just in that it refuses to admit deadness, one of a pair of opposites, it will also resemble the sort of things with which we first started, things like three and two, which 'while not being opposites, always have the opposites', and do not admit 'the character opposite to the one which is in them' (104b8–10). The passage at 105e10–106c7 confirms that it is with this class of things that Socrates ultimately wants to compare soul, rather than with the characters which 'occupy' them – as indeed we should expect, soul is not itself a character but a thing which has characters. He could not have started by classing soul with them without begging the question of its immortality; its inability to admit deadness has to be established by independent means, which are provided by a comparison of the consequences of its 'occupation' of a body to those of the 'occupation' of three, etc., by their essential characters. But if so, the whole argument will in fact finally depend on an analogy between the behaviour of soul and that of characters. The argument is this: (1) opposite characters will not admit each other, but must either get out of the way or perish on the advance of the other; (2) some things, though not themselves opposites, will similarly not admit certain opposites, and must therefore similarly either get out of the way or perish; (3) soul is one of these things, in that it will not admit deadness, so that the same must hold true of it; but (4) the second alternative, perishing, is out of the question in its case. (e6 takes us as far as the first part of step 3.)   **d6 ζωῆι:** if ζῶν εἶναι (c9–10) is parallel to e.g. θερμὸν εἶναι (b9), then ζωή here must mean 'aliveness', and θάνατος in d9 'deadness' (cf. 106b3–4).   **d10–11 οὐκοῦν**

ψυχὴ κτλ. 'Well then, soul will absolutely never admit (οὐ μή + aor. subj. expressing strong denial) the opposite to what it itself always brings, as is agreed from what we said before?' **d13–14 τὸ μὴ δεχόμ-ενον κτλ.:** 104e5 (with specific reference to three). **d16 τὸ δὲ δίκαιον κτλ.** 'And [what do we call] what does not admit [the] just, and what does not admit [the] musical?' The examples here are simple opposi-tions; S. is only concerned to establish the general principle that what does not admit *F*-ness is called ἀ-*F*, and opposites themselves do not admit each other.

e2 καλοῦμεν: future. **e6** I.e. soul can never come to be in a state of being dead (cf. d6n., or having died: 106b4); or, to use the formulation of 102e, it can never withstand and admit deadness, while still being what it is (soul). But Cebes originally demanded that it be shown to be ἀνώλεθρον as well as ἀθάνατον (88b, 95b–e); and it has been agreed that whatever cannot admit an opposite will *either* get out of the way *or* perish when it advances (102d–103a, 103d–e). It must therefore be established that only the first alternative is available in the case of soul – which is S.'s next task (e10–107a1). **e8 τοῦτο μὲν δὴ ἀποδεδεῖχθαι φῶμεν;** 'Are we to say that this much has been proved?' μέν, strength-ened by δή (see *GP* 258–9), implicitly contrasts τοῦτο with what has (perhaps) yet to be proved. **e10–106a1 εἰ τῶι ἀναρτίωι κτλ.** 'If it were necessary for what is un-even (ἀνάρτιος as at 105d15) to be im-perishable, three would surely be imperishable?'

106a8 κἂν εἰ = καὶ εἰ, 'even if', with ἄν anticipating the ἂν ἀπεσβέν-νυτο of the apodosis.

b1 καὶ ὧδε . . . περὶ τοῦ ἀθανάτου 'in this way about what is ἀθάνατος too'. **b2 εἰ μὲν . . . ἐστιν:** 'if τὸ ἀθάνατον *is* also imperishable' con-trasts with the previous 'if the un-even [etc.] *were to be* imperishable', suggesting at least a higher degree of probability. μέν: the answering δέ does not occur until d1, after a repetition of the proposition of b2–3 (c9–10), which is necessitated by S.'s expansion of b2–3 in b3–c7. **b3 ὅταν θάνατος ἐπ' αὐτὴν ἴηι** 'when death attacks it': the context leaves no doubt about the hostile sense of ἰέναι ἐπί here, as of ἐπιέναι at 104b10 (contrast 105a3). What is presumably meant is when someone dies; according to Cebes' scenario, at least, this will always be a threat-ening time for the soul. **b3–4 θάνατον μὲν γὰρ . . . οὐ δέξεται** 'for it certainly won't admit death [deadness]', sc. whatever else happens to it (μὲν δή as at 105e8), so that it will be ἀθάνατος (and if what is ἀθάνατον is ἀνώλεθρον, also ἀνώλεθρον). **b4 οὐδ' ἔσται τεθνηκυῖα:** S. here states precisely what the argument has given him. **b5–6 ὥσπερ τὰ τρία οὐκ ... ἄρτιον, οὐδέ γ' αὖ τὸ περιττόν κτλ.:** for the strategy, see 105d1n. **b7–8 τί κωλύει ... ἄρτιον μὲν τὸ περιττὸν μὴ γίγνεσθαι** lit. 'what prevents the odd's [i.e. the odd in three] not becoming even' (ὥσπερ ὡμολόγηται, i.e. just as we agreed that it could not, but instead ...). **ἐπίοντος τοῦ ἀρτίου:** as e.g. when three is doubled (cf. 105a).

c1 αὐτοῦ ἀντ' ἐκείνου: both αὐτοῦ and ἐκείνου refer to τὸ περιττόν (ἄρτιον = τὸ ἄρτιον).

d1 ἂν δέοι 'we would need'. **d2 τούτου γε ἔνεκα** 'so far as this goes'. **d2–4 σχολῆι γὰρ ἂν κτλ.** 'For anything else would hardly be able to escape perishing (on σχολῆι + μή + potential opt., see *MT* 293), if what is ἀθάνατον (γε), being everlasting, is going to turn out to admit perishing.' The grounds for Cebes' assumption that τὸ ἀθάνατον is everlasting (and therefore imperishable) are perhaps that the description ἀθάνατος will only be applicable to something which is alive, and that the only way in which what is alive can come to an end is by dying, and so becoming dead instead of alive. **d5–7 ὁ δέ γε θεός κτλ.** 'Yes, and god [i.e. any and every god: cf. 60c2n., 67a6] and the form of life [i.e. of aliveness: cf. 105d6n.], itself, and anything else there may be which is ἀθάνατον would be agreed by everyone never to perish.' S. offers circumstantial evidence in favour of Cebes' concession: everything else that is ἀθάνατος is certainly immune to perishing. 'Everyone' may have a different reference in the two cases specified: literally everyone in the first (because, standardly, οἱ θεοί = οἱ ἀθάνατοι), and all philosophers in the second, since only they have any direct interest in forms as such (but see 65d4–5n.). That the form of aliveness is ἀθάνατον will follow from the principles (*a*) that the *F* (any form) is itself *F* (whatever it is the form of), and (*b*) that 'no opposite will become opposite to itself, either the one in us or the one in nature' (103b5); and it cannot perish in so far as all forms are absolutely unchanging (78d). Unless it were actually a living thing, S. could not argue directly from its being ἀθάνατον to its imperishability, and in fact he shows no sign of wanting to do so; nevertheless it could still be said that, for anything alive, perishing was equivalent to dying (see preceding n.). (That it is alive *qua* living thing is surely something he would reject, if the forms are unchanging, and if being a living thing entails the capacity for activity and change. But if so, this will count as further evidence against interpreting the 'is' in the formula 'the *F* [any form] is *F* [whatever it is the form of]' generally as the copula: see 74d6–7n., 102d9–e2n.) **d8–9 παρὰ πάντων μέντοι νὴ Δί' . . . ἀνθρώπων τέ γε κτλ.** 'Yes, certainly, by everyone – and not only by men but still more, I think, by gods.' (γε goes with the τε, emphasising the conjunction: men *and* gods. See *GP* lviii.) A light touch; the gods certainly wouldn't deny their own imperishability.

ει ὁπότε: here causal. **ἀδιάφθορον** = ἀνώλεθρον. **e5–6 τὸ μὲν θνητόν . . . αὐτοῦ ἀποθνήισκει** 'his mortal [part] dies'. If in the case of living things death is synonymous with perishing (cf. d2–4n.), then it is natural enough to speak of the body as dying, and to contrast it with the soul's going off 'intact and *imperishable*' (e6–7, i.e. in any death: cf. 88a–b). **e9–107a1** It is strictly only at this point that the conclusion 'soul is immortal' is reached, i.e. after being ἀθάνατον has been seen to entail being ἀνώλεθρον (cf. 105e6n.). καὶ τῶι ὄντι κτλ. recalls the opening of the first argument (70c4–5). Whether we are more convinced by the present argument than by the others (and the long build-up to it suggests that it is meant to be S.'s *pièce de résistance*) will depend on the following: whether we are prepared to accept – like Cebes – the continuing treatment of soul as a thing in itself, and whether we are swayed by the attempt to assimilate what looks like a causal relationship between it and the living body to the logical relationship between characters (properties?) – or, better, S.'s tendency to regard characters/properties as object-like entities inhabiting things (see esp. 105d1n.). This latter issue will take us into the area of the 'initial hypotheses' of 102a–b, which S. says 'must be examined more clearly' (107b5–6), though he for his part suggests that such further examination will actually lead to greater confidence in the argument (b6–9). παντὸς μᾶλλον ('more than anything') here in 106e9 itself constitutes a strong assertion of its force. Nevertheless, he simultaneously accepts Simmias' reiterated warning about the limits of human understanding (a9–b3; cf. 85c–d).

107a2–3 οὔκουν ἔγωγε . . . ἔχω κτλ. 'Well, *I* don't have anything else to add, nor [can I] in any way disbelieve what has been said.' (ἀλλ' εἰ δή κτλ. 'On the other hand, if . . .') **a5–7** I.e. there's no time like the present – but especially since one of the main participants is about to die. (*MT* 241 gives parallels for the omission of ἄν with the potential opt. ἀναβάλλοιτο after constructions similar to οὐκ οἶδα κτλ.) **a8 ἀλλὰ μήν . . . οὐδ' αὐτός . . . 9 λεγομένων** 'No, certainly (ἀλλὰ μήν as at e.g. 58d7), neither do I myself any longer have any way of disbelieving [the conclusion], at least on the basis of what is being said', i.e. now – but (ὑπὸ μέντοι . . .) there may still be other things to be said. τὰ λεγόμενα has the same reference as οἱ λόγοι in a3, b1, and τὰ εἰρημένα in b2–3. **a9–b1 περὶ ὧν** = τούτων περὶ ὧν.

b2 παρ' ἐμαυτῶι 'in my own mind'. **b4 οὐ μόνον γ' . . . ἀλλὰ . . . 6 σαφέστερον** 'Right (γε¹): not only [that] . . . but – both that is well said, and what's more (καὶ . . . γε), our initial hypotheses, even if they carry conviction with you, still, they must be examined more clearly' (we should expect ἐπισκεπτέον, but 'our initial hypotheses', having become subject of the conditional clause, stay as subject of the apodosis). The disturbed syntax perhaps reflects S.'s quick acceptance of Simmias' point; he goes on in b6–9 to rephrase his verdict on the argument in the light of that. **b7 διέλητε** 'analyse'. The only specific issue relating to the hypotheses (of 102a–b) which has openly been left for further discussion is that of the precise way in which forms come to be 'in' particulars (see 100d4–6n., 102b5–6n.); but there are certainly other things on which greater clarity is needed, for example about how the *F* (and so the *F* 'in us') 'is' itself *F* (cf. 74d6–7n., 102d9–e2n., 106d5–7n.). **τῶι λόγωι** 'the argument', i.e. the one that will establish (within the limits of human capacity) the soul's immortality – but that will evidently be a variant of the one just completed. **b8–9 κἂν τοῦτο αὐτὸ σαφὲς γένηται** 'and if this very thing becomes clear': since it is natural to connect σαφές with b6 σαφέστερον, τοῦτο αὐτό should probably be taken as referring to the results of the further examination of the hypotheses, together with their consequences for the argument.

107c1–115a8: Socrates tells a story

If the soul really is immortal, Socrates goes on, then there will be added reason to look after it; death will not wipe out our wrongdoings and the misery they bring us. The only way out is to become as good and wise as possible, which will ensure that we go to the best of the regions of the earth that receive the souls of the dead. He gives a long, imaginative description of these regions, and the judgement, rewards and punishments that await us. On the status of the whole account (or μῦθος, 'story': 110b), see 114d1–7. The effect is to locate human existence within the larger framework of a cosmos which he sees as governed by order and justice.

107c1 ἀλλὰ τόδε γ' . . . δίκαιον διανοηθῆναι 'But this much it's right to have in mind' (i.e. whatever we may say about the strength of the preceding argument; ἀλλά . . . γε as at e.g. 74a5).   **c2 εἴπερ** 'if . . . really'. If the soul is immortal, then we shall have to carry the consequence of not 'caring for our souls', i.e. κακία (c6–8), not only now but for all time to come: the burden, S. implies, might be tolerable for a time, if one knew that it would be removed at death, but not if one had to bear it for eternity. He has not argued for the claim that vice in the soul is bad for the person who has it, still less that such a person will recognise that it is (though he does argue for these claims, at length, in *Rep.*). His earlier 'defence', however, pictured people in general as placing importance on (what they called) virtue, and associated true virtue with wisdom, i.e. a proper understanding of what is really desirable (68c–69d). Part of the function of the myth as a whole is to return us once more to the themes of that defence, after the completion of the arguments for the survival of the soul to which it originally gave rise.   **c3 ἐν ὧι καλοῦμεν τὸ ζῆν:** i.e. in which what we call 'life' occurs. What we call life turns out to be only a short episode in the existence of the soul, just as the geographical area we inhabit is only a small and insignificant part of the earth (109a–b).   **c4 νῦν δή:** i.e. given the premiss that the soul *is* immortal.   **καὶ δόξειεν . . . εἶναι** 'really would appear to be terrible' (cf. καί at 62a1, 69c3).   **c5 ἀμελήσει:** the emphatic fut. in the condition underlines the threat (see *MT* 447).   **c6 ἀπαλλαγή** 'separation', since as the apodosis in c6–8 shows, S. is referring back to the original definition of death at 64c ('if death were separation from everything', sc. and not just from the body); c7 ἀπηλλάχθαι, however, will be ambiguous between separation and escape (d1 ἀποφυγή; cf. 64c5n).   **c8 νῦν . . . οὖσα** 'but as it is, since it is manifestly immortal'.

d1 κακῶν: i.e. the evils which are either constituted by or follow from κακία.   **d3–4 τῆς παιδείας τε καὶ τροφῆς** 'their education and nurture', i.e. the dispositions they have acquired during life (τροφή as at

81d8). Cf. *Gorg.* 523a–525a, where the souls of the dead arrive in Hades, and 'everything is open to view in the soul, when it is stripped of the body, both what belongs to its nature and the conditions (παθήματα: cf. *Phd.* 79d6) which the person acquired in his soul through the practice of each thing', i.e. through what he did during his lifetime. The difference is that here in *Phd.* S. makes no reference to what we are born with, putting all the emphasis on what we have 'learned' to be, through our neglect or care of our souls. **d4 ἃ δὴ . . . βλάπτειν** 'which are the very things which are said to do the greatest good or harm'. 'Are said': the idea of a judgement of the dead may be as old as Hom. (*Od.* 11.576–600), and in any case certainly pre-existed Plato (Burkert 1985, 197–8); but despite the repeated λέγεται (d5), the expansion of the idea which now follows is likely to owe at least something, both in its details and in its general shape, to Plato's own invention (see next n., and cf. Dodds 1959, 372–6, on the myth in *Gorg.*). **d6 ἄρα:** as at 97c1, apparently implying the newness to S. (and/or to his audience) of what he is about to relate. That each person has a δαίμων who has acquired him by lot as his charge during life was probably a familiar notion: Heraclitus' ἦθος ἀνθρώπωι δαίμων ('man's character is his δαίμων', DK 22 A 119) is a response to it (Burkert 1985, 181), as – in similar vein – is *Rep.* 617e1 (addressed to souls about to be reborn) οὐχ ὑμᾶς δαίμων λήξεται, ἀλλ' ὑμεῖς δαίμονα αἱρήσεσθε (because each person will choose the kind of life and the degree of virtue which he will have). What will have been less familiar is the suggestion that it is its δαίμων which leads the soul to Hades. S. perhaps hints at its newness in e1–2 μετὰ ἡγεμόνος ἐκείνου ὧι δὴ προστέτακται κτλ.: it is *that* guide, he insists (with δή emphasising the antecedent, as at e.g. 72a7), who has the appointed function of leading the soul, sc. rather than the better-known guide of the dead, Hermes (*Od.* 24.1–14). (On S.'s account, only a certain category of souls will find themselves travelling in the company of gods: 108c3–5.) If we are to make this idea consistent with c1–d2, the δαίμων ought to represent the choices made by the soul in life, as he does in the *Rep.* passage; that he is said to have acquired his particular charge by lot (d7) may be regarded as part of the story P. is adapting. 'Another guide' brings souls back into this world (e3–4; i.e. into another body) perhaps because their choices will have been changed by their long experiences in Hades. All of this is consistent with the detailed account of the journeys of the dead in

113d–114c. **d7 ἐπιχειρεῖ** 'undertakes' (cf. 73b9n.). **d7–8 εἰς δή τινα τόπον** 'to a certain place', with δή stressing τινα (*GP* 212). The place may be unknown, but its existence is assured: it is the place of judgement (d8 διαδικασαμένους, 'after submitting themselves to trial'), from which there lead the many different routes to 'Hades', each for a different category of soul (e4ff.). Some of these routes lead upwards rather than downwards (114b–c; cf. 8od).

e1 δή: cf. 72a7–8n. **e2 τυχόντας:** sc. αὐτούς. **e3 ἄλλος . . . ἡγεμών:** see d6n. **e4 ἐν . . . περιόδοις** 'after many long cycles of time' (for this use of ἐν, cf. 58b8). According to *Rep.* 615a and *Phdr.* 249a, the period of time between death and rebirth is a thousand years (described in *Phdr.* as a περίοδος χιλιετής); here in *Phd.* it is simply measured in unspecified περίοδοι longer than years. **e5 ἄρα:** apparently used much as at d6 ('the journey is not, after all, . . .'). **ὡς ὁ Αἰσχύλου Τήλεφος λέγει:** apparently in a lost play of the same name (=fr. 239 Radt).

108a1 ἁπλῆν 'simple', 'straightforward' (that, at least, is how S. takes it, as a2–3 shows). **a2–3 οὐδὲ γὰρ ἂν ἡγεμόνων ἔδει** 'For [in that case] neither would there be a need for guides.' The same reasoning would of course apply even if there were only one guide (cf. 107d6n.). **a3 που:** as at 70d1. **a4 τριόδους:** the MSS all have περιόδους, but τριόδους (places where a road forks) neatly explains σχίσεις, and a5–6 seems in any case to refer to things that happen at such places (the making of offerings, especially to Hecate, who has the ability to enter Hades: Burkert 1985, 171, 200, 222). For the same general idea of the forking of the road travelled after death, cf. *Gorg.* 524a. **a7 τὰ παρόντα** 'its present circumstances' (as at *Crit.* 120e–121a, compared by Verdenius): the good and wise follow easily because they know what is happening to them and why, i.e. that it is for the best – recalling S.'s own attitude towards death. **a8 ἐν τῶι ἔμπροσθεν:** 81c–d. The earlier passage appeared to suggest that this type of soul remains in the realm of the visible until its next reincarnation; that impression is now corrected.

b1 ἐπτοημένη: cf. 68c9–10, where ἐπτοῆσθαι περὶ τὰς ἐπιθυμίας is contrasted with ὀλιγώρως ἔχειν καὶ κοσμίως, just as here ἡ ἐπιθυμητικῶς τοῦ σώματος ἔχουσα (ψυχή) is contrasted with ἡ κοσμία (a6). **πολλά:** internal acc. after ἀντιτείνασα. **b2–3 ὑπὸ τοῦ προστεταγμένου**

δαίμονος: on the interpretation suggested above (107d6n.), the force exerted by 'the appointed δαίμων' will stand for the necessary consequences of this soul's previous choice of life; it will go first to the place of judgement (ὅθιπερ αἱ ἄλλαι, b4), and from there to whichever destination in the underworld is appropriate to it. **b3 ἀφικομένην:** sc. τὴν ψυχήν (of either type), to which b4 τὴν μὲν ἀκάθαρτον (the second type, 'unpurified' from bodily influences) is in apposition, which leads us to expect an answering τὴν δὲ καθαράν, and a common subject and verb governing both; instead, the subject and verb turn out to be appropriate only to the former, which means that a new start is necessary to introduce the second half of the contrast (c3 ἡ δὲ καθαρῶς κτλ.). The second μέν, in b7, is merely a repetition of the first, made necessary by the long intervening description. **b5 τοιοῦτον:** i.e. of the kind immediately to be described (φόνοι ἄδικοι). To the κοσμία τε καὶ φρόνιμος ψυχή S. naturally opposes some of the worst representatives of the 'unpurified': the net result is that we have an indication of the most important bifurcation of the roads to the underworld, with the good and wise and the bad and foolish going to unspecified, but emphatically different, destinations (c2–3, 5). **b7–c3** These lines prepare the way for the reappearance in c3–5 of one of the leading motifs of S.'s 'defence', that the philosopher will find himself, after death, in the company of the gods (b8 οὔτε συνέμπορος οὔτε ἡγεμὼν ἐθέλει γίγνεσθαι, contrasting with c4–5 συνεμπόρων καὶ ἡγεμόνων θεῶν τυχοῦσα); they also reintroduce the idea of the 'wandering' of unpurified souls (81d–e; cf. a8n.), by using the motif of the guide in a literal way (such souls are shunned even by their appointed guides). c2–3 leaves their destination vague; 113d–114b divides them up into sub-groups, with widely differing fates. **b8 αὐτή** 'by itself'.

c1 δή τινες: cf. 107d7–8n. The periods of time, χρόνοι, here are to be distinguished from the περίοδοι of 107e4. **c5 ᾤκησεν:** gnomic aorist. **τὸν αὐτῆι ἑκάστηι τόπον προσήκοντα** 'the place appropriate to each': cf. 114b–c. For the combination of αὐτῆι ('it') and ἑκάστηι, Verdenius compares *Soph.* 266b, *Laws* 795e. **c6 τῆς γῆς τόποι:** the transition is natural enough, since S. is at least starting from traditional ideas, and both Hades, where the dead traditionally go, and Elysium, where human beings may occasionally go as an alternative to death, may both be described as earthly: the second is on the same plane as the world inhabited by the living, the first either on the same plane or, more usually, under the surface of the earth (for sources, see Burkert 1985, ch. 4.2). **c7 οὔτε ὅση:** i.e., as it turns out, not as small. **c8 ὑπό τινος πέπεισμαι:** it is probably useless for us to try to identify the τις with any known person. P. in any case regularly invents sources for ideas of his own which he attributes to S. (who of course knows nothing himself); and it is safe to assume that that is what he is doing here (cf. Furley 1989, 18, and 108e4–109a6n.).

d2 τοι: see 60c9n. **d2–3 οὐ μέντοι . . . πείθει:** Simmias has heard of no radical theories, of the kind that S. has promised. **d4 ἀλλὰ μέντοι . . . γε** 'Well, yes (I shall tell you, because …)'; see *GP* 411. **d4–5 οὐχ ἡ Γλαύκου τέχνη γέ μοι δοκεῖ εἶναι διηγήσασθαι ἅ γ' ἐστίν** 'it doesn't seem to me to be [a matter for] the art of Glaucus to explain what, at any rate, [the theories I have heard] are' (even if showing that they are true is too hard for such a skill, d5–6). The harshness of the construction (οὐχ . . . τέχνη . . . διηγήσασθαι) is explained if οὐχ ἡ Γλαύκου τέχνη is a traditional, proverbial expression ('it doesn't take a genius to …': see Burnet *ad loc.*, with his Appendix II); in that case, there will also be no necessity, in order to understand the present context, to try to decide which Glaucus is meant. (Sedley 1989–90, 389–90 suggests – following Gaiser – that the relevant Glaucus is the one named in Hdt. 1.25 as the inventor of the art of welding. According to Sedley's attractively ingenious view, the myth contains traces of the kind of teleological explanation that S. earlier said that he hankered after – one which showed how 'the good … *binds and holds things together*' (99c5–6) – but could not find; d4–6 hints at this, but also contains a confession that proving such an explanation *true* is still beyond him. See further e4–109a6n., 110e2–6n., 112a7–b2n. For other speculations on the identity of Glaucus, see Clay 1985.) **d5 ὡς . . . ἀληθῆ:** sc. ἐστι. **d7–8 ἅμα μὲν . . . ἠπιστάμην** 'not only would I perhaps not even be capable of doing it, but also, even if I did know how to …': in the light of the counterfactual 'if I did know how to', ἴσως probably does not indicate any real doubt about his lack of the relevant skill (cf. 67b1n.). S. will not, in any case, commit himself to the truth of his description: 114d. **d8–9 ὁ βίος . . . οὐκ ἐξαρκεῖν:** cf. *Phdr.* 246a4–6 οἷον μέν ἐστι, πάντηι πάντως θείας εἶναι καὶ μακρᾶς διηγήσεως, ὧι δὲ ἔοικεν, ἀνθρωπίνης τε καὶ ἐλάττονος.   **d9 ἰδέαν** 'visible form' (cf. Ross 1951, 13–14).

e3 καὶ ταῦτα 'even this'.   **e4 τοίνυν** 'Well, . . .' (cf. 60d8n.); echoed at 109a6.   **πρῶτον μέν** is answered by 109a9 ἔτι.   **e4–109a6** The theory advanced here has usually been attributed to Anaximander, mainly on the basis of Arist. *DC* 295b10–16. But Furley 1989 suggests that it is essentially P.'s own: among other things, Anaximander seems to have thought that the earth was cylinder-shaped, not spherical (which in the context is what e5 περιφερής must mean). This suggestion looks consistent with the way S. introduces the theory. 'If [the earth] is in the middle, being round, [I am persuaded that] it needs neither air nor any other such force to prevent it from falling . . .': S. here refers back to his earlier attack on the natural scientists, which had as one of its prime exhibits what they said about the shape of the earth and why it stays where it is, ending with a 'contemptuous' reference (*HGP* I 294) to the idea that it rests on air 'like a flat kneading-trough' (99b). This ironic treatment of the flat-earthers is probably what enables him now to start from the earth's sphericity ('if . . . , being spherical'), flatness and sphericity having been raised as the only two options (97d8–e1); that the earth is in the centre, his other starting-point, was the normal assumption, and is in any case the only option S. has raised (97e3–4). The theory in question is thus presented as an argument whose only explicit premisses are embedded in the context of *Phd.* itself. The theory itself is an application of 'the principle of sufficient reason': 'the earth stays where it is because there is no *sufficient reason* for it to move in any direction' (Furley 17), being in itself uniformly balanced and uniformly related everywhere to the boundary of its uniformly spherical container, the heaven (ὁ οὐρανός, 109a3). See Barnes 1979, I 23–8. According to Sedley (1989–90, 364), 97–9 leads us to expect S. to substitute a teleological explanation for the mechanical one he is rejecting. On his view, 'the object of the passage is to explain teleologically the earth's spherical shape and central position. It does so by showing that these jointly constitute sufficient conditions for the earth's stability, which is itself taken to be the good end served', i.e. because contributing to the maintenance of overall cosmic order (365). But one might reply that after 99c, in which S. admitted his *failure* to find the kind of explanation he wanted, it would actually be rather surprising to discover him employing it (even in the rather covert and provisional way Sedley proposes). The crucial requirement is that S. should not be seen to rely on the sort of account he has criticised the scientists for using; from this point of view, the most important feature of the theory proposed is that it dispenses with material factors altogether. At the same time, the world which he describes is one within which teleological explanations will be possible, if symmetry and order are regarded as better than their opposites (a view which pervades *Tim*.; cf. Sedley 364). **e5 δεῖν:** e4 ὡς seems to be forgotten (cf. Verdenius *ad loc*.). (μηδέν: for the μή (after πέπεισμαι), see *MT* 685.)

109a1 ἀνάγκης 'force': cf. 97e1–2 τὴν αἰτίαν καὶ τὴν ἀνάγκην, with n. **a2 ἱκανὴν ... 4 ἰσορροπίαν** 'that the likeness everywhere of the heaven itself to itself [i.e. its uniformity] and the equilibrium of the earth itself are sufficient to hold it up'. **a4–6** For the underlying principle, see general n. on 108e4–109a6 above. (a6 ὁμοίως δ' ἔχον: i.e. if it is both in a uniform state itself and positioned uniformly in the middle of its (uniform) container.) **a8 καὶ ... γε:** as at 58d1, etc. **a9 ἔτι τοίνυν** 'Well then (τοίνυν, adding a new point: see *GP* 575–6), the next thing [I am persuaded of is that ...].' **αὐτό** 'it', i.e. the earth. **a9 ἡμᾶς ... b2 μορίωι** 'we – those from the River Phasis as far as the pillars of Heracles – inhabit a small part'. Aesch. fr. 191 Radt identifies the Phasis (modern Rion, flowing into the eastern Black Sea), as the boundary between Europe and Asia. Even taken together, the Mediterranean and the Black Sea are no more significant than any other of the many water-filled hollows over the surface of the earth (b4–6).

b2 μύρμηκας ἢ βατράχους: 'ants' emphasises 'our' insignificance; 'frogs' is more appropriate to the image of our seas as a τέλμα. **b5–6 παντοδαπὰ καὶ τὰς ἰδέας καὶ τὰ μεγέθη** 'of all sorts, in relation both to their shapes and their sizes'. **b6 συνερρυηκέναι:** sc. πέπεισμαι. **b7 αὐτὴν δὲ τὴν γῆν ... c1 τοιαῦτα** 'and that the earth itself [i.e. the real surface of the earth] is situated pure in the heaven, pure [itself], in which are the stars, the very [heaven] which (ὃν δή: cf. 72a7–8n.) the majority of those concerned with such things name "aether"'. The 'stars' include the 'wanderers', the planets: cf. c6–7, and *Tim*. 38c. The 'real earth' (cf. 110a1), S. suggests, belongs to the same 'pure' realm as the stars, which is the 'aether' talked about by 'most of those concerned with such things' (of whom, of course, he is not one: see *Ap.* 19b–d). The poets, especially Homer, regularly use the word αἰθήρ and a synonym for the sky or the heavens, the place of the stars and the gods; in Euripides, 'aether' is the stuff that encircles the earth, out of which – so Teiresias claims – Zeus made a phantom Dionysus (*Bacch.* 291ff.). Among the philosophers, Anaxagoras (DK 59 B 2 15) and Empedocles (DK 31 B 38) both employ the word to refer to cosmic fire (although in Empedocles it also appears as a synonym for ἀήρ: DK 31 B 100 *passim*). 'Aether', then, has a special status, which is enough to allow the next step in S.'s description: 'and it's of that that these [i.e. water, mist, and air] are the sediment (ὑποστάθμη), and are always flowing down together into the hollows of the earth' (c1–3). Here aether is already being treated as a stuff as well as a location, and one distinct from more familiar stuffs (cf. d7–8, 111b5–6; at *Tim* 58d, aether is the purest form of air).

c1 [εἰωθότων λέγειν]: these words (as Burnet suggests, followed by Verdenius) seem to be a copyist's insertion from 108c7; there are no other instances of λέγειν with περί + acc. in P. (and, one may add, probably few of repetitions of a phrase in such proximity, unless for effect). For οἱ περί + acc. ('those concerned with ...'), cf. *Phdr.* 272c. **c3 οὖν** perhaps merely marks a new stage in S.'s account ('this is how things really are. Now we don't realise this ...'). Cf. 58b4n.   **c4–5 ἐν μέσωι τῶι πυθμένι** 'in the middle of the bottom'.

d2 ἀφιγμένος: sc. εἴη. The perfect optatives indicate a hypothetical state ('as if someone had not reached the surface of the sea and so had not seen'). **ἐκδὺς καὶ ἀνακύψας** 'emerging and poking up his head'. **d3 ὅσωι ... 4 παρὰ σφίσι** 'how much purer and more beautiful it really is than their [region]', i.e. the place (supplying τόπου from d3) where the imaginary person and his kind live. **d4 μηδὲ ... 5 ἑωρακότος** 'and had not heard it from anyone else who had seen it' (?lit. 'from [someone] else, the one who had seen'). **d5–6 ταὐτὸν ... πεπονθέναι** '[I am persuaded that] it is this very thing, then (δή: cf. 71d5, etc.), that has happened to us.' **d7 ὡς ... 8 χωροῦντα** 'as if this [i.e. air] were the heaven, and the stars travelled through it' (cf. b7–c1n.). **d8 τὸ δὲ εἶναι ταὐτόν** 'but in fact (τὸ δέ: see 87c6n.) it is the same thing' (followed by acc. + inf. – 'that we are unable ...').

e2 ἐπ' ἔσχατον τὸν ἀέρα: cf. c4–5 ἐν μέσωι τῶι πυθμένι. **e3 κατιδεῖν ⟨ἂν⟩ ἀνακύψαντα:** the acc. + inf. construction penetrates here into a causal clause (e2 ἐπεί ...). The addition of ἂν (not found in any of the MSS) is necessary to supply the required apodosis of a future remote condition ('if someone were to ..., he *would* stick up his head and see'). Part of the apodosis is given here; then follows a comparison (e4–5 ὥσπερ ... τὰ ἐνθάδε), after which the apodosis appears in a fuller form (e5 οὕτως ... κατιδεῖν). For the image, cf. *Phdr.* 248aff., where the charioteer of the most godlike of non-divine souls flies up and manages to stick his head through the outermost rim of the universe, so glimpsing the true reality beyond (249c3–4 ἀνακύψασα (ἡ ψυχή) εἰς τὸ ὂν ὄντως, represented in this context by the forms); and the simile of the prisoners in the cave at *Rep.* 514a–517a, in which one of them finds himself freed and dragged up into the true light of the sun. Here in the *Phaedo*, as in the other two cases, there is reference to the difficulty of the process (e6): what S. is urging is a complete change of perspective.
e6 εἰ ἡ φύσις ἱκανὴ εἴη ἀνασχέσθαι θεωροῦσα 'if his nature were capable of holding up under the sight of them': in the first place he would, of course, be out of his element, like fish out of water; but there is also the suggestion that the sight itself would be overpowering (see preceding n.).

110a1 ἥδε μὲν γὰρ κτλ.: the acc. + inf. construction is finally abandoned, after the ὅτι-clause beginning in 109e7. **a5 πηλός** 'mud': listed at *Parm.* 130c6 among the least valuable of things. **a6 βόρβοροι:** βόρβορος, unlike πηλός (which can also mean 'potter's clay'), has entirely negative connotations (cf. 69c6). The plural, perhaps used partly for variation, may indicate different quantities/areas (or types?) of slime. **ὅπου ἂν καὶ ἡ γῆ ἦι** 'wherever the earth also is', the implication being that in the sea even the earth itself is rendered imperfect.
a7 πρὸς τὰ παρ' ἡμῖν κτλ. 'in no way at all worthy of being judged in relation to the beauties in our world'. **a8 ἐκεῖνα δὲ αὖ** 'But those things in their turn', i.e. the things on the surface of the 'true' earth.

b1 εἰ γὰρ δὴ καὶ μῦθον λέγειν καλόν 'for if [it is] right also to tell a story' (the alternative reading εἰ γὰρ δεῖ καὶ μῦθον λέγειν comes to much the same thing). The ἂν ... φανείη of a8 has already marked the new subject (ἐκεῖνα) as one that S. is less sure about than the things he has been saying, about which he is 'convinced'; describing it, he now admits, will be a matter of story-telling. The new part of his account in fact seems like a continuation of the preceding one, and hardly distinguishable from it in kind. The underlying message of both parts is that we have a false perception of the significance of our existence here 'on' the earth, which is certainly something of which the whole conversation proves S. to be in no doubt: if it is all a 'story', nevertheless it will contain truths (cf. 114d, with 70b6n., 61e1–2n., 61b5n., and Introduction §7). γὰρ δή: cf. 76a1n.   **b2 οἷα τυγχάνει κτλ.** 'what the things on the earth under the heaven actually are like' (i.e. the things that are on the real surface of the earth, under the real heaven).   **b3 ἀλλὰ μήν:** cf. 58d7n. (also for the γε).   **b5 λέγεται:** S. disowns responsibility even for his μῦθος; but by now the fiction that he is drawing on some unnamed source (see 108c8n.) is visibly wearing thin.   **b6 ἡ γῆ αὕτη** 'this earth', i.e. the one mentioned at b2, the real one.   **b6–7 ὥσπερ αἱ δωδεκάσκυτοι σφαῖραι:** as ancient as well as more modern craftsmen had evidently discovered, twelve pentagons of leather sewn together to form a dodecahedron will give the closest approximation to a sphere which can be constructed from flat surfaces. The dodecahedron is also, in mathematics, one of the five regular solids: at *Tim.* 55c, the Divine Craftsman, who is also a divine mathematician, having used up the other four in constructing the molecules of fire, air, water and earth, uses the dodecahedron for the construction of 'the whole', i.e. the cosmos itself. In the present context, however, as the rest of the sentence shows, the leading idea is not so much the shape of the earth – which has already been said to be spherical – as its appearance as a variegated (ποικίλη, b7) patchwork. Cf. Loriaux.   **b7 χρώμασιν διειλημμένη** 'picked out in different colours'.   **b8 εἶναι:** sc. λέγεται. **ὥσπερ δείγματα** 'like samples'. In this instance, as it will turn out to be the case in others, our world contains traces of the beauties to be found in the world above, just as it (in some sense: see 100d4–6n.) contains 'traces' of the forms, which can remind us of them. But it is, after all, a part of 'Hades' which S. is describing, which is where, if anywhere (according to his 'defence'), the philosopher will expect to achieve the knowledge for which he has striven during life. (The idea of 'our' colours as δείγματα of the real ones suggests a relationship based on likeness: see 100a1–3n. But it would be unwise to suppose that the present context – which is now, after all, explicitly one of story-telling – can really give us any further useful information about the form–particular hypothesis, much though we might wish for it.)

c1 ἐκ τοιούτων: i.e. out of such colours.   **c2–3 τὴν μὲν ... τὴν δὲ ... , τὴν δὲ ...** 'part of it ... another part ..., another ...'.
c3 ἀλουργῆ ... καὶ θαυμαστὴν τὸ κάλλος 'purple and wonderful in its beauty', i.e. of a wonderfully beautiful purple.   **c4 τὴν δὲ ... λευκοτέραν** 'another part, as much of it [sc. the earth] as is white, whiter than chalk or snow'.   **c6 καὶ γὰρ ... d3 φαντάζεσθαι** 'These very hollows in it, full to the brim as they are of water and air, offer an appearance (εἶδος, 'visible aspect': cf. ἰδέα at 108d9) of colour as they glitter among the variegated colours around them, so that its appearance is of one continuous variegated surface' (lit. 'so that one continuous variegated appearance of it is presented to the eye': εἶδος again). The idea of continuity is mimicked by the simple juxtaposition of the two adjectives (συνεχὲς ποικίλον) in the last part of the sentence, describing the whole, and the repetition of words and ideas from the first part, describing the hollows (αὐτῆς ... τι εἶδος ... ποικιλίαι / τι αὐτῆς εἶδος ... ποικίλον). Two things seem to be implied: (*a*) that the hollows, like the one in which we live, have no colour of their own, only reflecting the real colours around them; but (*b*) that this leaves the beauty of the upper surface itself undiminished.

d3 τοιαύτηι: i.e. so different from (and especially so much more beautiful than) our earth.   **d5 καὶ αὖ τὰ ὄρη ὡσαύτως** 'and similarly, in their turn, with the mountains': i.e., as is explained in καὶ τοὺς λίθους κτλ., they too show the same proportionate difference.   **d7 ὧν καί** 'and it is of these, in fact' (cf. *GP* 294–5).

e1 ἐκεῖ δὲ ... 2 καλλίω 'but there [there is] nothing [sc. of the relevant type: rocks or stones] which is not of this sort, and still more beautiful than these'.   **e2 τὸ δ' αἴτιον ... 6 παρέχει:** according to Sedley 1989–90, 371, there are two levels of explanation in this context, a materialistic one (represented by e2–6), and a deeper, teleological one, by which the difference between the higher realm and ours is for the sake of the greater happiness of those above (see esp. 111a2–3). But it would be simpler to read e2–6 as an application of the general principle that everything in the upper world is perfect, as it is not with us (something which Sedley's teleological αἴτιον seems not to explain).   **e4 ὥσπερ**

... 5 συνερρυηκότων 'as those here [have been corrupted and eaten up] by mildew and brine because of the things that have settled together here' (i.e. water, mist, and air: 109b6–7). **e5 καὶ γῆι:** cf. a6n.
e5–6 τοῖς ἄλλοις ζώιοις τε καὶ φυτοῖς 'and to animals and plants besides'. **e6 αἴσχη** 'uglinesses', i.e. forms of ugliness.

111a2 πανταχοῦ τῆς γῆς 'everywhere on the earth'. **a2 ὥστε ... 3 θεατῶν:** lit. 'so that to see it is a spectacle that belongs to fortunate spectators'. Cf. Hom. *Od.* 5.73–4 ἔνθα κ' ἔπειτα καὶ ἀθάνατός περ ἐπελθὼν | θηήσαιτο ἰδὼν καὶ τερφθείη φρεσὶν ἧισιν: of Calypso's cave and its surroundings, one of the many poetic descriptions of earthly paradises which are recalled by S.'s account. 'Belongs to fortunate spectators' – fortunate, of course, because of the beauty of the things seen, not because of their potential exchange value, in which those who live there will have no, or little, interest: the population consists of, or includes (see following n.) those of us who are judged previously to have lived exceptionally good lives (114b6–c2, though without having attained full 'purification' through philosophy, c2–5), which according to the implications of S.'s 'defence' (see 68c8–12, 68e2–69c3, 66c2–d3) is incompatible with any but the most moderate concern with material things. **a4 ἀνθρώπους:** i.e., presumably, combinations of soul and something which is at least comparable to our bodies, though its needs (a7–b1) and capacities (b2–6) are different. It seems to be only the perfectly purified philosophers who will have a wholly incorporeal existence (114c3–4 ἄνευ ... σωμάτων ζῶσι τὸ παράπαν); cf. the account of the fate of unpurified souls at 81b–e. Since other things, including plants and animals, are apparently permanent features of the upper world, it is natural to suppose the same to be true of the human beings referred to here, i.e. that they are a quite distinct race from us, who will be joined by some of the more fortunate of us from time to time; on the other hand, it may be more economical to identify the two groups with one another (if it is a separate race which lives on the 'real' earth, should we not need a separate eschatology for them?), and the phrasing of 114b6–c2 is certainly in favour of it ('those who seem to have lived exceptionally well are the ones who ...'). But we should be careful not to press S.'s 'story' too hard. The emphasis of the present context is on the superior quality of existence in the world above, and so on the inferiority of our own. The theme of the destinations of souls after death will be reintroduced only later. **a6–7 ἃς περιρρεῖν τὸν ἀέρα πρὸς τῆι ἠπείρωι οὔσας** 'around which the air flows, being close to the mainland'. As Burnet says, this is P.'s way of making room in his landscape for the Isles of the Blest (the traditional alternative destination to Hades for human beings above the common run): (νήσοις) ἃς ... ἀέρα is a neat, playful variation of Pindar's lines ἔνθα μακάρων | νᾶσον ὠκεανίδες | αὖραι περιπνέοισιν (*Ol.* 2.70–2). Burnet's explanation of S.'s stipulation of the nearness of the islands to the 'mainland' is probably also right – if they were further out, we should see them as we look up.   **a7 ἐνὶ λόγωι ... b1 τὸν αἰθέρα** 'in a word, what water and the sea are to us in relation to our needs, that air is there, and what air is to us, aether is to them'. 'In a word', because S. is both generalising – air there plays the role not just of the sea here, but of water as a whole (for this sort of use of τε ... καί, see *GP* 515) – and, in part, recapitulating, by reintroducing the subject of aether from 109b4–c3. 'In relation to our needs': presumably, then, the inhabitants of the upper world will 'fish' for birds, 'drink' air, and 'breathe' aether: just as in Hom., ichor, not blood, runs in the veins of the gods? S. continues in the light tone clearly identifiable in a6–7.

b1 τὰς δὲ ὥρας ... 2 τοιαύτην 'Their climate is such' (lit. 'the seasons for them have / are constituted by such a mix', sc. of hot, cold, dry, wet).   **b3 χρόνον ... ζῆν πολὺ πλείω:** if the inhabitants of the upper world do come from here, i.e. from our world (see a4n.), then their life would be equivalent to our death, and their 'dying' would be a matter of their returning here (see 107e2–4), and – as we call it – being born (again, into a new body). Cf. 107c3 ἐν ὧι καλοῦμεν τὸ ζῆν.   **b3 καὶ ὄψει ... 6 πρὸς καθαρότητα:** if their sensory faculties (πᾶσι τοῖς τοιούτοις = the other senses, apart from sight and hearing?) are superior to ours, because of the greater purity of the medium (aether as opposed to air, the difference being measured by that between water and air), then the point S. made in his defence about the obstruction caused by the senses to the acquisition of φρόνησις (65a9–b6) will be less applicable; indeed now – as he implies, by blandly listing φρόνησις along with them – the senses will even be an aid to its acquisition, since things are seen as they really are (c1–2).   **b6 καὶ δὴ καί** 'Moreover' (further evidence of the superiority of their existence).   **b7 ἐν οἷς τῶι ὄντι οἰκητὰς θεοὺς εἶναι:** this is perhaps one step short of the relationship with the gods referred to at 69c7 ('living with the gods') and 82b10 ('joining the race of the gods'), but consistent with what S. expects for himself at 63b5–c3 ('entering the presence of gods who are good and wise masters'). **b7–8 καὶ φήμας τε καὶ μαντείας καὶ αἰσθήσεις τῶν θεῶν:** sc. αὐτοῖς εἶναι. Lit. 'and [they have] utterances and prophecies and perceptions of the gods', i.e. utterances and prophecies from them, perceptions of them – all direct, as the preceding relative clause implies, and as is confirmed by what follows (καὶ τοιαύτας κτλ.).

c1 αὐτοῖς πρὸς αὐτούς: i.e. face to face.   **καὶ . . . γε:** 'what is more' (as at 58d1, etc.).   **c2–3 καὶ τὴν ἄλλην κτλ.** 'and their happiness in everything else is in accordance with these things', i.e. the ones last mentioned: knowledge, and proximity to the divine, are the things that S. thinks most desirable.   **c4–5 τὰ περὶ τὴν γῆν** 'the things around the earth', i.e. the things on its surface.   **c5 τόπους δ' . . . d2 πλατυτέρους** 'but there are places within it, in (κατά: see LSJ s.v. B.1.2) its hollows, many of them in a circle around the whole, some of them deeper and more widely spread out [i.e. with a broader opening] than the one in which we live, while others are deeper but have an opening smaller than ours has, and others (ἔστι δ' οὕς = τοὺς δέ) are shallower than ours and broader'. The interpretation of this passage, and especially the exact relation of the new 'places' to the hollows, is much disputed. But if we read back from what follows, we seem to discover that the places in question are (a) the locations of lakes and seas (112c6–7, 113a6–8), (b) the places from which or into which various rivers, etc. appear or disappear (e1–2, 112c8–d1, e4–113c8), and (c) other χάσματα, in the sense of 'chasms' or 'gulfs' (see e6–112a1, which introduces the χάσμα of Tartarus, by contrast with χάσμα here in c8 in the sense of 'opening'). (a), and the openings of (b) and (c), will probably as a rule be located within inhabited hollows like ours, but they may also be on the 'real' surface of the earth, as the two openings of Tartarus probably are (and it is doubtful whether there could be life around the lake of Pyriphlegethon, 113a6–8). In the latter case the 'places' in question can still reasonably be said to be κατὰ τὰ ἔγκοιλα τῆς γῆς, from the perspective of someone standing on the surface. Type (c), we may suppose, will be represented by those said to be deeper and wider than ours (c6–7), type (b) by those which are deeper and narrower (c7–d1), while those which are less deep and broader (d1–2) will be included in type (*a*). The main purpose of c4–d2, however, is to switch our attention from the things περὶ τὴν γῆν to those within it (ἐν αὐτῆι), while also indicating, in relation to these too, the insignificance of our region. (αὐτούς in c8 is strictly redundant, but may ease the change of construction back to acc. + inf.)

d2 τούτους δὲ πάντας ... 4 ἔχειν 'All these are connected to each other by numerous subterranean passages, both broader and narrower ones, and have ways through between them.'   **d5 καὶ ἀενάων ... 7 καὶ ψυχρῶν** 'and ever-flowing subterranean rivers, both of hot waters and of cold, of unimaginable size': explaining and expanding πολὺ ... ὕδωρ.   **d8 βορβορωδεστέρου:** cf. 110a6n.

e1–2 ὥσπερ ἐν Σικελίαι κτλ.: here, as with the references to hot waters and to a 'purer' type of mud (the latter, like the former, associated with volcanic springs?), P. anchors his detailed account of the underworld to known features of our world (there really are rivers of mud and of fire down there, just as we find them at Etna), while simultaneously suggesting 'explanations' of these features (for the tone cf. 112a7–b2n.). (See further 112b6–7n.) But in what follows his sources will more often be poetic and mythical.   **e2 ὧν δὴ καί:** tr. 'it is with these things' (i.e. water, fire, mud).   **e3 ὡς ... γιγνομένη** 'as the circling stream happens to reach each one on each occasion' (Gallop).   **e4–5 ὥσπερ αἰώραν τινά** 'as it were [the movement of] a kind of swing' (cf. *Laws* 789d3, and αἰωρεῖσθαι at 98d2), i.e. an oscillation (αἰώραν is subject).   **e5 ἔστι δὲ ἄρα ... :** ἄρα seems to mark an important new turn in the description (cf. *GP* 32–3, on ἄρα as 'expressing a lively feeling of interest'); at the same time S. finally abandons the acc. + inf. construction, even though what follows is doubtless still part of the μῦθος, and of what λέγεται (110b5). See further 112a7–b2n.   **e5–6 διὰ φύσιν τοιάνδε τινά** 'because of some sort of thing of the following kind'. For φύσις in the sense of 'sort', 'class', like εἶδος, see LSJ s.v. vi. But the choice of this word here may have a special significance. The explanation S. goes on to give is of a purely mechanistic kind – that is, of the kind offered by experts in 'that wisdom they call περὶ φύσεως ἱστορίαν', which he introduced at 96a and then went on to criticise (cf. 108e4–109a6n., 110e2–6n.). Is he perhaps now warning us, through a play on the term φύσις, that he is himself about to behave like the natural philosophers? See further 112a7–b2n., and 113d1 τούτων δ' οὕτως πεφυκότων (summarising the 'physical' account of the underworld). The phrase διὰ φύσιν τοιάνδε τινά in any case does not suggest any great confidence in the explanation to be offered. **e6 χασμάτων:** cf. c5–d2n. **e6 ἄλλως τε ... 112a2 γῆς:** lit. 'is actually largest both in other respects and in being bored right through the whole earth', i.e. it is not only the broadest but also the deepest, in that it is the only one which stretches from one side to the other. ('Right through the earth' might just mean 'right through to the centre', but this hardly seems the most obvious interpretation.) The openings of this χάσμα to the surface seem to play no role in the account, except to allow it to fit into the system of ἔγκοιλα/κοῖλα. It would fit nicely if it followed the line of axis of the earth (cf. *Rep.* 616b, and *Tim.* 40b, which at least according to Arist. (*DC* 293b30–2) talks of the earth's revolving); but there is no indication of this in the text.

112a3 = Hom. *Il.* 8.14. (βέρεθρον/βάραθρον, 'pit', suggests a τόπος which is open at least at one end: see preceding n.) **a4 ἄλλοθι ... ἄλλοι:** *Il.* 8.451; e.g. Hes. *Th.* 119. **a5 γάρ** seems to introduce the main part of the explanation promised in 111e5–6. **a6 γίγνονται ... 7 ῥέωσιν:** cf. Arist. *Meteor.* 356a12–14 (commenting on the present passage) τοὺς δὲ χυμοὺς καὶ τὰς χροίας ἴσχειν τὸ ὕδωρ δι' οἵας ἂν τύχωσι ῥέοντα γῆς (so e.g. the water may be either salt or fresh: cf. c7–8; for colour, see 113b8–c1). But there are also ποταμοί of fire and mud (111d7–8), and the same account is probably meant to be given of them: rivers of mud will flow through muddy regions, rivers of fire through fiery regions. The latter, however, are evidently not pure fire: both 111d–e and 113a–b associate them with lava-flows, and with mud; the second context also directly with water (111d7–e2; 113b5–6, a5–b1). Thus all rivers are still ultimately of water, and can be derived from waters of Tartarus: while at b2 these are referred to more vaguely as τὸ ὑγρὸν τοῦτο, 'this liquid' (perhaps because the rivers flowing *in* as well as out will have different characteristics), at c2 they become simply τὸ ὕδωρ. **a7 ἡ δὲ ... b2 τὸ ὑγρὸν τοῦτο** 'And the reason why the rivers flow out from there and flow in is that this liquid does not have a bottom or place to stand.' In fact, the full statement of the αἰτία extends considerably beyond this sentence: so, S. continues (i.e.

because it has no place where it could come to rest), 'it oscillates and surges to and fro / up and down' (b3; cf. c2–3n.), and as it comes to certain channels, fills these, from which it travels up to regions like ours, and then drains back down again (c1–e3). The obvious objections to this theory are made, after what is by and large (see preceding n.) a fair summary of it, in Arist. *Meteor.* 356a14–33 (e.g. Arist. says 'we shall get the proverbial rivers flowing upwards' – a traditional way of referring to the impossible: Eur. *Med.* 410). But we should remember again that the whole context is one of a μῦθος (110b1), and that S. himself will raise the question about how much of his story is to be believed (114d). The same point may help to weaken the obvious objection that S. now seems to be offering us an 'explanation' which is indistinguishable from the sorts of αἰτίαι – or αἴτια: if we compare αἰτία here at 112b1 with αἴτιον at 110e2, they appear (? *pace* Frede 1980) to be synonymous terms – which he earlier criticised the natural scientists for offering: cf. 111e5–6n. (and 108e4–109a6n., 110e2–6n.). Is he perhaps now parodying them, by producing the same sorts of speculations about the things under the earth as he reported them earlier as producing about the things over it? The parody would be given an additional slant by the fact that S. has suddenly started talking in direct speech: thus we seem to find him, just before his death, doing one of the things that at *Ap.* 19b–c he denies he ever did, but was wrongly accused of doing, ζητῶν τά τε ὑπὸ γῆς καὶ οὐράνια (cf. 26d6–9; for the status of S.'s account of his supposed early interest in science in 96–9, see 95e9n.). But of course we know all along that they are not really S.'s speculations; cf. 111e5–6n. The proper explanation for the movement of liquids within the earth, if S. is at all serious about these, would presumably be teleological: either it has still to be found (see 99c, 108e4–109a6n.), or, as Sedley suggests (1989–90, 369–70), it is connected with the scheme of punishments and rewards for souls outlined in 113d–114c.

b3 δή 'So'.   **b3–4 καὶ τὸ πνεῦμα:** πνεῦμα is air in motion (cf. *Crat.* 410b): wind, and esp. breath. Both meanings are in play in what follows.   **b5–6 εἰς τὸ ἐπ᾽ ἐκεῖνα τῆς γῆς . . . εἰς τὸ ἐπὶ τάδε:** lit. 'towards the [part] of the earth over there . . . towards the [part of the earth] over here' (cf. LSJ s.v. ἐπί c.3); i.e. away from us / towards us (which suggests that we are relatively close to one end of Tartarus: cf. Bluck

135). **b6 ὥσπερ τῶν ἀναπνεόντων ... 7 πνεῦμα:** lit. 'just as the breath of those [creatures] that breathe breathes out and in, flowing'.

c1 εἰσιὸν καὶ ἐξιόν: i.e. as it moves towards and away from the centre. **ὅταν τε οὖν:** οὖν is 'resumptive', as at 58b1 etc.; ὅταν τε is answered by its pair at c4. **c2 τὸν δὴ κάτω καλούμενον:** S. admits the parochialism of the perspective of b5–6; from opposite us, what we call 'down' would appear as 'up'. (*Pace GP* 235, the use of δή here seems comparable to its use after relatives, as e.g. at 72a7, 96a8: 'that place which we call "down"'.) **c2 τοῖς κατ᾽ ἐκεῖνα τὰ ῥεύματα ... 3 ὥσπερ οἱ ἐπαντλοῦντες:** lit. 'it flows into the streams in the [places] there through the earth, like those irrigating'; i.e. it flows into the empty channels there, filling them as in the process of irrigation. The simile does important work, referring to the *raising* of the water (which is what irrigators do): any movement away from the centre will be movement upwards in the absolute sense (as is implied by τὸν δὴ καλούμενον κάτω: see preceding n.). τὰ κατ᾽ ἐκεῖνα is a variation of b5 τὸ ἐπ᾽ ἐκεῖνα (τῆς γῆς), and has the same reference. **c4 ὅταν τε αὖ ἐκεῖθεν ... ἀπολίπηι** 'and when in turn its level falls (and it leaves) there', i.e. the hemisphere opposite ours (ἀπολείπειν is regularly used of rivers or streams failing). **c5 τὰ ἐνθάδε:** sc. ῥεύματα, those in our hemisphere corresponding to the ones mentioned in c2. **c6 καὶ διὰ τῆς γῆς** is perhaps added to make it clear that S. is still describing things underground. **c7 ὁδοποιεῖται** 'a way is made', maintaining the comparison with the process of irrigation begun in c3 (οἱ ἐπαντλοῦντες; cf. also c6 ὀχετῶν). **c7 θαλάττας ... 8 ποιεῖ:** cf. Arist. *Meteor.* 351a19ff. ('The same parts of the earth are not always moist or dry, but they change according as rivers come into existence and dry up. And so the relation of land to sea changes too and a place does not always remain land or sea throughout all time ...' But the reasons Arist. gives are, of course, different from S.'s: cf. a7–b2n.). Some rivers, at least, dry up annually in the Mediterranean. S. does not tell us what time-scale he has in mind, and perhaps we should not ask; to do so would be to imply that he is talking as historian and geographer rather than as story-teller. See further e6–7n.

d1 τὰ μὲν μακροτέρους ... 2 βραχυτέρους: lit. 'some [streams] travelling round longer and more numerous places, others fewer and shorter': μακροτέρους and βραχυτέρους suggest that τόπους refers to the channels themselves, as at 111e2 (cf. Robin). It is these 'places' which will turn out to be the main focus of interest, as the locations of the punishments of the dead (113c–114b). S. began at 108c5–6 by saying that εἰσὶν ... πολλοὶ καὶ θαυμαστοὶ τῆς γῆς τόποι; having dealt with those on or near the surface, he then turned to the τόποι ἐν αὐτῆι (111c5), and by stages he is now gradually identifying the important ones. **d3 κατωτέρω ἢ ἐπηντλεῖτο** 'further down than [the place at which] it was channelled off'. **d4 πάντα ... ἐκροῆς:** hydraulically speaking, this seems unnecessary (unless it is somehow to prevent a reversal of flow?); it does, however, help to justify the description of any river – seen as a single unit from its exit from Tartarus to its re-entrance there – as flowing *downwards*, a point of some importance in connection with the great rivers of Hades to be introduced in the next section (these are *infernal* rivers, despite the fact that part of their course is upwards). **d5 ἔνια μὲν ... 6 κατὰ τὸ αὐτὸ μέρος** 'some issued from opposite the [part] where they flow in, and some in the same part', i.e. some flow back into Tartarus on the other side of the earth's middle, some on the same side from which they started. **d8 εἰς τὸ δυνατὸν κάτω καθέντα πάλιν ἐμβάλλει** 'descending as far down as they can' (καθίημι used intransitively), i.e. in their circling; εἰς τὸ δυνατόν is then explained by e1–3 – they can go down as far as the middle, but not beyond it, because the other side, leading away from the middle, will be uphill.

e1 ἑκατέρωσε 'on either side': the reference is to the two sorts of river mentioned in d5–6 (cf. e2 ἀμφοτέροις). **e4 τὰ μὲν οὖν δὴ ... 5 ἐστι:** lit. 'The other rivers, then, are many and large and of all kinds.' μὲν οὖν δή is perhaps used like μὲν δή, to mark a transition (cf. 64a2n., and *GP* 258). **e5 δ' ἄρα:** see 111e5n. **e6–7 ἐξωτάτω ῥέον περὶ κύκλωι** 'flowing furthest out, around in a circle'. The encircling of earth by Oceanus was evidently a popular notion: see Hdt. 4.8, and cf. Hom. *Il.* 18.607–8. But according to *Il.* 21.195–7, it is Oceanus itself 'from which all rivers and all sea and all springs and deep wells flow'. By making Tartarus the source, S. appropriately gives the underworld a more immediate influence on our existence 'here'. In *Od.*, Oceanus seems to form the boundary between the world of the living and that of the dead: see 10.508–12, 11.155–9. **e7 τούτου δὲ καταντικρύ:** the reference seems to be to the points of exit of Oceanus and Acheron from Tartarus; but the important point is the opposition between the

two rivers in itself, emphasised by e8 ἐναντίως ῥέων – one being associated with the living, the other with the dead. The third river,
Pyriphlegethon, leaves Tartarus midway between Oceanus and Acheron
(113a5–6), and Cocytus, the fourth, opposite that: their exits will then
be like the four points of the compass somewhere on a horizontal plane
across the χάσμα of Tartarus. The other rivers apart from Oceanus all
form lakes, all apparently underground (see 113a1–2, a6–8n., c3n.);
later in their courses, Cocytus and Pyriplegethon then both approach
the lake of Acheron from opposite directions, but do not enter it. All of
this is built on *Od.* 10.508–15: 'When you cross Oceanus in your ship,
... yourself enter the dank house of Hades. There into Acheron flows
Pyriphlegethon, and that Cocytus which is a branch (ἀπορρώξ) of the
water of Styx; there is a rock and the meeting-place of two roaring
rivers.' Plato adds to and varies this picture both for the sake of symmetry, and to meet the demands of his elaborate eschatology: see esp.
113e6–114b6.

113a1 καὶ δὴ καί 'and in particular' (cf. 59d7–8n., 85d4). The
Acherusian lake is especially ἐρῆμος. **ὑπὸ γῆν ῥέων** may imply that it
previously flowed over the surface (or in a hollow), but need not do so;
what it certainly tells us is that the lake is underground. **a2–3 αἱ τῶν
τετελευτηκότων ψυχαὶ τῶν πολλῶν** 'the souls of most of those who
have died': these are the ones who have lived μέσως (d4–e1). **a5 εἰς
τὰς τῶν ζώιων γενέσεις:** this seems to refer back to 81e–82b; if so,
ζῶια includes ἄνθρωποι (see 82b6–8n., and cf. 94a8–10). See further
d6–e1n. **a6 ἐγγὺς τῆς ἐκβολῆς ... 7–8 τῆς παρ' ἡμῖν θαλάττης:** if
the ἐκβολή meant is that from Tartarus (which after the repeated use
of ἐμβάλλειν of rivers entering Tartarus, it surely must be: 112d3, 8,
113b4), then this new lake is also underground. This and the other two
lakes (the Acherusian, and Styx) seem to form a subterranean ana-
logue of the inhabited hollows above; each is a dwelling-place for a
different type of soul (cf. d7 οἰκοῦσι, with d6–e1n.; and 108c2, 5). That
the lake of Pyriplegethon is 'bigger than our sea' will then suggest a
rather large number of people beating their mothers or fathers (see
114a6); but then the earth is a big place (109a9, etc.)

b1 θολερός 'turbid'; also of mad passion – like the souls of those who
will find themselves in it (see preceding n.)? That it is literally fiery
does not need to be said, in view of its name, Πυριφλεγέθων. **b1–2**

περιελιττόμενος ... τῆι γῆι 'winding round in the earth'. **b3 οὐ συμμειγνύμενος τῶι ὕδατι:** for the idea, cf. *Il.* 2.753–4, where we are told that the water of the Titaressus, being a branch (ἀπορρώξ) of the Styx, will not mix with that of the Peneius. Cf. Hes. *Th.* 777 νόσφιν δὲ θεῶν ... ναίει, of the goddess Styx; both contexts support the connection of the name with στυγεῖν, 'hate'. **b4 κατωτέρω τοῦ Ταρτάρου** 'lower down in Tartarus', i.e. than its ἐκβολή (cf. 112d4). (For the genitive, cf. expressions like b6 ὅπηι ... τῆς γῆς.) **b5–6 οὗ καὶ κτλ.:** lit. 'whose lava-streams it is which blast up fragments [of it], wherever on earth they happen to do so', i.e. at various points. **b8–c1 χρῶμα δ᾽ ἔχοντα ὅλον οἷον ὁ κυανός** 'and all with a colour such as κυανός [has]': Theophr. (*De lap.* 37) identifies ('male') κυανός as similar to lapis lazuli; in Homer, the adj. κυάνεος indicates a deep blackness, which is what is intended here.

c1 ὄν refers to b7 τόπον. **c1–2 καὶ τὴν λίμνην ποιεῖ ὁ ποταμὸς ἐμβάλλων Στύγα** 'and the river creates the lake of Styx, into which it flows'. **c3 δεινὰς δυνάμεις λαβὼν ἐν τῶι ὕδατι** 'taking up terrible powers in its water': in Hes. *Th.* 775–806, the δεινή Styx is eldest daughter of Oceanus, and her 'famous, cold' water is what the gods swear by (cf. e.g. Hom. *Od.* 5.185–6); if they break their oath, punishment follows. Something so powerful must be terrible magic indeed. **c3 δὺς κατὰ τῆς γῆς** might, but need not, imply that the lake of Styx is on the surface (cf. Loriaux 155); if it were, how would the Stygian gloom be explained? **c6 οὐδενὶ μείγνυται:** cf. b3n. **c8 ὡς οἱ ποιηταὶ λέγουσιν:** cf. 112e7n. (κωκυτός = 'wailing'.)

d1 τούτων δὲ οὕτως πεφυκότων: cf. 111e5–6n. **d2 εἰς τὸν τόπον ... κομίζει:** cf. 107d5–e2, where the place is similarly left unspecified. **d3 διεδικάσαντο:** gnomic aor. ('submit themselves to judgement'). **d4 οἳ μὲν ἂν δόξωσι μέσως βεβιωκέναι:** i.e. the majority (a1–3). **d4 πορευθέντες ... 5–6 ὀχήματά ἐστιν:** the dead had traditionally to be ferried over the rivers of the underworld (see e.g. Aesch. *Sept.* 842, Ar. *Frogs*). But cf. also the metaphor of λόγοι as rafts (ὀχήματα) at 85c–d: the non-philosophical majority mount those ὀχήματα which are available to them; how much better if they had relied on ones of a different sort. **d6 ἐκεῖ ... e1 ἕκαστος:** lit. 'there they both (τε¹) dwell and in the process of their purification they both (τε²) are absolved of their crimes by paying penalties for them, if any of them has committed any crime, and (τε³) secure honours for their good deeds, each according to his desert'. Taken strictly, this suggests (*a*) that their existence in Hades is itself a kind of 'purification', with penalties for crimes being extra; probably (*b*) that not every soul that finds itself here will have committed crimes (they may just not have distinguished themselves πρὸς τὸ ὁσίως βιῶναι, like the next category up: 114b6–7); and possibly (*c*) that there is some kind of hierarchy among the inhabitants (τιμὰς φέρονται κτλ.) – which would in turn imply (*d*) that they form some kind of society (cf. Achilles' lament at *Od.* 11.489–91, that he would rather be a hired labourer on earth than *king* among the dead?). The last would not be surprising, since they will include, perhaps as the largest group among them (cf. 90a1–2), οἱ τὴν δημοτικὴν καὶ πολιτικὴν ἀρετὴν ἐπιτετηδευκότες (82a11–b1; for the connection with that context, see a5n.). All require 'purification' from their excessive attachment to the body (81b1–c6; including those who have practised δ. καὶ π. ἀρετή, as 68d–69a shows), although evidently the process is far from completed during their stay (see 81d–82b). Those who commit serious crimes, and go to worse places than the Acherusian lake (113e6–114a6), will only be reborn, if at all, after themselves being promoted there (114a7–b6); among these, presumably, will be the ones who find themselves back as the more savage animals (82a3–5). P. himself, however, prefers not to spell these details out – either because he prefers subtle economy to prosaic completeness, or because he means each of the two passages (i.e. the present one, and that at 81–2) to work its effect in its own context without encouraging us to dwell on the elaborateness of the eschatology involved, although as a careful writer he has ensured that all the details really do fit together; again there is a certain playfulness in the whole construction (cf. 81d1–2n., and e.g. 111a6–7n.).

e1–2 οἳ δ' ἂν δόξωσιν ἀνιάτως ἔχειν: like Tantalus, Sisyphus and Tityus (*Gorg.* 525e). **e5 δέ:** as at 78c8 (see n.); also at 114a3. **e7 οἷον** 'as for instance'.

114a1 μεταμέλον αὐτοῖς: acc. abs. **a2–3 τοιούτωι τινὶ ἄλλωι τρόπωι:** i.e. under other similar extenuating circumstances, including regret for the thing done (καὶ μεταμέλον κτλ.). **a6 πατραλοίας ... μητραλοίας** 'father-beaters ... mother-beaters'. **a7–8 κατὰ τὴν λίμνην τὴν Ἀχερουσιάδα:** cf. 113b2–3, c5. **a9 ὕβρισαν** 'assaulted'.

a9–b1 ἱκετεύουσι καὶ δέονται: at Athens, killers were evidently no longer liable to legal action or punishment if their victims forgave them before dying (Dem. 37.59).

b2–3 λήγουσι τῶν κακῶν: i.e. the extreme ones they encountered in Cocytus and Pyriphlegethon. **b6 ὑπὸ τῶν δικαστῶν:** cf. 113d3–4 (and *Gorg.* 523e–524a, *Ap.* 41a). **b6 οἳ δὲ δὴ ... 7 βιῶναι:** lit. 'But those who seem [to have lived] exceptionally in the direction of living virtuously'. δή marks out this οἳ δέ in contrast to the others (cf. 65a9n.); we here reach the climax of this section of S.'s story. ὁσίως = 'virtuously': ὁσιότης, more strictly 'piety', must here have a wider connotation, since it is opposed to criminal acts in general; and in P. generally it frequently stands for what we call the 'moral' virtues as a whole (as e.g. *passim* in *Euth.*). This category of people must be separate from οἱ τὴν δημοτικὴν καὶ πολιτικὴν ἀρετὴν ἐπιτετηδευκότες (82a11–b1), because it includes the philosophers (c2 τούτων δὲ αὐτῶν κτλ.), who were directly contrasted with them (68d–69a, which also described this sort of 'virtue' as bogus; cf. 113d6–e1n.). **b7–8 οἱ τῶνδε μὲν τῶν τόπων ... c1 ὥσπερ δεσμωτηρίων:** 'these places within the earth' must refer to Acheron, etc. (this category is not condemned, as it were, to the prisons below); but the following words recall the recurring image of the body as the prison of the soul (62b3–4, with 67d1–2, 81e1, 92a1). In fact, only a sub-group of the present category, οἱ φιλοσοφίαι ἱκανῶς καθηράμενοι, will get clear of *this* prison altogether (c2–6); but the others too will be close to such a state (see esp. 111b3–6n.). At the same time, there is also an allusion to S.'s own present position (in the prison of the body, which is itself in a real prison), which suggests that he is predicting this second grade of happiness for himself, rather than the first (cf. 111b7n.). If, as seems likely, what awaits the fully-fledged philosopher is actually becoming divine (see following n.), it would be surprising to find S., of all people, firmly expecting that future for himself (see 61d9n., 78a4n., 89c7–8n., 97b6–7, 108c8n.). On the other hand, *Phd.* seems to show him as having the relevant qualifications.

c1–2 ἄνω δὲ κτλ.: see 110b–111c. **c2 τούτων ... αὐτῶν:** i.e. of those introduced in b6–7 (οἳ ... βιῶναι). **c3 φιλοσοφίαι ἱκανῶς καθηράμενοι:** if οἱ ἐπὶ γῆς οἰκιζόμενοι possess real virtue (see b6n.), then they must be philosophers (69a–d, which represents ἀρετή and φρόνησις as two sides of a single coin: cf. 107d2, and c7 below); but, evidently, their rejection of the body was not as complete as it might have been (*total* separation from the body in life is of course impossible: 67c–d). **c3–4 τὸ παράπαν** qualifies ἄνευ ... σωμάτων ('absolument sans corps', Robin), and contrasts this group with the one before, who do have bodies of a sort (111a7–c3). **c4–5 οἰκήσεις ἔτι τούτων καλλίους:** i.e. even more beautiful than the ones referred to in c1–2. These are, presumably, the habitations of the gods: see 82b10–c1 εἰς δέ γε θεῶν γένος μὴ φιλοσοφήσαντι καὶ παντελῶς καθαρῶι ἀπιόντι οὐ θέμις ἀφικνεῖσθαι ἀλλ᾽ ἢ τῶι φιλομαθεῖ. **c5 οὔτε ὁ χρόνος κτλ.:** cf. 108d8–9, with the passage from *Phdr.* cited in the n. **c6 ἀλλὰ τούτων δὴ ἕνεκα χρὴ κτλ.:** for ἀλλὰ ... χρή, cf. ἀλλά + imperative at 91c6. δή is emphatic ('for the sake of *these* things': cf. 107c–d).

d1 μὲν οὖν: μέν is answered by d2 μέντοι; οὖν is merely transitional ('now'). Cf. e.g. 62b2n. **διισχυρίσασθαι:** cf. 100d7. **d3 ἐστίν** 'are the case'. **περὶ τὰς ψυχὰς ἡμῶν καὶ τὰς οἰκήσεις:** despite the fact that only one small category among the dead will be completely bodiless (c2–4, with e.g. 76b–c), all can still be described as (separated) ψυχαί, in accordance with the original definition of death at 64c, to the extent that all certainly leave corpses behind. That the souls of the dead retain some sort of bodily shape is part of the Homeric conception (see esp. *Od.* 11) which forms the backdrop to the arguments of the *Phaedo* (70a4–5n., 64c4–5n.); the reason why most Platonic 'dead' souls do so has of course been given at 81c–e. **d4 ἐπείπερ ... οὖσα** 'given that the soul is clearly [something] immortal': S. here reasserts his trust in the final argument (cf. 107c2 εἴπερ ἡ ψυχὴ ἀθάνατος). Further work needs to be done to it, but it is, he thinks, fundamentally sound: 107b4–9. (For ἐπείπερ ... γε, cf. 77d4 ἐπειδή γε.) The Homeric residents of Hades (see preceding n.) could not be described as ἀθάνατοι, even if they continued in existence for ever: the fact that they are *dead*, i.e. that they were once alive, are so no longer, and never will be again (unless through the intervention of a Heracles: see Eur. *Alc.*), is their main feature, reflected in their complete insubstantiality – which for Simmias and Cebes, at least, constitutes grounds for suggesting that they cease to exist altogether (70a1–6, 77b3–5, d5–e7). **d4 τοῦτο ... 6 ἔχειν** 'this it seems to me both to be fitting (sc. διισχυρίσασθαι) and to be worth risking (sc. διισχυρίσασθαι, or οἴεσθαι, or both) for

[someone] who thinks it to be so'.   **d6 καλὸς γὰρ ὁ κίνδυνος:** cf. c8
καλὸν ... τὸ ἄθλον.   **d6–7 ὥσπερ ἐπᾴδειν:** cf. 77e9, 78a5. In both
contexts, the reference is to ways of ridding oneself of fears about
death; the difference is that in the first these were apparently to be
rational arguments (paradoxically, since 'charms' or 'spells' would
normally be prime examples of the irrational), whereas here the
ἐπῳδαί are things that have not been rationally established. For S.,
they do somehow follow on from the conclusions of his arguments
(107c2, 114d4); they are underpinned by his belief that this is the best
of all possible worlds (cf. nn. to 108d4–5, 108e4–109a6, etc.), which
no doubt he would *hope* to see established. Meanwhile, however, his
reference to his μῦθος as a kind of ἐπῳδή (in the normal sense) reinforces his admission (d1–2) that it is not something on whose truth he,
or any sensible person, would insist.   **d7 διὸ δὴ κτλ.:** 'which is why I
myself have been spinning out my story for so long now' (as if the
words themselves would do the trick, as in a spell).   **d8 ἀλλὰ ... δή:**
cf. 78a10n.

e3 πλέον θάτερον: lit. 'more of the other', i.e. more which is κακόν
than good (an idiomatic expression: see Burnet).   **e2 τοὺς κόσμους**
'its adornments'.

115a2 περιμένει: cf. the original discussion of the prohibition on suicide (61d–62c).   **a5–6 ἐμὲ δὲ νῦν ἤδη ... ἡ εἱμαρμένη** 'And now it's
me that fate calls, [as] a man in a tragic play would say', which suggests
that he himself is in a 'tragic' or serious plight; but on his account, of
course, he is not – and so he goes on, 'and now I think it's just about
time for me to make for the bath' (a6), as if nothing out of the ordinary
were happening. Of course it is no ordinary bath (a7–8); at the same
time what is summoning him is nothing so grand as fate, but simple
questions of practical convenience. Alternatively, a6 σχεδόν τι ...
λουτρόν continues the reference to tragedy (cf. the hero's ritual cleans-
ing at Soph. *Ajax* 654–6); in which case the change of tone is effected
by a8 alone. *Symp.* 174a tells us that S.'s baths were infrequent; now he
takes one just when he is about to have no further use for his body.   **a7
δή** reinforces γάρ, as at 76a1, etc.   **a8 καὶ μὴ κτλ.** 'and not give the
women the trouble of washing a corpse' (λούειν is perhaps best treated
as an explanatory or 'limiting' inf.: cf. *MT* 763ff.).

115b1–end: Socrates dies

The tragicomic tone of 115a5–8 gives a foretaste of the final scene, in which S.'s cheerfulness in facing death is contrasted with the grief of everyone else. The grief is for different reasons: the jailer and the women, who have not heard S.'s arguments, are upset for S., as also, at least according to S., is Crito; while the others are upset, not for him but for themselves, because they are losing the companionship of such a man. The 'charms', then (114d7), have worked their effect – up to the point where he drinks the hemlock (117c–e; for another description of the state of those present prior to that moment, see 58e–59b).

115b3 ἄλλου του is probably neut.   **b3–4** ὅτι ἄν κτλ.: lit. 'by doing which we would do [what we do] most pleasingly to you'. For ἐν χάριτι, cf. e.g. ἐν βραχεῖ = βραχέως, and LSJ s.v. ἐν ιι.   **b5** οὐδὲν καινότερον 'nothing very new'.   **b6–7** καὶ ἐμοὶ καὶ τοῖς ἐμοῖς . . . ἐν χάριτι ποιήσετε 'pleasingly, to me and mine', because beneficially; because, by improving themselves (ὑμῶν αὐτῶν ἐπιμελούμενοι, i.e. caring for your real selves, your souls: cf. c4–116a1), they will to that degree be making the world a better place? But see further 116b6n.   **b8** μέν can be defended as 'solitary', suggesting '[and care for other things]': cf. 69d9–10n., and Verdenius. P. frequently prefers to avoid complete balance (ὑμῶν αὐτῶν ἐπιμελούμενοι / ὑμῶν αὐτῶν ἀμελῆτε).   **b10** ἐν τῶι ἔμπροσθεν χρόνωι once more S. emphasises the continuity of their present conversations with those they have had before (cf. 59a, 75d, 78c–d).   **b10–c1** οὐδὲ ἐὰν πολλὰ κτλ. 'even if you agree [sc. verbally, about what I say and have always said you should do] many times over, and vehemently, you will do no good [sc. to yourselves, still less to me]'.

c2 ταῦτα μὲν τοίνυν προθυμησόμεθα . . . οὕτω ποιεῖν 'Then we'll be keen to do this as you say.'   **c3** θάπτωμεν δέ σε τίνα τρόπον; Cf. 116a1. S. goes on (c4ff.) to pretend, jokingly, that this question shows that his arguments have not persuaded Crito (though there will turn out also to be a serious point: see e5–6n.). If S. really thought this, it is not clear that he would have regarded it as a laughing matter; and in fact Crito's question is a perfectly natural one, whether he is convinced or not. He is simply taking charge of practical matters (cf. 116a3, b3–4, d7–9, 118a7–8), as he has always done (59b7n.), and as S. knows (since he gives any subsequent directions to him). **c5** γελάσας ... **6** εἶπεν 'With a quiet laugh and a glance at us, he said.' **c7–8** διατάττων ἕκαστον τῶν λεγομένων 'setting out in order [the various parts of] each of the things said' (i.e. his arguments).

d1 δή introduces the ironic repetition of Crito's question. **d4** εἰς μακάρων δή τινας εὐδαιμονίας 'to certain states of happiness which belong to the blest'. For δή τινας, cf. 107d7–8n.; the studied vagueness of the expression – which also recalls, but significantly varies, Hes. *WD* 171 ἐν μακάρων νήσοισι – is consistent with what he said about his μῦθος at 114d (but cf. also 114b7–c1n.). **d4** ταῦτα ... **5** λέγειν 'I think I'm putting this to him in vain' (παραμυθούμενος κτλ.: so Crito has a sharper critical eye than all the rest of them?). **d7–8** ἦν οὗτος κτλ.: we have no information about such an event from outside *Phd.*; the best suggestion seems to be that Crito offered his guarantee (unsuccessfully – ἠγγυᾶτο, 'conative' impf.) if S. were to be spared waiting for his execution in prison (see Hackforth).

e5–6 τὸ μὴ καλῶς λέγειν κτλ.: i.e. if we speak imprecisely, that will cause us to think imprecisely too. (εἰς αὐτὸ τοῦτο means 'in regard to this very thing', i.e. in itself.)

116a1 νόμιμον 'customary', 'usual'. **a2** ἀνίστατο 'got up and went'. This and the following imperfects describe the actions involved as taking time (and as they would have appeared to an onlooker) rather than as simple events (cf. 59e8–60a1 ἐκέλευεν ... εἰσιόντες ... κατελαμβάνομεν). **a5** ἀνασκοποῦντες 'reviewing', 'going back over'. τοτὲ δ' αὖ 'and sometimes' ('as if τοτὲ μέν had preceded', Burnet). **a6** διεξιόντες 'going over'.

b3 ἐκεῖναι: i.e. Xanthippe (60a) and others. **b3** ἐναντίον τοῦ Κρίτωνος ... **4** ἐβούλετο: at least the main part of the conversation (διαλεχθείς) seems to have been practical (ἐπιστείλας), with Crito there as executor, and guardian of the children. **b6** χρόνον γὰρ πολὺν κτλ. suggests detailed discussion of practical arrangements for his family; contrast 115b5–8. **b7** λελουμένος: since we know why he went off for a bath, his sitting down 'freshly bathed' already indicates what is to come (b8 καὶ ἧκεν κτλ.). **b7** καὶ οὐ πολλὰ ... **8** καὶ ἧκεν ὁ τῶν ἕνδεκα ὑπηρέτης 'and he had said just a few things to us, when the agent of the Eleven came' (see *GP* 293). **b8–c1 στὰς παρ' αὐτόν** 'coming up to him'.

c1 γε emphasises the following σοῦ. **c4 καὶ ἄλλως ... 6–7 καὶ δὴ καὶ νῦν:** cf. 112e8–113a1. **c5 ἐν τούτωι τῶι χρόνωι:** i.e. during your time in prison. **c7–8 οὐκ ἐμοὶ κτλ.** 'you are not angry with me, since you recognise those responsible, but with them.'

d2 καὶ ἅμα κτλ. 'Bursting into tears as he said this, he turned and went away.' **d4 ἡμεῖς ταῦτα ποιήσομεν:** to anyone who has been listening to τὰ εἰρημένα (116a5), but not to the official, 'we [i.e. I] shall do this' will mean primarily χαιρήσομεν – what is about to happen will, he thinks, bring him happiness. **d5–6 καὶ παρὰ πάντα ... τὸν χρόνον ... 7 καὶ νῦν** 'both throughout (παρά) the whole time ..., and now ...' **d7 ὡς** is exclamatory. **d7–8 ἀλλ' ἄγε δή ... πειθώμεθα αὐτῶι** 'Come, then, let us do as he says.' 'Clearly a Homeric reminiscence', *GP* 14 (ἀλλ' ἄγε δή + 'hortative' subj., or imper., is common in Homer, which it is not in P.; the rhythm, too, is that of a hexameter). Cf. 115a5 (Hom., for P., is himself one of the tragic poets: see *Rep.* 595b–c).

e3 οἶδα ... 4 αὐτοῖς 'I know that others too drink [the hemlock] very late, when the order is given to them', i.e. that they delay doing so until long after the order is given. **e4–5 καὶ συγγενομένους γ' ἐνίους κτλ.** 'and what's more (καὶ ... γε) having had intercourse with those they happened to feel desire for': not that S. would want to do any of these things, nor is Crito suggesting it; his point is just about the time still available – or that, plus the *contrast* between what others want and what S. does. **e6 ἔτι ... ἐγχωρεῖ** 'there is still time'. **e7 εἰκότως γε ... 117a2 παρ' ἐμαυτῶι** 'It is with good reason (emphatic γε) both (τε) that those people that you refer to do this, for they think that they will gain by doing it; and I will not do this, with good reason, for I do not think that I gain anything at all by drinking a little later – anything else, that is (γε²), apart from making myself look ridiculous in my own eyes.' The introduction of οἴονται γὰρ ... ποιήσαντες slightly disturbs the syntax.

117a2–3 φειδόμενος οὐδενὸς ἔτι ἐνόντος 'being sparing when there is nothing more left in [the jar]': for the idea, evidently proverbial, cf. Hes. *WD* 368–9.

b1–2 αὐτὸ ποίησει 'it will do its work by itself.'   **b4** οὐδὲ διαφθείρας κτλ.: lit. 'and without losing [sc. οὐδέν] of his colour or of his face', i.e. keeping his colour and his composure.   **b5** ταυρηδὸν ὑποβλέψας: ταυρηδόν suggests menace, as can ὑποβλέπειν ('look out from under one's eyebrows'); but 'mischief' (Burnet, LSJ) seems more appropriate. For another typical (ὥσπερ εἰώθει) Socratic look, see 86d5–6. **b6–7** τί λέγεις . . . περὶ κτλ.: lit. 'What do you say about the drink as regards making a libation to someone? Is it permitted or not?' Xen. *Hell.* 2.3.56 reports Theramenes as making a different, and ironic, sort of gesture (ἀποκοτταβίζειν) with the remains of the hemlock towards the person responsible for his death; S.'s question merely combines piety with wit.   **b9** μέτριον 'in due measure'.

c1 ἀλλ' . . . γέ που 'but I suppose, at any rate'.   **c2** μετοίκησιν: cf. 61e1, 67c1 (ἀποδημεῖν), *Ap.* 40c (death is either extinction, or μεταβολή τις . . . καὶ μετοίκησις τῆι ψυχῆι τοῦ τόπου τοῦ ἐνθένδε εἰς ἄλλον τόπον). **c3** ἃ δὴ κτλ.: for a more expansive prayer, in a more leisurely context, see *Phdr.* 279b–c. **c3–5** καὶ ἅμα κτλ. 'And with these words, he put [the cup] to [his lips], and drained it dry quite (καὶ μάλα) without flinching or distaste.' **c5** τέως 'for a time'. ἐπιεικῶς 'fairly well'. **c6** κατέχειν τὸ μὴ δακρύειν 'to restrain their tears', with μή reinforcing the negative implied in κατέχειν (see *MT* 811). **c7** ἐμοῦ γε βίαι καὶ αὐτοῦ 'in my case (γε), quite against my own will'. **c8–9** οὐ γὰρ δὴ ἐκεῖνόν γε 'for it was certainly not for *him*'. **c9–d1** ἀλλὰ τὴν ἐμαυτοῦ τύχην κτλ. 'but for my own misfortune, [thinking] of what sort of man I had been deprived as a companion'.

d2 ἐξανέστη 'had got up and moved away'. **d3** Ἀπολλόδωρος: see 59a–b. **d4–6** ἀναβρυχησάμενος κτλ. 'bellowing out in his tears and distress, made every one of those present break down, except, that is, for S. himself'. **d7** θαυμάσιοι: θαυμάσιος, often used to address people, ranges in meaning from 'admirable' to 'odd', 'strange'. **d7–8** ἐγὼ μέντοι οὐχ ἥκιστα τούτου ἔνεκα 'It was for just this reason, you know, that I ...' (cf. *GP* 400).

e1–2 καὶ γὰρ κτλ.: for ἀκήκοα, cf. 61d9n. Burials, at least, would normally be accompanied by noisy lamentation; εὐφημία is rather a feature of approaches to the gods, prefacing prayer and accompanying sacrifice (Burkert 1985, 73, 199). But S.'s death, after all, is – he hopes

and expects – a matter of his entering the presence of the gods. **e5**
οὕτω γὰρ κτλ. 'for these were the man's orders' (a9–b1). Phaedo's
description of the event in e4–118a14 appears to omit some of the
more violent symptoms of hemlock poisoning (e.g. nausea, vomiting).
Burnet (Appendix 1), supposing the description to be historically accurate, relies on the suggestion that the symptoms might vary with different individuals; more plausibly, Gill 1973 argues that the symptoms
have been deliberately selected (*a*) to show S.'s physical toughness, (*b*)
for aesthetic reasons, and (*c*) to 'illuminate, in visual form' the account
of death given earlier in the dialogue, as the purification and liberation
of the soul from the body (hence the stress on the numbness spreading
upwards into the trunk, the loss of sensation indicating the departure
of the soul). But see following n. **e6 καὶ ἅμα ... 7 τὰ σκέλη** 'and at
the same time this person, the one who had given him the poison, took
hold of him, and after a while (διαλιπὼν χρόνον) examined his feet
and his legs'. ἐφάπτεσθαι is 'lay hold of', not 'feel' (e.g. Hackforth,
Gallop), among other things because this would make nonsense of the
sequence of events indicated by ἅμα and διαλιπὼν χρόνον (the ἐπισκοπεῖν must itself have been by feel); ἐφαπτόμενος αὐτοῦ is a delicate way
of alluding to the less pleasant effects of the poison, which 'often' include convulsions (Gill 25; cf. 118a12 ἐκινήθη, and the reference to the
covering of S.'s face in 118a6). The man takes the precaution of holding S. down, though Phaedo does not say it directly, nor why he has to
do it. Cf. 118a3n.

118a1 καὶ μετὰ τοῦτο κτλ. 'And after this, in turn, [he squeezed]
his shins.' **a3 αὐτὸς ἥπτετο** 'he himself kept hold of [him]'. **a1–2**
ἐπανιὼν οὕτως 'going up in this way'. **a3–4 ἐπειδὰν πρὸς τῆι καρδίαι**
γένηται αὐτῶι 'when it reached his heart'. **a4 οἰχήσεται** 'he will
die/go' (cf. 117e5n., Gill 1973, 27). **a5 ἤδη ... 6 καὶ ἐκκαλυψάμενος**
'Well, it was by now pretty well the region around his [lower] abdo-
men that was getting cold, when (καί: cf. 116b7–8n.), uncovering his
face ...' **a7–8 τῶι Ἀσκληπιῶι κτλ.:** the 'usual' interpretation of this
(Gill 28 n.1) is that S. is thanking the god of healing for his recovery
from the sickness of life. Hackforth, following Wilamowitz, objects that
Phd. does not portray life as a sickness – though in fact S. does attribute
such an idea to Cebes at 95d; Gallop adds that it would be incompatible with 90e–91a. But these objections are prosaic (why should S. not

momentarily compare the happiness he expects with that of someone recovered from illness?), and the alternative explanation – that S. is referring to an actual debt – presupposes an interest in historicity on P.'s part which is little in evidence elsewhere in the dialogue. **a11 ταῦτα . . . ἀπεκρίνατο:** lit. 'When he [Crito] asked this, he [S.] answered nothing further.' **a12 ἐκινήθη:** see 117e6–7n. **a13 καὶ ὅς τὰ ὄμματα ἔστησεν:** lit. 'and he [S.] fixed his eyes', i.e. his eyes became fixed. **a15 ἡμῖν:** ethic dat. **a16 ὧν ἐπειράθημεν** 'of whom we had had experience'. **a17 καὶ ἄλλως:** not 'and besides' – since according to *Phd.* being just is part of being good, and φρόνησις is a necessary concomitant of the [other] virtues (69a–c) – but 'and otherwise', i.e. even apart from the comparison with those Phaedo and the others had known (cf. Burnet). **καὶ δικαιοτάτου:** the dialogue thus ends on the same ironic note that it began – that S., who deserved it least of all, should have been condemned to death.

INDEXES TO THE INTRODUCTION
AND COMMENTARY

1 **General**

2 Proper names

3 Greek words